THROUGH
FORTRESS AND
ROCK

THROUGH FORTRESS AND ROCK

The Story of Gencor
1895-1995

JDF JONES

JONATHAN BALL PUBLISHERS
Johannesburg

Published in 1995 by
Jonathan Ball Publishers (Pty) Ltd
P O Box 33977
Jeppestown 2043

ISBN 1 86842 029 9

Design by Michael Barnett
Maps by Ian Carter, Johannesburg
Typesetting and reproduction of text by Book Productions, Pretoria
Reproduction of photographic sections and cover by RT Sparhams, Johannesburg
Index by Naomi Musiker, Johannesburg
Printed and bound by National Book Printers; Drukkery St, Goodwood, Western Cape

CONTENTS

FOREWORD

It seemed like a good idea at the time – to compile a corporate history to mark Gencor's centenary. So I asked JDF Jones to take up the task and I set only one condition: no dry organisational chronicle, please, but rather a gripping tale that would appeal to employees and the general public alike.

I fear he has succeeded too well. With unlimited access to our archives and exceptional co-operation from industry colleagues and group executives (both present and former) in wide-ranging interviews, he has unearthed much that will stir old emotions. If we believed in censorship, I would probably have welshed on the whole deal. But it is difficult to put the genie back in the bottle; and in any event, the modern Gencor is noted for openness and – in the modern idiom – transparency. I have therefore not asked JDF to retract or soften anything that he has written.

I apologise in advance to those who will find painful the arousal of ancient passions.

Brian Gilbertson
1995

PREFACE

The Albu brothers and Adolf Goerz are the least celebrated of the 'Rand-lords', the mining magnates who laid the foundations of the modern South African economy during the extraordinary years which spanned the discovery of gold on the Witwatersrand in 1886 and the Anglo-Boer War. In comparison with Cecil Rhodes and Barney Barnato, Alfred Beit and Julius Wernher, JB Robinson and all the other famous names, they are shadows. They have no biographers, few anecdotes cast light on their personalities, and the archives they have left behind are so scanty that a proper history is hardly possible.

But the Albus – George and Leopold – who created General Mining, and Adolf Goerz, whose legacy was Union Corporation, were arguably as interesting and as significant as any of their more colourful and better record-ed colleagues. General Mining and Union Corporation eventually came together to form present-day Gencor – and Gencor today is a South African-based international group second in size and scope and importance only to the Oppenheimer family's Anglo American complex.

Even more interesting, the story of the Albu family and the bachelor Adolf Goerz and their successors casts fresh light on the events of South Africa's development. After the Boer War and Goerz's premature death, the story of the two mining-cum-industrial groups, with all their ups and downs, illustrates uncannily well the story of South Africa itself through the dramas of the twentieth century. The history of a commercial organisation cannot be read in isolation from the political, economic and racial history of the same period. Thus, the Gencor story – which covers the 100 years from the registration of the Albus' General Mining and Finance Corporation on 30 December 1895 (literally the day after Dr Jameson launched his Raid on the Transvaal), through to the arrival of a majority-rule South Africa, unimaginable to so many of the characters in the tale that follows – can only make sense if it is related to the story of the South African nation, painful, anguished, sometimes bloody as it has been.

Many millions of words have been spent on the dramas of South Africa in this century, particularly since the institutionalisation of apartheid in 1948. The history of these past 100 years may well be illustrated, and perhaps illuminated, by a record of the changes that took place in one very large organisation over those same 100 years – or rather, in the various elements that eventually came together to make up that one organisation called Gencor. The intention of this book, whose publication coincides with Gencor's centenary, is not to present a conventional corporate history (with its careful record of the minutiae of the firm's activities) so much as to offer a microcosm of South Africa over 100 dramatic years – 1895-1995.

This book could not have been written without total reliance on Keith Wallis's *The Progenitors*, an unpublished history of the group which focuses in particular, Mr Wallis will agree, on Union Corporation. Similarly, though to a far lesser degree, I have benefited from another unpublished manuscript history of General Mining by Eric Rosenthal (evidently never taken beyond an early draft but enjoying various sources which have since been lost) and a lucid memorandum on Union Corporation's early history by William Randerson, and I have also relied heavily on Dr Grietjie Verhoef's recent manuscript history of Federale Mynbou. Mr Wallis and Dr Verhoef have been extremely generous and helpful.

I need to emphasise that the archival material is patchy, usually inadequate and often non-existent, thanks to heavy 'weeding', war damage and, too often, deliberate destruction of files by senior figures from Sir Henry Strakosch to Dr Wim de Villiers. The archive is so frail that the narrative that follows would better be described as 'scenes from' the story of Gencor. In an attempt to make this history accessible to lay readers in particular, I have deliberately omitted the sort of detail – especially of finance, management or mining technology – which would only be valued by, or meaningful to, the specialist, who is asked to consult the manuscripts of Mr Wallis or Dr Verhoef at the Gencor offices in Johannesburg or London, and at various libraries in South Africa. I ought to add that Gencor has been expanding world-wide so rapidly this year that I have had to draw the line at 1 August, so this book may already be out of date.

I am most grateful to Lesley Lambert, Frances Murray, Helen Parsons, Pam Agnew, Caron dos Santos, Francie Whitley, Ian Carter and their colleagues in Johannesburg, to Gerhard Kirsten in Bellville, to Joanna Wilson and Sandra Butcher in London, and to Jim and Frances Jones, Neil Viljoen,

Naas Steenkamp and Michael Coulson, among many others. Various members of the Albu family have co-operated enthusiastically, in particular Julia Albu, Sir George and Lady Albu, Ann Boyd, Kathleen Forsyth, Allan Goodman, Charles Goodman, Peter Railing and David and Susan Stapleton-Cotton. I am also indebted to the staff at the Brenthurst Library, at the Chamber of Mines Library, at MuseumAfrica, at the African Studies Department of the Public Library (formerly called the Strange Archives) – all in Johannesburg – and at the Sanlam Archive in Bellville and the London Library.

Brian Gilbertson, today's Executive Chairman of Gencor, gave me free rein and urged me to write a frank, readable and accessible book. His predecessors, Derek Keys and Ted Pavitt, were among many Gencor executives, both present and retired – it would be invidious to list them – who were also generous with their time, their memories, and their candour. Harry Oppenheimer, too, generously gave me permission to quote from historical letters.

I rather hope that none of the above will be too distressed by what follows ...

JDFJ, September 1995

CHAPTER ONE

THE GERMAN RANDLORDS

It is easy to underestimate the role of Germans in the creation of modern South Africa. Because they played no significant political role, their interest and involvement in the shaping of events before the First World War – and before the Anglo-Boer War – have sometimes been forgotten. It is less common to understate the role of European Jews in South Africa's economic, if not political, development: sometimes the Jewish presence is *over*-stressed – the Randlords, for instance, were by no means uniformly Jewish. However, it has been calculated that of the 25 leading entrepreneurs who were involved in the opening up of the Rand goldfields, 15 were Jewish, 11 of the total were from Germany or Austria, and 9 of that latter category were also Jewish. The brothers George and Leopold Albu were Jewish; they and Adolf Goerz were German. The Albus and Goerz were the creators respectively of General Mining and Union Corporation, which many years later were to merge and to become Gencor.

German entrepreneurs, bankers, industrialists and investors had been vigorously interested in South Africa since shortly after the discovery of diamonds in Kimberley in 1869. The Albu brothers and Adolf Goerz, coming from different backgrounds, represent two different varieties of German venturers. George and Leopold Albu had been brought up in a suburb of Berlin where their father, Simon, was a builder and repairer of coaches. They were Sephardic Jews who traced their origins – or so they would later claim – to a mediaeval rabbi who had lived under the protection of the Spanish dukes of Alba and had translated the Pentateuch into Spanish; hence one possible explanation of the family's unusual name. There were four boys, George (born in 1857), Leopold (1859), Felix and Eugen, and two girls, Regina and Eveline. Next to nothing is known about the detail of their childhood in the years when the Prussian army was creating the German Empire. Simon was apparently injured in his work and the family was in difficulty, though

5

the boys were properly educated. George was apprenticed to a haberdasher in Silesia, and it was Leopold, always to be the more impatient of the two, who was the first to respond to the suggestion of their uncle in Kimberley that he come out to see if he could make his fortune on the new diamond fields.

There is a mystery about this uncle. The only Albu known to have been in Kimberley at the time was the first Rabbi of the town's synagogue, which was consecrated in 1876, whom Louis Cohen in his *Reminiscences of Kimberley* specifically insists was the uncle of George and Leopold. The *Reminiscences* is one of the most readable (and mischievous) books ever written about South Africa, but Louis Cohen certainly should not be relied upon for perfect accuracy, and his libellous description of a charity concert at the Theatre Royal may be a touch exaggerated: 'The old humbug advanced to the footlights, glared, glinted, and blew his spongy nose with a debauched red handkerchief... Slowly and gravely, with much professional precision, he landed his violin on his left shoulder and played remarkably well a difficult number resplendent with crescendos, quavers and grimaces. Then he stopped to blow his nose again, and waited for applause. It is sad to chronicle that at this particular moment some of the chosen of his flock commenced to hiss, at which the grave and reverend pastor paused and, glowering angrily at the aristocratic assemblage, visited his nose again with thunderous effect. This was too much. We had come to hear Schubert, not sneezing and, the hisses redoubling, the sacred Albu, with eyes flashing like those of a wild cat, deliberately turned his back to the immaculate audience, lifted up the coat-tails of his highly respectable black dress-coat, and applauded himself on that portion of his body which ought to have been well smacked earlier in life...'

Worse was to come – the Rabbi Albu was fired, but, as Louis Cohen continues, 'the Holy Man got his revenge. He took a single-roomed office in Endell Street, where he ate, drank, and slept, shaking his elbow all the time, and regularly on a Saturday, as his whilom flock wended their way to *shool*, he would stand at his habitation's door, kissing his fingers to them, unkempt, dirty and unshaven, smoking a filthy old pipe, and puffing like a steam boat. It is asserted, too, that on a certain eventful Yom Kippur morning he was seen vigorously cutting into a ham, and exclaiming with gusto as he did so "I'll show you how to keep Yom Kippur"...'

At least this gives the flavour of life in early Kimberley: the Rabbi does not feature again in the family archives, which is probably not surprising.

This must have been the man whose invitation was taken up by Leopold, who sailed for the Cape in 1875. In May 1876 George followed him. His first job (though he was afterwards rather reticent about it) was with the well-known firm of drapers, Stuttaford, in Cape Town, and a cousin named Barnet Leon – great-grandfather of the Democratic Party's leader, Tony Leon – gave him a few trinkets of jewellery to sell. His brother was already in the provisions business in the same town. In Louis Cohen's words, 'The proud and 'aughty Leopold honoured the same sea port with his presence, where, on the market place each morning, he trafficked with the Boers in forage, mealies, etc. This particular commercial spot was an African Rialto, and it would be unfair not to mention the important and solid fact that the versatile Leo was looked up to as a marvel of cleverness and honesty...' George would later reminisce about the peaceful atmosphere of Cape Town in those days and of how the grass grew in Adderley Street.

But soon the brothers went north on the 28-day wagon journey to Kimberley. There they set up as produce dealers, though they had their eye on the diamond trade. They were still in their teens.

Adolf Goerz was the same age as George Albu, though his background was distinctly more privileged. He was born in 1857 in Mainz, son of a member of the Reichstag who had been chief justice of the Grand Duchy of Hesse. He was trained as a mining engineer in the respected School of Mines at Freiburg – and, equally (or more) important for the future, his sister married Dr Georg von Siemens, the prominent industrialist who was also founding chairman of Deutsche Bank in Berlin.

Goerz had established himself in Berlin as a consultant mining engineer when, in 1888, the Deutsche Bank was approached by Edward Lippert, a Transvaal businessman who had particularly close links with President Kruger (thanks to which he held the dynamite monopoly concession which was so to enrage the Randlords over the next decade). Lippert was himself German and thought he might be able to persuade the President to put a banking concession in the way of Deutsche Bank. Evidently it was necessary to take expert advice on the potential of the Witwatersrand goldfield which had been discovered in 1886, so it made sense to send out Adolf Goerz.

Goerz spent a good part of 1888 in the Transvaal and, although nothing came of the banking concession, reported back to Berlin. As a result, Deutsche Bank (with Berliner Handelsgesellschaft and Jacob HS Stern of Frankfurt) formed a syndicate with capital of £100 000 for him to invest. Goerz then returned to South Africa and, helped by a share slump in 1890, was able to pick up a profitable portfolio of shares and claims. As a highly qualified mining engineer he quickly made his name as a consultant and collected various directorships. He also joined the new Johannesburg Stock Exchange, but – unlike the Albus, and indeed most of the Randlords – he was always to be more involved and active as an engineer than as a stockbroker or share dealer. So here was Goerz, in his early thirties, fast established in the new goldfield while the Albus had only recently moved their base from Kimberley to Johannesburg.

George Albu had been living in Kimberley for over 10 years and had become a respected and successful local businessman. He had married Gertrude Rosendorff, having returned to Berlin to collect his childhood girlfriend, and they were beginning to produce their six children. The brothers had started as *kopje wallopers* (middlemen buying stones from the men on the diggings) and then became licensed diamond brokers and dealers before expanding by buying claims and promoting several small companies, but with no great success: they were already discovering that the consolidation and amalgamation of the diggings into the hands of the big boys – most notably De Beers – meant that they were competing out of their class. George Albu nevertheless became a director of several small mines: he would always remain attached to, and modestly involved in, Kimberley's diamonds. Restive Leopold went off in 1884 to the new goldfield in the Eastern Transvaal, settling at Barberton as a produce dealer and stockbroker. He moved on to Johannesburg in 1887. George visited him there and was unimpressed, but the writing was on the wall. The future evidently lay not in Kimberley but on the Rand. The incentive for George to move was that the Albus had become associated with various Kimberley businesses in some small outcrop mines on the central Rand – in particular, the 'Meyer and Charlton', always to be known as 'the Meyer', which was to be one of the projects which turned George Albu from a modest Kimberley diamond dealer into a Randlord.

Both the Albus and Goerz arrived a little late on the Rand. After the frantic excitement of the first gold rush, the point was quickly taken that this field had nothing in common with the alluvial diggings of California and elsewhere. The reef, it was soon discovered, went deep: exploitation would need major finance. The millionaires from Kimberley – Rhodes, Rudd, Robinson, Barnato, etc – were soon on the spot (though some of them were less enthusiastic and less convinced than others). Goerz, when he arrived, would have access to German finance; the Albus would have to progress more modestly. George Albu's tactic in these early years was to focus on smaller-scale projects and to teach himself enough about mining to be able to trust his own judgement. He became known for an unusual willingness to go underground – Louis Cohen in *Reminiscences of Johannesburg* describes him as 'quiet, unassuming George Albu, his clothes smeared with gilded mud, showing that he had been fossicking in the Meyer and Charlton mines'.

The Albus would specialise in reconstruction of precarious companies. The Meyer was the best example of this. Formed in 1888, its claim area was minute, but it produced 6 500 oz in the first year, and promised to be very low cost. The second year was disappointing and some of the Kimberley investors (including Barnato and Joel) pulled out. George Albu was prepared to support another share-issue and thereby became a Director. He was soon to be Chairman and Managing Director, consolidating and extending the area, raising more capital, putting in a main incline shaft. The dividends did not falter and the Meyer was to be known as 'the Jewel Box of the Rand' (the metaphor makes the point that it was always small). It prospered for many years.

There was a similar story for another outcrop mine, Roodepoort United Main Reef, this time west of the central Rand, where George Albu became Managing Director in 1892 and dividends began to be paid in 1894; it was extended in 1895-8 and became another Albu mainstay, as did Goch Amalgamated Gold Mining, near the Meyer. And, ominously for the future, the Albu brothers had decided to take over flotation of one of the earliest deep-level prospects, Cinderella Deep, some kilometres to the east. In addition, the Steyn Estate Gold Mining Company had already been reconstructed as the New Steyn, near Roodepoort, most of the new shares being taken up by President Gold Mining (which the Albus had floated earlier): the dramatic 'Kaffir boom' in the markets in 1895 gave Leopold Albu the opportunity to turn President's £16 000 share portfolio into £250 000.

The brothers reckoned they were ready to establish their master company along the lines common to the Randlords at the time. It would be called General Mining and Finance Corporation. For this, they needed European financing – and the Albus naturally looked to Germany, no doubt very conscious of how the Deutsche Bank connection was smoothing Adolf Goerz's progress. In 1893 George Albu had gone to Europe to woo German finance: the attempt was premature, though important contacts were established. With the successes of 1895 apparent, the Dresdner Bank – the rival of Deutsche Bank – was prepared to back a new Albu company. Since the Albus were aiming for a £1 million capital base, the bank brought in Berlin Disconto Gesellschaft and S Bleichroder as partners, with of course the brothers as major subscribers in exchange for their existing assets (the precise details have been lost).

The General Mining and Finance Corporation Limited was registered in the Transvaal on 30 December 1895; its authorised capital was £1 250 000 (the equivalent of the value 100 years later would be to multiply at least 25-30 times), of which 250 000 £1 shares were held in reserve. In April, Leopold Albu went off to Britain, as 'Managing Director, London', to take responsibility for the new Corporation's access to the European market: he was to remain based there for more than 40 years, returning only occasionally to Johannesburg, several times to allow his brother – who had taken the title 'Managing Director, Johannesburg' (and, in due course, 'Chairman') – to take home leave in Europe. Dresdner seconded a senior man, Martin Luebeck, as Manager and Director, no doubt to keep an eye on the brothers.

During the period before General Mining's creation, there was a substantial degree of co-operation between the brothers and the Goerz operation. However, as the decade continued, the strains – in effect, the rivalry between them, perhaps exacerbated by the competition between the two German parent banks – became more and more apparent until, after the end of the Anglo-Boer War, the bad feeling was undisguised. The atmosphere improved between the two world wars but this early experience was hardly propitious for their future relationship.

By 1891 Adolf Goerz had directorships in May Consolidated Mines, Crown Reef, the Meyer, and Princess Estate. His engineers were intimately involved in the development of electricity on the Rand, thanks to his connections with Siemens-Halske, which won the concession for the Brakpan power station in 1894. Directorships with Metropolitan Gold Mining and New Rietfontein Estate and South West Africa Company followed. On the grounds of his rapid success the original syndicate was turned into a private company, Ad Goerz and Co, in 1892; with initial capital equivalent to £160 000 and another £160 000 available, Goerz could now start to build up significant shareholdings and think of floating new and deep-level mines. Of course, although he had a substantial holding himself, control remained with Deutsche Bank and its German partners.

Keith Wallis has described the situation on the Rand in the early days in the following way: 'The "real" money to be made out of the Witwatersrand was from the formation and flotation on the Stock Exchange of new mines and the reconstruction and refinancing of old ones. The promoters issued substantial quantities of "vendor" shares to themselves as owners of the property on which a new mine was to be established, probably subscribed another tranche of shares cheaply, and then offered "working capital" shares to the public at a large premium. With luck and a certain amount of pump priming, the market could be stimulated to such an extent that a good proportion of the vendor and cheap shares could be sold at the same time as the working capital was raised, leaving the promoters with a handsome profit which more than covered the cost of their remaining shareholdings.'

Adolf Goerz's strategy, as a comparative latecomer, was to look to the fringes, first on the West Rand, and, for longer-term ambitions, on the East Rand. On the West Rand, in 1894 the new company created a handsome profit out of a share issue for Princess Estate (near General Mining's Roodepoort

United Main Reef); it then bought more claims in the same area (to be called Roodepoort Central Deep) while targeting the so-called Botha Reef and planning two new deep-level mines towards Krugersdorp to be called Lancaster and Lancaster West Mining Companies respectively. Between Lancaster and Roodepoort Central Deep Goerz was committing £350 000: the new Ad Goerz and Co with its £320 000 base was committing its survival to these two mines.

Both mine companies had successful flotations in London, Germany and France: they went to healthy premiums and in 1895 Ad Goerz and Co paid an £80 000 dividend. The next stage of Goerz's strategy was to persuade his German principals to agree to a larger investment – which would mean a public company. The eventual and successful outcome was the transfer of Ad Goerz's business into A Goerz and Co Ltd in 1897, with an injection of new capital. The company was registered in South Africa, that is to say in Pretoria, but its direction – and this was to be important for the future – was firmly established in London. One reason was that Goerz himself in 1895 had decided that he wanted to live in Britain: perhaps he felt that he would not be so much under the thumb of Deutsche Bank, and he was now rich enough to humour his own preferences as he entered middle age. Conceivably his health may have been a factor. He is also on record as showing interest in extending his Group outside South Africa.

In 1897 Goerz was appointed Managing Director and another German, Amandus Brakhan, who had been recruited in 1892, became Managing Director in South Africa. Of eight other directors, four were resident in Germany. The Chairman was an English peer, Lord Battersea (of the famous Flowers beer family – though it may have helped that his wife was a Rothschild). The overwhelming majority of the staff came from Germany or Austria. And, of course, the Germans still had the controlling voice – which was significant because German investors traditionally attached greater importance to regular dividend payments than did their British equivalents, who were less inclined to 'stay' with a share over the long-term. For years to come the Goerz group was to feel the need for a larger capital base.

The offering of 200 000 shares at 32/6d in March 1898 earned a sour response in some quarters – the *Pall Mall Gazette*, for example, said: 'It was made in Germany (and the Transvaal – nice mixture!) and should be left alone for Teutonic digestion...' Nevertheless, the issue was substantially oversubscribed.

The second part of Adolf Goerz's development plan was to look East – to Modderfontein and to Geduld (on one of President Kruger's farms). Brakhan was an enthusiast for Geduld and managed to persuade Goerz to agree; a young manager named Henry Strakosch had to make a special trip to Cape Town to collect £10 000 in gold sovereigns, which was the only currency the Transvaal leader would accept. A Goerz and Co therefore went ahead with Geduld with a management contract and a 20 per cent shareholding: it was floated in March 1899, and Goerz realised £180 000 in share profits. Three shafts were planned. But war was to end all that, and to pose some worrying questions for the future.

Indeed, the management would have had good reason for alarm if it had had the gift of foresight. Three of the Goerz flotations mentioned above – Roodepoort Central Deep, Lancaster and Lancaster West – were ultimately to prove failures since the values at the far western end of the Rand, while encouraging at first, proved too inconsistent to maintain a supply of profitable ore. This experience did no good to the Goerz reputation in the years ahead. The outcrop propositions did better, especially the holding in Meyer and Charlton, but in 1899 the simmering rivalry between the Albu and Goerz groups suffered one of its eruptions and Goerz lost its part in the Meyer in consequence of a squabble over who should succeed Adolf Goerz himself as consulting engineer to the Meyer. The Albus, for whatever reason – pressure from Dresdner? awareness of the Meyer's importance? – decided to put up their own George Denny in preference to the Goerz nominee. Brakhan and Goerz resigned in a fury and the episode was not forgotten in the years ahead.

But these financial strategies and corporate rivalries, which by the turn of the century had established two new members in the first division of the Randlords, had been interrupted, and could have been thrown off course, by one of the most dramatic political events in South Africa's history: the Jameson Raid. It is relevant to this story not just because, as everyone knows, it was to lead inexorably to the Anglo-Boer War, but also because it casts interesting light on the Anglo-German tensions in South Africa's business development at that period, and in particular on the relationship between George Albu and his fellow Randlords.

Adolf Goerz, by moving to live in England in 1895 (he was to make only one more visit to Johannesburg), was better able than George Albu to keep out of the fast-growing political confrontations in the Transvaal between President Kruger's government in Pretoria and the 'Uitlanders' in Johannesburg. From now on he was to be represented in the Transvaal by Amandus Brakhan, who had become 'Managing Director in South Africa' with the registration of the public company A Goerz and Co Ltd in Pretoria in December 1897. Lord Battersea was still Chairman but Adolf Goerz was evidently in command in London.

The detail of the Jameson Raid has been endlessly researched, analysed and debated; the full truth will never be known. The essence, it can be agreed, is that some of the Randlords – not all of them – conspired with the colonial authorities to attempt to bring down the Kruger government by sending a mounted force from the Bechuanaland border to the alleged 'rescue' of the Uitlanders, who were supposed to stage a 'rising' in Johannesburg. Dr Leander Starr Jameson's invasion was a catastrophe with elements of farce. Kruger was fully aware of what he was up to; Jameson had fewer than 400 men when he finally crossed the border on 29 December 1895, and his drunken troopers didn't even manage to cut the telegraph line to Pretoria. There was no rising in Johannesburg; Jameson ignored all messages telling him to turn back, and the conspirators – the 'Reformers' – gathered at the Rand Club to await their fate. On 9 January, 64 of them were arrested, courteously enough in the circumstances, and taken off to jail in Pretoria. Four of their leaders were sentenced to death, to the scarcely justified shock and horror of the Uitlanders, but the sentences were commuted on payment of £25 000 each. The Kaiser sent an indiscreet cable of congratulation to Kruger which caused much anger in Britain. The young Jan Smuts later said that 'the Raid was the real declaration of war in the great Anglo-Boer conflict'.

Historians used to concentrate on the precise responsibility of Cecil Rhodes (he was of course the leading conspirator and had to resign as Prime Minister of the Cape in consequence) and of the British Colonial Secretary Joseph Chamberlain (who, while certainly part of the plot, managed to extricate himself and was actually acquitted of any responsibility by the Committee of Inquiry in London). The debate has more recently shifted to the wider role, and responsibility, of the Randlords. Who was on which side? Were they divided along lines of nationality or of business interests? Were the 'outcrop' men at odds with the 'deep-level' owners? And were the 'Germans' on Kruger's side while the English stood behind Rhodes and the British Empire? The most convincing answer is that nothing was so clear-cut. No doubt all the mine-owners were exasperated, to one degree or other, by the restraints and costs imposed on them by the policies of the Kruger government, just as they would have sympathised – again to varying degrees – with the Uitlanders' anger that they had no franchise. Some of them, and certainly George Albu, were deeply critical of any recourse to insurrection, yet the evidence hardly confirms an English-German split.

The two most committed and influential conspirators were Rhodes and Alfred Beit – but the German Beit was surely not an Imperial agent of Britain. The other leading conspirators arguably came under the influence of either Rhodes (Jameson, Hammond, and his brother Frank, for example) or of Beit (Lionel Phillips, Percy FitzPatrick, George Farrar). It is even unconvincing to argue, as Mendelsohn has, that the conspirators were committed to 'long-range mining programmes' while their opponents 'were either pre-occupied with stock-jobbing or were content with modest holding operations' – the examples of the Albu and the Goerz groups seem to run counter to that. No doubt George Albu (and Amandus Brakhan) were closer to Pretoria than, say, Phillips or FitzPatrick: they both seem to have got on well with President Kruger and with his associates like Edward Lippert; they would have had no particular loyalty to Britain (at that period); they both had an interest in building up German exports through their agency representation of companies like the arms-making Krupp. Finally, there must be the element of personal character. Rhodes was a gambler, whereas George Albu was more cautious and more realistic, less inclined to take risks. And it should not be forgotten that, on the very week that Dr Jameson rode into the Transvaal, the Albus were preoccupied with completing the registration of their General Mining and Finance Corporation, the result of nearly 20 years of hard work.

One immediate result of the Raid, unsurprisingly, was that there was a breakaway from the Chamber of Mines of, in the main, companies which disapproved of the conspiracy – the 'Cosmopolitans', as they were dubbed. George Albu was prominent in the founding of the Association of Mines of the South African Republic in April 1896. Its 26 members included Goerz, the maverick JB Robinson and Barney Barnato. But another of their motives was certainly that they also hoped to benefit at the expense of their competitors by extracting rewards from Kruger for their loyalty. Amandus Brakhan told Georges Rouliot, a senior Wernher, Beit partner, that he hoped for favoured treatment, and Rouliot wrote to Wernher to warn him that 'the German section' was lobbying for harsh measures against their group.

In the event, Pretoria did not come up with rewards and the Randlords' split was healed quite soon. The main reason was that the government had set up an Industrial Commission of Inquiry in March 1897 which was to investigate the state of affairs of the mining industry: it promised to be important and the mine-owners, with George Albu's active support, decided they would be wise to make peace amongst themselves and present a common front. Indeed, in business as opposed to political matters, George Albu, who had become the second Chairman of the Association, had in 1897 emerged as a prominent (and increasingly long-winded) spokesman for the gold mines. In his evidence to the Industrial Commission in May we find the most lucid, candid and effective explanation that we have of the problems and grievances, the prejudices and concerns, of the industry not just at the time but as they had been experienced over the decade.

It is hardly too much to say that George Albu dominated the proceedings of the Inquiry; in a sense, it was the high point of his career, as he spoke on behalf of the entire industry. He was rapidly co-opted as an advisory member of the Commission, joining Amandus Brakhan, who had been there from the beginning. 'The mining industry is at present ailing,' George Albu said in his opening statement. He emphasised that he spoke 'unbiased by any party feeling'. He urged the Commissioners to understand that 'an industry like the one in the Transvaal has never existed before in the world. You must further understand that we have been novices in working this industry. We could only gain our experience by the capital which we have put into the mines... The two questions which affect the ultimate effect of the mining industry are the Railway question and the Dynamite question ... that is the seat of the disease...'

He deluged the Commission with statistics to make the point that elsewhere in the world governments went to great pains to minimise rail freight charges for the sake of their industries. 'You must always consider, gentlemen, it is not the railways which make the gold mines, it is the gold mines which make the railways. If we had no gold mines here we would have no railways...' The size of the railway tariffs meant that the cost of essential supplies from Europe was increased by 100 per cent. He moved on to the second great grievance, the dynamite concession: 'The Transvaal is about the largest consumer in the world of this article, and must not we look idiotically foolish that we, as the largest consumer, pay (for an article that costs 18s. 6d. at home) 85s., and when the government only makes 5s. per case over that... I don't know whether you are aware that we are at present in a condition of great depression, and there is no improvement in the state of affairs, as the European capitalists are tired of putting in more money in a place which has to pay enormous prices for its principal commodity, dynamite, and where such extraordinary tariffs exist as those shown by our railway tariff. As a friend of the government I can only point out to you, gentlemen, that if this depression lasts you will soon feel the effects in your own budgets...'

George Albu then turned to what he described as 'a few minor questions', by which he meant the Liquor Law and the administration of the law. 'The drink, gentlemen, is the curse of the place, and unless the law is strengthened ... the traffic will continue rampant...' He threw in for good measure an appeal for an honest Detective Department. But it was when he turned, under questioning, to the labour question that George Albu nailed the Randlords' true colours to the mast. 'The native at the present moment receives a wage which is far in excess of the exigencies of his existence. The native earns between 50s. and 60s. per month and then he pays nothing for food or lodging, in fact he can save almost the whole amount he receives... If the native can save £20 a year, it is almost sufficient for him to go home and live on the fat of his land. In five or six years' time the native population will have saved enough money to make it unnecessary to them to work any more. The consequences of this will be most disastrous for the industry and the State... I think if the native gets sufficient pay to save £5 a year, that sum is quite enough for his requirements, and will prevent natives from becoming rich in a short space of time.'

When the Commissioners inquired what George Albu would do about this, he replied, nothing daunted, 'The only remedy I can suggest is that we pay the native a wage which, whilst enabling him to save money, will hinder him becoming exceptionally rich...' To the obvious question, why were the wages not reduced before, George Albu replied, 'For years and years we were labouring under a scarcity of native labour, which to a great extent is now abated. At the present moment we have sufficient labour. Secondly, we have come to the conclusion that it is absolutely impossible to pay these high wages. We have either to reduce our expenses, or we have to shut down the greater number of our mines.' He went on to explain the problem the industry had with recruitment: 'The native, as a rule, who wants to come down to work, has no money, and the mining industry has to advance his fares; and when the native comes here, we have so little control over him that he can easily desert. It has occurred to companies who have brought down five hundred natives at a cost of £1,250 that three hundred have deserted after a week.'

Later, the Commissioners returned to this subject, where George Albu was of course reaching to the very heart of the issue of colonial and racial exploitation and speaking with a rare candour.

'How do you intend to cheapen kaffir labour?'

'By simply telling the boys that their wages are reduced. The maximum at present is 2s. 3d. a shift and we can reduce that to 1s. 6d., that is for skilled labour. Ordinary labour 1s. or less for the shift...'

'Suppose the kaffirs retire back to their kraals? ... Would you be in favour of asking the government to enforce the labour?'

'Certainly. A kaffir cannot live on nothing.'

'You would make it compulsory?'

'Yes, I would make it compulsory and without using force. A tax could be levied. If a white man loiters about without doing anything he is run in. Why should a nigger be allowed to do nothing? If there is a famine in a district, then government has to pay for it, and that falls back again on the industry. Therefore, I think a kaffir should be compelled to work in order to earn his living.'

'Would it not be called slavery?'

'Not so long as the men earned a certain amount of money.'

'If a man can live without work, how can you force him to work?'

'Tax him then.'

Another Commissioner asked the question which would feature promi-
nently in the years ahead: 'Is it possible to replace kaffir labour by [white]
miners?'

George Albu replied: 'That is not possible. I don't think a white man can
do considerably more work than a skilled kaffir.'

The Commissioners, evidently either fascinated or made nervous by the
brusqueness of George Albu's opinions, returned once more to his thoughts
about native recruitment.

'Is there a law in England to get forced labour?'

'No; nowhere in the world as far as I know... I, as an employer of labour,
say it would be a good thing to have forced labour, but another question is
whether you could get it.'

'Do you think the people would consent to such a [tax] law?'

'I do not know ... the law is not the same for the kaffir as for the white
man.'

'How can you say so?'

'The native, for instance, has to wear a badge, and he must not be out after
9 o'clock...'

A Commissioner pointed out that two-thirds of the natives in the mines
were not subjects of the State: 'How can we go and tax natives who are not
our subjects?'

'No, of course not. The native who comes here would not get taxed. He
works.'

After he had sat down, George Albu took a lively part in the cross-ex-
amination of other witnesses and did not hesitate to express his own tren-
chant opinions. For example, in questioning the Chairman of the Transvaal
Licensed Victuallers Association, he declared: 'My experience is that ... to
supply natives with drink in fair measures or indiscriminately, as during the
past eight years, is simply a dark blot on humanity. I shall ever advocate the
total abolition of the sale of drink to natives...'

Here, as elsewhere, George Albu appears to have been reporting the
unanimous view of the mine-owners. The director of the dynamite concession, for example, in which Nobel had a principal stake, was given a fear-
ful hammering by the Commissioners, including a blazing row with George
Albu, who became positively witty at one point: 'You know, the whole thing
would be a very good subject of Gilbert, the author [of "and Sullivan"]. For
this Commission, it is sufficient to know that dynamite is sold at Home at
23s., and that this enormous interest is to pay 85s. Where does the difference go to? Somebody must make a profit...'

It had been widely supposed that the government had planned for the Industrial Commission to expose that the depression in the mines (half of them were working at a loss at the time) was caused by financial sharp practice by the owners rather than by state abuses. If so, Pretoria's strategy misfired: the Report of the Commission delivered a series of recommendations and conclusions which were overwhelmingly sympathetic to the industry's evidence and arguments. The Randlords might have been justified in claiming a famous victory, with battle honours for George Albu and Amandus Brakhan. In actuality, the Kruger government did almost nothing beyond a few minor reductions of the rail rates and the price of dynamite. The tension between the Uitlanders and Pretoria seemed certain to increase again, as even Boers protested at Kruger's disregard of the Industrial Commission, but in February 1898 he achieved a sweeping victory in the presidential election in which one of his opponents was the respected Chairman of the Commission, who stood on a platform of industrial reform. Sir Alfred Milner had arrived in Cape Town from London the previous May as Governor of the Cape and High Commissioner of South Africa. In November the mineowners had agreed to a re-amalgamated organisation, to be re-titled the Chamber of Mines of the South African Republic. Albu and Brakhan were asked to join the Executive on behalf of the General Mining and Goerz groups, and the country proceeded towards war.

O*ne hundred years ago, the Johannesburg where the Albus were to make their fortune was a rough, tough, noisy and dusty place. The stamp batteries set up a constant hubbub, the dirt roads and the mine-dumps created a pervading swirl of dust, and the frequent accidents on the mines were matched by a constant and inescapable prevalence of disease.*

Even a Randlord-in-embryo had to concern himself with the day-to-day detail of administration, hygiene and basic services, as George Albu's letters demonstrate. For example, on 21 March 1894, he politely asks his landlord to provide electric light to his office – one bulb in each of the four rooms – 'as the days are getting very short already'. On 30 March 1895 he is upbraiding the Secretary of the Johannesburg Waterworks Company: 'In spite of repeated requests to use the pump which is specially attached to the pit they persist in not doing so (and never clean the pit) consequently causing great inconvenience. I have also frequently observed the men on duty, instead of putting a clean bucket down each bin, simply emptying the old one and putting it back again...'

On 10 June 1895, he complains in person to the Head Director of the Telegraph Department about the late delivery of cables to his office. In August a Telegraphic Code Book is introduced, with special alterations, to allow confidential communication with the London Office which Leopold

Albu was opening. In January 1896 he orders a special new filing cabinet to be shipped from London, 'Fitted for Foolscap files'. George Albu also had to do battle with the authorities on the matter of his own house: on 17 June 1896, 'I am sorry to have to call your attention again to the deplorable state of the street in front of my house and of End Street generally. During the dry season the dust was unbelievable and now after the rains the dust has turned into a thick paste...' (He was right to be annoyed because on 2 April he had been promised that a kerb and gutter would be laid in front of his house immediately.)

On 27 July 1897 – a great day! – he was ordering a telephone for the General Mining office – 'The wires are already laid.' (In February 1898 he would be complaining furiously that a new line had not yet been installed at his own home.)

Sometimes the letters show how his brother Leopold was already developing the miserly streak which was to become evident in the years ahead. In November 1903 the Johannesburg office has to devote pages of an inter-office letter to London to sort out whether or not Mr Leopold agrees with one bill, whether 'the charges for the cigarette box and sandwich box are absurdly high' (he offered to pay half), whether the china on order from London has been received in good order, and 'he has no recollection of having contracted such a large liability to Maples'. As for the repairs to the Victoria carriage ordered by him from Hooper, 'The spring of the Victoria broke during the first two days trial of the carriage, and Mr Leopold Albu desires that you will bring this before Messrs Hooper and Co and request them to refund to you the amount of £5.18.6 being the expenses incurred by Mr Albu in repairing the damage...' (4 January 1904).

But civilisation was coming fast to Johannesburg. On 5 November 1907 General Mining writes to the Johannesburg Municipality: 'The General Mining building having been connected up with the Town Sewerage System, yesterday morning, we shall be glad if you would discontinue the Tank Wagon service after tomorrow morning.' Even more dramatic – on 5 February 1908 – 'We shall be glad to hear from you at your early convenience when the Otis Elevator which you are installing is likely to be completed...'

The modern age had arrived. There were electric broughams to join the horse trams and cabs; there were Zoo Lake, the Wanderers Club, theatres and the races for (white) social life. Society dressed formally and elegantly on every such occasion. The Albus would soon be moving into Northwards, high on the Parktown Ridge. And below the Ridge, early every morning, the ox-wagons could be heard creaking up Oxford Road, bringing their produce to Johannesburg's Market Square.

CHAPTER TWO

THE ANGLO-
BOER WAR

George Albu's letters to his brother chart the tragedy. On 21 February 1898, he wrote: 'The outlook of the political situation in the Transvaal is not at all bright and we go further and fear very grave complications between that State and Great Britain. The government of this Republic appears thoroughly tired out by the continual nagging tone of Mr Chamberlain's despatches and will we fear take the invitation to throw down the gauntlet. You can well imagine what that would mean. It is an actual fact that loads of arms and ammunition have been sent over from Pretoria this week and taken to the Johannesburg Fort. It is an equally well known fact that Great Britain has sent out troops lately to South Africa... British prestige in this country does not admit of any other solution of the question. If Great Britain again retires with the tail between its legs then goodbye to British prestige in South Africa... Whether our prognostications be too pessimistic or no, we cannot too strongly recommend to you to abstain from further fresh business for the present...'

A month later, on 14 March, upset by the murder of Woolf Joel, Barney Barnato's heir at 'Johnnies' – ('the moving spirit in that firm. The firm is extremely sad and it appears that the house of Barnato Bros is now doomed to decay'), he was reporting that 'as far as the political outlook is concerned, we are living in a state of unrest and anxiety... We are afraid we shall not have any rest for a long time to come and until then it is ridiculous to expect decent times... Life in the Transvaal has become a burden, the people having become hardened and callous through the many reverses they have experienced.' His pessimism encouraged him to talk in subsequent letters of selling out, or running down, various holdings, for example in George Goch or in Rand Mines: 'Statistics have proved that very few men in the world have acquired fortunes by speculating and we must therefore conclude that there are but few men that are imbued with that true instinct of gauging the effects of political or financial consequences and we regret to say that we do not belong to those few. In any case we must not lose the opportunity of disposing of our holdings in the above companies this time...'

On 31 December 1898, he was writing to London: 'Everything is being done to incense Pretoria against the "Uitlander" and the whole position can only be compared to a Powder Magazine requiring but a spark to cause an explosion. It is quite evident England wants this eventuality, and will get it sooner or later, by foul or fair means; all the more so because Rhodesia as a mining country is apparently an utter failure and the Transvaal the only State in South Africa which supports the whole of the Cape...' He granted that Leopold might think him too gloomy, but 'holding the opinions we do, we are in favour of realising whatever we can.'

Evidently the Dresdner Bank, watching the political deterioration, had been losing its nerve, to George's irritation and depression: 'It seems to me, judging from the letter the Dresdner Bank wrote to us, that they somewhat regretted having ventured a South African speculation through the medium of our firm. Now, we feel that the results so far obtained perfectly justified them, but that G and L Albu too have the right to feel dissatisfied with the results. At the same time, as little as we blame the Dresdner Bank, as little have they the right to blame us.'

On 20 March 1899, George was briefly more cheerful because he could report that the government 'is desirous to come to a thorough understanding with the mining industries and Uitlanders in order to establish peace.' A week later – this was the month, curiously enough, when his office acquired a typewriter for the first time, to the relief of subsequent historical researchers! – he was still in a hopeful mood, insisting that General Mining's company funds should be placed on call with the Dresdner Bank ('We cannot compare our Corporation with Wernher, Beit and Co or the Goldfields...') and adding that Brakhan had resigned from New Goch so that the company was now entirely under Albu control.

But by May 1899 it was clear to George that Britain was intent on war and that Kruger would refuse to make enough concessions to avert it. 'The attitude taken up by Mr Chamberlain is sufficient indication at this time that Great Britain means business and will if possible make war with the Transvaal. There is only one way by which such a calamity can be averted, and that is if Paul Kruger concedes all the demands made by the so-called Uitlander population. We know that the Transvaal government will go to a great length to satisfy these demands, but they will not do anything that may in time to come endanger the independence of this State. They would sooner fight the English and are fully determined to defend themselves.

'It is quite clear that Chamberlain does not care a fig for any reforms. What he and Rhodes want is the country, and under such circumstances the gloomy views taken by everyone here are quite justified. You will readily understand the worry this unfortunate condition of affairs is causing our Mr Albu, and that it is difficult for him under the circumstances to clearly discuss business...' (There was throughout this period a convention that George's letters referred to himself in the third person.)

Leopold in London apparently thought he knew better and was still arguing in July that war was out of the question. 'We differ from you entirely,' replied George on 3 July 1899, 'and so do all the other big houses, as is clearly demonstrated by the fact that every one of them has taken the precaution to send away their own and their Company's securities. We think we are the only group on these fields who have not done so yet, although we have everything put together in such a manner that it can be sent, at a moment's notice, to a place which is more secure than Johannesburg.'

By late September George was reporting: 'The white miners are gradually leaving the Mines owing to the war scare. The different groups endeavoured to stop the exodus by offering the men who are willing to stay a bonus of £25 in terms of enclosed circulars, but the same has seemingly had very little effect as they continue to leave. If this goes on nearly every mine on the Rand will be compelled to shut down'. On 2 October, he was writing: 'The situation is getting more critical every day and the Boer Commandos are massing on the Border. The British government, no doubt due to the idea that the Boers would climb down, has not taken the precaution to send sufficient troops to South Africa, and if – in the case of hostilities actually breaking out – the Boers should win the first battle or two, the whole of the Cape and the Natal Dutch are likely to rise, thus most seriously complicating the position.'

And then, on 25 October 1899, George was suddenly writing from Cape Town in the heat of war, scrawling a long and urgent letter to his brother in London: his immediate concern was to report on the value of the Corporation's gold, which had been either commandeered by the Transvaal government or left behind, and to explain how men had been left in place to run the mine pumps: 'It is very difficult at present to prognosticate when the end will be. Three months is probably the longest time the Boers can hold out.'

George Albu was one of the last of the mine-owners to retreat from Johannesburg to the safety of the Cape: he left on 16 October 1899, long after 40 000 other whites had fled the city on overcrowded refugee trains; war had been declared on 11 October. He fretted in Cape Town, where he opened an office in Mansion House Chambers and was concerned to correct an over-embellished London press account of his escape, which he described as 'a concoction of the inventive brain of a liar'. The truth was, he explained, that 'The train consisted of several First and Second Saloon carriages and about eight coal trucks, carrying in all about 1,200 passengers. The Boers neither searched Mr Albu nor asked him for money, and he ascertained at the time that neither personal effects nor money were commandeered from any of the passengers on the train. Travelling through the Transvaal and the Free State the Boers behaved most friendly and went even so far as to help the women to carry their luggage down the embankment on which the train had stopped by reason of the rails having been taken up...'

As we have seen, he was still expecting an absence from the Rand of only three months. Eventually, it was the Group's most reliable property, the Meyer, which was to be the first mine to reopen – but that was not until 4 May 1901. The frustrations – and the losses – were made worse because for 11 of those 19 months, despite the Rand's reoccupation by the British forces, the Generals refused to let the miners return.

George Albu spent part of his time in Cape Town sending a stream of often irritable letters to Leopold in London (who, as always, replied in kind). 'If you entertain the idea that our supposed leisure in Cape Town induces us to indulge in criticism or harpings on your transactions, you are mistaken...' he had the grace to concede in May 1900. The only positive value of this period was that the brothers were able to think through, and debate by sea-mail, the future policy of their group, whose public flotation in London would have been at the turn of the century if the war had not intervened.

Some of the German nationals who had been left behind on the Rand because they were considered 'neutral' were to have a more exciting time. George Albu's brother-in-law, Hans Rosendorff, for instance, commanded a section of the Mine Guards who were set up to attempt to protect the properties from the widely feared danger of Boer raids. The manager of the Van Ryn, another German national called Wentz, had a close encounter with Boer commandos in January 1900. He smuggled out a personal note to George Albu: 'I am sorry having to report that the Boers succeeded again in raiding our district on January 29. This time they came with the sole purpose of burning everything down... In the Battery Engine Room three dynamite charges had been laid ... the high-pressure cylinder and guide piece of the engine was seriously damaged and so was the casting with the tubes of the condenser. The third charge in the compressor not going off, the secretary and myself succeeded in dissuading the raiders from renewing the charge, which I afterwards was able to extract, and so save the compressor. At the eastern section the head-gear and the Main Shaft Number 4, as well as the crusher station and the workshops, were burned down to the ground. The Estate Battery had already been set on fire at five different places and the front entrance was guarded by the armed raiders. With two of my men – at the risk of our lives – I entered the Battery from the back, unobserved by the Boers, and we were lucky enough to put a few buckets of water on the fire. Whilst doing this the raiders were recalled and thus the mill was saved. The Engine House at Number 4 shaft had been set on fire too, but it was quenched by the mine captain and myself...'

But the most important German 'neutral' to stay behind was not a General Mining employee but Amandus Brakhan, the Managing Director of A Goerz and Co. The most senior of the mine managers to remain in Johannesburg, Brakhan was particularly involved in protecting the interests of German shareholders, and he was the Transvaal representative of the Committee which had been set up in Berlin for that purpose. He and his colleagues had as their priorities the pumping of the mines, their protection against casual damage, the recruitment of Mine Police, and an attempt to keep Cape Town informed of the situation behind the lines. He also had an important diplomatic role – to persuade the Pretoria government to hold back from the destruction of the installations which was being urged by some of President Kruger's followers as they were forced back by the irresistible weight of massive British reinforcements. Brakhan was able to employ the effective argument that sympathy for the Boer cause in Germany and France, where there were many shareholders, would be alienated if Continental investments were damaged. This point had been appreciated even before the war. Brakhan had reported in a letter dated 22 July 1899: 'We feel pretty sure that a certain section among the Boers will try to prevent any serious damage being done to property which is controlled by German or French firms, if one may speak of any French firms here at all.'

On 9 September he wrote, 'We are having some dozens of German flags made in order that 3 or 4 of them may be flown in the case of necessity at each of the properties in which we are interested.' The same letter described the other arrangements that had been made for the safety of the mines: 'Each mine will retain a month's supply of coal based on present requirements. This of course is with a view to continuing pumping operations. Suitable pipes are being prepared, together with caps which can easily be soldered on, in order to contain the mine plans which, in case of necessity, can be lowered into the shaft... Lead-lined wooden boxes are being made to contain the mine books, which are either to be lowered into the shaft or buried. Preparations will also be made for filling in a portion of the shafts at a depth, say, of 75 feet in the case of vertical and 100 feet in the case of incline shafts. This will be done by means of lagging, consisting of deals being put across the sett nearest to a bearer, upon which will be placed 6 to 8 feet of wooden blocks and chips and refuse, and then on this, say, 6 feet of well-sifted ashes. The idea is that if the shafts are set on fire, this layer will stop its progress, while it will also minimise and localise the damage done in the event of dynamite being used...'

In the event, these fears proved exaggerated. British army forces reoccupied Johannesburg on 31 May 1900, eight months after the outbreak of war. The town saw no fighting because Lord Roberts agreed to Dr FET Krause's proposal of a 24-hour delay to allow the Boers to withdraw: Krause had earlier had to use physical force to foil an attempt by Judge AF Koch to destroy the mines. Engineers sent up from Cape Town were able to confirm in due course that there was no serious damage.

But it was a closer-run thing than this summary suggests, and the dangers were certainly not over. At the turn of the year, State Secretary Reitz had caused a panic in Europe by warning that as a last resort the Republic was planning to blow up the mines as part of a scorched-earth policy. In March 1900, the Mines Police discovered that preparations were being made to dynamite the various shafts. George Albu and Henry Strakosch in Cape Town lobbied Lord Milner and a Proclamation was published on 26 May promising retaliation against anyone responsible for 'wanton destruction and damage'.

Brakhan had again been instrumental in protecting the mines, according to a report from Henry Strakosch to London dated 2 May 1900: 'At the time when Mr Munnik ordered the laying of mines in some of the shafts ... Mr Brakhan immediately made representations to the government and also protested against Mr Munnik's doings with the Commander of the Republican Forces, Mr Louis Botha, who is personally known to Mr Brakhan. Mr Botha is supposed to have, immediately upon receipt of Mr Brakhan's telegram, wired to President Kruger informing him that he would resign his position as Commander of the Republican Forces if the preparations for the destruction of the mines were not immediately stopped. We have therefore to a great extent to thank Mr Brakhan for his prompt action.'

Now, in the anti-climactic 12 months during which the Boer commandos tied down the British army while the mine-owners fumed in Cape Town, forbidden by Lord Kitchener to return to the Rand, the Boers – and General Smuts in particular – changed their mind about the mines and decided to target them. Modderfontein and New Kleinfontein were attacked in December 1900, the latter by a 350-strong commando. The Chamber of Mines, meeting in its Cape exile, won Lord Milner's agreement to set up a Rand Rifles Mines Division, to be manned by former miners and funded by the Chamber, with the specific task of defending the installations (this funding rapidly became a matter of controversy, with George Albu among the loudest complainants). Albu and Brakhan had a particular interest – the mills at Van Ryn and Modderfontein were attacked and burned in January 1901, and the Rand Electric Company (which powered the all-important pumps) was also damaged. Perhaps the Boer commandos had left their change of tactic too late. The Mine Guard rushed to the north, did its job successfully and was eventually disbanded in December 1901.

On 4 May 1901 George and Leopold Albu were to preside over the dropping of stamps at the Meyer, but only after a period of long and intense frustration. Notwithstanding the British occupation of the Rand, the companies, of course, did not get off scot-free. They lost production for between 18 and 36 months; worse, nine of them were commandeered by the Boers for more than six months and their production largely funded the war. The National Bank in Pretoria had had its gold and coin reserves removed by Smuts – to inspire the later fantasy tales of the mysterious and hidden 'Kruger's Gold' – and, of more direct concern to owners like Albu and Brakhan, at the start of the fighting some (not all) of the bar gold at the mines was confiscated and the plates scraped. The attempt to recover the value of this scraped or commandeered gold from the European insurance companies was to consume much tedious correspondence in the months, even years, ahead.

The mining houses, like almost everyone else, underestimated the capacity of the Transvaal to resist the British army, and therefore never dreamed that the industry would be closed for up to a couple of years. Even the normally hard-headed young Henry Strakosch, reporting intelligently to London on the significance of British reverses in the opening weeks of the war – 'The moral effect of these British defeats upon the Boers will be to induce them to go on fighting to the end' – admitted that his previous calculation of a return to the Rand 'about March or the beginning of April' might be over-sanguine, and added, 'Under present circumstances it is very difficult to foresee when a settlement of this unfortunate War will take place ... we still think that unless some decisive victories are achieved by the British troops normal conditions will not be restored until well into the second half of next year' (by which he meant 1900).

No one appreciated that the war would drag on another two years. George Albu, writing to Leopold in London at the end of May 1900, reported: 'There are rumours this morning that Lord Roberts has entered Johannesburg and found the mines undisturbed and undamaged. We should therefore regard the campaign as almost concluded.' By his weekly mailship letter the following week, he was explaining, 'Now that the War seems to be practically at an end, we expect the government will make some arrangements enabling anyhow some of us to return to Johannesburg almost immediately'. On 13 June 1900, he was writing: 'Negotiations for our return to Johannesburg were progressing favourably and everybody was in hopes of starting by about the end of this week. But yesterday we were informed ... that all arrangements for the despatch of mining trains are off. The matter may therefore be regarded as postponed *sine die.*'

The rest of 1900 was to be a period of misery and despair for the Albus and their colleagues. George Albu, always prone to depression, took a gloomy view of the future. He seems to have seen the writing on the wall at the beginning of that year: 'From what we can learn, the Boers are determined to fight to the bitter end and the War might therefore last fully another six months longer.' His views were evidently coloured by his private sympathy for the Boers. On 27 June 1900 he was writing to his brother in London: 'We fear that the greater portion of the expenditure caused by the War will have to be borne by the Mines, and that our taxation will therefore be, contrary to what it was prior to the War and under the Dutch regime, a comparatively heavy one. This may or may not be counterbalanced by better administration of the country, but with views such as we hold, namely that our economic grievances were nil, we must necessarily come to the conclusion that taxation will affect us in a manner that will add to the cost of production.'

His sympathies were not entirely a secret, as he would surely have wished them to be. On 18 April 1900 Henry Strakosch had written to the Goerz office in London: 'We are much interested to read in your letter that there is considerable feeling against the Albus in City circles. It seems not unlikely that this is caused by the very open pro-Boer attitude taken up by this firm. Mr George Albu quite openly expresses his pro-Boer feelings; but hardly anybody in Cape Town takes any notice of him now. The other groups like ourselves, ignore him, and you will have noticed from the letters which were addressed to the Governor that he was not asked to sign them. We thought this the most advisable course, because the people at Government House know Mr Albu's sympathies, and the Governor might therefore not have liked to have his signature on documents of this kind.'

The bad feeling between the Albu and Goerz camps – which were still assumed by the outside world to be German allies – was no longer in doubt; never again would relations be as amicable and co-operative as in the early 1890s. The role played by Amandus Brakhan in Johannesburg seems to have irritated the Albus: already in November 1899 George Albu was pouring out his heart to Leopold: 'That firm [i.e. Goerz] is anything but popular... It is amusing to read in the *African Review* how Brakhan and Goerz are constantly appearing before the public in print... To take notice of this craving for self-advertisement would simply be foolish and we see no reason why we should introduce articles which would only help to bring about the effects desired by Goerz and Co...' By 24 January 1900, he was positively vitriolic when reporting on the recent appointment of the Mine Police: 'Brakhan had no more to do with the formation of the Corps than our Mr Albu had. All the credit for initiating the movement is due only to the gentlemen aforementioned and to nobody else. Goerz and Co and we, the same as the other groups, only joined after the idea of starting the Corps had assumed some tangible form... If Mr Goerz at home delights in advertising himself we should not deprive him of that pleasure, as small things always amuse small minds.'

George curtly dismissed his brother's suggestion that he come home to London: 'He wants to be as near to Johannesburg as possible in order to be one of the first there again, when that time comes. We can assure you that it is no pleasure to be here at the present moment and a few months at home would be very nice, but his first duty is to look after our interests.' On a technical issue concerning a Deutsche Bank bond guarantee to the Violet mine, he was flying off the handle in a 4 April letter to Leopold in a way which again demonstrated the growing antipathy between the two groups. He poured scorn on Henry Strakosch who, he said, was simply trying to prove his sagacity to his employers in London: 'The spirit of vanity which pervades the members of the firm Goerz and Co is ever apparent and, whilst we were weak enough to humour him, we were not foolish enough to let him score a success over us.'

One reason for George Albu's bad temper at the time was that he was beginning to realise that there was no sign of an end to the fighting. By April 1900 his pessimism, or rather his realism, had been confirmed: in his words, 'That the market is stagnant must be attributed to the fear entertained by most of us here that the War may last very much longer yet than anticipated. It is said that General Roberts does not intend to make a move for another month, and we believe that the Transvaal Boers will fight to the bitter end, even after Pretoria has fallen, for stores and ammunition, we hear, are being sent to the Spelonken, situated somewhere in the low country, a district which affords them on account of its mountainous formation the opportunity for carrying on guerrilla warfare of the very worst description. We warn therefore of our opinion that it is absolutely premature to talk at the present moment about the introduction of shares or of already providing the necessary supplies for the Mines.'

The Albus' sympathy for the Boers, which had become more and more apparent after their discretion in the aftermath of the Jameson Raid, is noteworthy because it corrects the common impression that the Randlords unanimously welcomed the war, or that they were universally pro-war and pro-British. For example, in the first, hurried, letter George Albu sent to Leopold on his arrival in Cape Town, dated 25 October 1899, he acknowledged the friendly reception he had received on his final visit to Pretoria when attempting to salvage the company's gold ('They assured Mr Albu that the government will repay us every penny after the termination of War, but that they find it impossible to treat us differently from others. If they returned the gold to us they would have to do likewise for Goerz and other firms and this they could not do at all...')

In the first weeks of his exile in Cape Town, George was quite straightforward in a letter to Leopold – 'Our own sympathies with the Boers prompt us to desire for a speedy cessation of hostilities. They fought bravely and well... It has been always beyond our comprehension how the Transvaal and Free State could take up the attitude they did towards Britain, it can only be explained by the fact that those whom the "Gods wished to destroy they first strike with blindness". Whether the Boers have deserved this fate or whether the War is a just one is now too late to discuss. The fat, vulgarly speaking, is already in the fire and must burn to cinders... One thing is certain, namely that the British Public will at last gradually become large shareholders in our industry, and we for ourselves ought to be willing to sell them all they want to buy...'

The re-unification of the mining industry with the formation of the Chamber of Mines of the South African Republic in November 1897 had not meant that the Randlords thereafter agreed on everything. On the contrary, Albu and Brakhan, and also Wernher and Eckstein, had been unhappy with the gung-ho line taken by Percy FitzPatrick, who was very much under the influence of some of the others, including Beit. This tension within the ranks of the Randlords intensified as the war proceeded. On 14 March 1900, for example, George in a technical letter to London lashed out at his fellow Randlords: 'They and their gang were powerful enough to bring about this frightful war and their influence in the South African Market is equally powerful...' On 28 March 1900 he was insisting that the Boers were not going to damage the mines as so many of his colleagues feared ('We have not the slightest hesitation in giving it as our opinion that the Boers will not do any damage to our properties on the Rand. No matter what happens, their past and present actions prove conclusively that it is not their intention to wreak vengeance against Johannesburg. The origin of this fear must be traced to us Uitlanders, because, if the case had been reversed, we would probably not have left one stone on the top of another.')

As the months dragged by, George Albu became increasingly jaundiced.

On 18 July his weekly letter to Leopold illustrated his pessimism for the future and also his sympathy for the Boers, bringing together many of his grievances and also revealing the tension which frequently coloured the warm relations between the two brothers: 'The dragging character which the prosecution of this War has assumed makes it utterly impossible for us to give you any forecast as to the time when we will be allowed to return to the Rand en masse but, taking the most favourable view of the course of events, we do not think we are likely to get back before another two or three months... Foodstuffs in Johannesburg are very scarce, whilst butter, milk and flour are almost unobtainable. The military authorities show no desire whatever to permit any influx of people to the Rand, probably fearing the same disastrous results as were experienced in Bloemfontein in the shape of a serious outbreak of enteric fever epidemic and kindred elements... This War, although it has lasted already nine months, is not yet at an end and, though one should imagine that the courage of the Boers should by now be completely broken, they still show a desire to continue the fight. This is simply marvellous, if one considers the small number of men they have left. Some people, who have lately left the Transvaal, state that the opinion prevailing amongst the Boers – ridiculous as it may sound – is that the War is now only beginning.'

By 22 August, George Albu was again magnanimous to the Boers, scathing about the British politicians and also his colleagues, and pessimistic about future prospects. By now he was way out of line with the majority of his colleagues on the Chamber of Mines: 'In our opinion, the cost of this War will exceed £100 million, the greater portion of which will be saddled on the mines... We have no desire to detract from the Field Marshall's magnificent work, but, had the Boers contemplated a wholesale destruction of Mines and Works on the Rand, time would not have prevented them from doing so, as they have plenty of it. One must give the devil his due and recognise that the Boers have not carried on the War with the intention of destroying property. They did not destroy Koffiefontein, nor Jagersfontein, nor Kampfersdam and the Kimberley Waterworks. They had plenty of time to do these things and yet abstained. The same reasons prevented them from destroying Johannesburg. The reports that we have to thank Lord Roberts for finding our Works intact are spread for the purpose of saddling the mining industry with as big a share of the War Expenditure as possible.' George went on to dismiss claims that Mr Chamberlain had made about the dynamite concession: 'A few prevarications and lies more or less do not matter to an ambitious statesman.'

Some of what George was writing to his brother under the pressure of an unending war no longer tallied with his evidence to the Commission in 1897:

for example, 'We do not hold a brief for the Netherlands Railway, nor do we have any interest in it, but we deny that it was badly and expensively managed... The attitude people take up ... against the Netherlands Railway is frightfully unfair...' He went on to add, 'Conversations we had with men who returned lately from the Rand go a long way to prove that things are not as rosy up there as the public is made to believe through the medium of the press. The conditions prevailing are such that we cannot entertain the idea of a speedy return.'

George's letter of 7 November 1900, as the Boers were stepping up their sabotage of the railway lines, deserves to be quoted at length, because in this private outburst to his brother he was again betraying a position and indeed a passion very different from the stereotype of a Randlord: 'Feeling, and knowing full well, that there was no conspiracy to drive the British into the sea, that our cry for the franchise was only a sham, that our grievances – especially the economic ones – were nil, that the government – corrupt as some of its members may have been – gave us mining and mineral laws of such liberal nature, the like of which cannot be found in any country. Please mark our words, "the chickens will come home to roost" and the mining industry will have to suffer. Has it never occurred to you that the British government and the nation, despite all the jingoistic show, hate the present War, the cost of which they were assured would not be more than £10 million, and the operations of which would simply consist in a walkover. Underlying all this patriotic outburst, you find the impotent rage which every Englishman feels in the losses of men and money and, more than anything else, the loss of prestige. 250,000 have not been able to terminate a War against two small republics. In this time the Military now even go to the extent of adopting measures in order to finish the campaign which are disallowed by the so-called Geneva Convention, in as much as they wreak their vengeance against women and children and burn homesteads and farms by the thousands. No, they hate us for being the immediate cause...'

A year earlier, Lord Roberts's arrival in Johannesburg in May 1900, eventually followed by President Kruger's departure for European exile (in September), had opened another period of frustration and delay in which the Chamber of Mines, exiled in Cape Town, continued to put forward lists of names of the mining employees it urged to be the first to return in order to prepare for the speediest resumption of the industry. Roberts, conscious of the uncertain military situation, the shortage of provisions on the Rand, and the other demands on rolling stock, had put his foot down. Eventually a mere 20 engineers went north on 28 June – including George Denny, for General Mining, and Captain James for A Goerz and Co – only to be stranded for three days in Bloemfontein before being allowed up to Johannesburg for 10 days to prepare their reports.

Denny reported on 15 July 1900 from the Rand Club (which had managed to remain open throughout the war) to give a practical view of the situation on the ground: 'The Mines, some of them at least, were within an ace of being wrecked, and had not Dr Krause stepped in and arrested Judge Koch, we should not have found things in the condition they are in today. I visited the Goch yesterday and had a thorough look all around the surface works. I must express my great satisfaction at the condition of things. McDowell has been a brick, and has given very particular attention to everything in his charge... Of course we are handicapped in doing any work by a proclamation which states that only pumping may be done... As far as I can see there is nothing to prevent an immediate start if we had the men and materials to work with... The town is empty, saving for an occasional vehicle or passer-by in the midst of the town. One would think the whole place deserted. Everything at the office is just as I left it, and I can say the same of my house, not a thing destroyed or lost. There has been considerable looting however... Your house is intact, your horses are as well as when you left... As far as I can judge there is no likelihood of sending our workmen forward for the next couple of months, although rumour has it that Lord Roberts is about to begin his final coup, which will annihilate any further resistance on the part of the Boers...'

The other mining houses were in the same position. Henry Strakosch was trying, and failing, to get permission to go north. Brakhan, who could not risk coming down to Cape Town because he might not be able to get back to Johannesburg, was having problems with the Censor as he tried to send a wire in July to A Goerz and Co – not dreaming that Adolf Goerz was to die that very week, on holiday in Switzerland, at the early age of 43.

As the year passed, the flow of Uitlander refugees returning home from the coast to the Transvaal began to pick up very slowly. The situation in Johannesburg improved and the British generals gained confidence. In November 1900, Lord Milner agreed that every mine could send up one man. The Chamber of Mines was allowed by Kitchener to send a trainload of stores, but the rail service was still erratic. (George Albu wrote to London on 17 October that 'The railway line is by no means safe ... people may talk of peace, but as long as the country remains in the present disturbed state there can be no real peace.') Just a week later he reported that 'Matters seem even to be looking slightly worse now and our return appears as far off as ever... Fighting is reported from different quarters, town guards are being formed in the frontier towns and telegraphic communication with Johannesburg is again temporarily suspended...' There were frequent shortages of food in Johannesburg: the authorities limited distribution of food to burghers and men in the Rand Rifles (all British males allowed back to the Rand were required to join the Corps), with the result that other foreigners were seriously deprived; this led to a diplomatic contretemps with the German government in particular. Destitute foreigners, particularly Jews, were deported. The rule of the Uitlanders seemed to have arrived with a vengeance.

The scale of the problem should not be denied. Milner estimated in October 1900 that between 30 000 and 40 000 whites had been 'exiled from Johannesburg', usually to the coast, for more than a year and were getting to the end of their tether, yet the army continued to postpone permission for their return home. The authorities agreed that there should be a careful control of who should be authorised to 'come up', and when: in mid-1900, for example, George Albu had been included on an official list of Randlords who should *not* be given a permit at present.

George Albu was to continue trying to travel north. As he explained in a December 1900 letter to London, he was 'eager to proceed to the Rand after the New Year, but it seems somewhat unlikely that he will succeed in procuring a permit. On the other hand, he being a British subject, it may please the Military Authorities in Johannesburg to enrol him in the "Rand Rifles", a Corps which had ostensibly been formed for the purpose of guarding the town, but is at the same time liable for service anywhere in South Africa. As our Mr Albu has no desire to be placed in a position where he is obliged to shoot at Boers or to be shot at by them, he will very likely have to postpone the trip...'

He was still deeply pessimistic: 'It appears that the Boer leaders have made up their minds to fight to the bitter end. We can therefore only guess as to the moment when that bitter end has arrived... Let us hope that the reforms of which we have promised ourselves such grand results, will not disappoint our expectations, but recompense the Mining Industry for the big losses it has already sustained.' He was presumably attempting irony.

George Albu's exasperation seems understandable: in early January 1901 he reported that Lord Kitchener was declining to give military protection to the mines. As he commented in his weekly letter to London: 'In order to guard the Mines effectively we require to send forward about 3,000 men, which are to be drawn from former employees of the various companies. We doubt very much whether we can get anything like this number and to send less would only endanger our mines in case of an attack.' George seems to have changed his mind about Boer tactics, because he went on, 'Our own opinion is that the Boers, wherever they get a chance will destroy property, and to have but an inadequate number defending the Mines would simply mean to jeopardise the lives of those poor devils as well... We can only tell you that Kitchener's action proves that we have not misjudged the feelings of the military leaders towards us. He does not care a hang for our properties! His duty is to finish the War, and if we have not enough men to guard our Mines they will simply be left to the mercy of the Boers, to whom an excellent lesson was given in the destruction of property – a lesson they will not forget... It is our opinion that the darkest days in this campaign have yet to come, and we have a feeling that the British Army is nonplussed and, what is worse, disorganised. Time in South Africa has been put back at least a quarter of a century, and though the War may cease peace will never come. We are not in a pessimistic mood but the feeling of bitterness permeating the Cape Dutch, who form, after all, the majority and settled population in this country, is now so full of hatred against everything British that a real peace can never be re-established, and commerce and industry can only advance in countries that are settled and peaceful.'

And then, on 30 January 1901, General Mining in London received a message from the Cape Town office – 'We cabled this morning the fact that Mr Albu is leaving for Johannesburg.' By January and February of 1901, temporary permits were at last being issued to mine managers and other essential members of the vanguard of a general return, such as boarding-house keepers (an important profession in a town of bachelor white miners). There was also a problem to be sorted out about the pay of these white miners: the military authorities tried to insist that they be paid no more than the men on active service at 5 shillings a day, which was substantially less than their pre-war rate on the mines (8s 6d). The men threatened to stop work, which put at risk the pumping operations, as Brakhan explained to London on 9 April ('Figures received from Johannesburg show that about 875 workmen are employed in pumping and maintenance work, about half of whom are British subjects, 125 Americans, and the remainder of various nationalities. The British workmen can no doubt be prevailed upon in one way or another to keep on working; but on the other hand the mines might have to face a possible shortage of 300 men...') The solution, approved by Milner in May, was to pay the balance directly to a Mines Fund which paid 'allowances' to families and dependants.

Still, the Boer commandos were too active for the mine-owners' comfort. On 2 January 1901 Strakosch had reported to London that: 'The invading Boer commandos have been successful in pushing forward still further south, doing a good deal of damage to the Railway and private property... Another most unsatisfactory feature during the last week has been the attack upon the New Kleinfontein mine, which resulted in the burning down of the mill and crusher house.' In April George Albu reported another attack on Van Ryn and in July Brakhan wrote of an attack on Roodepoort ('An attempt was also made by the Boers to set fire to the coal bunkers of the Roodepoort United Main at that company's new incline shaft, and it is fortunate that this attempt was only made just prior to the Boers withdrawing, otherwise great damage might have been the result, for we understand that the Mine Guards adopted a very cautious policy (putting it mildly). There were about 17 mounted police belonging to the Johannesburg District located in the barracks and these, reinforced by about half-a-dozen volunteers from the Mine Guards, staved off the rush of the Boers on the barracks and, through their volley firing, held the enemy to retire... Altogether it appears that people are beginning to lose heart as regards the military operations... The opinion is held in leading circles here that the War may spin out for a fairly long time yet, and we must own that we are very much surprised that the cold weather has not influenced more Boers to surrender.'

Slowly – very slowly – the situation in Johannesburg was improving. Before the end of the month, the Chamber of Mines Executive Committee had visited Johannesburg to see Sir Alfred Milner and on 1 June 1901 the *Johannesburg Gazette* carried an official announcement of the resumption of mining.

General Mining's Meyer and Charlton had already won the race to be the first mine to resume production, although there was some muttering from rival houses because there had been a plan to have a simultaneous re-opening of three of the seven mines that were permitted to start. They were chosen because of their proximity to Johannesburg, as George Albu had been told during his reconnaissance to the Rand in January. George Albu's speech on the occasion of the dropping of the stamps and the re-opening of the milling plants at the Meyer was one of the most important and widely reported of his career, the equal of his evidence to the 1897 Commission of Inquiry. He had to choose his words carefully because, as his enemies no doubt observed at the time, he had to re-ingratiate himself with the victors, who knew perfectly well of his earlier and continuing sympathies for the vanquished.

He was as verbose as ever: '... a feeling of deep gratification ... epoch making period in the industry of South Africa ... pregnant with destiny ... how much meaning there is in the present re-starting of the industry ... preface of a new chapter ... fullness of sentiment ... a matter for congratulation ... the sounds emitted from the iron throats of the stamp battery, which to the untutored ear are harsh and grating, are to the nerves of the long-tried disciples of this particular musical school, soothing and satisfying to a high degree. They tell of the transition from the gloomy minor to the joyous and triumphant major passages, and ease the tension upon the strings, for long at breaking point...' [George Albu was musical] – and so on and so forth. 'During the past eighteen months, the supporters of this industry, be they masters or workmen, have suffered heavily... Can any parallel be found to the steadiness of the values of our mining companies' securities through the recent critical times? ... But yet there was no wavering...'

George Albu at last got to his message for his distinguished guests: 'Before the cessation of activity we had to face many problems in the development of the industry, and we find ourselves still confronted by the majority of them, though we expect to find that the advent of an enlightened administration will minimise them in our future operations.' He hoped that 'questions of taxation may be re-arranged', and added, 'The native labour question, with its accompanying drink bug-bear, the matter of the tariff, the reduction of living costs, the dynamite question, and the other difficulties that have been household words in the past, are real obstacles that are not to be settled without the employment of much time and perseverance. The government and the industry must work together for their mutual benefit...'

Lord Kitchener replied graciously, there were various toasts, and Mrs Wybergh (wife of the Acting Commissioner of Mines) was invited to break a bottle of champagne against the first of the stamps to be set in motion. Photographs were taken and gold medals presented. And as Amandus Brakhan observed caustically, in his letter to London on 10 May, 'It is generally held that the speeches of Mr Albu were much too voluminous and a little peculiar in view of the political position he has, even in Cape Town, been taking up' – an opinion to be confirmed by Henry Strakosch on 1 June, telling Joseph Kitchen in London that the newly ennobled Lord Milner 'has a poor opinion of Mr Albu and considers that, as is shown in part by his speech at the re-starting of the Meyer and Charlton mills, he shifts his ground'.

It is not surprising that the Albus have not usually been associated by historians with Eckstein, Beit, FitzPatrick, Farrar, Bailey, Rhodes and the other Randlords who contributed, either financially or on the field, to the British victory. There is a famous, and anti-Semitic, poem by Hilaire Belloc, which mocks the Randlords:

> *We also know the sacred height*
> *Upon Tugela side,*
> *Where those 300 fought with Beit*
> *And fair young Wernher died ...*
>
> *... The little mound where Eckstein stood*
> *And gallant Albu fell*

A South African Corporation

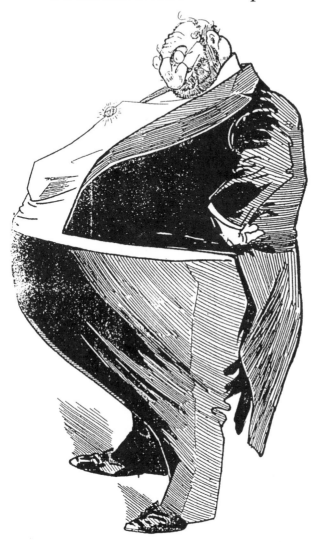

ITS LIMIT

'I am of the opinion that when the war . . . is over
. . . there will be no limit to the size of these
corporations' – John Morley

The Owl, published in Cape Town, produced a number of anti-Semitic cartoons. This one, from its Christmas number, December 1901, would have been seen by Johannesburgers as many were still refugees in Cape Town at this time.

And Oppenheim half-blind with blood
Went fording through the rising flood –
My lord, we know them well.

... The little empty homes forlorn
The ruined synagogues that mourn
In Frankfurt and Berlin ...

George Albu was, surely, libelled.

In the light of all this, George Albu must have felt himself in a diplomatically delicate position when the British authorities at last allowed the miners to return to the Rand and when – ironically, we may now think – he and Leopold presided over the re-opening of the Meyer and Charlton on 4 May 1901. This was a considerable publicity coup for the Albus, and the brothers made the most of it, but it is not surprising that George's effusive speech of gratitude to the authorities, here represented by Lord Kitchener himself, caused a certain raising of eyebrows in the industry, and indeed in Sunnyside, where Lord Milner had established his Johannesburg headquarters.

CHAPTER THREE

THE PEACE

On 31 May 1902, 12 months after the re-opening of the Meyer, the Treaty of Vereeniging was at last agreed. In contrast with the scenes of celebration in London, there was little enthusiasm visible in Johannesburg, according to the report to headquarters from the Goerz office. The mines were being re-opened steadily. Seven were operating, with 350 stamps, by early June 1901; another eight before the end of the year. Black labour doubled to 18 000 over that period. As early as July Lord Kitchener told the Chamber of Mines in confidence that he intended shortly to disband the Mine Guards (whose cost of 8s 6d a day was a grievance with the mine-owners). Various other problems were being sorted out – military escorts for the train to convey the gold to the coast (and who to pay for it, and who to insure it); recovery of commandeered gold bars; the shortage of trucks for transport of coal and supplies; protests about premature withdrawal of troops from outlying areas; permits to get skilled men back from the Cape; arguments about bureaucratic form-filling; the shortage of 'boys'.

The Goerz properties were in the rear of this process. As Brakhan reported on 24 May, 'There have been a thousand and one minor difficulties to contend with, but it is useless to trouble you with all these matters, beyond stating that they required not only a lot of time but also a great deal of trouble and tact.' Already the nature of future problems was clear. The first was the matter of *white* labour shortages; for example, Brakhan wrote to London on 31 May, 'The fact that on the Geldenhuis Deep, where all its 100 permits have been exhausted in bringing up men, there are too many men of certain trades while others are absolutely lacking, is no doubt due to insufficient care having been taken in the selection of the men... A large number of Rand rock drill men have died during the war, the cause of trouble being lung trouble, which has set in in consequence of the damp winter atmosphere in England, and even in Cape Town. The Mines, therefore, will in this respect, apparently meet with some trouble for the first year or two...'

Nor was the security situation without worries: again in Brakhan's words, dated 12 July 1901: 'We hear that it will now be very stringently enforced that every British subject who has not joined the Rand Rifles has to do so at once, or anyone of British or of other nationality who has joined has to comply very strictly with all regulations regarding drill and musketry practice, and that anyone who neglects his duty in this respect is to be sent over the Border...' But although Brakhan suggested that 'the War may spin out for a fairly long time yet', its practical effect for the mining industry was over. Now the Randlords confronted the problems of the Peace. The Johannesburg Stock Exchange re-opened on 17 December, with a celebration attended by a small but enthusiastic gathering. By December Kitchener was authorising the starting of another 500 stamps and Brakhan was beginning to report to his London Board on the alarming implications of the shortage of black labour. Commercial considerations were also re-emerging: 'It will be in our interest to assist Mr Albu to obtain permission to re-start as soon as possible, for we have observed that the shares of a mine about to re-start work are in demand.'

The principal problem of the peace was the disappearance of the labour which was the fundamental and essential requirement of the industry. In the middle of the war, in April 1900, Henry Strakosch had written from Cape Town to London trying hard to look on the bright side – 'One of the advantages which the mining industry may derive from British rule is of course a reduction in the price of dynamite, as well as a reduction in Railway rates, which however seems to us a trifling item in comparison with the advantages the industry will derive from a good and honest administration of the Native Pass, Liquor and Illicit Diamond Buying Laws, and the assistance on the part of the Government to supply the mines with natives.'

Dynamite and rail tariffs were indeed now going to be less important than the availability of native labour; everyone knew it. Brakhan, for instance, reporting to London on 13 December 1901, concerning the Chamber of Mines' attempt to get Lord Kitchener's agreement to restart 1 000 stamps, added: 'Everything, of course, depends on the influx of native labour and seeing that so far the Northern Transvaal is only available, whilst in future also some boys may be obtainable from the district line between Middelburg and Lydenburg, we are afraid that unless we soon obtain boys from the East Coast, it will be impossible to start 100 stamps per week, which would mean 6,000 boys per month, or double the quantity as forecast as likely obtainable.' As Brakhan had pointed out the previous month, the situation was awkward because 'Lord Kitchener has on several occasions expressed himself as somewhat displeased that the delay in starting up Mines, for which he has given his permission, is to his mind excessive; this gave him the impression that the Industry was clamouring for an expansion of Milling operations although the Mines were not as yet ready to start.'

The mines could not resume operations at their pre-war level because 100 000 black workers had been dispersed by the war and most of them were in no hurry to return to a wage which the Chamber of Mines had decided to reduce to 30 shillings a month from the pre-war rate of 43 shillings. This extraordinary decision, taken in the unreal atmosphere of Cape Town in late 1900, influenced no doubt by a euphoric determination to put the industry onto a profitable and businesslike footing, was unanimous; it was described as 'reasonable' and it was emphasised that this was a guaranteed wage free of deductions. But it misjudged the mood of a black population which had been disrupted and intimidated by the fighting, had plenty of alternative employment possibilities in the post-war reconstruction, had enjoyed several good rainy seasons, and was not over-disposed to leave the kraals. So, as the British army slowly mopped up the *bitter-einder* Boers and the mine managers made their plans, the black workers simply did not turn up. In other words, the first thing the Randlords did after they had won 'their' war was to shoot themselves in the foot. They spent much of the next decade coping with the consequences.

Lord Milner's administration allowed no doubt of its determination to see a speedy resumption of the mining industry. As George Albu had gloomily forecast, the mines were to be the milch-cow of the new South Africa, and the Randlords would soon look back with mixed feelings on the tax demands of the Transvaal Republic. But at least the grievances of the Uitlanders had not been forgotten: the Chamber gave evidence in October 1900 in Cape Town to the Lyttelton Commission, which had been set up by the British government to inquire into the Kruger government's concessions and, in due course, the explosives and liquor monopolies were cancelled and the Railways nationalised. Milner and the Chamber held amicable meetings. The Chamber, with most of its members back in Johannesburg, held its first post-hostilities Annual General Meeting on 3 April 1902 and heard that the Boer authorities had had 'access' to gold worth £2 690 000, of which £582 310-worth had 'vanished'. (The AGM minutes record 'laughter' – presumably of the pained variety.) More seriously, the losses sustained by the mines in cash divestments or costs as a result of the war were estimated at £3,4 million.

The Goerz group entered the post-war era confronted with problems greater than, and different from, the rest of the industry. It had the temporary difficulty that, for accidental reasons of geography, British troops were quartered longest on two of its properties on opposite sides of the Rand (Lancaster and Geduld). The Goerz mines were not given a high priority for reopening, perhaps for political reasons. The new management was conscious that its shareholders, of whom a large proportion were connected with Deutsche Bank, attached great importance to dividends, whereas development spending might have made better long-term sense. The underlying concern, of course, was to install and establish the new management team after the founder's death.

Adolf Goerz is fated to remain the most obscure of the Randlords. Comparatively little is known about him. It is thought that he might have had a history of heart disease, but none of his London colleagues can have imagined, when he set off on holiday to St Moritz in July 1900, that he was about to cable for his doctor, return to Lucerne and Lake Brienz, and die there at the age of 43. He was a bachelor who had established himself in London, in preference to Johannesburg, for some years. He was not really a 'Randlord' – he was more of a technical man, an engineer not a financier by background; he lived modestly (in St John's Wood) by Randlord standards. He was, one imagines, a more sophisticated, educated, discriminating, balanced man than many of the others, and he left £97 000, a third of it to his housekeeper, the rest to family in Germany and to various charities. (In 1900 this was by no means poverty, but needs to be compared with Alfred Beit's £8 million and Julius Wernher's £14 million.)

The obituaries were effusive and seemed to be making a point: for example, 'Mr Goerz was a rich man and a powerful one in the financial world but he was ever modest and retiring. Of all the Kaffir magnates he was decidedly the most simple and the most loveable. He was the soul of honour and a true friend' – or, 'He kept no yachts and wrote no letters to the newspapers... Not one penny of his wealth was amassed by trickery or any other than a legitimate manner' – or, 'Even of mind, philosophic of temperament, sober of judgement, painstaking and enterprising...' The *Daily Mail* was more down-to-earth: 'Mr Goerz was an unusually tall man and fairly robust, but for some time past he had been distinctly out of health...'

A sheaf of letters of commiseration has survived in the archives. His Chairman, Lord Battersea, wrote, 'I am quite horrified and very, very distressed... The loss to me personally and from a business point of view is very great – firstly, I had become very much attached to Mr Goerz for his kind courtesy and then I had learnt to trust his great intelligence and appreciate his honourable views and great devotion to work. We shall miss him very much. Indeed, I do not know to whom we shall have to entrust the destinies of our companies. I confess ... that I was *very anxious* about Mr Goerz's health

George Albu, the elder of the Albu brothers who left Germany for South Africa in the mid-1870s
to seek their fortune, eventually founding General Mining and Finance Corporation in Johannesburg
in 1895.

Leopold Albu co-managed General Mining and Finance Corporation from London and worked closely with his brother George for 50 years.

Adolf Goerz, the mining engineer from Mainz who founded AD Goerz & Co,
later to become Union Corporation. He died young in 1900.

Left: Leopold and George Albu with their extended family, together in the Johannesburg suburb of Doornfontein, c.1911: (left to right) unidentified, Nanny, Adelaide holding Veronica, Leopold, Alice (seated), unidentified, unidentified, George Werner (seated), Fanny, unidentified, unidentified, Charlotte, Kitty (seated), George, Ginny, Bobby, Walter.

Below left: Ginny Rosendorff, George Albu's childhood sweetheart and then wife. She was to be the head of the Albu family in Johannesburg until 1950.

Below centre: Adelaide, the young wife of Leopold Albu. She esteemed her beauty – and her jewels.

Below right: Leopold and Adelaide Albu with their baby daughter, Veronica. After their separation Adelaide would live mainly in Paris, while Veronica was brought up by her father.

Right: Leopold and George with their horses and dogs in Johannesburg, c. 1910.

Below: Leopold Albu poses on horseback while Adelaide, who was a distinguished horsewoman, looks on.

Left: Amandus Brakhan was recruited in 1892 and appointed Managing Director of A Goerz & Co in South Africa in 1897. He remained in Johannesburg throughout the Anglo-Boer War and played an important role there before returning to London.

Below left: Lord Battersea, an English peer related to the Flowers beer family, became A Goerz & Co's first Chairman in London at the turn of the century.

Below right: The young Henry Strakosch, A Goerz and Co's manager in Johannesburg and then Managing Director in London, who would become a leading international financial diplomat.

Sir Henry Strakosch, who ran Union Corporation for nearly 40 years, was awarded three separate orders of knighthood for his assistance on economic policy to the South African, Indian and British governments.

Top: Miners seeking their fortunes in the Transvaal crossed rugged terrain by oxwagon to get there in the 1880s. The Albu brothers followed this same route on the 28-day journey from Cape Town to Kimberley.

Bottom: An early view of Barberton (1885), where Leopold Albu attempted to join the gold rush before deciding to try his luck in Johannesburg.

Top: Early days at the Meyer and Charlton gold mine on the Witwatersrand. It was this small mining project which transformed the Albus from modest Kimberley diamond dealers into Randlords (1888).

Bottom: The Meyer and Charlton – 'the jewel box of the Rand' – was one of the earliest workings of the outcrop reef, very near the heart of Johannesburg.

Top: The first office of the Meyer and Charlton. George Albu was responsible for transforming this modest operation into a long-life and profitable mine.

Bottom: The second office of the Meyer and Charlton. The headgear and manager's buildings still survive, not far from Johannesburg's M2 motorway, as photographed in 1995 for the jacket of this book.

Top: Early Johannesburg (Fox Street) in 1898 – a rough and dusty place to do business. Even the Randlords had to exert themselves to receive adequate service.

Bottom: An early mining house on the Meyer and Charlton, typical of managers' accommodation throughout the Rand.

Top: The gold mines were an occasional target of guerrilla activity during the Anglo-Boer War.

Bottom: One example – from Potchefstroom – of the concentration camps set up during the Anglo-Boer War, which did so much to damage future relationships between Afrikaners and the British authorities.

Top left: Barricaded buildings in a deserted
Pritchard Street before the British occupation of
Johannesburg. The British army re-took this
town on 31 May 1900 as the Boer units
withdrew to continue their campaign.

Top right: British army units were posted at the
gold mines after the occupation of the Rand to
help the Mine Guards defend the properties
against attack by Boer commandos.

Bottom left: On 4 May 1901, after a long period of frustration, George Albu delivers his address at the re-opening of the Meyer and Charlton, the first Rand mine to resume operations after the war. George Albu is on the left, Leopold far right and Kitchener is seated centre.

Bottom right: Mr Joseph Chamberlain, the British Colonial Secretary, made a long and important visit to South Africa in early 1903 to plan the future of the country. Here he is seen making a speech in Johannesburg.

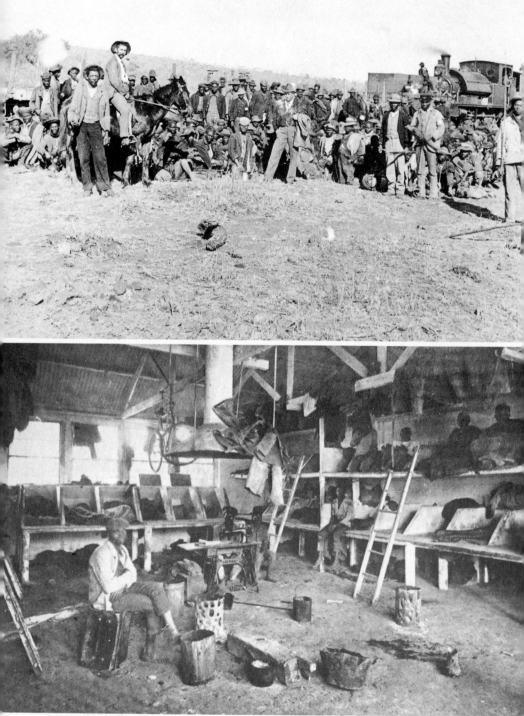

Top: A typical scene from the early 1900s, recruiting black labour for the gold mines.

Bottom: Cramped hostels with concrete bunks for beds were typical of the conditions in which black mine labour was expected to live in the first half of this century.

– if you remember, I expressed my anxiety and diagnosed to myself his condition as serious...'

George Albu, cabling from Johannesburg, was as brief as courtesy would permit:

'GOERZ LONDON

SINCERE REGRET

GEORGE ALBU'

Leopold Albu from London provided a longer and more conventional appreciation: '...His sudden removal in his prime of life is a loss which I feel very keenly. His genial nature and numerous good qualities commanded the respect of all with whom he came in contact, and he has left a gap in South African circles which will not readily be filled.'

The truest memorial of Adolf Goerz must be that his creation, Union Corporation, for much of the following century had a pre-eminent reputation for its mining and exploration skills.

In this emergency, with no succession laid down, the obvious solution was to summon Amandus Brakhan – who was in the throes of the dramas in Johannesburg at the time. Eventually Brakhan managed to get out of Johannesburg in September and travel to London to sort out the consequences of the founder's death. He returned to South Africa in January 1901 as Managing Director while the 30-year-old Henry Strakosch was brought back to London in 1901 as Manager of the office there with the promise of the London managing directorship (and a seat on the Board) the next year. The other London Manager, Joseph Kitchin, a former journalist, became Strakosch's long-serving right-hand man. The detail is important because Brakhan/Kitchin were to run the Goerz group with Strakosch for more than 40 years, and Strakosch, set free from the daily responsibilities on the Rand, was to become one of the most influential backstage financial diplomats of the century.

The Goerz group evidently had problems. It had four established mines on the West Rand, but both the Lancaster mines, having started well, were faltering. Its most promising and ambitious prospects in the East Rand basin were Modderfontein Deep, where Goerz had taken a stake in 1894, and, more ambitiously, the neighbouring Geduld. The new Goerz team decided that the West Rand had to be the priority and advanced £200 000 to Lancaster, Roodepoort Central Deep and Princess. Deutsche Bank swallowed the refusal of a dividend for 1900 – which hardly seems surprising in that of all years – but insisted on 10 per cent for 1901. 'Self-flotation' in Geduld helped out in 1902, but 1903 was difficult, with the producing mines calling for funds.

Rescue came with the 1904 flotation of Van Dyk Proprietary Mines, on an East Rand farm between Boksburg and Brakpan, where Adolf Goerz had taken options in 1898. Although the Goerz management was unconvinced about the East Rand – they had been sitting on Modder Deep for some years and Geduld still had no shaft – Deutsche Bank reckoned a flotation was possible and also agreed to underwrite a rights issue, which raised £550 000. After a great deal of hyping, the Van Dyk flotation in October 1904 was a success and Goerz cleared a profit of £243 000, so that the company celebrated by paying out a 15 per cent dividend for 1904. Then, sober reality returned. No dividends would be declared again until 1910.

As Henry Strakosch, in August 1905, wrote to Brakhan (who the next year would insist on moving, with the chairmanship, from Johannesburg to London): 'The present position is that our four producing West Rand companies are most seriously indebted to us and there is no prospect of reducing their liabilities except by some form of share issue, combined in all probability with drastic reconstructions... Now, the position has changed considerably for the worst. In the first place, the companies are, generally speaking, no longer making any profit and secondly the making of further share issues is not only made extremely difficult by the state of the market, but almost impossible by reason of the bad results of the companies themselves... We are drifting into a very unsound position...' On the insistence of Deutsche Bank there was a financial clamp-down. The immediate result was that Tudor, the Group's most recent western Rand flotation, was suspended forever, even before the shaft had reached the Reef. The rest of the story on the West Rand was also bleak: Lancaster merged with Lancaster West in 1908 and struggled on until 1913; Roodepoort Central Deep amalgamated with Princess in 1911 and managed to keep going until 1920. The problems were, quite simply, the labour shortage, the dearth of working capital, and the on-going need to fund debenture finance.

The depressing situation on the West Rand made it all the more important to press through with the shaft sinking on Geduld. Great embarrassment was caused in December 1905 when the assay samples were 'salted', to the fury of European investors. As Strakosch wrote to Johannesburg, 'the position was as bad and regrettable as it could well be... The past few days have been most unpleasant for us...'

The result of this succession of headaches was that the Goerz group – in a policy decision that was to distinguish it, for years to come, from the Albus' General Mining – decided to turn its attention outside and beyond South Africa. Their founder would probably have approved. During the war he had investigated pearl fisheries off German East Africa, gold in Hyderabad, lead in Spain and copper in South West Africa – none of which came to anything.

He may even have retreated to London in order to liberate himself from South Africa. Now – and repeatedly in the years to come – his Group was thinking internationally, not least in Mexico, where it was fated to find exciting times – and where, nearly 90 years later, Gencor would eventually return. Union Corporation was always inclined to think 'offshore'.

Meanwhile, the Albu brothers were also trying to re-establish their fortunes. Only days after the ceremonial opening of the Meyer, George and Leopold sailed together to Europe to restructure their finances, leaving the South African operations in the charge of George Denny and his brother Harry, their well-regarded consulting engineers who had learned their trade in the Australian goldfields.

The Albus had now been in South Africa for 25 years and they had the opportunity, in the weekly correspondence they exchanged between Johannesburg and London, to work out a sort of business philosophy. Their talents were complementary. George was the hands-on executive, the Managing Director who had taught himself to understand mining technology; Leopold in London was the financial man, at ease in the European markets, suspected by some of his counterparts (such as Sir Ernest Oppenheimer, for example) of being the sharper, better businessman; but he was more erratic, more effervescent, more alarmist (whereas George showed signs of being a depressive), less generous than his brother, more of a bully. Some contemporaries thought it was Leopold who had had the 'vision' of General Mining. Sometimes they swapped jobs, when Leopold in Johannesburg (as office folklore has it) would lose his temper, behave outrageously, fire the whole staff overnight. George by contrast seems to have been held in affection as well as respect.

In this age, before the international telephone, they were forced to conduct their arguments either by the weekly mailship letter or, when emotion overruled parsimony, by the cabled telegrams which, if they were at all confidential (as they usually were) had to be wearisomely translated into code. This running debate between the Albu brothers over many years casts light on the very development of South Africa, as well as giving us more than a passing glimpse of a saga of a German-Jewish family which sometimes seems worthy of Thomas Mann.

The trigger to the resurrection of the Albus' fortunes was the 1901 negotiation with Dresdner Bank and other German, French and British investors. The placing of 300 000 shares with a syndicate that included Dresdner, Disconto Gesellschaft and Bleichroder (and, of course, G & L Albu) raised £675 000. The two brothers owned about 50 per cent of General Mining, whose value at the time of the April 1902 Annual General Meeting had risen to £2,75 million. Most of General Mining's holdings were in the mines of the Group: unlike the Goerz group, the usual practice was to own about 25 per cent of each company. The old faithfuls at the heart of the portfolio were still the Meyer and Charlton and Roodepoort United, which were to pay dividends for years to come. Then there were three more outcrop mines – Aurora West, New Goch and Van Ryn – and the two deep-level prospects where George Albu and George Denny thought that the future lay: Cinderella Deep and New Steyn, to the east and west of Johannesburg respectively. Finally, there were ambitions on the West Rand. All of this was to spell trouble ahead.

The starting point for the Albus' post-war ambition to enter the big league on the West Rand was their taking control of two existing outcrop mines near Krugersdorp, West Rand Mines and Violet Consolidated Gold Mining Company. The Albu and Denny quartet decided to re-finance them and then to consolidate them in 1902 as West Rand Consolidated Mines, bringing together various owners of claims including Goerz. Old shafts were de-watered and extended, two large vertical shafts were planned; West Rand Consolidated was eventually to be the salvation of the Group, but not before some alarming years had passed.

All this was happening in the post-war boom years of 1902-4 when the market was strong (which meant that Leopold Albu was in his share-dealing element in London), General Mining was paying 20 per cent dividends, the holders of founders' shares prospered mightily, and the future seemed bright. Then, reality caught up with the victorious Randlords, to whose ranks the Albu brothers now definitely belonged, and for many of them things were never quite the same again. But in the immediate post-war euphoria, it is hardly surprising that the Chamber of Mines and Lord Milner were at one in their determination to regain as quickly as possible the pre-war level of gold production. Milner needed their taxes to fuel his reconstruction of South Africa; the mining financiers needed to make up for lost time. The trouble was, they didn't have the labour.

It had always been understood by the wiser of the Randlords, a sub-category which included the Albus and Adolf Goerz, that the future strength of the industry lay in the region's enormous reserves of low-grade, deep-level ore. To extract this ore required an assured and self-replenishing supply of cheap labour, never mind if it was unskilled. If the labour had not existed, the reserves would have been too low-grade to justify extraction. (One historian has pointed out, in illustration, that if an ore body similar to South Africa's had been discovered in North America or Australia, it would have been left in the ground.)

The fundamental realities of South Africa's gold mining industry could never be ignored. As Keith Wallis, Gencor's historian and a long-serving senior executive, has put it: 'The economics of gold mining on the Rand at the beginning of the 20th century can be fairly simply stated. An ounce of gold fetched just over £4 and the benchmark for working costs was around £1 a ton. A mining company had therefore to win ¼ oz of gold (5 dwt or 8 grammes) per ton merely to cover its day-to-day costs. A good margin above this figure was needed to remunerate both the capital spent on opening up the mine and that required from time to time to extend the working area, gain access to other reefs, increase mill recovery and improve safety and working conditions. Although special factors somewhat muddy the comparisons, such as the ability in some areas to sort and discard substantial tonnages of waste rock before milling, it is a fair generalisation to say that a mine consistently yielding 8dwt (12 grammes) or better, was likely to be a winner, while one yielding significantly less would in all probability lurch from crisis to crisis.'

Hence the ongoing value to General Mining of outcrop mines like the Meyer and Van Ryn, which had higher than 8 dwt recovery – but in Van Ryn, to take just one example, in December 1902 there were only 464 blacks on the property compared with the pre-war level of 2 500. In the middle of that year the Group as a whole was trying to operate with only 30 per cent of its required labour force. Leopold Albu was already publicly urging importation of Chinese. His views seem to have been in advance of those of his colleagues: the Chamber of Mines was divided on the issue, with flamboyant leaders like Sir Percy FitzPatrick, its President, insisting that Africa was its own adequate reservoir, but even after the Chamber had reversed its attempt to cut wages, and had in fact raised them, the workers still did not turn up. In mid-1903 there were scarcely half of the 90 000 black labourers who had been at work in the industry in the middle of 1899. The reports, speeches and letters of the period are littered with despair.

A more radical solution had not been ignored: why not forget about black labour – leave it to work on the farms and elsewhere in the new economy – and run the mines with whites who by definition would be more skilled (if not all 'skilled') and much more productive although, of course, they would be more expensive? This idea had been raised by the Commission of Inquiry in 1897 and scorned by George Albu. FitzPatrick was attracted, briefly, by this solution, and its most enthusiastic advocate was a mine manager, Colonel FHP Creswell (later to have an important political career), but experiments in replacing the non-appearing blacks with unskilled whites were not encouraging: the attempt was expensive, it threatened tension between skilled and unskilled whites, it led to fears of labour agitation. However, some of the mine-owners were convinced that the solution lay in a more efficient system of recruitment of labour from within Southern Africa. They were assured of the support of Milner – no one was more anxious to get the industry back on its feet – and, in the end, they were to be proved right.

Even before the Chamber moved back to Johannesburg, the existing re-cruitment organisations had been reconstituted as the Witwatersrand Native Labour Association – to be famous in Africa for the rest of the century as 'Wenela'. The intention was to regulate and discipline the pre-war recruit-ment network so as to control the chaotic system of 'runners' and independent 'touts' and 'advances', and, by so doing, to reduce the costs of finding labour. From 1902, Wenela was given exclusive rights to recruit in southern Mozam-bique – always the most important single source of labour – thanks to Lord Milner's willingness to renew the old rail and customs preferences with the Portuguese for the sake of access to the vital labour supply. Thereafter Wenela spread its net northwards into East and Central Africa, but it was to be years before the doctors on the mines were able to cope with the ap-palling mortality rates of these 'tropicals' brought to the Highveld.

Still the labour shortfall persisted (George Albu's private opinions may be imagined in the light of his vigorous espousal of forced labour in his ev-idence to the 1897 Commission). Milner was convinced of the necessity for a Chinese solution by 1903: In April he wrote, ' I am coming to the con-clusion that in all probability we must have some Asiatics – not necessari-ly Chinese – here for our industrial development. I am dead against the Asi-atic settler and trader, but I do not believe that the indentured Asiatic would prove uncontrollable. And, without the impetus he would give, I do not see how we are to have that great influx of British population – for the superi-or skilled work, trades, professions and agriculture, which is the ultimate salvation.' But Joseph Chamberlain, the Colonial Secretary in London, who had visited South Africa earlier that year, continued to resist: with the hindsight of history, we may see that his intuition told him what were to be the consequences for British politics.

One explanation for the long debate was simple racial prejudice. There was at the time widespread popular fear of the 'Yellow Peril' – of yellow men with pigtails, incomprehensible language and inscrutable customs. In addition to this, all thoughtful South Africans were worried about the in-troduction of another cultural strand into the country (the Indian population of Natal was growing fast). General Smuts spoke of 'this sacrilege of Chi-nese importation'; General Botha warned that it would lead to a breach be-tween the mines and the Transvaal. Other, less alarming, sources of labour had in the meantime been considered: Italians, for example, and West Indians, Hungarians, Finns, Serbians, Syrians, even Red Indians. But China was famous for being a very cheap and inexhaustible source of coolies. The Transvaal Labour Commission, meeting in late 1903, decided by a large majority that white unskilled labour was not practicable – that 'the demand for native labour for the Transvaal mining industry is in excess of the present supply by about 129,000 labourers', and that 'there is no adequate supply of labour in Central and Southern Africa to meet requirements'.

At the very end of 1903 the Chamber of Mines decided to ask the government to be permitted to recruit in China. It fell to the irrepressible Leopold Albu, chairing the General Mining AGM on 26 May 1904 in the absence of his brother George, who was on holiday in Europe, to betray the racial stereotyping typical of the time. Leopold started by referring to the Corporation's experiment with unskilled whites: 'The experience was simply that the white men did less work than the native at an enormously increased cost. Calculations which were made at the time showed that on the basis of unskilled white labour as a substitute for native labour, the mines of the Witwatersrand were, with very few exceptions, quite unpayable.'

Leopold went on: 'The first need of an industry ... is a labour supply, always available up to its fullest needs. As an industry becomes established, so in equal measure it is necessary that its organisation should become susceptible of a high degree of training and fitness for the work. Here I believe the Kaffir, at least for some generations to come, will fail. His idea of work is for the most part to secure means wherewith to purchase wives, and when he has obtained the position of a wife owner, he is to all intents and purposes lost to the industrial world, for the reason that thereafter his wives work for him. A change in the *personnel* of Kaffirs is therefore constant and inevitable. He works for short periods at most, and returns to his native state to unlearn, by a life of indolent ease, everything that has been taught him. At any given time, therefore, the total number of workers is made up of a few more or less efficient, a number of learners, and a number quite ignorant... We have, therefore, turned to the Chinaman.' Leopold explained that the Chinese coolie preferred task work, so proper bonus and piece work systems could be introduced. 'It is certain that the industrious nature of the Chinaman will permit of a large *per caput* reduction in the mines' labour complement when compared with the Kaffir labourer.'

With that disposed of, Leopold Albu went on to tackle Mr Chamberlain, who 'by his eloquence and personal influence, obtained promises and guarantees from men who, sick of war, and well-nigh ruined as a consequence thereof, reluctantly consented to enter into such an undertaking [he was referring to the mining companies' agreement to put up a £10 million loan] in the hope that some finality, some definite knowledge of the worst, could

be arrived at, and some hope of renewed activity obtained... But', asked
Leopold, 'should the Government insist?' He ended his colourful speech with
a plea for a reduction in the size of the South African Constabulary in
order to reduce costs.

The first thousand Chinese arrived in June 1904. Eventually there were to
be more than 50 000. The Albus were among the first of the mining groups
to indent for them (their London office had been lobbying General Botha
to speak up in favour of the experiment 'in view of the prevailing great anxiety and disastrous depression') and were enthusiastic in their praise: for example, on 4 July 1904 George Albu wrote to a business contact in Cape Town:
'The newly arrived batch of Chinese is proving highly satisfactory as a labour
unit and, as the great obstacle of late years to the progress of the industry
(want of labour) looks like being surmounted, there is every reason that we
shall steadily improve our profit earning capacity – and that as a consequence
general interest in mining securities will gradually revive.'

To stay with the example of the Van Ryn mine, 1 500 of General Mining's initial allocation were sent to Van Ryn and arrangements had been made
for another 6 000 to be sent to West Rand Mines, Violet Consolidated, New
Steyn Estate, Roodepoort United Main Reef, Aurora West United, and
Rand Collieries. On 22 November 1904 George Albu told Van Ryn shareholders: '...the experiment of supplementing the deficient Kaffir supply with
Asiatics has proved an undoubted success. The present complement of
1,150 coolies will shortly be augmented by the arrival of a further 450 Northern Chinamen who are on the water and expected to arrive in the course of
the next few weeks. The intention is to gradually replace the Kaffirs now
engaged, and to work the Mine entirely by means of coolie labour. The Chinese labourer has, after a surprisingly short period of training, shown himself to be a willing and efficient worker, and it has already been demonstrated
beyond doubt that the Mines can be worked as economically and effectively
with the coolie as with the best class of Native. Moreover, in view of the fact
that the coolies will remain for 3 years, they will have an opportunity of gradually attaining to a level of skills in the performance of their duties which
it is impossible for the constantly shifting Kaffir labourer to reach.' He admitted that, 'As might be expected in handling a large number of Asiatics,
a few disturbances have occurred, one of them unfortunately resulting in the
death of three Coolies...'

There had, in fact, in the early months of the Chinese influx, been a lot
of public nervousness. Although the Chinese were kept in their compounds
and had little to do with the rest of the population – and there was next to
no 'desertion' because there was no way a Chinese could vanish into the veld

– these newcomers (who, after all, were there in substantial numbers, were known to contain a criminal element, had strange habits, were frequently addicted to gambling and to opium) were at first widely assumed to be dangerous. The President of the Chamber in February 1906 had to point out: 'The total number of persons who are known to have been killed by Chinese coolies ... from the arrival of the first batch of coolies in June 1904 to the present time, when there are 49,100 coolies on the fields, is 19, all of whom were men. Of this number, 8 were white men...'

Gradually the 'Celestials', as they were called, seem to have settled down; the mining house records are full of references to labourers who, while by no means slaves, were certainly described as though they were sub-human – for example, 'We hereby give you an undertaking not to remove any of the 1,200 who are being imported for the Van Ryn Company ... without first obtaining your written sanction' (letter from General Mining to the Foreign Labour Department in Johannesburg on June 1904); 'The Corporation is receiving 475 coolies per S.S. Sikh, 12th shipment. Will you kindly issue us a licence for the employment of these coolies on the Van Ryn...'(5 October 1904); 'Account for £199 13s 7d for passport fees for 498 Chinese labourers...' These were happy days for any white man who had lived out East and had picked up the languages: the main problem underground was communication, and the Albus were not alone in setting up language classes to teach white supervisors some scraps of 'the Chinese language'. To illustrate the racial mix, in mid-1906 there were 17 500 whites on the South African gold mines, averaging £26 15 shillings a month, 102 000 blacks at an average wage of 52/3d, and 53 000 Chinese at 41/6d.

From one point of view, the Chinese experiment was successful, and can be said to have given the mines their post-war lift-off. Pre-war production had peaked at 3,56 million fine ounces; in 1903 it had fallen to 2,86 million ounces. The arrival of the Chinese in 1904 lifted production at once to 3,65 million and by 1907 it was 6,22 million. The Transvaal was the world's top gold producer. And coincidentally, as a consequence of several years of drought bringing distress to the kraals, the black workers began to return to the mines.

The end had been there from the beginning. As early as March 1904, Sir Henry Campbell-Bannerman had tabled a Liberal censure motion in London's House of Commons indicting the Unionist government for permitting a system akin to slavery (which Winston Churchill later admitted, in a famous phrase, was 'a terminological inexactitude'). The Non-conformist conscience of the British middle classes was set alight. It became the great political issue of the 1900s: in January 1906 Campbell-Bannerman won a landslide election victory and Chinese recruitment was suspended. The coolies were repatriated at the end of the first period of their three-year agreement, and the last Chinese mineworkers went home in 1910.

Curiously enough, George Albu, having been an enthusiast, was among the first to cool. He had always been conscious of the costs, which included a capitation charge of £11 10s 0d collected by the Chamber in advance and a £3 or £4 levy on arrival in Natal. In George's words, 'The cost of a Chinaman, compared with the best class of Kaffir labourer, is undoubtedly heavier, due chiefly to the additional supervision required and the increased cost of feeding...' Soon after the 1906 election George Albu said wryly, 'I now have to deal with an aspect of our business which may be considered more or less political in character... If against our strenuous protests the Chinese coolies are wholly or partly repatriated, conditions might conceivably arise which would necessitate shutting down certain low-grade and developing properties, but I have no fear of such a calamity being forced upon us.'

Contrast this with the continuing enthusiasm of the Goerz group in a letter to London as late as 7 January 1907: 'The case for the retention of the present number of Coolies is all the more strong when it is remembered that the 53,000 Chinamen we have here at present are the most efficient body of unskilled workers we have ever had on these fields. They came in the first instance for a fixed period of 3 years ... and it is reckoned that at least 80 percent of those now here will be desirous of renewing their contracts... To get a permanent substitute, even if same were obtainable, to replace our 53,000 efficient Chinamen, or even 80 percent thereof, would mean the recruitment of something like 3 times that number of Kaffirs in order to keep the menage going on its present basis... A logical solution would be to run the whole of the Gold Mines with Chinese labour, thus freeing Kaffir labour as much as possible for the purposes of these other industries, and the mere fact of such a step being taken would tend to lower the Kaffir's idea of what he is worth, and thus save the employers of Kaffir labour in the Colony a very material sum per annum...'

In contrast, on 12 June 1907 Leopold Albu in London was cabling his brother in Johannesburg with a canny suggestion about delaying the announcement of the West Rand Consolidated dividend:

'IN VIEW OF VERY UNSATISFACTORY ECONOMICAL AND FINANCIAL OUTLOOK GENERALLY EXISTING SOUTH AFRICA WE SHOULD RESTRICT EXPENDITURE EVERYWHERE AND AWAIT DEVELOPMENT IN SHAFT WHEN WE WILL BE IN A POSITION BETTER TO JUDGE PROSPECT MINE WRITE STOP WE SHOULD DECLARE OUR DIVIDEND NOT BEFORE 20 JUNE WHICH WILL BE AFTER GOVERNMENT DECLARATION POLICY CHINESE LABOUR OUR ACTION WILL BE REGARDED BY OTHERS AS DEMONSTRATION OF OUR CONFIDENCE SATISFACTORY LABOUR QUESTION DESPITE REPATRIATION OF CHI-

NESE AND WILL COUNTERACT GREATLY PUBLIC ANXIETY WHICH GOVERNMENT DE-
CLARATION MAY CREATE OTHERWISE STOP'

Leopold added, in remarks in London, 'We can but regret the repealing of
the Labour Ordinance, but we felt that no good could be done by crying over
spilt milk. What we have to do is to meet the difficulty promptly if we are
not to suffer great loss.' Suddenly, and unlike most of the other mining houses, General Mining decided to switch back to black labour.

T*he conditions of life and work on a South African gold mine in the
early years of this century should not be glossed over. They have
been eloquently described by a respected historian, Dr Alan H
Jeeves, so much so that there is no point in paraphrasing his own words, an
extended quotation can serve.*

The working environment of the mines, he writes in Migrant Labour in
South Africa's Mining Economy, *was 'dangerous, brutal and onerous... On
arrival in Johannesburg, the recruit was taken to a central depot to await
assignment to his particular mine. At the depot he received a cursory medical
examination by being paraded with all of the other recent arrivals past a
medical officer who rejected few of the recruits that he saw... After a short
period at the government compound at Driehoek or Germiston, the recruit
would be picked up by a black official, an "induna" or "police boy", of the
mine to which he was contracted, and taken to the compound. Depending on
the size of the mine, this could be a rough collection of huts housing a small
group of workers or a complex of barracks housing several thousand. The
worker would be assigned to a room housing typically from 20 to 50 of his
fellows and given one of the tiered concrete bunks which would be "home"
for the contract period... Movement in and out was carefully monitored by the
compound police... Many of the older compounds remained dark, unsanitary
and overcrowded... The staple mealie meal porridge was now augmented with
fresh vegetables and meat, but these regulations were loosely enforced at
best...*

*'Most of the workers on the mines were recruited for underground mining
which in comparison with surface work was onerous, dangerous, and
therefore very unpopular ... the principal underground task was hand-drilling
in the stopes to prepare the ore bodies to be charged with dynamite and
blasted. The day's work began at four or five a.m. when the compound police
rousted the workers out of their bunks and began moving them to the shaft
head for the trip below ground. At some mines there would be an issue of
mealie meal porridge or bread and perhaps tea before work began, but at
others no food at all was given in the morning... Once underground the
miners faced a wait of two or three hours before work could begin ... the
whites did not begin to go underground until perhaps 7 o'clock... The
"hammer boys" used a sharpened piece of drill steel and a hammer. They*

worked in a crowded, narrow stope which offered, if they were lucky, perhaps three or four feet of head room. Ventilation was rudimentary, the stope dusty from the broken ore and usually very hot. In all but the best mines sanitary arrangements were practically non-existent... They worked in the dark with only a few candles providing dim illumination... Most of the workers would not get back to the surface earlier than late afternoon... The overheated workers returned to the compound dressed in ragged shorts which is all that most of them wore underground. In winter this contributed to the very high incidence of pneumonia which carried off high numbers, particularly of the so-called "tropical migrants" from the regions north of 22 degrees. The main meal, usually a shovel of mealie meal with perhaps a scattering of vegetables and some rough meat or offal on Saturday, came after work... The harsh working conditions, poor food, excessive liquor and beer consumption and unhealthy compound environment contributed to very high rates of illness, accident and death...'

This was the life for which men were arriving from the kraals to offer their labour as the Celestials began to go home.

CHAPTER FOUR

THE MINERS' STRIKES

The 'Chinese slavery' issue is of central importance in these post-war years, not just because of its political consequences – it brought down the government in London and led directly to the 1907 victory of the Botha/Smuts Het Volk coalition in the Transvaal – but also because it focused attention on the fundamental matter that the government and the industry would have to face: the country's future labour supply. With the distraction of the 'coolie' option disposed of, South Africa, as so often in the century ahead, had to debate the division of functions between white and black. But first, even as the black workers began to drift back to 'Egoli' or 'Gauteng' (depending on whether they spoke Xhosa/Zulu or Sotho) from the kraals, and Wenela extended its recruiting net, there had to be a resolution of the distinction between skilled and unskilled *whites*.

There was an extra dimension to the question of whether the answer to the industry's labour problems might lie in a white as opposed to black workforce – the skilled men were frequently of European background, heirs to the mining traditions of Cornwall or Wales or wherever, whereas the 'unskilled' men were often Afrikaners, tempted in from the farms, willing to accept lower pay and to be used as strike-breakers. Understandably, the former group saw the latter as a threat to their comparatively high-wage status, and they organised themselves into unions to protect their skilled and semi-skilled status. The result was to be the 1907 strike.

To the mine-owners, the issue was all about costs – it was their constant obsession – and in these next years the industry prepared a profoundly important, generational change: to go big, and to go deep. The Albus were in the vanguard of that development, with the eventual result that they overextended themselves. They would have argued that they had no option. Leopold Albu, as we have seen at the May 1904 Annual General Meeting of General Mining, correctly pointed out that the Labour Commission had

After the 1907 Strike Afrikaners began to replace British immigrants as miners. (Frank Holland: <u>The Star</u>)

gone into the possibility of employing unskilled whites to do the work of blacks, that experiments had been carried out, and that they had failed. At the following year's meeting, George Albu hammered home his conviction that the only course for the industry was to reduce costs so as to exploit the low-grade ores: 'I have always said that the problem that we have to solve on these fields is to treat low-grade ores at a profit. There are millions upon millions of tons of Main Reef standing in the outcrop mines today, virtually developed, which are regarded as unpayable, and therefore left untouched. Their value is probably anything from 3-6 dwts per ton. To mine and mill it at a profit with 50, 100 or even 200 stamps may not today be possible, but if the deductions of our Consulting Engineer are correct, with larger mills, say, of 500, 750 or 1,000 stamps, provided with tube mills and the latest appliances for extracting the gold from the tailings, and the mines equipped with labour-saving devices, now being constantly introduced, these low-grade ores, if taken out at the same time as the higher-grade bodies, should yield handsome profits.'

The Albus were alert to technical change (they pioneered the tube mill, for instance) and were in these years prepared to attempt deeds as well as deliver words – though George was usually the bolder, Leopold the more concerned about economy. As early as 21 March 1898, for instance, George had been waxing eloquent about the attraction of the deep levels ('The question of raising sufficient working capital to work this tremendous deep level block can be arranged when times are good again. Viewing it as a mining proposition the same appears so favourable that no difficulty need be anticipated... You may regard all these things as mere theory but you can accept as a fact that it will not be difficult to mine at 5,000 or 6,000 feet depth...' he wrote to his brother, sounding almost like a visionary). This was the time when George Albu was planning his strategy and thinking very big indeed – too big, as events were to prove. In effect anticipating the role of the next generation, he planned a series of major consolidations and at the same time committed the Group to a combination of deep-level prospects that would have been risky even for a much larger group.

Of the 'pre-war' generation of mines, Van Ryn and the Meyer were steady earners, New Goch struggled for years, and Aurora West could not survive its low grades and was closed in 1906. In the Roodepoort area, Albu put through a complicated consolidation programme based on an enlarged Roodepoort United linked to a major deep-level plan for New Steyn, but it was to be hard hit by the labour shortages. The biggest consolidation plan was to bring together West Rand Consolidated, West Rand Mines, and Violet in the Krugersdorp district; it was to be a long, difficult slog, and eventually was the salvation of the Group. Finally, and at the same time, the Albus were trying to push through two other – and major – deep-level prospects, Cinderella Deep and Rand Collieries. Cinderella Deep near Boksburg, where the Albus sank the first 4 000-foot shaft on the Rand, was probably to be inscribed on George's heart.

The West Rand Consolidated was first conceived in 1899, when the adjoining Violet Consolidated, which had opened in 1894, got into financial difficulties. Albu and his consulting engineer George Denny decided that the only solution was a reconstruction on a major scale, with a very big milling plant to handle a whole group of mines. In his retirement, Denny would remember telling the nervous Leopold Albu that it was essential that the enterprise be so big because the property was too low grade otherwise to become payable. Denny recalled that his first estimate, to mill 1 000 tons a day, was regarded as a record for the gold industry at that time. By 1906 they were indeed planning a monster mill of 1 000 stamps (in fact it never had more than 600).

At this point, to the Albus' disgust, politics intervened again with the Liberal Party victory in Britain and the subsequent ban on coolie labour. Fearing for the secure supply of labour, the expansion plans were cut back. The project went ahead but the result was not as good as had been hoped, and Leopold Albu's apprehensions were reinforced. On 10 June 1907, for example, he was cabling his brother in Johannesburg from London (in the ornate private code that was used at the time):

'EXPERIENCE HAS COMPLETELY OPENED OUR EYES TO ENORMOUS RISK DEEP LEVEL STOP WE ARE OPPOSED ABSOLUTELY ACQUIRING ANY DEEP LEVEL CLAIMS FOR MORE THAN NOMINAL CONSIDERATION THEREFORE IMPLORE FINALLY ABANDON IDEA...'

Two days later he was repeating the same sort of message –

'IN VIEW OF VERY UNSATISFACTORY ECONOMIC AND FINANCIAL OUTLOOK GENERALLY EXISTING SOUTH AFRICA WE SHOULD TO THE CONTRARY RESTRICT EXPENDITURE EVERYWHERE AND AWAIT DEVELOPMENT IN SHAFT...'

Leopold Albu was right to be worried about expenditure because the Group's most ambitious project, Cinderella Deep, was indeed giving cause for concern.

Despite Leopold's insistence on vigorous economies – most dramatically, the departure from the firm in 1906 of the distinguished mining engineers George Denny and his brother, who were so central to the development projects and yet whom Leopold insisted were grossly overpaid – the Albus had to go back to Germany to raise more money. The General Mining share price (£4 in 1902) had dropped to 27/6d in end-1906 and the £687 000 raised in 1902 was exhausted. The Dresdner syndicate agreed to take up £625 000 of new shares at 25 shillings to raise £780 000. The condition was that the new members of the syndicate required a seat on the Board, which meant that the Albus could in future be outvoted. Less symbolically, and more practically, consultation in Berlin, usually by Leopold from his London base, became more frequent and more important.

In the middle of the difficult years of 1904-8, with senior managers and owners deeply worried about the balance sheet, many smaller operations being amalgamated to form large mines, major development projects seemingly bogged down, and no clear solution in sight to the fundamental problem of an assured supply of cheap labour, the London office of General Mining received an urgent cable on 22 May 1907 from Johannesburg:

'UNDERGROUND MEN NEW GOCH MEYER AND CHARLTON ROODEPOORT HAVE STRUCK ARE ENDEAVOURING KEEP MILL RUNNING VAN RYN IS LIKELY TO FOLLOW NUMEROUS OTHER MINES HAVE STRUCK...'

The next day it was updated:

'VAN RYN UNDERGROUND MEN HAVE STRUCK STOP ALL OUR MINES UP TO THE PRESENT FULL STAMPS RUNNING WITH THE AID OF SURFACE MEN AND STAFF STOP STRIKE GENERAL PRINCIPALLY OWING TO INTIMIDATION WE HAVE APPLIED TO GOVERNMENT TO AFFORD PROTECTION AS MANY MEN COERCED SOUTH AFRICA CONSTABULARY ARRIVING STOP WHAT ARE LLOYDS RATE OF INSURANCE FIRE RESULTING FROM DISTURBANCE...'

and on May 25 -

'FULL MILLS WILL CONTINUE RUNNING UNDER DIFFICULTIES CINDERELLA DEEP THREATENS IF STRIKE SHALL SHUT DOWN STRUGGLE MAY BE PROLONGED GROUPS RESOLVE STAND FIRM.'

Although the *general* strike called by the Transvaal Miners Association (TMA) was not observed, the strike among white miners spread until 4 000 miners were out and 49 mines were affected. Botha's government responded firmly, sending in the cavalry, and before the end of July it was over. George Albu, addressing his AGM in the middle of the dispute, was forceful and unusually to the point. He explained that the industry was involved in its first serious dispute with white workers and that the occasion for the strike appeared to be management's requirements that the men in future supervise three drills, not two. 'There is an endeavour, however, to widen the dispute on the part of certain misguided people who desire to set up a standard of the number of the white men to be employed on each mine, irrespective of its profit earning capacity and the conditions involved,' Albu told his shareholders.

'This section dreams of both the coolie and Kaffir being ultimately supplanted by white labour... I may be called brutal for stating the facts, but it is invariably wiser to speak frankly in order to pave the way for a settlement.

Have the men earning £1 per shift, who have gone out in sympathy with the rock-drill contractor, acted wisely? I venture to say no. For a long time past we have realised that a large proportion of the miners are grossly inefficient, and further, that the number of white men employed underground on the mines is excessive in proportion to the work performed. Whether the excessive number of men employed led to the inefficiency, or whether the inefficiency was the cause of the large number of men being engaged, I will not debate, but the broad fact remains that a radical change must be affected. Yet the mining houses – strange as it may sound to those who vilify them – swayed largely by sentimental reasons, continue to employ this unnecessary surplus of white labour because they desire to avoid discharging men... The men have now themselves solved the difficulty by going on strike, and have thus eliminated the sentimental factor.'

In the tone of voice familiar from management in countless strikes throughout this century, George Albu went on: 'After thousands of white men have vacated their positions, we find the stamps running as merrily as ever, and if this strike has taught one lesson, it is that in the past our mines have been greatly over-staffed with so-called 'skilled' labour. I venture to predict that in the future, on an average, it will be found that mines will be run with from 15 percent to 20 percent less highly paid labourers, and with a corresponding decrease in working costs...'

The 1907 strike in fact turned out to be a comparatively minor episode, but it was also a harbinger of the far more dramatic events of 1913 and 1922. The issue, again and again, was to be the privileged role of *white* labour in the South African gold industry. Lionel Phillips of Corner House summed up the affair in a letter to Julius Wernher with a wit which was beyond the Albu style: 'The whole position is really getting topsy-turvy; a Boer government calling out British troops to keep English miners in order while the Dutchmen are replacing them in the mines...'

At General Mining the Albus had been worrying about practicalities. A cable from Johannesburg on 27 May said:

'ENDEAVOUR TAKE OUT ONE MONTH GENERAL POLICY STERLING 200,000 WITHOUT AVERAGE CLAUSE COVERING ALL OUR MINES SO THAT INSURANCE PAID ANY MINE UP TO TOTAL AMOUNT POLICY STOP IN VIEW OF LARGE NUMBER TROOPS ARRIVING RATE SHOULD BE CHEAPER THAN ONE PERCENT...'

The reply from London came the same evening from Leopold -

'IN VIEW OF MILITARY PROTECTION DO NOT THINK RISKS WARRANT SUCH LARGE EXPENDITURE ON INSURANCE...'

Fortunately for morale and for the shareholders, the market managed a brief recovery in 1908-9 and Leopold was able to place shares and restore liquidity. Dividends of 5 per cent, 15 per cent and 7,5 per cent were paid for

1908-10 and the long-deferred development projects were pushed ahead. At the AGM of May 1909, George Albu was in unusually cheerful form: 'Gentlemen, in the long years in which I have been associated with this industry, I have never known such a bright outlook as that before us at the present time...' He promised that for once he would make no comment on public affairs, though he allowed himself a mention of the prevalence of gold stealing in the reduction works.

It was not to last. The deep-level projects were swallowing cash. Leopold blocked George's wish to start shaft-sinking at New Steyn, Rand Collieries took £250 000, and it became clear that Cinderella needed £1 million (an enormous sum for those days). Throughout these years, Cinderella was dogged with constant and expensive problems. The first shaft had been completed in 1906 but the original plan relied on driving a very long crosscut to the neighbouring ERPM for the provision of the necessary second (emergency) exit and proper ventilation. In 1909 completion of this project was at least two years off, working conditions becoming steadily more appalling as the crosscut got further away from the only source of air. It became clear that a second shaft, and a very substantial increase in the lease area, were needed if the mine was to be put onto a profitable basis. Leopold in Europe had to use all his skills to persuade the European investors to put up the funds, but while work was proceeding on the second shaft, working profits continued to drift lower. In the end, time – and money – ran out and with the European war approaching there was no serious prospect of a further major refinancing. To the brothers' distress and embarrassment, milling was suspended in June 1913 and the shaft sinking ended later that year, only 100 metres short of the reef. No single factor was more responsible than Cinderella for the perilous state in which General Mining entered the First World War.

By this time, the Albu and Goerz groups, still sometimes associated by outside commentators as the 'Continentals' and assumed therefore to be allies, were in fact continuing to grow apart, notwithstanding their common involvement in West Rand Consolidated and Roodepoort. In 1903 Goerz turned down an offered participation by Albu in Rand Collieries; Leopold thereupon objected to the Goerz proposals for a reconstruction at Princess Estate. The two groups were ever more deeply tied to the two German banking groups, Dresdner and Deutsche. The Albus were also still linked with the Krupp group, through United Engineering. Some of the leadership of both groups, German (or Austrian) in origin, had taken British papers and were based in London, but both organisations were still essentially 'German'.

Notwithstanding the increasing difficulties and set-backs, and the helpless sense of depression as the world drifted towards European war, this was the heyday of the Randlords, or rather, perhaps, their last fling. As in so many other ways, the Albus were not entirely typical in this world of immensely rich millionaires in their grand Park Lane mansions and their English country estates: men like Robinson, Wernher, Otto Beit, Phillips and Neumann cut far more of a dash than stolid George Albu and his nattier brother – and anyhow George was usually in Johannesburg, though he bought a house in Grosvenor Place, a stone's throw from Hyde Park and from his brother Leopold in Hamilton Place. Young Henry Strakosch at Goerz had not yet entered the period of his international distinction.

After the delicate time of the Anglo-Boer War, when George Albu's Boer sympathies were rather too well known, he seems to have resolved to stand back from the political stage. Perhaps he accepted that he was never to be one of the inner core of the Randlords; or perhaps he didn't really wish to be one of them. In 1906 he was sounded out to take his turn as annual President of the Chamber of Mines, but he pleaded overwork, to his brother's mixed feelings. Instead, George Albu became something of an honorary Englishman – despite his accent! As the years went by, and as he endured the particular difficulties of the Anglo-German War, he saw to it that his business, his household, his family, his tastes, his loyalties were British by adoption.

George Albu was a classic Edwardian paterfamilias. He had six children by his wife Gertrude (known as Ginny) – four girls and two boys. In 1912 he moved from The Turrets, a fairly grand house at Doornfontein, to one of Johannesburg's most distinctive Randlord mansions, Northwards, which sits high on the Ridge to the north of Johannesburg and looks out over what were then the young forests of Saxonwold, first planted by George Albu's friend Edward Lippert, and which today make up the luxuriant green panorama of Johannesburg's northern suburbs. (Northwards still dominates the Ridge: it immediately adjoins – was nearly swallowed up by – the motorway to Pretoria). The house, which is imposing and superbly positioned though not particularly elegant, had been built in 1903 by the distinguished architect Herbert Baker for Colonel John Dale Lace and his sensational – some would say notorious – beauty of a wife, José. The Albus took over the house after a serious fire in 1912 and turned it into a family home where they were to remain until 1951; Northwards deserves to be associated far more with the Albu family than with the Dale Laces, with whom it is still often coupled.

George was not concerned only for his immediate family. His younger brother, Leopold, was of course in daily contact from London. There was their youngest brother, Eugen, an actor and impresario in Germany, and another brother, Felix, who came out to South Africa to join his brothers, married his London cousin, Evelina, in 1888, but died in Cape Town in 1895 (George had to send his effects back to Europe): there were two sons of this marriage, Vivian and Cecil, and a daughter Ethel, and the office files show that Uncle George kept an eye on them, sending the boys cigarettes at the Front, making share allocations. Then there were two sisters, Evelina, who married Professor Theodore Flatau and remained in Germany and then the South of France, and Regina, who married Joseph Freudenthal, who was to be the Albus' right-hand man in the London office for a generation. Their son Norman served in the Grenadier Guards in the First War, refusing to change his German name despite the suggestion of his monarch; *his* son Peter succeeded him both in the Grenadiers (under the sensibly adjusted name of Railing in the *Second* War) and in the General Mining London office for many years. In other words, this was a family dynasty, as George knew full well.

The term 'Randlords' is, of course, a misnomer because they were not lords but baronets and knights – they should have been called 'Randbarts'! (The most hated of them, JB Robinson, got a peerage from Lloyd George but was forced to return it by the outraged House of Lords). In the years before the First World War, baronetcies or knighthoods were handed out to Sir Julius Wernher, Sir Percy FitzPatrick, Sir George Farrar, Sir Frederick Eckstein, Sir Joseph Robinson, Sir Lionel Phillips, Sir Otto Beit (Alfred Beit had died), Sir Sigismund Neumann, Sir Max Michaelis, and Sir George Albu. Why? Their enemies – of whom there were many – said they had bought them, but that would be very hard to prove, especially in the case of someone like George Albu. They all, of course, contributed enormously to 'charities'; some of them – Phillips and FitzPatrick, for instance – had political careers which would have merited reward whatever their trade. George Albu was deeply gratified by his title, awarded in 1912, and became an even more patriotic Englishman. Lady Phillips, whose husband Lionel was honoured at the same time, was furious, asking what Albu had done in comparison with her husband. Only a few months later, Sir George Albu was awarded the honour of the Königlichen Kronen Orden (Third Class) by the Kaiser, which was more than Sir Lionel could hope for...

These changing allegiances exacted their price. The Randlords suffered for years, both in actuality and in the history books, from anti-Semitic abuse – the taunt of 'Hoggenheimer' endured until fairly recently, as the Oppenheimer family can testify. One absurdity of this is revealed by the fact that many of the original mine-owners were not Jewish, whatever their names suggest to the illiterate: for instance, Eckstein and Wernher were not Jewish, they were Christian-German, and Beit's family had become Christian before his birth. George Albu's wife, Gertrude Rosendorff, seems to have become either Lutheran or Anglican, and brought up her children as Chris-

The Albu Family

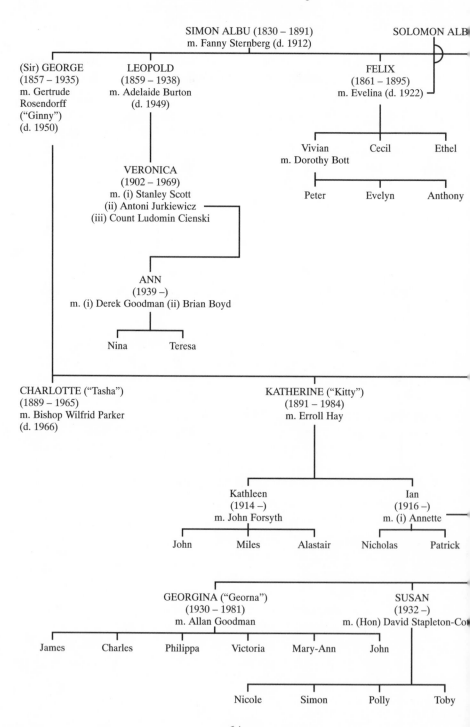

SIMON ALBU (1830 – 1891)
m. Fanny Sternberg (d. 1912)

SOLOMON ALB

(Sir) GEORGE
(1857 – 1935)
m. Gertrude
Rosendorff
("Ginny")
(d. 1950)

LEOPOLD
(1859 – 1938)
m. Adelaide Burton
(d. 1949)

FELIX
(1861 – 1895)
m. Evelina (d. 1922)

Vivian
m. Dorothy Bott

Cecil

Ethel

Peter

Evelyn

Anthony

VERONICA
(1902 – 1969)
m. (i) Stanley Scott
(ii) Antoni Jurkiewicz
(iii) Count Ludomin Cienski

ANN
(1939 –)
m. (i) Derek Goodman (ii) Brian Boyd

Nina

Teresa

CHARLOTTE ("Tasha")
(1889 – 1965)
m. Bishop Wilfrid Parker
(d. 1966)

KATHERINE ("Kitty")
(1891 – 1984)
m. Erroll Hay

Kathleen
(1914 –)
m. John Forsyth

Ian
(1916 –)
m. (i) Annette

John

Miles

Alastair

Nicholas

Patrick

GEORGINA ("Georna")
(1930 – 1981)
m. Allan Goodman

SUSAN
(1932 –)
m. (Hon) David Stapleton-Co

James

Charles

Philippa

Victoria

Mary-Ann

John

Nicole

Simon

Polly

Toby

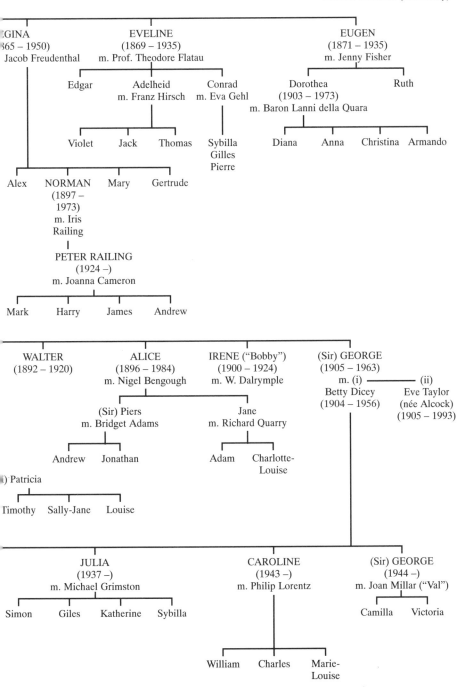

RABBI B ALBU (Kimberley)

GINA
(1865 – 1950)
Jacob Freudenthal

EVELINE
(1869 – 1935)
m. Prof. Theodore Flatau

EUGEN
(1871 – 1935)
m. Jenny Fisher

Edgar   Adelheid   Conrad
m. Franz Hirsch   m. Eva Gehl

Dorothea
(1903 – 1973)
m. Baron Lanni della Quara

Ruth

Violet   Jack   Thomas   Sybilla
Gilles
Pierre

Diana   Anna   Christina   Armando

Alex   NORMAN   Mary   Gertrude
(1897 –
1973)
m. Iris
Railing

PETER RAILING
(1924 –)
m. Joanna Cameron

Mark   Harry   James   Andrew

WALTER
(1892 – 1920)

ALICE
(1896 – 1984)
m. Nigel Bengough

IRENE ("Bobby")
(1900 – 1924)
m. W. Dalrymple

(Sir) GEORGE
(1905 – 1963)
m. (i) ———— (ii)
Betty Dicey   Eve Taylor
(1904 – 1956)   (née Alcock)
(1905 – 1993)

(Sir) Piers
m. Bridget Adams

Jane
m. Richard Quarry

Andrew   Jonathan

Adam   Charlotte-
Louise

(i) Patricia

Timothy   Sally-Jane   Louise

JULIA
(1937 –)
m. Michael Grimston

CAROLINE
(1943 –)
m. Philip Lorentz

(Sir) GEORGE
(1944 –)
m. Joan Millar ("Val")

Simon   Giles   Katherine   Sybilla

Camilla   Victoria

William   Charles   Marie-
Louise

tians, and it is impossible to be certain at this remove whether Adolf Goerz, or his successor, Henry Strakosch, were Jewish or Christian, or whether it had ceased to matter to them. Smears of this sort, which were not reserved for their South African enemies (see, for instance, the anti-Semitic tone of so much anti-Randlord abuse in Parliament in London during the Boer War), must have been painful enough, but for some of them – like the Albus and the Oppenheimers – it was the German association which was to become more dangerous.

B*ehind his gruff, Teutonic exterior, Sir George Albu was a charitable man, a Randlord who accepted his obligations to his own community. His private letter books show the range of his interests: he was always sending a cheque to a hard-up case ('for absolutely the last time'), accepting a vice-presidency of the West Rand Poultry Club, the Rand Polo Club, the South African Aeronautical Society (promising 'either to demonstrate my right to be considered an active member of your Society or else to perish in the attempt'!) He commiserates with Lionel Phillips about the constant 'calls on my purse' which they share, and agrees to support the formidable Lady Phillips as she sets up the Johannesburg Art Gallery (cannily choosing to contribute some of his own paintings rather than cash). He is active in setting up the German Hospital in Johannesburg, serving as Chairman of the Founding Committee in 1904. He writes references, placates managers' wives when they are required to postpone home leave, makes introductions, provides a car for Phillips's 1910 election campaign, promises his wife's subscription to innumerable good causes, and just very occasionally he jibes ('Mrs Albu also regrets that she does not see her way to supply ice-cream for the children's supper. The demands made upon her are very heavy and your Orphanage has received more than its share of the contributions to such institutions... She feels that it is taxing her resources too much to ask her to provide ice-cream for two hundred children, especially in view of the fact that there are hundreds in this town who lack even bread and the bare necessaries of life...') When the World War came, he made over his London house for a hospital – and when his brother Leopold, the miser, withdrew his promised contribution, George immediately made good the shortfall.*

This is a man who was shedding his German nationality. His letters with his brother were conducted in English almost from the beginning, breaking into German only in crisis. His children were firmly brought up as English-speaking South Africans (though their mother sometimes spoke German at home). The Albus entertained lavishly, were musical and well-read, generous, unostentatious – and entirely respectable.

More delicate is the matter of the Jewish background. In the earlier years in Johannesburg, George is frequently spotted in involvement with the Jewish community: for instance, he was centrally involved in the setting up and funding of a Jewish orphanage. He was not to be the first of the mining magnates whose Jewish blood seemed to thin in the South African climate. One critical event may have been the marriage of his eldest daughter, Charlotte, from Northwards in 1933 to Wilfrid Parker, who was to become Anglican Bishop of Pretoria, a wedding which occasioned a crisis in the local Jewish community when her father declined to forbid the marriage of a daughter who was, after all, in her forties. There is a family legend that George spent the night before the wedding in the synagogue, seeking to come to terms with his daughter's desertion of the faith: the next day he attended the ceremony, and he was eventually to be buried in a Christian cemetery in Johannesburg. George Albu's grandchildren were all to be active Anglicans. One thinks of the Oppenheimer family: Sir Ernest converted after a sequence of family tragedies, and his son, Harry, was to be a life-long practising Anglican.

CHAPTER FIVE

WORLD WAR AND REBELLION

In 1914 George Albu sent his eldest son Walter, aged 22, on active service: first in German South West Africa and then in France with the British Forces, where he transferred to the Royal Flying Corps. Two of his daughters went to Europe to nurse the wounded. His Grosvenor Place home became a hospital, largely funded by him. Walter came out of the war in 1918 so damaged, in a variety of ways, that he died in 1920 (the detail is hard to understand: the death certificate refers to 'Septicaemia/Influenza/Thrombosis Leg').

In May 1915 the *Lusitania* was sunk by a German U-boat with the loss of 1 198 lives. Its loss provoked a fury of anti-German rioting in South Africa, which turned indiscriminately on every identifiable German family or business. In Kimberley, Ernest Oppenheimer – the Mayor of the town as well as master of De Beers – was lucky to escape with his life and never lived there again. In Johannesburg the General Mining offices were just one of the targets of the mob. Various first-hand accounts agree that the total destruction of the building was only averted thanks to the courage of a senior clerk who, as the mob ransacked the ground floor and then Sir George's office, shouted at them that the Albu son and daughters were fighting for the Allied cause. There was a moment that evening when the mob set off up the Ridge to attack Northwards and other German houses: they were diverted just in time as the Albu servants assembled a modest armoury and George wrote a hurried Will. Hans Rosendorff's home in Parktown was looted on the way.

Sir George had his extended family to worry about. His brother-in-law, Hans Rosendorff, for example, having neglected to change his German papers, was forced to leave Johannesburg in 1915 after this episode. He went to Mozambique where he was interned in a Portuguese camp. Sir George pulled strings to have him exchanged and supported him when he was allowed back into South Africa on parole – and he promptly repeated the manoeuvre on behalf of two more of what he described to the Minister as 'the better class of German subjects'. And Sir George was still a part of the Jewish community. In March 1916 he was writing about his concern for the relief of poor Jews in the 'Russian war zone' and sending a cheque.

The Albu brothers had taken British nationality many years before in Kimberley, proving themselves wiser than their counterparts at Goerz. Henry Strakosch became a British subject in 1907, as did his colleague Hans Neuhaus, but five of the six German-born members of the London staff of Goerz in 1914 were interned or deported and even Amandus Brakhan had to call for help from his grandest friends in London to escape the same fate.

Not surprisingly the Goerz companies were in the same difficult situation as the Albus. As early as 21 August 1914 the London office had warned Johannesburg that a certain Francis J Dormer (who was a former editor of the Johannesburg *Star*) 'is again on the war path and is urging that the control of the Rand industry should be taken out of the hands of directors and responsible officials of German nationality... Dormer's objection to Germans seems to be directed also against naturalised British subjects of German nationality, and therefore against such groups as ourselves, the General Mining and also the Central Mining...' (Dormer had written to the *Financial Times* on 14 August 1914 calling for the retirement of directors 'shielding behind naturalisation that was only intended to secure certain titular and other advantages in this country.') Hans Neuhaus, now rejoicing in the name Henry Newhouse, replied to Strakosch on 9 September from Johannesburg, 'We are very interested in your remarks as to the position of alien enemies. Local Germans and Austrians are being treated apparently differently to those at Home. None of them are allowed to leave the Union without a permit and such of them as are Reservists have been arrested and confined in the Agricultural Show Grounds. These men are still being collected from all over South Africa and Rhodesia for this purpose. The others are not being interfered with at all.'

By 6 January 1915 Newhouse was evidently worried: 'We occasionally have difficulty in convincing people that we are not a German firm... And even when people are convinced that we are English, or rather a Transvaal company, they are still inclined to look upon any actions of ours with suspicion, as they consider that even if technically we are British, we are German in sympathy...' In the *Lusitania* riots in May 1915 at least 65 fires were started by the anti-German mob; the Goerz offices did not suffer as much damage as General Mining's.

These difficult days might have been less alarming if the two groups had gone into the war in stronger shape. As early as 1912, for instance, the two Albu brothers had become very worried. On 14 December Leopold poured his heart out to George in a letter phrased in typically extreme language, rich in mixed metaphors: 'South Africa to all intents and purposes is dead in the eyes of the European public and financiers. Wild cats in Timbuktu, I am sure, have greater chance. It is heartbreaking to have to admit this sad state of things, but it is no use playing Micawber any longer and waiting and hoping for things that will never come again. Of course we have closed our eyes too long to the state of affairs; we have not realised that the continued failures of a great many of the mines for which we entertained and expressed sanguine hopes and expectations must gradually undermine the confidence and enthusiasm not only of the public but some of our more intimate friends and associates, and not only in the industry but, what is worse, in our own judgement and abilities. So we cannot be surprised to see even our staunch believers and supporters at last leaving the sinking ship... The cream has been skimmed, the richest mines have been worked out, and who is left likely to risk and provide the millions required to work the poor areas?'

The suspension of operations at Cinderella Deep brought them to the brink of despair: the two brothers travelled to Berlin but the Dresdner and the other banks, pointing to the miners' strike in 1913 (and no doubt very conscious of the parlous diplomatic situation in Europe) refused to provide a rescue package. The speech that year to the AGM of George Nathan, in the Chair, was a masterpiece of looking on the bright side, assuring shareholders that all the separate mines were doing as well as could be expected. The fact was that Rand Collieries – another risky deep-level project – had been suspended, New Steyn was still undeveloped, Roodepoort United, West Rand Consolidated and New Goch were still absorbing development funds and would soon be showing losses. Only the faithful Meyer, Aurora West (heavily in debt) and Van Ryn were generating profits. The collapse of stock markets had eroded reserves and ended hopes of dealing profits. Net assets were down to £1 million at the start of 1914, a figure to be compared with the £2,5 million that shareholders had subscribed in the three General Mining issues since 1895; dividends could be forgotten. Costs had already been rigorously pruned (Sir George volunteered not to draw part of his remuneration, Leopold refused to do the same). At the 1914 AGM Sir George said he was unable to retire and 'to devote most of the remaining years of my life to the public affairs and commonweal of this country' because he felt that he could only do so at a time of assured prosperity for the Corporation. (Since he was to continue in the Chair for another 20 years, it may be permitted to disbelieve him.)

The Goerz group was hardly in better shape. The West Rand mines had all been struggling for years: Lancaster West gave up in 1913; Roodepoort Central Deep amalgamated with Princess in 1911 and kept going only until 1920; Van Dyk had run out of money in 1910 and closed (to the particular fury of the German syndicate involved); Geduld had a host of problems still but began to show profits; Modder Deep was not yet in production. In Mexico the Group's projects had, by 1914, been submerged in revolution.

Curiously enough, the German financial underpinning of the South African groups continued up to the very brink of war. Goerz, for example, had made an attempt in mid-year to raise £400 000 to bring Modder Deep – always seen as vital to the future – into production: the German directors vetoed the scheme for a capital issue but promised that Deutsche Bank would if necessary provide funds to complete the job. Then, in July 1914, the Bank advanced £40 000 in a draft which Henry Strakosch personally presented just before the banks closed for the Bank Holiday weekend on Friday, 1 August. War was declared on Monday, 4 August!

In Johannesburg that same week, Henry Newhouse urgently needed local funds for Modder Deep. The local bank refused, so – on his own initiative – he went off to the local subsidiary of a German industrial company associated with Deutsche Bank, Orenstein-Arthur Koppel, and negotiated a £100 000 loan repayable on 1 January 1915. Goerz's Berlin office meanwhile secured the approval of Koppel in Germany on the strength of a Deutsche Bank guarantee, and the go-ahead was cabled from Berlin to Johannesburg on 3 August! Modder Deep came into production in January 1915 and, with Geduld, carried A Goerz and Co through the war. It was the last and greatest favour from Deutsche Bank.

It seems extraordinary that businessmen could continue committing themselves in such a way while Europe was manifestly accelerating into war, but this was to be the first 'total' war – in previous conflicts, many kinds of communication had remained open, and few can have realised that the German banks' deep, indeed fundamental, involvement in both these German-sired mining houses would never be so close again. Both companies actually continued to have a Berlin office through the war, though they soon discovered that they would have no contact with them for four years. Henry Strakosch, in a letter dated 23 October 1914, revealed a keen understanding of the new world: 'In view of the predominant number of alien enemy directors on our Board and the fact that we are known to have important German connections, we, as also all the other prominent officials of the company, are in a particularly delicate situation, and I feel we should do nothing which could in any way be misconstrued by the authorities... May I say that so strongly do I feel on this subject that I have not even attempted to communicate with my nearest relatives in Austria since the outbreak of War.'

Strakosch went on to tell Newhouse of an incident affecting an employee of the company in London whose teenage son had rigged up a wireless apparatus in their Chiselhurst garden in Kent. The police arrived, the house was searched, some firearms and foodstuffs confiscated, and the innocent Mr Francke was temporarily detained. 'The feeling in this country in regard to German and Austrian subjects has recently become exceedingly acute.' Three directors of Goerz resident in Germany were immediately removed from the Board; two other German nationals resident in Paris and London (the latter was indeed Brakhan) resigned after the May 1915 riots. The moral was clear to the small number of remaining directors, and eventually it was Neuhaus/Newhouse who in August 1918 proposed that A Goerz and Co be renamed 'Union Corporation Limited'. The disentanglement took a little longer and had to wait until the Berlin office was once again able to make contact in August 1919 – when Strakosch was told that the whole staff had been transferred to the Deutsche Bank.

The full facts of the ownership of the two groups, which had been such a delicate matter during the war years, were not easy to track down, but it eventually emerged that 55 per cent of A Goerz and Co was held either by or on behalf of German and Austrian investors in 1914. For General Mining, the proportion was only slightly lower – 'enemy-held shares' were later calculated to total 46 per cent of the corporation's issued capital. Seen in the light of a violently inflamed political xenophobia, both groups were evidently in a dangerously exposed position (the May 1915 riots were to remind them of that), and there were ominous questions being asked in the British Parliament.

The outcome was legislation vesting enemy-held shares in the British and South African 'Custodians of Enemy Property'. This was also dangerous for the companies because it raised the possibility that other mining houses, not tarred with the German brush, might try to purchase these shares from the Custodians. The issue was evidently extremely complex because the legislation specifically permitted companies to buy these 'enemy' shares in themselves. In the end, the successful solution, for Goerz, was to raise a loan in 1917 to bid for the shares held by the South African Custodian, amounting to 25 per cent of the issue capital.

Crucially, Henry Strakosch managed to persuade General Smuts to rule against open tender for the shares (on the argument that this might have led to an additional concentration of control on the Rand). A further 30 per cent of the share capital was thereafter purchased from the British Authority, and these shares were to be sold on over the years to come. A 14 per cent rump of 200 000 shares was put into a new investment trust, the Bay Hall Trust, which was also to be a support in future times of trouble.

The Albus took a slightly more relaxed approach. They waited, calculating that stagnant market conditions were on their side. In May 1921 they did a deal with the British and South African Custodians of Enemy Property, who sold 861 041 shares (46 per cent) to General Mining at the give-away price of 2 shillings each, which represented more than 6 shillings of assets. These shares were thereupon cancelled and a year later the asset value per share had recovered to its £1 par value. Down in the mines, the Albus still had their problems, but as financiers they had pulled the chestnuts out of the fire. At the 1922 AGM the acting Chairman, Arthur French, was understandably elated, even though he had just been reporting on the recent rebellion of white miners: 'I have indicated the vastly improved prospects of your Corporation as the result of several causes. Most important of these is the effect of the purchase of the ex-enemy shares of our group of companies, which has greatly strengthened our position and enhanced the value of our assets. The probable entire elimination in the near future of the depreciation of over £1,000,000, which we have had to show in our balance sheets in recent years in respect of our investments, is a most gratifying feature, especially as the wiping out of this large deficit would release future profits for distribution to shareholders.'

It is one of the supreme ironies of South Africa's commercial history that the Albu and Goerz groups were both saved by the defeat in the First World War of the nation which had supplied their founders, their shareholders and their managers.

There was unfinished business to be dealt with. Back in 1907, the strike by white miners had in essence been a protest by skilled and comparatively highly paid men against attempts by the mine-owners to cut costs and experiment with 'unskilled' and under-paid whites. The state had demonstrated its willingness to support the mine-owners. The 1913 General Strike was a much more serious matter. The failure of 1907 had led to the creation of the South African Labour Party, whose fundamental tenet was the protection of the white worker against 'cheap' (which usually meant black) labour. As South Africa moved into Union in 1910 and the 1911 Mines and Works Act enshrined a colour bar, the mining houses and the new trade unionists locked onto a collision course.

By 1913 relations between management and white underground labour were, in the words of the official history of the Chamber of Mines, 'abysmal ... the militant response of the trade unions ... mirrored the industrial unrest of America, Australia and Europe. In South Africa, however, underlying fear of the black masses and agitation about unfair competition in the workplace, added a cutting edge to the clash of management and labour.'

The description given by George Nathan, reporting as Acting Chairman to the General Mining AGM, of the spark that fired the General Strike in May 1913 was not inaccurate: 'This strike is probably without a parallel – certainly in this country – in that there is absolutely no dispute between the employers and employees, nor, as admitted by the latter, have they any hardship to redress...' Nathan explained that there had been an attempt to change the hours of a small number of underground mechanics to coincide with the hours worked by miners. The situation escalated rapidly, undoubtedly thanks in part to the efforts of certain 'labour agitators'. The Strike spread from Kleinfontein to Van Ryn on 19 June, when a large majority of the men voted against a strike but were later persuaded or intimidated into changing their minds. Nathan here allowed himself a little licence: 'I must confess I find it impossible to understand how intelligent workmen can allow themselves to be so readily influenced by the violent and fiery speeches of so-called leaders who have for the most part done little manual labour themselves for years past, and who are simply fooling the men with promises and prospects which they must know quite well can't possibly be realised...'

The climax came on 4-5 July with anarchy in central Johannesburg. The Rand Club was attacked, British troops were called out. Generals Botha and Smuts, Prime Minister and Minister of Mines respectively, came to the Carlton Hotel, met the strike leaders, gave in, and signed what Smuts was to describe as 'a humiliation'. The atmosphere in Johannesburg at that time is evoked in the Albu papers. Sir George appears to have been making frantic efforts to increase his domestic insurance, to which his agent replied, on 8 July 1913: 'As we were ordered yesterday by the authorities to cease business and leave the premises, it was impossible for us to cable home and have the insurance of £5000 effected on the residence of Sir George Albu, Bart... In view of the fact that conditions in the city are now once more normal, we have no doubt you will be pleased that this insurance was not effected...'

So, in 1913 the strikers won. But the next year the government cracked down when the railway workers called a general strike: the ringleaders were rushed to Durban and Smuts deported them to England whence they had come. Soon there was war in Europe, and the ultimate confrontation between white labour, the mining houses – and the state – was postponed.

Leopold Albu, back in South Africa for the first time in 15 years, was in typically outspoken form when he addressed the General Mining AGM on 25 August 1921. He spoke of the crisis confronting the industry but chose to reserve his most provocative remarks for the labour situation: 'It is becoming increasingly evident that the operation of the so-called colour bar is more and more unjustifiable, and that in the future the native, as his intelligence permits, must be given more responsible work in order to develop the resources of this country economically. I feel certain that the abolition of the colour bar would scarcely affect the white man at the present moment, and would in the end, by enlarging the sphere of employment, provide work for many more than are now employed. If the labour unions would only take this long view, their members would, I am sure, come to the conclusion that this artificial barrier is very detrimental to their own best interests, as it undoubtedly is to the interests of the country at large. Besides, I do not see how this bar to the advancement of the natives can be justified on moral grounds, and already there are definite signs that the native himself is waking up to a sense of this injustice. The fact is that the native of South Africa is becoming educated. Through education his ambition is being developed, and unless an outlet is provided for that ambition, which the present restrictions prevent, there can be but little doubt that the time will come when the native himself will force the issue.'

Leopold Albu hastened to add that he did not suggest 'that the white man and the native should be placed on terms of social equality – that, of course, is unthinkable –', but some of his audience might have been struck by the development in his political sensibility in the course of his long absence overseas. What Leopold did not say, and perhaps did not know, was that the white workforce now contained an element intent on revolution: it needs to be remembered that this was a time when, in the aftermath of the Bolshevik takeover of Russia in 1917, Marxist revolution was on everyone's mind. However, Leopold had pointed out in the same speech that the gold industry had come through the war very badly: 'Whilst the price of gold, in contrast to any other commodity, remained stationary during the War, the cost of production continually mounted up, owing to colossal increases in wages, materials, plant and everything in connection with mining'; hence, he could argue, the gravity of the deterioration in the efficiency of the workers.

The danger of this rise in costs for the mines had been camouflaged in the immediate post-war years by the 'premium' on the gold price compared with the pre-war price of 85 shillings an ounce. By the end of 1921, with the premium reduced so the price was 97/6, the true picture was emerging. At 95 shillings an ounce, at least seven mines were running at a loss and another 15 were in danger if costs rose any higher. General Smuts, now Prime Minister, called a conference of the Chamber of Mines and the Mine Workers Union. Smuts had been aware of the situation from early on: 'The gold industry is a wasting industry,' he warned. 'As things are today, we watch, not slowly, but fairly rapidly, a creeping paralysis coming over it and, unless we are careful about the restoration of normal conditions in the world, and the disappearance of the premium, the risk is very grave indeed that you may have a cataclysm on the Witwatersrand.'

All the mining leaders echoed him: for example, the Chairman of General Mining's Van Ryn warned: 'Producers of raw materials such as we are have to choose between working at a loss or closing down operations, and there is only one of these alternatives open to them unless they are philanthropists.' As the gold premium continued to fall, PM Anderson, who had just taken over the Union Corporation office in Johannesburg, wrote to London on 19 October 1921 in his weekly mailship letter – 'There is a general feeling among the Groups that we are still a long way from having control of the mines and that, sooner or later, there must be a trial of strength in the form of a general strike or a general lock-out, so as to clear up the position.' Arthur French, chairing the earlier General Mining AGM, had declared, 'Many of our mines are simply living on the premium...' At a conference between unions and Chamber on 15 December, the Chamber explained that at the current price of 96 shillings an ounce there were eight mines producing at a loss and that if it dropped to its normal 85 shillings the unprofitable mines would be joined by another 16, spanning the whole of the Rand.

A further drop in the gold price on 21 December 1921 convinced the mining houses that they had to act at once to cut costs: they arbitrarily gave notice of wage reductions involving gold mines, collieries, the Power Company and the engineers. The result was a general strike from 22 January 1922 in which 22 000 men stopped work in mines, engineering works and power stations. By March the protest had become rebellion – civil war – with commandos of workers confronting the full force of the state. It was to be one of the most cathartic events in South Africa's history.

PM Anderson of Union Corporation in his letters to London reflected the fears that the mines would be flooded: on 11 January 1922 he described the attitude of underground and surface officials as 'very wobbly' and said it was not clear how far they would stand by the management. But the situation was to be saved by these officials, who, reported Anderson shortly afterwards, 'have completely changed their attitude and are now rendering very loyal service without demur.'

By March, there was revolution, to which the government responded with martial law. On 15 March 1922 Anderson reported again on the view from the Chamber: 'Since writing last week ... the Rand has passed through one of the most fateful periods in its history. On Thursday morning rioting took place in Benoni and shooting at sight became general. Disturbances were also in progress in other parts of the Rand ... on Friday a commando of about

700 mounted and armed men took possession of the Brakpan Mines. The officials put up a resistance lasting at least one hour. Unfortunately, no police appeared on the scene and the mine officials had to surrender for the want of ammunition... A body of revolutionaries, among whom were many well-known strikers, thereupon submitted the 31 defenders to the most brutal treatment. A number of them were clubbed to death...' And so on.

In the end, 230 lives were lost and four of the labour leaders were hanged for treason and murder. In London boardrooms, these events would have seemed near-incomprehensible. Henry Strakosch wrote to PM Anderson on 23 March 1922: 'Dear Anderson, my thoughts have been with you all during the troublous times that you have been passing, and I need not tell you what a relief it was to hear from your cable that you and all our people were safe and well. The to me always incomprehensible attitude of the Labour leaders is now, in the light of the events which have happened, adequately explained. It was always a puzzle to me why all along, at the various conferences, they refused to tackle the real issue... It is evident now that the leaders were merely preparing the ground for their revolutionary onslaught. It may interest you to know that I have heard here from a reliable source that the English Secret Service was able to intercept correspondence which clearly showed that the revolutionary movement was planned to take place early in March. Now that this ghastly affair has been successfully suppressed, I sincerely hope that punishment of the severest kind will be meted out to the leaders, and that the unions will be purged of the Bolshevik element by which they appear to have been dominated these last few years. The Chamber's decision to have nothing further to do with the Federation is a very wise one. It always seemed to me incongruous that we should be held, figuratively speaking, to negotiate with butchers and bakers regarding work on the mines!'

Strakosch, always a cool head with an eye for the bottom line, added: 'By the time this letter reaches you, you will no doubt be in a position to gauge the situation sufficiently to be able to form a view as to the effect which the post-strike working conditions will have on working costs... I hope that the lowering of costs will be well reflected in the working results of the second half of this year...'

(Anderson was coincidentally rewarded with a special participation in the 'Enemy Shares' which had been secured at such a low price, thanks to his efforts, from the Custodian of Enemy Property – and, on 11 May, a note from Strakosch cautioned him that he should not expect the same exceptional treatment next time!)

The industry had been at a standstill for 76 days (Geduld, for instance, had been cut off at one time); the improvement came immediately. The most effective consequence was the slashing of white wages, which fell from 24,8 per cent of gold mining revenue in 1921 to 18 per cent in the following year; the proportion of black workers to whites soared, as did the proportion of blacks underground – which did not mean that the colour bar was ended. Sir George Albu (to take again the example of Van Ryn) reported that working costs which in 1921 had averaged 25/9d per ton and had reached 26/2d in 1922 had fallen to 19/10d a year later.

Leopold Albu, as usual, put it more bluntly: 'The ugly episode is over ... and has taught several cogent lessons to South Africa... We re-started after the strike with a slate wiped clean of the restraints forced gradually upon the mines by the demands of the trade unions during the stress and difficulties of the War period and after, which made it impossible for a manager to keep control... Let us hope that the lessons of the strike will be taken to heart by the genuine worker. They will of course have no effect on the Communistic crank and agitator who desires to participate in the benefits of industry without working for it. If the real worker learns from this lesson the folly of regarding as gospel the speakers' argument of his "International" brother, and of putting his trust in him, the strike and the lives lost, however regrettable, will not have been in vain.'

A recent historian, David Yudelman, has summed up the aftermath of the 1922 Strike in a more sober and more helpful way: 'The combined effect of the reorganisation (of labour) and the technological revolution led to an unbroken decade of increases in labour productivity and restored the prosperity, or at least the viability, of the industry.'

The conventional view of the 1922 Rebellion and the election of the 1924 'Pact' government of the National and Labour parties which was its direct consequence used to be that this was the culmination of a conflict between labour and capital in which highly paid 'white labour' won an essentially racial struggle against the capitalist mine-owners who had, for a generation, been trying to substitute low-paid black labour. According to this thesis, the capitalists won in 1922 but lost in 1924 with the election of a coalition of Afrikaner nationalists and white workers.

Revisionist historians have now challenged this interpretation. Yudelman, for instance, has argued persuasively that the arrival of the 'Pact' government was not a major turning point in South Africa's history. He starts from the position that the smashing of the 1922 strike dealt white miners a blow from which they would not recover until the Second World War. He shows, for instance, that the proportion of blacks to whites in the industry – generally seen as the cause of 1922 – increased sharply; over the next 18 years strikes were almost unheard of; working costs on the gold mines fell *below 20 shillings a ton milled and stayed low: 'The mining capitalists benefited considerably from the aftermath of the 1922 revolt at the expense of white miners' – and the mine-owners continued their recovery for the first five years of a Pact government representing Afrikaner nationalists and white labour, as proved by growth of the revenue, profits, dividends and ore tonnages. Yudelman points out that, in fact as opposed to mythology, the Pact government, with its 'civilised labour policy', shifted the expensive burden of sheltered white employment from the mining industry (contrary to the Chamber's public complaints!) and transferred it to the manufacturing and state sectors. In Yudelman's words: 'The results of 1922 were far from being a defeat for the gold-mining capitalists. They did suffer a limited loss of autonomy in the sphere of collective bargaining, but ... there can be no doubt that the increased role of the state did bring a virtual end to militant white worker resistance... The white miners ... suffered as a result of the 1922 revolt and continued to do so throughout the two terms of the Pact Government.'*

Quietly and quickly, the Pact government understood that the low-paid gold industry could not be milked beyond a certain limit: the real 'turning point' was to be the international convulsion that led to the near-doubling of the gold price in 1933.

CHAPTER SIX

THE
GOLD PRICE

The story of General Mining and Union Corporation in the years that followed the 1922 Rebellion goes a long way to support the 'revisionist' thesis. Of course, there were special – coincidental – factors at work. The financial situation of Union Corporation, for example, improved consistently, thanks to the steady results from Modder Deep and Geduld (and the regular liquidation through the market of 'Enemy Shares'). General Mining, once it had got its chronic Cinderella problem off its hands in 1926 – thanks to a government-inspired deal (designed to secure a political benefit from the Boksburg electorate) to merge with ERPM, bringing a rights issue which gave Cinderella a second shaft and a new life – also resumed a dividend-paying progress, in this case thanks to the coming-good at last of West Rand Consolidated.

But behind the dramas underground during this period, and the best endeavours of brilliant engineers like Stowe McLean at West Rand Consolidated, there was the more important tale of the gold price – the Gold Standard – and Sir Henry Strakosch's rarely sung contribution to international diplomacy between the wars.

Henry Strakosch was born in Austria in 1871 to a family which had prospered in the sugar-beet industry. He became a banker, flourished, was transferred by the Anglo-Austrian Bank to London, tired of the profession and went out to South Africa in 1895, where he soon joined Adolf Goerz. He was Manager in Cape Town at the height of the war from October 1899 to December 1900, was recalled to Britain as Managing Director (London) after Goerz's death and – as sole Managing Director and, from 1923, also Chairman – was in undisputed control of the Group from January 1908 until 1943. His right-hand man for many years in London was Joseph Kitchin, and even the formalities of post-Victorian correspondence betray an affection between

80

them. He cannot have been an easy man to know: he was a bachelor until, very late in life, he married the widow of a former Union Corporation director and Chairman, Joseph Temperley. He was an entirely cosmopolitan and multilingual European, who travelled constantly. He took British citizenship in 1907 but did not become well known until after the First World War. He became a very rich man. Apart from his collection of historic banknotes, his only known passion was for automobiles – he used to tour the Continent in the latest high-speed vehicle, to the apprehension of Mr Kitchin, a non-driver.

After his transfer to London in 1901, he visited Africa only three times, a habit – or rather, an omission – which was undoubtedly to help create a certain gap between the Union Corporation management in London and Johannesburg. He was courteous, but he was not famous for fraternising with his staff in either country: many of them would not have recognised him, yet he was to make a large personal donation to the setting up of a staff pension fund.

His peculiar role in the between-war years was his extraordinary knowledge of, and expertise in, international currency – a distinction testified by his being awarded three separate Orders of Knighthood, for his assistance to the South African, Indian and British governments respectively. Notwithstanding frequent ill health, he seems constantly to have been travelling, accompanied always by his private secretary, Arthur Goldup, and his manservant: his correspondence to head office arrived from a galaxy of Europe's first-class hotels. During these years there was no apparent attempt to distinguish between his work as head of Union Corporation and his role as monetary statesman – no one seems ever to have made the distinction, presumably because his mixing with statesmen and financiers was central to his value to the Group. (It was also possible to justify this because he had a strong if subservient team in London and, from 1921 in Johannesburg, a powerful manager, PM Anderson, who was to be one of the most respected of South Africa's industrial leaders.)

The end of the First World War had brought the collapse of the Gold Standard which had been a comforting certainty for so many years. This has been explained very lucidly by Keith Wallis: 'Historically, gold was the medium for settling international debts and silver was that of national coinage. While silver currency was continually debased, gold changed hands on the basis of weight rather than face value and therefore stayed above national politics... The 'guinea'... was fixed as legal tender on the basis of 21/- for over a hundred years when it ceased to be minted and was replaced by the sovereign containing 0.235 ounces of gold, which held sway over the remainder of the 19th century and became synonymous with the £ sterling.

The Industrial Revolution, however, required much more lubrication by way of money supply than could be provided in the form of gold coinage despite the gold finds in the United States, Australia and South Africa. As goldsmiths and money-lenders turned into bankers, taking deposits and lending out other people's money as well as their own, a balance had to be struck between the cost of holding unremunerative gold in the vaults and the imperative need to convince every depositor that his money could be paid out in gold coin on demand. In other words, banks had to keep a proportion of their assets in the form of gold. If their stocks of metal increased, they could be more liberal in their lending policy, thereby effectively creating more money, more trade and more employment: if the stocks decreased they had to pull in their horns, the money supply was restricted and activity was cramped...

'The mechanism worked as well as it did because the European banking structure was reasonably efficient at moving gold by way of loans from countries with surpluses to those with deficits, and also due to the fact that, in the latter part of the century, the nation with the biggest balance of payments surplus – Great Britain – had a strong propensity for reinvesting the resulting inflow in the developing areas of the world... The 1914-18 War brought this state of affairs to an abrupt end. The balance of trade of the warring European countries went sharply into deficit and all their gold resources had to be mobilised to pay for war materials, the main recipient being the United States... In Britain, gold coinage was replaced by Treasury notes but for foreign transactions the gold parity was held until the War ended. In the end the controls which had enabled it to be maintained had to be relaxed and the Bank of England could no longer keep the window open and gold moved to a premium in London and elsewhere...'

After the First World War Henry Strakosch started to publish a series of influential pamphlets from the Union Corporation offices in London. His duties for Union Corporation had brought him into contact with John Maynard Keynes (who was managing the Treasury Gold Division during the war) and with General Smuts, who had joined the War Cabinet. Strakosch began to advise the Treasury on a part-time basis. Immediately after the war, when the gold price had moved to its premium, he and Keynes worked out a scheme for marketing South African gold, but this was turned down by the South African government.

However, the premium had revealed an impossible position for the South African banks, who were required to exchange paper for gold at the standard gold price, and Smuts invited Keynes to visit South Africa to make proposals to a Commission. Keynes declined and Smuts asked Strakosch to fill his shoes. Strakosch had already published a monograph, *The Value of Gold in Our Economic System*, in 1918. He now produced *The South*

African Currency and Exchange Problem as he spent many months in South Africa. His return to London was postponed again and again, and his letters to Joseph Kitchin must have been exasperating to that solid professional, judging by the latter's response – for example: 'I should be glad if you could let me know as soon as possible of the probable time of your return as we have many enquiries and certain business matters to an extent depend upon it' (18 March 1920).

Strakosch, from the Mount Nelson Hotel in Cape Town, was clearly relishing his new importance ('I am told that I have almost beaten the record for the length of examination before a Select Committee. My examination was concluded on the 5th inst., but the Select Committee desired me to be re-examined... I believe I have made good headway in converting even some of the most stubborn opponents (the Nationalists) of my proposal' (7 May 1920); 'I need hardly say I am getting rather tired with these constant delays, on the other hand I fear that it would have been impossible to refuse General Smuts's request' (20 May); 'I have no doubt you will be interested and pleased to hear that the Union Government have appointed me their Financial Advisor to attend at the International Financial Conference in Brussels' (6 September), etc.) Kitchin sometimes may betray his deeper feelings: for instance, 'I enclose an invitation to you to take part in the International Economic Conference ... you will note ... that the people connected with the Conference, who include Mr Keynes, are a very mixed lot, and I should think it would be best for you not to accept...') There is never any doubt who was the boss. For instance, in September 1921 Strakosch was in Geneva and found time to write to London – 'MacFarlane is not a desirable Manager... The Dick Turpin methods which he employs condemn him entirely in my view as a man who can be entrusted with the running of affairs at the Mine and I am more than ever convinced that he should be got rid of at the earliest possible moment... P.S. Your telegram urging my early return has just reached me... I don't quite follow in what respect the position has become "very difficult"...' To which the wretched Kitchin replied, 'Almost every day problems arise for settlement: in fact we have had four or five formal or informal board meetings this week. I feel the difficulty sometimes of meeting these problems without having an opportunity of consulting you ...' Strakosch was still in Geneva when he had Kitchin's telegram telling him that the Managing Director in Johannesburg, Michael McCormack, had died unexpectedly very soon after his appointment –

'IN VIEW OF URGENT QUESTIONS THERE ... ASKING ANDERSON TAKE CHARGE FOR PRESENT THINK POTT SHOULD NOT CANCEL MEXICAN JOURNEY IN VIEW OF URGENT QUESTIONS THERE BUT COULD BE RECALLED IF NECESSARY THINK ADVISABLE TO VISIT JOHANNESBURG FAIRLY SOON...'

Strakosch replied reassuringly that there was no need for panic but no doubt it would be necessary for someone to go out to Johannesburg to choose a new Manager. (In the event, Anderson got the job.) All of this is a small example of the detail of correspondence between the London office and the peripatetic Strakosch: it may be understandable, with all these glittering distractions, why the between-war reign of Strakosch and Kitchin was a touch short on imaginative risk and drive insofar as the affairs of the company were concerned.

The South African Currency and Exchange Problem, after endorsement and much applause by Select Committee and Union government as well as Keynes himself, led directly to the South African Currency and Banking Act and, therefore, to the establishment of the South African Reserve Bank, which was to be the first central bank in the British Dominions. Smuts got Strakosch a knighthood in the 1921 Honours List.

Over the next 15 years Sir Henry was repeatedly engaged in currency diplomacy. He attended, as we have seen, the International Finance Committee at Brussels and Geneva in 1920. This led to his membership – and chairmanship – of the Economic and Finance Committee of the League of Nations (he was a member for 16 years). Throughout the 1920s he was Financial Advisor to the South African government, with all the travel and conferences that entailed. He advised the Portuguese government. (In 1929 he even sat on Britain's first Channel Tunnel Committee!) He was awarded a KBE by the British government in 1924.

India then became important in his life. He went there in 1925 as a member of the Royal Commission on Indian Currency and Finance and wrote to Kitchin from Government House, Bombay, on 17 December 1925: 'In point of fact my work here is so absorbing, and so strenuous, that I have not really been able to give any thought to anything else... The climate at Delhi while we were there was delightful and somewhat reminiscent of the winter months in Johannesburg, but Bombay is most trying, the temperature, though perhaps not inordinately high (usually about 85 during the day) is made rather unbearable by the intense humidity of the atmosphere. I shall not be sorry to leave the place...' Later in the month, and not for the first time, the London office had a cable saying that Sir Henry was ill and his return would be delayed: on 31 December the faithful Goldup, the private secretary, wrote to Kitchin from a hill station reporting that 'Sir Henry stood the journey remarkably well and, although still exceedingly weak, already seems distinctly better for the improved climactic conditions.'

The London and indeed Johannesburg staffs might have had their private thoughts from time to time: Kitchin wrote to Anderson on 1 July 1926 (he had just been made Assistant Managing Director in London) – 'Sir Henry does not propose to withdraw even in slightest measure from his activities in connection with the Corporation and I am sure that none of us would wish him to do so. Of course a good deal of his time has been taken up lately with work of a public character, but we always live in hopes that this will make less claim upon his time...' Presumably there had been speculation that Kitchin was to take over from Strakosch, because Strakosch on the same day wrote to Anderson in Johannesburg, 'I hope, on the contrary, that public affairs will in the future occupy far less of my time than they have in the past, especially during the last eight months in connection with India.' The result of this last episode was the setting up of the Reserve Bank of India (and another Knighthood, this time a GBE) for Sir Henry; he sat for many years as Finance Member of the Council of India and represented India at the Imperial Economic Conference in Ottawa in 1932 and the London Monetary and Economic Conference in 1933.

Leaving to one side this glittering career, what did he do with Union Corporation, whose activities on the ground he hardly ever visited? After the First World War, the mining activities of the Corporation were focused on the East Rand, where A Goerz and Co had pioneered exploration north of Springs on President Kruger's farm Geduld. This development was one of the series of great extensions of the South African gold industry which were to characterise the century, and between the wars the Corporation's prosperity depended on Modderfontein Deep Levels, Geduld, and, from 1926, the adjoining East Geduld.

Sir Henry was a man who must have found it hard to accept other opinions, and his natural caution stiffened with the years: nevertheless, since he so rarely visited South Africa, and was also so frequently preoccupied with international affairs, the Union Corporation team in Johannesburg was most important. Once Sir Henry had decided who to trust, the same men stayed in place until the Second World War. The leader was a young South African, the former Consulting Engineer, Peter von Maltitz Anderson (note again the German element, though he quietly dropped the *von* during the war), who was confirmed as Johannesburg Manager in 1921 and who became a member of the Board in 1927. One of his sub-managers was Sir Henry's brother Paul.

Anderson, an engineer, was born in the Free State in 1879. He had worked at Princess and Geduld and he was principally responsible for reviving and sustaining the Goerz tradition of technical drive and excellence which was the pride of Union Corporation for so many years. He was to become a dominant figure in the South African mining industry over the next generation, serving no fewer than five times as President of the Chamber of Mines, and founding a veritable mining dynasty – his son Colin would be President four times after the war, also representing Union Corporation, and another son Peter (of Rand Mines) would be President twice. 'PM' would be increasingly respected and (by many) feared as the inter-war years went by, but his relationship with his London head office was not always easy. There Strakosch had taken over the chairmanship from Joseph Temperley in 1923. Joseph Kitchin, as we have seen, was in due course confirmed as Assistant Managing Director.

While PM Anderson took the helm of Union Corporation in South Africa, Kitchin handled London and Sir Henry travelled the world, the rather frail situation of both the Corporation and General Mining was about to be restored by the good fortune of events on the international stage: that is to say, the miraculous transformation of the gold price. The post-war gold premium had been falling by 1921 and South African mines were closing in consequence (including Princess Estate). The Chamber reckoned that of the 39 mines remaining, 13 were making a loss in February 1921. There was a deep economic depression in South Africa, particularly in agriculture and diamonds. This had been the background to the 1922 Rebellion. But when Britain returned to the Gold Standard on 28 April 1925, South Africa followed suit, and – with the crushing of the Rebellion and the reassuring policies of the 1924 Pact government – the economics of the mines began to look up. Working costs were massively reduced, thanks in particular to rapid improvements in technology, including the introduction of new jack-hammers, and the end of any shortage of black labour. With the (unexpected) support of the Pact government, white wages were held down: the average shift-worker's wage in 1930 was 22/6d compared with 30/3d in 1921. Arthur French of General Mining, in his annual presidential address to the Chamber of Mines on 27 March 1925 said: 'Our relations with Ministers ... have been of the pleasantest description.'

Even as the Great Depression engulfed the world, South Africa's gold production – selling at the standard price of £4 4s 11½d an ounce – continued to rise steeply. Nevertheless, there were fears that, at the present working cost and the traditional world price, the industry might shortly go into decline. The government's response was to set up the 1930 Low Grade Ore Commission. The fears were dramatically to be proved premature. On 21 September 1931, Britain went off the Gold Standard and devalued, thus posing the South African government with a major question – what to do? Sir Henry Strakosch at this point got it wrong, and his contribution to the crisis may be thought to have had unfortunate consequences, though it was not entirely his fault.

Sir Henry's first thought (and his opinions in this field carried immense weight by now) was that South Africa should *not* follow London. He immediately cabled Anderson telling him to urge the government that:

'THERE IS NO DOUBT ABOUT IT IN MY MIND THAT IT IS IN THE INTEREST OF SOUTH AFRICA TO REMAIN ON THE GOLD STANDARD BECAUSE OF ITS OUTSTANDING INTEREST IN GOLD MINING AND ITS CONSTANT INTEREST IN SEEING THAT GOLD STANDARD IS MAINTAINED WHENEVER POSSIBLE AND RESTORED AS SOON AS POSSIBLE WHEN CRISIS OVER STOP EVEN IF S A RESERVE BANK INCUR LOSS ON THEIR STERLING BALANCE IT IS BETTER THAT UNION GOVERNMENT MAKE GOOD LOSS RATHER THAN ABANDON GOLD STANDARD STOP LINKING SOUTH AFRICAN CURRENCY WITH ENGLISH STERLING WOULD PROBABLY INVOLVE EARLY SUBSTANTIAL RISES IN PRICE SOUTH AFRICA WHICH WOULD UNDOUBTEDLY LEAD TO DEMAND OF INCREASE OF WAGES AND CONSEQUENT UNREST STOP...'

Anderson sent a brief acknowledgement and telephoned the Minister.

At the same time, General Smuts, who was visiting London and, of course, was in Opposition, sent a telegram to Pretoria urging that South Africa should *follow* Britain's example and join the new Sterling Area (it is hard to imagine that Strakosch and Smuts did not discuss the topic, and it is interesting that they disagreed). The South African Finance Minister, NC Havenga, not surprisingly declined to accept the advice of his opponent and declared that the Union would *remain* on the Gold Standard. At this point, the Chamber of Mines thought again and came to the conclusion that it would be wiser for South Africa to *follow* Britain; its two-man delegation who argued the case before Havenga included PM Anderson – who later admitted his embarrassment at having to put to the Minister the opposite of the message he had passed on from Sir Henry a fortnight previously.

In fact, Sir Henry was also having second thoughts – he now wanted Britain to return as soon as possible to the Gold Standard but at a much lower parity; the British devaluation had settled at about 30 per cent and, if South Africa could follow, there was an obvious attraction to Sir Henry of gaining that degree of revenue increase. The South African government, however, was not disposed to be seen to change course: there was a political dimension to the debate, with the Hertzog government anxious to be seen to be truly its own men. Havenga actually quoted Sir Henry's telegram in his speech to Parliament, though he had the grace not to name the author. In the event, the South African authorities insisted on staying with gold for another 15 months. Sticking with the old parity probably cost the industry £20 million in working profits. For South African exporters, the consequences were catastrophic and there was an unstoppable flight of South African currency. Eventually, Havenga had to yield, at the very end of 1932, when the South African pound was freed and quickly reached parity with sterling. As

Keith Wallis has pointed out, it would have been better for everyone if Strakosch and Smuts had each signed the other's cables!

There was a happy ending to the drama. In April 1933 Franklin D Roosevelt devalued the dollar and the gold price rose to $35 an ounce. It was, in the historian Kiewiet's much-quoted phrase, 'a windfall, the greatest perhaps of [South Africa's] career'. No one had imagined a 45 per cent increase in the gold price in their wildest dreams. Within just a few years, the results were evident. On the fiftieth anniversary of the Chamber of Mines, in 1936, its President could report that 15 new mines were in the process of being opened up, with 23 new main shafts. The economics of the industry had been transformed overnight. Immense quantities of low-grade ore – standing either in existing mines or in new fields – suddenly became available. Inevitably the government would take its share of the new profits, with fundamental consequences for state finances.

Union Corporation and General Mining shared in the bonanza – and not before time. Union Corporation had managed to rebuild itself after the war, but in 1930 it still had only two producing mines and one developing one. Geduld and Modder Deep now carried the Corporation's fortunes. These two had proved the consistent nature of this part of the East Rand basin, making it far less risky than in the far West to rely on values continuing into adjacent properties. This is what had made it possible for Union Corporation to push ahead with East Geduld well before there was any question of a higher gold price, and to be in a position to take full advantage of the rise when it came. East Geduld in fact came into production in mid-1931 and, east again, there was Grootvlei where Union Corporation had taken control in 1930. With the support of the new gold price, the development programme could be accelerated and production eventually started in 1938, the beginning of a long and profitable operation. Another happy result of the gold price hike for Union Corporation in the East Rand was the reopening in 1938 of the old Van Dyk, closed down in 1911, as the expanded and amalgamated Van Dyk Consolidated Mines. Finally, Marievale Consolidated Mines was developed very fast and came into production just as the Second World War broke out. So, Union Corporation in the 1930s added four mines to its existing two and, all in all, could show that it had expanded twice as fast as the industry as a whole and that working profits had soared.

Most important of all, the new gold price had inspired the mining houses to start thinking more ambitiously of more distant extensions of the existing ore-bodies – of *new* gold fields – and this new spirit extended to Union Corporation, whose devotion to exploration had not been forgotten, though not exactly conspicuous since Adolf Goerz's day. The fortunate result was that in 1936 a Union Corporation geologist called Alfred Frost began to look in south-west Transvaal and the northern Orange Free State, soon focusing on the Sand River district. The basic problem was that there was no outcrop to help the geologists and Union Corporation was not going to be in the expensive business of 'wild cat' drilling. In Keith Wallis's words: 'Frost's task was to find places where gold-bearing reefs might 'sub-outcrop' relatively close to the surface so that exploration proper could be carried out by sinking reasonably shallow, and therefore affordable, shafts – preferably inclined ones. The science of geophysics had by that time developed gravity and magnetic techniques, which between them gave some indication of both the characteristics and thicknesses of the rock formations underlying particular areas. The reef itself was not detectable magnetically, but was usually quite closely associated with a stratum of magnetic material, so this 'proxy' bed became the geologist's target. No surface techniques existed which would give any indication whatsoever of the thickness, richness or even existence of the gold-bearing reef itself.'

In the meantime, Frost was keeping in touch with Western Holdings, at that time controlled by Sir Abe Bailey, whose physicist, Oscar Weiss, had been carrying out a big programme of gravity and magnetic surveys using the torsion balance which could establish the thickness of underlying strata so that boreholes could be drilled in places which would avoid the 1 500 metre thick lavas of the north-western Free State. Union Corporation had taken a large stake in Western Holdings in 1937, and Frost and Weiss were therefore able to co-operate. The result – in April 1939 – was that a Western Holdings borehole on a farm called St Helena struck the basal reef at just over 350 metres and gave a yield *15 times* the minimum payable level. This sensational result heralded a new goldfield (an elderly Union Corporation director in London is reported to have concluded, after a good boardroom lunch, that gold had been found on the South Atlantic island of that name). There was a poetic justice in this – A Goerz and Co had only just missed a strike beyond Potchefstroom in the far west as long ago as 1902. This time the Corporation realised it did not hold enough ground under option in the area and therefore reached an alliance with Western Holdings; thereupon, Strakosch did a deal with Chester Beatty's Selection Trust to pool their Orange Free State interests. The result was that the Union Corporation involvement in the new gold field was diluted from the beginning, even though it would have the distinction of opening the first mine, St Helena.

But the war had to be fought first.

During these years, the Union Corporation was showing itself a rather different creature from General Mining in one important – and adventurous –

way: it was diversifying away from mining. Union Corporation – and indeed Adolf Goerz in the old days – had always been prepared to look outside Southern Africa. During the Boer War, for example, Goerz had investigated a wide range of 'offshore' prospects and he was also starting to get interested in Australia.

The story of Union Corporation in Mexico needs a separate book, but the essence is that in 1908 Henry Strakosch committed the Corporation to a risky silver venture in the central Mexican state of Zacatecas, about 800 kilometres from Mexico City. He actually visited the country in person in 1909. The La Fe venture, as it came to be called, absorbed £250 000 of the Group's money (nearly a fifth of its already depleted assets at the time) and collapsed in 1914 in the chaos of Mexican revolution after the overthrow of President Porfirio Diaz. However, its successor project, San Francisco Mines, became one of the Group's most fascinating stories and was to deliver profits for many years.

There had been dramatic and dangerous events at La Fe in 1914, when foreigners had to be evacuated (the Union Corporation Manager, Cyrus Pott, is supposed to have saved an American lady missionary by passing her off as his wife). The Mexican staff cowered underground – though keeping the pumps going – while the battle raged above their heads: they eventually managed to put the mine on a care-and-maintenance basis. Production actually resumed in 1920 but it became clear that the problems of the ore body were too great – not to speak of the problems of operating in Mexico at that time – and La Fe was closed in 1924. Meanwhile, as early as 1912, Cyrus Pott had found the San Francisco del Oro Syndicate which owned a silver-lead-zinc mine in the State of Chihuahua in north Mexico, and this was to be where the Corporation's curiosity in Mexico was to pay off. The 1930s were desperately difficult but after the Second World War San Francisco would once again be a substantial contributor of profits until, in the 1960s, the charms of Mexicanisation became inescapable; the last Union Corporation shareholding would be sold off in the late 1970s.

Apart from Mexican mining, Union Corporation was also interested in diversifying into industry, and here the results were to be more problematical. In 1925, for instance, the Corporation introduced the Enka Rayon Company of Holland to Britain, with 'British Enka' opening a factory at Aintree, but the company never flourished – and there was frequent tension with the Dutch directors – although it persevered until the 1950s when Union Corporation extracted itself. In 1928 the Corporation helped introduce to the London market Polyphonwerke AG, later to become Deutsche Grammophon: in this case it got out in 1935. A third example, more happily, was a major investment in Haggie, Son and Love, a wire-drawing and wire-rope business serving the South African mines, which, as the listed company Haggie, is still part-owned by Gencor, sharing control with Anglo American.

At this point Sir Henry laid down an 'industrial policy' which was to set guidelines for the future. These were that: (1) the business should be potentially large enough to warrant public flotation; (2) it should, from a manufacturing point of view, justify at least one factory of sufficient size to take advantage of the most economic processes available; (3) it should be simple. In consequence, there was to be only one major industrial project in these between-the-wars years – a domestic South African pulp and paper industry, to be known as Sappi. The company was announced in 1936 and the early years were difficult; the success story of Sappi would have to wait until long after the war.

I *was put onto shift bossing at the princely sum of £35 per month with a possible bonus of £5. At first it was all night shift work and when we started stoping I was put on to day shift. On night shift I had my one and only clash with a Basuto lashing gang. We were sinking a 15 degree incline haulage and my job on night shift was to see that it was cleaned out. But the gang started a go-slow routine and I couldn't understand why. Certain members of the gang were pointedly insolent and the trammer was frightened of the gang. I had been told that you had to show a Basuto who was the boss or they treated you with contempt. So I decided on a showdown and told the trammer if necessary to come to my rescue.*

The lashers were all bunched together throwing the broken rock back into the two cars on the winch rope, and taking their time. I asked one of them why he wasn't working. He spat. And I hit him. There were some 12 lashers and they came at me with their spades. I had taken the precaution of leaving a short drillsteel against the sidewall. I grabbed this and sailed into them with maniacal fury driving them back towards the face. They were all bunched together and couldn't wield their spades. The bossboy interceded and probably saved my life.

I now found out that they had not been paid a bonus they were entitled to. I told them I would accompany them to the compound to find out why they had not been paid. They set to with a will and soon had the end cleaned. I had made a significant gesture in throwing the drillsteel away and accompanied them to the shaft and got into the same deck of the cage with them. Without changing I went straight to the compound and led the gang into the Compound Manager's office. We sorted out the trouble and went into our several beds. That night it was all smiles and the end was cleaned in good time.

This same gang was to come to my help several weeks later when there was a mudrush on the conveyor belt crosscut. The various levels were connected by 60 degree ore and waste passes down which the ore or waste

*would pass to the conveyor belt crosscut which was fed into the shaft
measuring bins for hoisting to surface. Should water get into the system,
there was a great danger that the fines would be washed out and accumulated
and finally rush out as mud at the bottom. And that is what happened, the
whole of the crosscut being filled with mud to the hanging and surging to
within feet of the shaft. And there was no sign of the three or four operatives
of the conveyor belt, which was of course buried in mud. Were they also
buried? There was no other exit.*

    *My Basuto gang being nearest to the shaft were called to the rescue and
worked like Trojans while I collected other gangs. There is nothing so
frustrating as trying to shovel mud. At best you can shove it along. We found
the missing persons unharmed at the back of the crosscut. Never a dull
moment. And I had made good friends with my Basuto gang and learned once
more how not to do things...*

'Life at Van Dyk in the 1930s',
from an unpublished memoir by Bob Fourie

*(Bob Fourie was later to be nicknamed 'The Undertaker' because, as a
Union Corporation mine manager, he was eventually to close down Van Dyk,
Geduld and East Geduld.)*

CHAPTER SEVEN

SECOND GENERATION

General Mining had also benefited greatly from the 1933 rise in the gold price. In 1930 its situation had not looked promising: only three of the Group's turn-of-the-century mines were still in production – West Rand Cons, Van Ryn and the Meyer – and of these the Meyer was at last coming to its end, cleaning up its reduction works. Van Ryn was still in full production and therefore was well placed to benefit from a higher gold price. But the greatest beneficiary was West Rand Consolidated, where Stowe McLean was making his name.

McLean was one of the great characters of the South African industry. He was a Canadian who came out to South Africa in 1910 and later realised how much money he could make as a 'rock breaker' rather than as a shift-boss. He therefore became one of only two future presidents of the Chamber of Mines to have been a member of the Mine Workers Union, which landed him in a tricky position during the 1922 Strike: his solution was secretly to arrange for his car to be commandeered by the military with himself as driver. In 1923 he was sent to West Rand Consolidated by Sir George – he used to claim that his brief was to close it down – and stayed there for 13 years. He turned the mine round, planned a major vertical shaft, and, in 1933, as the gold price rocketed, he had broken various shaft-sinking records and was at last, with excellent timing, in a position to exploit the enormous ore reserves which he had established there – results which had made it possible for the Albus to raise more finance (and, indeed, had also restored the brothers' faith in their own projects). The Albus had earlier been rescued, with somewhat mixed feelings, from their long-running problems with Cinderella, though General Mining maintained a large shareholding. Of the other two deep-level prospects which had been such a concern, New Steyn had been merged with Durban Roodepoort, and Rand Collieries, renamed Witpoort Gold Areas, had been sold.

So, in the 1930s, the prospects for General Mining were mixed. In strictly financial terms, all was well, but the Corporation was hardly in a position to compete with other, more vigorous companies in the setting up of future ventures. The Albus' interest in original exploration is illustrated by the fact that in 1932 'exploration' costs totalled £40! This need not be surprising. The Albu brothers were tired and, as they grew older, their instinctive caution strengthened. Perhaps their nerve was running frail after the tensions and dangers of more than half a century. The two brothers understood how close they had sailed to disaster. Now they appreciated what they owed to Stowe McLean's rescue of West Rand Consolidated. They had made their name and fortune as specialists in small-scale outcrop operations and had flirted dangerously with deep shafts; now they could demonstrate, with West Rand Consolidated, after many years of problems, that they had an ambition and an ability to think big that made them the equal of their colleagues.

The brothers continued to run the Group by a process of debate and, frequently, argument. In the days before the international telephone, they spent their days arguing with each other by letter (allowing three weeks for arrival by Union Castle), cable (entailing fiddly translation into code and out of it), and, only later, by airmail. Leopold was the money man always, jealous of his expertise and instinct in the markets, quick to protest if his elder brother interfered from Johannesburg. Sir George was much more the hands-on Executive Chairman, always emphasising that he was on the spot and so, by implication, knew better: it had been George after all who taught himself mining in the early years and was noteworthy in the Rand Club in the 1880s and 90s for his dedication in inspecting his own underground properties.

There was an interesting exchange in September 1907, after the Strike, when Leopold commented bitterly to his brother: 'To think that this golden opportunity of reorganising the [white labour] matter on a sounder and more reasonable basis is now likely to be lost by the petty jealousies of the Groups makes one really feel discouraged for the future...' He developed the Albus' shared suspicions of their Randlord colleagues in a handwritten postscript – 'I think that you should quietly withdraw from that body [the Chamber of Mines], at first by constantly remaining away from their meetings and then resigning altogether ... we have all along been used only as padding in all the attitudes and actions of the Chamber to show to the Govt and the public the harmony of the mining houses, our views have hardly ever found an effective hearing unless they just happened to coincide with those of Eckstein, Farrar, and the Gold Fields... I warned you at the time not to join the Chamber in any other capacity except as President...' Perhaps the Albus always felt themselves, to some degree, to be outside the charmed circle...

The brothers knew, and had long agreed, their separate responsibilities, but this did not stop them scrapping: thus, for example, a cable from Leopold to George on 12 April 1911 –

'YOUR ATTITUDE PREPOSTEROUS RENDERING MY LIFE AND POSITION QUITE UN-BEARABLE YOUR REQUEST TO BE GUIDED BY YOU ADDS INSULT TO INJURY I CLAIM ABSOLUTE INDEPENDENCE ACTION MY DEPARTMENT WHICH IS ON FINANCE AND SHARE POLICY AND MUST PROTEST AGAINST THIS SYSTEMATIC INTERFERENCE YOUR DEPARTMENT WHICH IS ON TECHNICAL MANAGEMENT AND CONTROL MUST BE OB-VIOUS TO YOU ABSOLUTELY IMPOSSIBLE CARRY OUT ANY BUSINESS UNLESS OUR RESPECTIVE SPHERES AUTHORITY ARE CLEARLY DEFINED AND SCRUPULOUSLY RESPECTED BY EACH OTHER OTHERWISE IRRITATING DELAYS UNAVOIDABLE DEAD-LOCKS WHICH MUST BE INJURIOUS CORPORATION THIS EVENTUALITY I AM NOT PREPARED TO FACE THEREFORE MUST ASK YOU TO ABANDON NEW ACQUISITIONS OR SCHEMES INVOLVING INCREASING COMMITMENTS UNTIL YOUR RETURN TO LONDON WHICH I HOPE YOU WILL HASTEN AS MUCH AS POSSIBLE...'

This outburst is not entirely typical of their 40-year correspondence, but it rings true enough.

The most frequent purpose of their private correspondence and cables was of course to liaise on market tactics and to exchange, in code, useful confidential information. In the pre-1914 days, for instance, they needed to consult as to how to treat their German backers, as in a London-Johannesburg telegram on 10 March 1911:

'OUR BERLIN FRIENDS UNANIMOUSLY OF OPINION DIVIDEND MUST BE PAID THEY SAY THAT ACCORDING TO THEIR IDEA PROFIT MUST BE DISTRIBUTED WHATEVER FUTURE PROSPECT... STRONGLY OF OPINION PASSING DIVIDEND FOR LAST YEAR WILL ABSOLUTELY DESTROY CONFIDENCE ... CONSIDERING GERMANY OUR BIGGEST CLIEN-TELE AND THAT SHARES HELD THERE PRINCIPALLY FOR INVESTMENT SEE NO OTHER COURSE BUT TO ACT UPON CAREFULLY CONSIDERED VIEWS LEADING BANKS GERMANY WITH REGARD OUR POLICY...'

But this correspondence also has its fascination in revealing the brothers' discussion of changing situations. George, for example, would indulge his natural pessimism (13 April 1932) –

'IN MY OPINION WORLD CONDITIONS HOPELESS AND PRICES WILL EVENTUALLY GO MUCH LOWER'.

and Leopold a sometimes blind optimism (23 July 1932) –

'I AM CONVINCED HAVE SEEN THE WORST AND THERE IS EVERY LIKELIHOOD OF GRADUAL IMPROVEMENT STOP POLITICAL SITUATION IN GERMANY NOT AT ALL ALARMING...'.

The arguments went on all their lives and sometimes the disagreements were impassioned. In February 1933, to take just one instance, there was a plan for New Steyn to acquire Roodepoort Utd and Leopold objected to the terms –

'ON NO ACCOUNT WILL I AGREE TO LESS AMOUNT THAN 200,000 IT WOULD APPEAR THAT IN ALL CASES YOU REFUSE TO BE INFLUENCED BY MY ADVICE EMPLOYING ARGUMENTS WHICH ARE FALLACIOUS AND FAR FETCHED AND ACT DIRECTLY IN OPPOSITION THERETO WITH SERIOUS CONSEQUENCES TO OUR INTERESTS...'

and so on and so forth, day after day, until he got his way on March 24:

'IT APPEARS YOU ARE REVERTING USELESS CONTROVERSY WITH RESULTANT AND UNNECESSARY DELAY...'

Leopold seems always to have been complaining to and about the Johannesburg office: on 14 September 1928, in a typical example –

'MUST REPEAT WHAT WE HAVE SO OFTEN EMPHASISED AND MUST BE OBVIOUS TO YOU THAT IT CANNOT BE GOOD POLICY FOR YOU TO SELL OCCASIONAL SMALL PARCELS ESPECIALLY IN FALLING MARKET...'

or on 19 August 1932:

'I MUST AGAIN POINT OUT WHAT I HAVE SO OFTEN DONE THAT IT IS IMPOSSIBLE TO CARRY OUT SUCCESSFUL SHARE MARKET POLICY IF EACH OF US ACTS INDEPENDENTLY AND POSSIBLY WITH DIVERGENT AIM FROM OTHER... I AM CONVINCED THAT OUR ONLY POLICY IS TO LEAVE JOHANNESBURG MARKET ALONE AND GIVE ARBITRAGE A CHANCE AND NOT INTERFERE WITH MY MANAGEMENT OF MARKET...

Sometimes the brothers could not contain their exasperation, and their nerves, and resorted to the lengthy cables whose expense they quickly regretted afterwards. For example, on 9 April 1927, Leopold cabled –

'I AM NOT AT ALL SURPRISED BY OR ALARMED BY DEADLOCK BETWEEN YOU AND CENTRAL MINING BUT WHAT CAUSES GREAT ANXIETY IS THE DEADLOCK BETWEEN OURSELVES AND THE IMPOSSIBLE POSITION CREATED THEREBY WHICH CANNOT BUT HAVE THE MOST FAR REACHING CONSEQUENCES UPON THE SUCCESS OF GENERAL MINING...'

They were still at odds in their seventies: on 27 January 1934 Leopold sent a telegram:

'MY SILENCE SOLELY DUE TO FACT THAT HAVING EXHAUSTED ALL MY REASONS IN FAVOUR OF INDEPENDENT SCHEME AND HAVING APPARENTLY FAILED CONVINCE YOU WE APPEAR TO HAVE REACHED DEADLOCK... FACT THAT WE ARE BOTH OLD MEN DOES NOT JUSTIFY US SACRIFICING FUTURE STATUS AND PROSPERITY OF GENERAL MINING BY DISPOSING FEW REMAINING MINING ASSETS ONE AFTER THE OTHER...'

Always there was affection, apology, family love. They were constantly asking about the children, sending presents, planning holidays together, even apologising: see Leopold to George in December 1931, when there had been a bad row about the 'Witpoort proposal' concerning Rand Collieries, to which George must have reacted with distress –

'TERRIBLY SORRY THAT MY CABLES SHOULD HAVE CAUSED YOU SUCH UNHAPPINESS AND RESENTMENT PLEASE ACCEPT MY SINCEREST APOLOGIES AND ASSURANCE THAT NOTHING WAS NOR COULD HAVE BEEN FARTHER FROM MY INTENTION HOW-EVER SERIOUSLY OUR VIEWS AND OPINIONS MAY DIFFER NOTHING IN THE WORLD IS OR EVER CAN BE NEARER MY HEART THAN YOUR HAPPINESS WHATEVER MAY HAPPEN WISHING YOU ALL HAPPY NEW YEAR LOVE LEOPOLD.'

Who can doubt that Uncle Leopold meant it?

Their families had grown up surrounded by substantial though not grotesque luxury. Leopold lived in London's Mayfair, travelled frequently on the Continent and rarely to South Africa, and had what seems to have been an unhappy marriage to the much younger Adelaide, a beauty who was also an accomplished horsewoman and musician. Adelaide esteemed her looks, her dresses and her jewellery so much that, when they separated and Leopold asked whether she would take her daughter or her jewels, she opted for the latter, with the result that the only child, Veronica, was brought up by her father.

Veronica was to live an extravagant and dramatic life in which she got through a good part of her inheritance. Her first husband was a well-known theatrical impresario in London, Stanley Scott, whose productions she was thought to have bankrolled. The second husband was a Polish sculptor, An-toni Juskiewicz, who fathered her only child, Ann. Through the wartime world of Polish exiles she met her third husband, Count Ludomin Cienski, with whom after the war she returned to live in South Africa on the Cape wine estate L'Ormarins, which was later bought and developed by Anton Rupert's family.

Count Cienski had had his own wartime drama as a member of a group of Polish exile officers. In June 1943, he stood trial for the murder of his then wife's lover, pleaded not guilty and was discharged: in the laconic words of *The Times* of 2 June 1943, 'Lieut Buchowski was found shot dead in Lieut Cienski's flat on April 12. It was alleged that Lieut Buchowski had formed an attachment to Lt Cienski's wife, to which the accused objected...' Veronica thereafter married the Count. Her daughter, Ann, Leopold's only grand-daughter, was to make her life in Natal; she and her cousin 'Georna' Albu later married the two Goodman brothers, the dashing identical 'polo twins' of Johannesburg post-war society.

Before the war, Sir George and his family of six had continued to live in high-bourgeois comfort in Northwards on the Parktown Ridge. There were European servants (as well as scores of black staff), many entertainments, a farm outside town (but not too far – Sir George was not a country type), a busy social life mixing with high Johannesburg, and long visits to Europe where there was a house in Grosvenor Place. The formidable eldest daughter Charlotte, known as Tasha, was married to the Bishop of Pretoria; the second – Katherine (Kitty) – in 1913 married Erroll Hay, the Group's mining engineer, who was to join the Board and eventually leave it after a bitter row; Alice lived in England with her husband Nigel Bengough and her two children; Irene (Bobby) married Colonel Bill Dalrymple, wrote poetry and died in childbirth in 1924. As we have seen, there was another tragedy in that the elder son, Walter, had died in 1920, never having fully recovered from his war service. That left as successor to the firm the baby of the family, George Werner Albu, born in 1905, who was sent to Rugby and Cambridge. The Albu family had travelled quite a distance from the German Jewry of the mid-nineteenth century.

Sir George and Leopold accepted their family responsibilities to the end: thus, to give just one example, in September 1934, Leopold cabled George,

'IN CONSEQUENCE OF LETTER FROM ARTHUR ROSENDORFF [another brother-in-law] INFORMING ME LIFE IN GERMANY HAS BECOME INTOLERABLE AND SUGGESTING CLOSING BERLIN OFFICE HAVE INSTRUCTED HIM TO DO SO FORTHWITH AND THAT WE WILL ALLOW PENSIONS 300 PER ANNUM...'

It was time for a new generation. Jacob Freudenthal, the brother-in-law, had died in 1934, Arthur French in September 1935. Leopold Albu sailed to South Africa to discuss the succession in London and on 6 December the two brothers attended a Board meeting together – one of the very few occasions this had happened in 40 years. Sir George died in Johannesburg, quite suddenly, on 27 December 1935.

Leopold automatically moved into the Chair, and then realised that there might be a tax problem for the Corporation in consequence of his British residence. This, he declared, would be 'unthinkable' (he would have remembered how the brothers had won a law case 30 years previously to keep beyond the clutches of the UK taxman), and in June 1936 he therefore stepped aside, leaving Sir George's son – now known as Sir George W. Albu – aged only 30, to become Chairman. The uncle hailed his nephew in positively Victorian style: 'In handing over "the Mantle" which your father has carried for so many years with such outstanding distinction and honor [*sic*] and success I want to give expression to my affection for you and my confidence in your ability and integrity – and my hope that by constant attention to your work and duty you will eventually shape yourself in every respect so as to become worthy of bearing his name and Mantle!'

This was to be a tricky period. Leopold, increasingly crotchety, cautious and spendthrift in his old age, seems to have assumed that he would run things behind the scenes and he deluged young George in Johannesburg with a series of peremptory if affectionate instructions. On 14 May 1936, for example, he wrote: 'During my lifetime ... I rely on you that you will do nothing of importance without *previously* submitting it to me and be guided by my experience and judgment...' Or, in a letter urging his nephew to resist rashness: 'If you act accordingly and unwaveringly you will I am sure not have any cause for anxiety or regret. The future of the Corporation as well as your own will be as sure as anything in this world can be; and you will be happy in your position as chairman and you will maintain the proud reputation of the Corporation and the name of Albu...'

The new Sir George appears to have put up with this sort of thing with good grace – he had spent a lot of time with his uncle during his education in Britain and was evidently fond of him – but it must have been exasperating, in these depressing pre-war days, to cope with Leopold's caution and miserliness – the qualities which the old man had learned in his youth meant the difference between success and disaster. For example, Leopold made a great fuss about the cost of Stowe McLean's house in Johannesburg – 'I am rather afraid that the prodigality of the expenditure on the West Rand, where everything has been done regardless of expense and in a manner sumptuous enough for a king, may have influenced his judgment, and sense of fitness of things – and has obviously tempered the spirit of economy supposed to be inherent in one of his nationality...' (23 April 1936).

More importantly, Leopold resisted, or rather rejected, most of George's ideas (to the point where London managers wrote privately to George expressing sympathy). Again, George put up with this onslaught with remarkably good temper. There was, for example, an idea he had for a new process to manufacture castor oil. His uncle was scathing and sent a stream of telegrams in the familiar tone – for example, on 12 September, 'WE WOULD URGE YOU TO ADHERE TO RESOLUTION EXPRESSED IN ONE OF YOUR RECENT LETTERS WHICH HAS MY WHOLE HEARTED APPROVAL THAT YOU WILL NOT CONSIDER ANY NEW VENTURE UNLESS IT IS AN ELDORADO IT WOULD BE SHEER FOLLY AND ASKING FOR TROUBLE TO JEOPARDISE TECHNICAL AND FINANCIAL POSITION WHICH IS UNIQUE AND PRACTICALLY UNASSAILABLE BY EMBARKING ON VENTURES HOWEVER ATTRACTIVE THEY MAY LOOK THEORETICALLY OUR MOTTO MUST BE LEAVE WELL ALONE...'

George stuck to his guns on the oil project but nothing was to come of it. He had no better luck with his uncle either in a plan to build a new head office block in co-operation with Union Corporation or in other development projects: there is an unexplained cable from Leopold on 16 September: 'ORANGE FREE STATE – IT IS NOT ORIGINAL COST WITH WHICH WE ARE CONCERNED

BUT THE INDEFINITE EXPENDITURE INVOLVED IN PROSPECTING SUCH A LARGE AREA FOR THIS REASON CONFIRM OUR OPINION WE SHOULD NOT UNDERTAKE IT...'

It was precisely in the Free State that both Union Corporation and General Mining were to be overtaken by their rivals in the years ahead.

George was evidently casting around for avenues of diversification, since it was time for new thinking as the generations changed. At least the men at the head of the operation could now talk out their disagreements on the international telephone – there is a reference in one of George's letters in February 1936 to the benefit he had obtained from their conversation earlier that day, which had evidently been on the subject of a particularly painful row inside the family about Erroll Hay in the immediate aftermath of Sir George's death.

Hay was a highly respected mining engineer, manager and more recently director of the Corporation – and married to Sir George's daughter Kitty – who protested at Leopold's plans to cut his and other Johannesburg managers' remuneration and apparently threatened to make trouble at shareholders' meetings. George – who was much younger than Hay – was left to sort out the mess, and was thoroughly abused by his uncle for his decision to 'buy off' the family dissident. Thus Leopold wrote in a private letter, 'There seems to have been great laxity and unreasonable indulgency practised in your office in the past and this may have been due to family considerations... There must be discipline and authority in every establishment... If that is what you call an 'amicable' settlement I should like to know what would have been a forced one. A few more of such and we might as well close up shop...'

George replied firmly, in longhand, on 18 February 1936: 'It was a case of getting rid of him *à tout prix* – I have not in any way weakened nor have I been influenced by considerations of family ties... Immediately subsequent to your departure, Hay, enraged and bitter with a hatred of all things pertaining to Albu, sought a means of doing us harm... Although one hates having to 'buy' a man, it is sometimes the cleanest and best method, especially when dealing with a sadistic megalomaniac... With McLean here I have every hope – even to certainty – that the Corporation will go from strength to strength... *Au revoir*, old boy, and bless you...'

Leopold died on 19 March 1938, on a private visit to Rome. There is a family legend that he shot himself on the steps of the Grand Hotel, but this is certainly a confusion – there had a few years earlier been a dramatic scene when one of the nieces, Dorothea, daughter of Eugen, pleading with her uncle for help with her dressmaker's bills (or, possibly, to buy her Italian husband a castle – memories differ), staged a suicide on those same Rome hotel steps, not damaging herself seriously but almost frightening the life out of her elderly uncle. In fact, Leopold was in frail health at the time of his visit to Rome and he died of pneumonia. The widow, Adelaide, who in effect had been separated from Leopold for years and spent most of her time in Paris, sent a sad, heartbroken letter to young George: '...I am alone, *so alone*, parted from the being I loved most in the world and will love always. We had our differences earlier but we knew when the bitterness was past ... and that our love had withstood all the past storms which came from want of understanding of my youth and its necessities and his inability to show me that I was his dearest. I am so unhappy. I do not know how it happened, I only knew that he was so ill when they told me "while there is life there is hope" and that he would not know me if I came and that if he did know me it would frighten him as he knew I never travel... What an awful shock, for I saw him on his passing through Paris looking splendid and he was going to spend some days with me on his return... He passed here on his return journey. I met him at the station and as his train came in at 7.15 and stayed with him alone until he left at 8.30 – those moments the saddest of my life...'

Sir George Werner Albu was now in unhampered control of General Mining and Finance Corporation – if he wished to be. He had Stowe McLean, generally acknowledged as South Africa's top mining man, to run the show. The main business was the negotiation of an alliance with the remnants of the 'Corner House' group, Central Mining and Rand Mines. The two groups had been moving closer following the liaison achieved by the sale of Cinderella and New Steyn to ERPM and Durban Roodepoort, and in 1938 the link was signalled by an exchange of directorships. Central Mining may have been thinking of an attempt to absorb General Mining, but the war came first.

Sir George volunteered immediately war broke out and was to be one of the most senior figures in the mining industry to see active service (his friend Harry Oppenheimer was another). He went off to North Africa, as a Major in the Imperial Light Horse, with his black manservant and his pet monkey. In 1941 he was invalided home (still with servant, Thomas, and monkey, Topsy) suffering from cerebral malaria: his health never entirely recovered over the next 20 years.

Back in the Union Corporation headquarters in London, Sir Henry Strakosch had also been preoccupied with the approaching World War. He was excellently placed to follow and understand the gravity of the developments on Continental Europe – he travelled there frequently, some of his closest family still lived there, he had contacts at the highest level thanks to his years of financial statesmanship and his continued League of Nations committee work, and he also had the Intelligence Department of the Union Corporation at his command in London. Thus, Winston Churchill, in his *The Second World War*, recalls how he asked 'his friend Sir Henry Strakosch' to direct the brains of Union Corporation to analyse the 1936 German budget to work out how much Hitler was spending on re-armament: the answer, from Strakosch's bright young men, was £1 billion – and Churchill used that, and other information, in the House of Commons.

Churchill's biographer, Martin Gilbert, records that Strakosch produced figures showing that Germany was spending an average £800 million a year on raw material imports, a figure which Churchill challenged Prime Minister Chamberlain to contradict and received no answer. ('It is really very good of you to send me such a lucid, weighty paper... I think we have done a public service...' wrote Churchill to Strakosch, who continued to play this role in 1938 and 1939.) In the same period Strakosch had been centrally involved in the rescue of Churchill when he faced personal financial disaster. (Strakosch was by now a very wealthy man, witnessed by the fact that he personally underwrote 10 per cent of the 1937 rights issue.) Churchill's financial crisis in 1938 was very serious: he was threatened with having to leave public life and sell his house, Chartwell. Strakosch at once agreed to help. He wrote to Churchill on 28 March 1938: 'My dear Winston, I have today paid Vickers da Costa and Co £18,161/1/10 being the amount due by you to them... As agreed between us, I shall carry this position for three years, you giving me full discretion to sell or vary the holdings at any time, but on the understanding that you incur no further liability...' So it may be said that Strakosch was responsible for Churchill's survival as politician and statesman.

Sir Henry's domination of Union Corporation in these years was near complete. His trusted right-hand in London for many years, Joseph Kitchin, died in 1932 leaving a gap – a direct link with the increasingly remote Sir Henry – that could not be filled. Sir Henry did not visit South Africa between 1921 and 1939, but this did not mean that PM Anderson in Johannesburg had a free hand. On the contrary: it took years before Anderson – who had belatedly joined the Board, which met in London, in 1927 but was otherwise only rarely consulted on non-South African matters – was able to assert his own strong character. The inevitable gulf between the London and Johannesburg operations was to be an unfortunate legacy for the future. The directors seem to have had little influence on Sir Henry: they included distinguished grandees like Lord Buxton, Sir Reginald Mant and Sir Richard Horne (another of Churchill's circle). A more important recruit to the Board, in Sir Henry's final years, was one of Churchill's most fascinating and mysterious protégés, Brendan Bracken, who was to play an important part in the post-war story. At about the same time another substantial figure, Chester Beatty of Selection Trust, whom Sir Henry greatly admired, became a director. Younger City blood was belatedly introduced in 1939 in the shape of Charles Hambro.

The fact is that it was only in the last years that Sir Henry seemed to admit that his own powers might be failing. In this weary and depressing period he was concerning himself with the 'rescue' and re-establishment in Britain of European Jews (this raises again the question of Sir Henry's possibly Jewish blood). Just before the Anschluss, Sir Henry brought out his mother and sister from Austria, and the Gresham Street office of Union Corporation was to be employed in the task of facilitating and even accommodating refugees. (There is a famous Corporation story of an early-to-work female employee bumping into the pyjamaed – and famously libidinous – Tommy Balogh, the distinguished Hungarian economist, in the corridor.)

Sir Henry's final visit to South Africa in early 1939, as with so much of his international travel over 20 years, was not entirely dedicated to corporate affairs. He was ill for much of the trip and he was sounding out, for his London friends, whether South Africa would join the Allies in the approaching war with Germany. The British government was worried that the South African Prime Minister General Hertzog's preference for neutrality would deny Britain South Africa's gold, and also the important South Atlantic naval bases. Sir Henry's contribution is not clear, but in the event, on 4 September, the South African Parliament voted to declare war on Germany and General Smuts became Prime Minister.

Here, as in General Mining, a generation was handing over. Paul Strakosch, Sir Henry's brother and a Johannesburg manager, died in 1941, followed by his Johannesburg colleague Vernon Ronketti in 1943. Senior executives like PM Anderson, TP Stratten and HR Hill were diverted on government missions. The mines, cut off from their European supplies of machinery and parts, were in constant difficulty even as their production was declared vital for the war effort and most of their engineers were forbidden to enlist. They had the additional burden of being required to dedicate their workshops to producing military hardware, and, of course, despite the ban the mines supplied a large contingent to the armed forces, not all of whom would come home. (In lighter vein, the irrepressible Stowe McLean spent his spare time raising war funds by running a mobile roulette game among the affluent of Johannesburg's northern suburbs. It was entirely against the law but the authorities turned a blind eye and McLean raised a small fortune for the war effort.)

In London, Charles Hambro was sent off to Washington on government business, Joseph Temperley died in 1941, and Sir Henry Strakosch promptly married his widow. In September 1942 Sir Henry fell ill and cancer was diagnosed. He and his wife spent the next eight months in the south of the United States, returned to England in June 1943, and he died at his Walton-on-the-Hill home on 30 October. In an elegant obituary tribute in *The Times*, Brendan Bracken wrote, 'Henry Strakosch was a man of great business. His indefatigable industry, the clearness of his reason, and a generous fermenting in blood enabled him to do the work of many men... A good nature, we are told, pities the miserable, rescues the oppressed, and makes everyone's condition as tolerable as he can. So strove Henry Strakosch...'

Sir Henry left an estate valued at £2,5 million: after various unforeseen legal complications a part of this went to a Memorial Trust to fund contacts between British and South African graduates and which continues today: it was a reminder of the warmer, more charitable aspect of a man of somewhat forbidding privacy.

The succession had not been settled and it appears scarcely to have been discussed. It is possible – we cannot be sure – that Sir Henry had wanted Chester Beatty to succeed him, but PM Anderson and Cyrus Pott (who were joint Managing Directors) blocked this. Anderson and Pott also discussed the wisdom of a full merger with Central Mining, which in 1938 had developed its alliance with General Mining. Anderson managed to get to London and the future structure was agreed: Pott would retire (in 1945), Anderson would continue as sole Managing Director in Johannesburg, a new generation of managers was appointed, and the Board was re-manned. But the chairmanship and the Board – that is to say, Union Corporation and its image – would remain in London. In the area that mattered much more – on the ground, and under the ground – Anderson was in charge, and he would remain there until he died, in November 1954.

Two episodes catch the eye before the shutters of world war came down and General Smuts led South Africa by only a narrow parliamentary majority into the conflict on the side of the Allies. The first has its funny side. The Defence Force was understandably concerned that there might be German sympathisers placed in strategic positions on the mines, which had been such an important Allied interest in the First War. On 12 and 16 May 1939, Sir George received letters from a Colonel Thwaite, Deputy Director of Intelligence in the Union Defence Force, reprimanding him for having omitted to mark his correspondence 'Confidential' and instructing him, if he could provide any information about subversive elements, 'to write same on plain paper, without any address, merely giving the date and sign yourself '23'...'

Second Generation

Sir George, thereupon appointed as a Captain on the Reserve List, presumably being happy to help, replied with the sensible suggestion that 'aliens employed in the Mining Industry will not be directly concerned with sabotage, but will employ for this purpose the poorer elements among the employees, who are Union Nationals and who would be ready to commit acts of sabotage in return for small pecuniary remuneration. I am at present attempting to ascertain the mines on which this class of individual is working but have so far been unable to collect sufficient information...' Colonel Thwaite continued this rather surreal correspondence – which discussed such matters as the possible undermining of the Mineworker's Union, not to speak of the allegation that the students of Pretoria University were hiding revolvers in their lockers – until conventional soldiering intervened.

A second, sadder and more serious pre-war incident concerned a substantial oil company controlled by General Mining in Romania, Phoenix Oil and Transport Company, formed in 1920 with a refinery in Constanza, installations at Ploesti and a one million ton production. Leopold Albu had been particularly keen on its potential and had been Chairman since 1932. In 1938 there was a flurry of correspondence: a Mr RA Thomson, who probably had British Intelligence connections, wrote from Zagreb after the Anschluss, when Hitler's armies took over Austria, to tell the London managers of the new situation. The director, Mr Drucker, had been required to leave by the new 'Government Trustee'.

Mr Thomson wrote: 'As Mr Drucker possessed a high personal reputation amongst the whole of his staff he continued to be respected by all grades so that he was enabled to liquidate his position at the Office – as prescribed by the G.T.'s ultimatum – with as much dignity as the, for him unfortunate, circumstances allowed. There are numerous cases where gentlemen holding similar managerial positions have fared far worse as, for example, the General Manager of the Austrian Benzine Cartel who has, from the beginning, been in preventive arrest for reasons not yet published... Taking things altogether, I think the Vienna organisation has been able to establish its "Aryan" status in a comparatively comfortable manner, much as the personal sacrifices are to be deeply regretted...' He added that he was less optimistic about the situation of Phoenix's solicitor, Dr Herlinger, who could no longer expect to do well in court cases involving 'Aryan defendants'.

These people were of course Jews, presumably German in origin. The Albus – Jews from 1880s Germany, made good (and rich) in South Africa – accepted Mr Thomson's analysis. No doubt there was nothing they could do. After the war, in which the Phoenix installations were bombed by the Americans and then seized by the Russians who claimed the remaining output as war reparations, General Mining was happy to sell out.

CHAPTER EIGHT

BEYOND GOLD

Sir Henry Strakosch had brought Brendan Bracken onto the Union Corporation Board in 1940 as part of his policy of giving non-executive directorships to a small number of distinguished Englishmen in public affairs. The connection was rather closer than that sounds, because Strakosch and Bracken had been friends for some years: it was Bracken who had introduced the Austrian businessman to the circle of Winston Churchill, at a time when the statesman was in political exile. For instance, in January 1937 Bracken wrote to Churchill in the South of France suggesting he look up Sir Henry – 'a lonely old bird'. As we have seen, Churchill in Opposition benefited from the research assistance of Union Corporation's London office, and had also profited from Strakosch's private financial advice. (Moreover, in his Will, Sir Henry left Churchill £20 000 as well as Bracken £2 500, General Smuts £10 000 and Union Corporation staff £20 000.)

Brendan Bracken was one of the most remarkable characters of the age. He was eccentric, mysterious, mischievous, and not at all a conventional member of the British Establishment which supplied most of Sir Henry's non-executive directors. His principal interests were politics and journalism rather than business: most of all, he worshipped Churchill and devoted the earlier part of his short life to serving him. He made a great secret of his background. Biographers have since discovered that he was born in Ireland in 1901 and left his family when he was 15 to go to Australia. He never ever admitted to this Irish upbringing. When he returned to Britain he bought himself a brief public school education and then set himself to infiltrating British society, soon hitching his wagon to Churchill's star: his relationship with Churchill became so close that the absurd rumour grew that he was Churchill's natural son. He became an MP in 1929, joined Churchill in Downing Street in May 1940 as one of the inner and informal kitchen Cabinet that was said to run the war, and in 1941 he was made Minister of Information.

Above: General Mining and Finance Corporation's first headquarters in Johannesburg, the Grusonwerk Building, which would be substantially renovated in 1903. *Left:* The renovated General Mining and Finance Corporation headquarters shortly before demolition in 1951 to make way for a new corporate home. The complex of buildings would be re-fashioned yet again in 1995.

STRIKE JAN 1914.

Top: General Mining's West Rand Consolidated gold mine, seen here with a temporary headgear in 1907, was to play a major role in the fortunes of the group throughout the century.

Bottom: A 'human engine' gets to work during the 1914 miners' strike, which repeated the issues of the 1913 strike – the respective roles of white and black labour on the gold mines.

Top: The arrival of a detachment of Chinese labour on the mines in 1909. Their importation was to cease in 1910.

Bottom: The sinking of the *Lusitania* by a German U-boat in 1915 provoked a fury of anti-German rioting in South Africa, in which the General Mining and Goerz offices were both attacked. This picture shows a Johannesburg episode.

Opposite page
Top: Early days of construction work on Union Corporation's Modder Deep mine in the 1920s.
Bottom: Johannesburg in the 1930s had become a sophisticated city. This is the view looking north up Hollard Street from the General Mining building in 1936.
Above: Sir George Albu and members of his family out riding in Johannesburg's Saxonwold: (left to right) Kitty, Alice, George, Georna, Walter.
Left: An ageing Sir George (left) with his wife, Ginny (right) and his daughter-in-law Betty.

Opposite page
George Werner Albu took over the reins at General Mining at the age of 30 after Sir George's death in 1935. He never enjoyed the role of businessman. *Left:* Sir George Werner Albu with his daughters at Northwards, which was to be their home for many years.

Above: George Albu's eldest son, Walter, who died as a result of injuries sustained during the First World War.

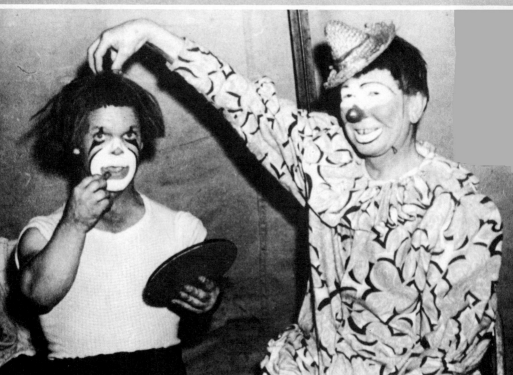

Top: Sir George Werner Albu's wife, Betty, with some of their children in their goat carriage at Northwards. The Albus had a passion for animals.

Bottom: Sir George Albu clowning with the famous Boswell Wilkie circus clown, Tickie (left).

Top: An aerial view of Vaalbosch, the Albus' bush farm and hunting lodge near Warmbaths.

Bottom left: George and Betty Albu enjoyed hunting, and Betty was a crack shot – here she shows off one of her prizes.

Bottom right: The Randlords at play: George and Betty Albu, with their eldest daughter, Georna (below), on a skiing holiday at Kitzbühel, Austria.

Top:
(left to right):
Stowe McLean, the Canadian-born mining engineer who rescued and gave vigorous life to West Rand Consolidated. He went on to become Chairman of General Mining in 1963 and President of the Chamber of Mines.

P M Anderson, who effectively ran Union Corporation from 1921 until his death in 1954, was the dominant figure of his generation in the South African gold mining industry.

Brendan Bracken, protégé of Winston Churchill, was one of the most extraordinarily eccentric and talented members of the British Establishment. He was Chairman of Union Corporation after the war.

Tommy Stratten, the right-hand man and successor of PM Anderson in 1954, was perhaps the most respected of all of Union Corporation's leaders.

Bottom far left: The first gold pour at St Helena in 1951. This was the pioneering achievement of Union Corporation in the Free State.

Left: Jack Scott, whose Strathmore group joined forces with General Mining in 1954, examines the first gold bar produced at Stilfontein. Scott was Deputy Chairman for years and then went off to pursue his obsession with diamonds.

Top: Tommy Stratten with Lord Bracken and Hugh Munro (right), taking some refreshment on site as they inspect progress at Evander.

Bottom: Again on site: Tommy Stratten and Jeff Goode discuss plans for the new Kinross mine with the visiting director Charles Hambro (centre).

Top: South Africa's first uranium plant was opened by Prime Minister D F Malan (right) at General Mining's West Rand Consolidated in 1952. Sir George Werner Albu was the host (left).

Bottom: William Bedford Coetzer, Managing Director and Chairman of Federale Volksbeleggings from 1956, realised his vision of an Afrikaner mining house in Federale Mynbou. He was to succeed Stowe McLean as Chairman of General Mining.

Above:
(left to right)
Naas Steenkamp,
George Clark,
Graham Boustred
of Anglo
American and
Donald Gordon of
Liberty Life at the
Matla opening.
Centre:
Wim de Villiers
(right) with
colleagues Tom de
Beer (left) and
Johan Fritz at a
General Mining
cocktail party
after the General
Mining take-over
of Union
Corporation.
Right:
Wim de Villiers,
who succeeded
Tom Muller as
Executive
Chairman of
General Mining,
was to re-fashion
his group but
would be brought
down by a
catastrophic
'Broedertwis'
clash in 1981–2.

Top: The 'Committee of Five' of the early 1980s at Gencor: (left to right) Hugh Smith, Ted Pavitt (Non-Executive Chairman), Tom de Beer, Johan Fritz, George Clark, Basil Landau.

Bottom: Derek Keys, Executive Chairman of Gencor (right), leads his colleagues at the memorial service for victims of the Kinross disaster, which claimed 177 lives in September 1986.

Derek Keys (left) and Brian Gilbertson, Executive Chairman of Gencor, celebrate Keys's return to Gencor in a new role as Chairman of Billiton in October 1994 after his term as Minister of Finance.

He therefore had to resign from the Union Corporation Board. With the rejection of Churchill by the electorate in 1945, and his own parliamentary defeat, Bracken was available to return to Union Corporation as Sir Henry would certainly have intended.

No one ever claimed that Bracken knew anything in particular about the mining industry. His business gifts lay in journalism: in a dramatically successful youthful role with Eyre and Spottiswood, he had created *The Banker* and acquired first the *Financial News* and then the *Investors Chronicle*. His friendship with Strakosch began when they found themselves bidding against each other for *The Economist* in 1928. The editor of that distinguished journal suggested that Bracken's backers and the syndicate led by Sir Henry should take 50 per cent each – a solution which has survived in approximately that form, and worked well, to this day. In 1945 Bracken was to achieve his biggest coup when he took over the *Financial Times* and merged it with the *Financial News* under the former title.

Union Corporation had been without a Chairman since Sir Henry's death in October 1943. When Cyrus Pott retired in 1945, Anderson was left as sole Managing Director – but the chairmanship would stay in London. Lord Harlech was brought onto the Board as the traditional Establishment non-executive director. A month after the arrival of a Labour government in July 1945, Brendan Bracken was invited by the Union Corporation directors to take the chairmanship. Anderson, who does not seem to have been consulted, was appointed Deputy Chairman. In fact, Anderson was to be the dominant figure in Union Corporation until he died in 1954.

Bracken, whose passion for politics began to fade after the electoral rejection of his beloved hero, had more than enough on his plate, since before the end of the year he was back in Parliament (and active in Opposition) and much taken with his chairmanship of the *Financial Times* (to which he was also a regular contributor). He was never to be a rich man like Sir Henry; indeed, he had to borrow from his great friend, the newspaper tycoon Lord Beaverbrook, to meet the qualification which, since the days of A Goerz and Co, required directors to hold at least a thousand shares. 'Lord B has bought eight hundred UC shares which he has instructed me to have registered in your name ... you will appreciate, of course, that these shares are merely on loan to you,' wrote a company official. Bracken repaid them before the end of the year: his Chairman's remuneration, according to his biographer, was in five figures – a substantial sum in those days.

He was not really an Executive Chairman, although he used the Gresham Street office of Union Corporation as his base rather than the *Financial Times*. His most valuable role was probably his unmatched access to well-placed contacts in politics as well as in finance. His principled insistence on the independence of good journalism meant that he managed to escape any conflict of interest between his two chairmanships: only once did he have to sue for libel – a magazine said he caused the *Financial Times* to puff St Helena shares and then sold his own; he was awarded damages which he chose not to enforce.

This is not to suggest that he did not take his role in the Corporation seriously. In particular, and in contrast with Sir Henry's record, he made a point of visiting South Africa at least once a year while his health permitted. These visits became a famous trial for his hosts, because they seem to have brought out his mischievous, inconsiderate and bullying side. For many years afterwards he was remembered by local Union Corporation managers for his informality, for his passionate interest in ordinary people and his memory of them, and, it must be said, for his taste for gin. His letters from Johannesburg to his friends in London start off with a touch of amused condescension, but as he got to know the country better his interest and involvement grew.

'My Dear Max,' he wrote to Beaverbrook from Johannesburg's Carlton Hotel on 31 August 1947, 'This country is roaringly prosperous. It abounds in exotic and small producing industries. They will suffer greatly when a slump comes. The owners, most of whom crossed the Red Sea with dry feet, have taken the precaution of placing blocks of their shares with the trusting British investors. I grieve for them. Johannesburg is acclaimed or condemned for its vivid way of life. It is, in fact, less lively than Dundee. There is no night life. Nor is there a good restaurant in this large City. Most of the population lives in its expensive suburbs where they, I am told, give large and very genteel dinner parties...'

In 1948 he presided over the Annual General Meeting and wrote home – 'My views are not fashionable in Johannesburg. I gave them at some length to the shareholders. I also expressed some doubts about the miraculous Orange Free State...' (That must be one of the most wrong-headed remarks of all time from the head of a mining house).

In January 1949 he wrote to Beaverbrook, 'I derived great amusement from the town we are establishing in the middle of the bush in the OFS. When I saw it last it consisted of three houses. It has now 22 streets of well-built houses and a school building that the University of New Brunswick might envy. It is a strange experience to have lived in a town that is only a year and a half old ... I greatly enjoyed myself.' Bracken was also learning about the political climate and getting it right: 'South Africa is in a rare mess. Smuts has little or no hope of ever returning to power...'

His handling of AGMs was neither conventional nor boring. To Anderson's horror he told one questioner – on the eve of Chamber of Mines pay negotiations – that all the miners, white and black, were grossly underpaid. To another shareholder asking in 1955 for more detail about the important but secret developments on the Far East Rand, Bracken replied, 'Why should I give you free information for which our rivals would pay me thousands?' One of the mines on this development near Bethal was later to be called Bracken, so his name is commemorated in South Africa today more dramatically than it is in Britain.

PM Anderson over the years had become the leading figure in the industry. He occupied a host of public positions in Johannesburg and – as Ted Pavitt would afterwards recall – many of his staff (not to speak of his sons) were 'petrified' by him: he was a rigorous, demanding man, much respected. He and Bracken were very different characters and never really got on. Anderson was increasingly disposed to go his own way without caring too much for the London Board. He had completed 43 years with Union Corporation when he died in November 1954.

There was no doubting his successor. Tommy Stratten, his right-hand man since the war, was looked up to and admired by all his colleagues. An electrical engineer, born in 1904, a Rhodes scholar at Oxford and a natural leader, he had been seconded to government for the duration of the war in the important job of Director of War Supplies (Technical). When he returned to Union Corporation and the long wait for the succession which would evidently be his, he acted as a useful foil to Anderson's more abrasive personality: he was Deputy Managing Director from 1950. One of Peter Anderson's sons, Colin, had also joined the Board, not without provoking murmurs about nepotism. More important was the appointment as Consulting Engineer of Hugh Monro, whose career had been slow to take off from the difficult days of the Depression but whose brilliance was never in doubt.

Bracken's health was failing, though he was only in his mid-fifties. He and Tommy Stratten, who was immediately made Managing Director on Anderson's death, succeeded in working together, though – as with Anderson – the geographical distance between them must have helped. Stratten said of his Chairman that 'his chief value to the Corporation was the warmth and enthusiasm he engendered with most people, high and low'. Bracken wrote, in May 1955, 'Stratten is doing a splendid job here. In a quiet but very effective way he has reorganised this Head Office... Of equal importance is the happy, zealous spirit which pervades this office.'

But the need to travel to Africa, even if less frequently than in the late 1940s, was getting too much for Bracken, who was being treated for a cancer of the throat. By 1957 he seems to have been thinking of stepping down and going back to his first love, newspapers; he wrote to one friend that he was longing to say 'Farewell Africa: Africa farewell'. Knowing he was mortally sick, he planned a final visit to the AGM in May 1958, but the doctors forbade it and he died on 8 August. His own paper, the *Financial Times*, wrote in its obituary: 'Vigour was an outstanding characteristic, instantly striking at the first moment of meeting him. His large, robust frame was surrounded by a mass of red hair, silvering in his later years, but always vivid. He spoke and gestured incisively. Great powers of aggression were at the service of a rapid, leaping mind...' Many people who encountered him, in the world of politics or of business, found him impossible, but no one could be indifferent to him. Several of the obituarists described him, with affection, as a 'buccaneer'.

Sir Charles Hambro agreed with Stratten to take over temporarily, but, as Stratten understood, and would enforce, it was time for the Chair, and Union Corporation, to move to Johannesburg.

Sir George Werner Albu had returned from the war to take up his inheritance as one of the inner group of second-generation Randlords. Sir George, like his father before him, was a family man. He and his wife Betty had four daughters and one son, the youngest, inevitably named George, in 1944. Northwards continued in the role of family home – spacious but not overwhelmingly grand, with gardens and stables galore – to which it had been moulded by the elder Sir George in the years after 1912 when he had bought the burned-out shell from the frivolous and fun-loving Dale Laces. There was also a farm, Rietvallei, on the northern outskirts of Johannesburg, and a bush farm and hunting lodge, loved by the family and called Vaalbosch, near Warmbad. The Grosvenor Place house in London had been sold.

The worm in the apple was that Sir George had not inherited his father's relish for the business world: in a word, he was uncomfortable with what Leopold had called 'the mantle of the Albus'. This is a classic story. George, the baby of the family, had not been expected to be the heir. His brother Walter, 13 years the elder, would have inherited if it were not for the World War and his early death in 1920. Thereafter, George was trapped. Through the next 20 years, as General Mining prospered briefly and then faltered until its fate was all too evidently at the disposal of Harry Oppenheimer, Sir George can be glimpsed undertaking his role with increasing reluctance and, it must be surmised, unhappiness (he would one day confirm this to his own son). His health was poor, a legacy of the war, though the diagnosis was not always clear. He suffered from filariasis (a rather obscure tropical illness affecting the lymph glands and related to elephantiasis) and from depression. His wife died prematurely in 1956. He drank heavily. In the end, on

18 February 1963, he was to shoot himself when terminally ill.

But this classic tragedy is only a one-sided view of life in Northwards. For the children, although some of them were frightened of their moody father, there are happy memories of carefree years of parties and ponies, of excursions and excitement, and of the extraordinary generosity of their parents. Sir George was in fact notorious throughout Johannesburg for his generosity. (One explanation of the mystery of what happened to the Albu fortune is that Sir George gave it away! There is another persistent rumour that George and Leopold lost a lot of money before the war in German bonds.) Perhaps he and his wife were typical of the second generation: they impressed on their children that to talk about money was bad form. If friends, or mere acquaintances, requested a loan, it was given, and never asked for again. And of course, life in Northwards was extremely expensive in these post-war years, with many servants (mostly black after the war), 42 gardeners, a dozen horses, foreign travel, new cars, balls, parties, musical recitals, constant entertainment.

Sir George had his eccentricities. A love of animals does not necessarily qualify, but Northwards had far more than an average South African household, with a lion cub, lots of monkeys, buck, owls, dogs, cats, horses, white mice. At one point Sir George was on the point of acquiring a giraffe for the gardens.

Undeniably eccentric was Sir George's interest in the paranormal. For a period of years Northwards was to be attended every Tuesday evening by a Mr Leonard Barrett, a spirit medium. The children and house guests would be ushered into a small sitting room, every light in the house would be turned off, and Mr Barrett would call on the guidance of the spirits, usually that of Sir George Albu senior, to whom he would address lists of questions often relating to the business decisions to be made by General Mining – 'Father, what shall I do about the Interim Dividend?', that sort of thing. Mr Barrett relayed answers. (This style of management, if generally known, would scarcely have helped the share price. There is a famous story of Sir Ernest Oppenheimer requiring a decision of George and, upon being told he must go home to consult his father – who was of course long dead – replied, 'If I were you, George, I'd contact your uncle – he was the better businessman'.) The young son and present baronet, George, has a vivid memory of a seance when he can have been only five or six years old, at which his grandfather was summoned, 'an apparition, exactly like his portrait', and *actually approached* the child in the front row to introduce himself in a benevolent manner to 'little George', the grandson whom, in this world, he had never met. One of the daughters remembers being reunited with a deceased favourite puppy who licked her leg under the table. After a violent encounter with a poltergeist, George Werner Albu gave up spiritualism in the 1950s but resumed after his wife's death. He told his daughter Julia he would try to make contact with her after he died. She has heard nothing.

The high life in Johannesburg's northern suburbs did not ignore the political dramas that were overtaking South Africa. With the death of old Sir George, the Albus had become conspicuously 'English', though they could all speak German. The new head of the family was strongly opposed to the incoming National Party, was a Municipal Councillor and himself sought nomination for a parliamentary seat on behalf of the United Party in 1948. Though defeated, he continued to back the United Party. The son of a German immigrant, he was nevertheless fiercely anti-German: he would not have a Mercedes or any such import, and he was also, of course, anti-Afrikaner. For some mysterious reason he was Denmark's honorary consul. A more lively interest was the Transvaal Association of Boys Clubs, which he founded (it was in some ways a counterpart to the Oppenheimers' Boys Town); he built a club house for the boys on the Transvaal farm.

By this time, the family had left behind its Jewish faith and affiliations (again there are parallels here with the Oppenheimer family), perhaps in part under the influence of Sir George's eldest sister, Charlotte, who had married the Bishop of Pretoria. Charlotte and her husband, the Rt Revd Wilfrid Parker, were to be conspicuous in the anti-apartheid movement. (The best man at the wedding was Father Trevor Huddleston.) Her sister Kitty, who was severely injured in a riding accident, was the wife of Erroll Hay, the General Mining director who had broken with Leopold and with his brother-in-law George in 1936; they lived, in style, in Inanda and outside Durban. Erroll was a dapper and fastidious man, a dandy, famous in the family for insisting that the beach in front of his house be raked every morning and furnished with ash-trays. He died of pneumoconiosis which he must have contracted in his days underground as a young mining engineer. The next daughter, Alice, had moved to England where she settled in high society and never revisited South Africa, and the youngest daughter, Irene (Bobby) had died very young in childbirth. The next generation was to be solidly Anglican, unmistakably 'English' South Africans.

The head of the family had been the formidable widow of the first Sir George – Ginny. She lived out her life, much loved by her grandchildren, in a Parktown house adjoining The Wilds, on the perimeter of the present Johannesburg Hospital in Ubla Lane: 'Ubla' was the original telegraphic address of General Mining. After she died in 1950 the Albus, faced with the construction of the motorway to Pretoria which would run across their garden, left Northwards, and moved to a sequence of houses before they settled, in Sir George's last years of sickness, on the Rietvallei farm north of

Johannesburg. After Betty's early death he had remarried – to Elsie Violet (known as Eve) Taylor, formerly governess to the Oppenheimer family. She had met a senior businessman from Mauritius at the Oppenheimers' table, married him, and then been widowed. George met her in Mauritius a couple of years after he had himself been widowed. The children tell a typical story of fighting with their stepmother, a strong-willed lady, but in later years they grew close to her. She died in 1993 in Parktown North.

With Sir George's death the Albus' personal involvement in the affairs of General Mining came to an end. The employment in London of their cousin Peter Railing (grandson of Jacob Freudenthal, brother-in-law of George and Leopold), ended at this same time in 1965. The title was passed to the next Sir George, who today lives outside Richmond, in Natal. None of this generation has any connection with Gencor.

Northwards was sold to the South African Broadcasting Corporation and then to the Transvaal Provincial Authority, which leased it to the Johannesburg College of Education, to be used first for student accommodation and then, from the mid-sixties, as headquarters of the Transvaal Schools Inspectorate. Inevitably these bureaucratic uses brought a rapid deterioration in the fabric. After a further period as the office of the South African Institute of Architects, it was transferred to the JCE Trust, which later leased the house to Gencor, which uses it for functions. In 1994 Gencor agreed to finance a major refurbishment programme to restore the house to its former condition and status, and Northwards was its old self in time for the centenary celebrations in late 1995.

Neither Union Corporation nor General Mining came out of the Second World War in a strong position: both of them would go through dramatic – and life-saving – developments in the gold mining sector. The gold price was to remain at $35 an ounce for more than 20 years. There was no need to market the stuff, it simply went to the Reserve Bank in Pretoria and then to the Bank of England, but costs were rising and this generation of managers was to be obsessed with inflation. Of course, it was a dollar, not a sterling price, so the exchange rate was the true fundamental. In 1939, for example, the gold price had been £7,5 an ounce; in 1945 it had risen only to £8,6, so costs were already squeezing. In 1949 the devaluation of sterling (and therefore of the South African pound) brought welcome relief, raising the $35-equivalent by nearly half to £12,4 and providing momentum for dramatic expansion in the 1950s. But inflation would always lie in ambush.

Union Corporation had started the 1930s with just two producing mines on the East Rand – Geduld and Modder Deep – with East Geduld coming into production in 1931. A potentially important developing mine farther east was Grootvlei, next door to East Geduld, where production started in 1938 and was to continue for many years. (Anglo American always had a significant holding in Grootvlei, though Union Corporation was the operating company.) Furthermore, in 1934 Union Corporation launched Marievale (also on the East Rand) and had it running in November 1939: again, it was to become an important and long-lived mine with a sentimental place in Gencor's history. The Group also rescued and revived Van Dyk, which had been closed down as long ago as 1911: production resumed in 1938. In other words, in the course of the 1930s Union Corporation added four mines to its two producers and was accounting for 10 per cent of the nation's industry tonnage.

But after 1945, while the East Rand was bound to remain far and away the most important source of company revenue, it was essential to focus on the exciting prospects in the Orange Free State, where prospecting had been suspended in 1941 after potentially dramatic borehole results at St Helena. This was to be a brand new, virgin gold field, as PM Anderson told the first General Meeting of St Helena in 1946: 'Water will probably have to be brought 50 miles from the Vaal River and the nearest electric power station is about 120 miles from the property, so that the supply of water and power become a serious undertaking. Fortunately, there are a number of potential mining areas in our immediate vicinity which will need similar services at an early date...'

Indeed, Union Corporation was no longer alone in the Free State. General Mining, for instance, had floated 'Geoffries' (General Exploration OFS Ltd) to look into the area. Union Corporation's pre-war exploration in the area had been in conjunction with Abe Bailey's Western Holdings, but after Sir Abe's death in 1940 Sir Ernest Oppenheimer took control of Western Holdings and the upshot was that Union Corporation started off the development of its 'own' St Helena with only 18 per cent of the shareholding. Nevertheless, the Group needed a rights issue (for £880 000) to coincide with the public flotation of St Helena Gold Mines, London's first gold mining flotation after the war – and the result was a fiasco because demand totally outstripped the shares on offer, to PM Anderson's distant fury.

The subsequent difficulties of opening St Helena have been described by Keith Wallis: 'The initial problem was that in that part of the Orange Free State there was nothing except wide open spaces of parched and dusty land. There was no power, no water, no hills, no trees, no roads, no houses and no workforce. To attract a workforce, St Helena needed houses, but for houses one needed roads and water – quite apart from building materials and fitments which were still in severe short supply following the War. Because of the drought and flatness of the countryside, the area was subject to ferocious dust storms. To help combat these, it was necessary to plant trees – but to plant trees one needs water...

'Everything came back to water and it was not long before water was being found in embarrassingly large quantities underground as progress was made with first the incline shaft and then the first vertical shaft. Ironically, however, the underground water turned out to be quite disgustingly salty and instead of being an asset became a considerable liability, not only because of the need to pump and to cement against waterbearing fissures, but also because of the problem of disposal of well over 15 million litres of water daily. With the flat terrain, water pumped to surface and allowed to run off followed storm water courses and had a habit of ending up far away where it always seemed to have a fatal attraction for the best and most valuable of the farmer's livestock.

'Extensive evaporating pans had therefore to be constructed hurriedly to deal with the unwanted water, while the mine still waited for its proper water supply to be piped in from the Vaal River (this eventually happened in 1950). One unexpected bonus which arose from the need to evaporate salty water was the way in which it attracted huge flocks of flamingos, which at least brought a splash of colour to an otherwise dreary landscape.

'In addition to the underground water (which occasionally got out of hand and necessitated keeping a boat underground to get access to the face of the incline) another serious and unpredicted hazard turned out to be methane gas which bubbled out of the water, causing a number of accidents and requiring the mine to be treated as if it were a coal mine, with an absolute ban on naked flames.'

The result of all this, coupled with a large and unexpected loss of land due to faulting, was another rights issue, in March 1952, to raise £1,7 million, which just about carried St Helena through to be the first Orange Free State mine to pour gold, in November 1951. Union Corporation managers were to reminisce for years about the opening-up of St Helena. Ted Pavitt, for instance, still tells of Hugh Monro stripping off all his clothes and wading up to his neck through the water. It would continue to be a difficult mine.

But Union Corporation had another major project in mind. The management realised that Modder Deep was slowly running down, and also that the re-opened Van Dyk – which had been given an extra and exceptionally deep shaft of 2 440 metres in 1950 – was probably going to be disappointing. One part of the response was to relish the success of Union Corporation's recent 10 per cent participation in the Tsumeb copper/lead/silver mine in South West Africa, in partnership with Newmont Mining and American Metal Company. Much more importantly, Union Corporation had been looking very secretly at what became known as the Far East Rand – the Reef extension east of the East Rand Basin, 80 kilometres east of Springs. This was one of the highlights of the history of Union Corporation, a company which had prided itself since its foundation by Adolf Goerz on its predominance in exploration and technology.

Hugh Monro, who was consulting engineer in the 1950s, always gave the credit to Alfred Frost, the chief geologist, who hailed originally from the north of England and had been crucial to the pre-war discoveries in the Orange Free State, and who was prepared to back his hunches by pestering even directors as forbidding as Anderson. Frost had been impressed by the new post-war magnetic prospecting techniques which had been pioneered by the geophysicist Oscar Weiss. An aircraft stripped of magnetic material was flown over large stretches of the Transvaal in search of the emergence of the Wits System – and produced anomalies to the East, near Kinross. After a certain hesitation (because Union Corporation was involved in a substantial exploration in Tanganyika at the time), and extensive drilling in the area, it was accepted that this was indeed the Kimberley Reef. For once, Union Corporation was out in the clear, ahead of the other mining houses, and Anderson and his team were able to seize mineral rights over a large part of what was at this stage called the Bethal area. Security was intense. Only in 1953 was the company prepared to admit 'some encouraging gold values...'

Here was a new gold field, perhaps Union Corporation's finest achievement. There would be four mines in due course, to be developed between 1954 and 1962. The Johannesburg managers had the pleasant task of deciding what to call their new mines. The obvious solution was 'Anderson', after the long-serving and titanic Managing Director who had just died in November 1954, still in harness at the age of 74, after serving the Group for more than 40 years. But there was a superstitious feeling that it would be unfair to the great man if the mine turned out to be a flop. The second proposal was to commemorate one of Adolf Goerz's colleagues with the title of 'Kuntz Gold Mines' – but after a moment's reflection it was agreed that this might be unfortunate in the vulgar world of the gold markets. The solution was Winkelhaak, the name of the local farm, and Winkelhaak thereby became one of South Africa's largest, most successful, and longest living gold mines. It was followed (in 1959) by Bracken (named after the late Chairman – who would have been amused), and by Leslie and Kinross, named after nearby communities, where production started in the early 1960s. PM Anderson was commemorated in due course by naming the new township – and the whole gold field – after his second wife Eve: Evander. (It is not clear whether the Group understood that Evander has a second meaning: it is a Greek mythological reference to the family of Bacchus – which might, of course, have been deliberate.)

To do all this, Union Corporation needed funds. A 1950 rights issue raised another £2,3 million, but Anderson and his successor, Tommy Stratten, continued to keep a tight grip on dividends. Stratten was also on the look-out for partners in the Far East Rand, though only Anglo American turned out to be seriously interested. Evander never suffered from the Orange Free State problems of extreme inaccessibility, but that did not mean it was as convenient as downtown Johannesburg – there was a problem with the black-turf soil, for example, and, as apartheid developed, the mining engineers found they were having to cope with bureaucratic interference with the racial zoning of townships and, for that matter, the actual mine shafts. Eventually the Group raised the necessary funds by direct fixed-term loans. Bracken and Leslie were simpler: they were pouring gold as early as 1962, and paying dividends in 1963. That meant it had taken just eight years to create a new gold field of three profitable mines out of the empty veld. Not bad?

So – to sum up – Union Corporation had come out of the war to develop the Orange Free State, and it also found the Far East Rand (Kinross would be added, eight years after Winkelhaak); it therefore had four new mines plus St Helena, though elsewhere its older properties were fading, or at least would do so if the gold price did not rise. But so long as the price was stuck at $35 it was impossible for the mining houses to develop new mines. Therefore they looked to other things – and ran into problems such as they had never imagined.

The story of General Mining over this same period is not so very different. Coming out of the war, General Mining had no Free State prospects under its belt – indeed, it was looking pretty puny. The long-term stalwart, Van Ryn, had closed at last, as had the Meyer some years before. The only serious property was West Rand Consolidated (in which the Group in fact had a minority holding), which had been rescued and given vigorous life by Stowe McLean.

General Mining, like Union Corporation, needed money, and in 1949 raised £2 million in a rights issue. (It is possible that this was the moment when the Albu family's stake in the Group began to be diluted in an irreparable way.) As a result, General Mining bought control of the so-called Ohlthaver group, which included Lydenburg Platinum, various industrial interests – a clue to the future – and also South Roodepoort Main Reef Areas Mine. But this was a sideshow, because the future of General Mining was about to be transformed, firstly by uranium, and secondly by Jack Scott in Strathmore.

The story of uranium will be told in a moment. In essence, West Rand Cons would become South Africa's first uranium producer, in 1952. Leaving aside the contribution of secret uranium purchases by America and

Britain to the General Mining finances, they also helped ensure a future for that mine longer than its gold output could have justified in the days of the $35 price. The deal with Jack Scott was even more important. It is hardly too much to say that without Scott, and Strathmore, General Mining would not have endured to become the parent of Gencor.

Back in 1887 Klerksdorp, about 100 kilometres west of the Central Rand reef, had flourished briefly when the idea caught on that it was the site of a second Johannesburg. Miners, geologists, financiers and con-men poured in: more than 150 companies were registered; there was even a local stock exchange for a year or two; and then the boom collapsed. But some people continued to believe that there was gold in the hills that surrounded the long-established village of Klerksdorp. One of them was George Denny, the Albus' famous mining engineer, who wrote a little book to argue the case; another was Dr Louis Nel of the State Geological Survey, whose researches eventually, many years later, led to Anglo American's major commitment to the area; but the most sympathetic – and in another way successful – enthusiast was a certain Charles Scott, who, in 1888, discovered and worked an outcropping reef on his farm 'Strathmore', on Klerksdorp's southern boundary. Serious faulting of the reef frustrated his search for the continuation of his find, but after his death in 1933 his son, Jack, dedicated himself to the same search.

Jack Scott was a powerful personality. Born in 1903, a qualified engineer, he had a distinguished war and was decorated in the field; he became a passionate pilot, married a well-known British actress (who would die in childbirth), and in 1947, resuming his odyssey, he found the Strathmore Reef (later to be called the Vaal Reef) at a little over 800 metres. The Stilfontein Gold Mining Company was registered in April 1949, the Charles and Margaret shafts (named after the twin children of his dead wife) began sinking in May of the same year, and the Stilfontein mine came into production in July 1952. Here was yet another new gold field.

Jack Scott needed financial muscle if he was to develop the field. He was able to start up his own, smaller operation at Ellaton but the more important prospect, Buffelsfontein, would be deeper and would be beyond his powers. Sir Ernest Oppenheimer had become conscious of the political delicacy of overdeveloping his visible dominance of the industry, and he was an old friend of the Albus. In summary, the upshot, in 1954, was that General Mining – with the benevolent brokerage of Sir Ernest and his son Harry – took over the Strathmore group, and Buffelsfontein would come into production in 1957.

This was a turning point in General Mining's history; it brought three new gold mines and added 50 per cent to the equity capital – as well as Jack Scott himself, as an additional Deputy Chairman to the main Board. Scott was one of the characters of the South African mining world, a secretive, charming man, capable of enlisting the loyalty of his colleagues just as he had as a colonel in the war. He married again, to a famous beauty, Toni Frost, and was to remain a vigorous and opinionated figure in General Mining councils: the least of his influence was seen in the helipad he insisted on installing on top of the new General Mining headquarters building in downtown Johannesburg in 1959, to the horror of his Union Corporation counterparts in the building opposite. He never got on with Harry Oppenheimer, an antipathy which eventually seems to have played an awkward role in the tensions that lay not so far ahead, when General Mining's very existence came under challenge and Harry Oppenheimer chose to use Anglo's major shareholding in a very deliberate way.

After this episode, Scott, although he remained a non-executive director of Genmin until the late 1970s, became increasingly preoccupied with diamonds, particularly in Basutoland and, eventually, in South West Africa. He devoted more and more of his energy to a personal search for the diamond mother-lode in the mountains of Basutoland. (To jump ahead for a moment, this passion for diamonds was to ruin Scott, because after he left General Mining in the mid-1960s he was parted from his money in a series of diamond ventures into which he had been led – the parallel with Sir George Albu is striking – by a susceptibility to the paranormal which he shared with his first wife. He stood guarantor for very substantial sums and in his old age was threatened with poverty, from which Gencor's Ted Pavitt rescued him by arranging for him to become, appropriately enough, President of Stilfontein. Gencor continued to watch over him in his old age. And in 1989 Derek Keys, as Chairman of Gencor, was visited by the octogenarian Jack Scott, who tried to convince him that there was still plenty of gold to be found at Klerksdorp and that Gencor should act at once.)

To return to the 1950s, it emerged that uranium was an important by-product of the Klerksdorp field. It had been an important revenue source for all the local mines since 1953 (the detailed figures were censored) but the significance of the district was revealed in 1961 when, with the cutback in uranium demand world-wide, it was announced that under the new contracts with Britain and America Klerksdorp would increase its contribution from 38 per cent to 46 per cent of South Africa's total production.

In the closing months of the Second World War, Stowe McLean, the Deputy Chairman of General Mining, who was currently serving as President of the Chamber of Mines, was summoned to Pretoria by the Prime Minister, Field-Marshall Smuts, to discuss a matter of vital importance to the country. Years later, when the blanket of secrecy could be lifted just a little, McLean recorded, 'I found that he wished to ascertain the magnitude of uranium deposits in the Witwatersrand ores, and how these deposits could be best developed.' The consequence, inspired by the Western powers' new awareness, as the Cold War beckoned, that the free world's uranium reserves must be harnessed to their nuclear weapons programme, or at least denied to their enemies, was to be the development, at scarcely credible speed, of a major new South African industry. McLean's own favourite mine, West Rand Consolidated, was to be in the vanguard when the Bird Reef series, which had been opened up by McLean himself in the early 1930s, turned out (despite the exaggerated effect of a portable geiger counter) to have higher than normal uranium levels.

The uranium for the first atomic bombs had been drawn from Canada and the then Belgian Congo, but new reserves were urgently required. Professor GW Bain of Amherst College, Massachusetts, had been working on the Manhattan Project, the code name for the development of the A-bomb, and remembered that he had some specimens of Witwatersrand ores in his private collection in his laboratory; it had been known for years that there was uranium oxide in some of the Wits Reefs. Shortly after McLean's meeting with Smuts, Dr Bain and his British counterpart, Dr CH Davidson, arrived in South Africa with a geiger counter to collect samples from various mines. They concluded that the Rand might be one of the largest low-grade uranium fields in the world. The operative adjective was 'low-grade'. In the US, a typical uranium deposit yielded 5 pounds to the ton; in South Africa, it was closer to 9 ounces. But the point was that the uranium could be extracted from the gold-mines' slimes *after* the ore had been milled and the gold removed. In other words, the mining effort – the investment, the labour – had already been directed to and justified by the gold: the uranium in the slimes was a waste-product, an extraordinary bonus.

Little wonder that Washington and London decided that the solution to the coming arms race might lie in South Africa, and that they wanted a 10-year agreement. It only remained to enlist the Chamber of Mines, under a cloak of the densest secrecy, and create a new extractive industry overnight.

Not quite overnight, but South Africa's first uranium plant was opened by the Prime Minster, Dr DF Malan, at General Mining's West Rand Consolidated in October 1952. By 1960, 26 gold mines had been authorised to produce uranium from 17 extraction plants and were producing 6 200 tons of uranium oxide. The construction programme had delivered a dramatic boost to the country's industrial economy, and the mines' revenue was estimated to be an additional £50 million a year. The financing of this project had to be swathed in secrecy. The Americans and the British provided loans for the development costs, and paid a 'price' which included an allowance for 'profit'.

One unforeseen result of the arrival of uranium was that some of the older, and faltering, gold mines received a new lease of life – JCI's Randfontein Estates, for instance, and West Rand Cons would also benefit dramatically. (West Rand Cons had almost lost out when the initial samples were disappointing: the geologists then turned back to the Bird Reef and took 34 000 samples to prove the mine's potential).

This might be seen as the first generation of the South African uranium industry. As the 1950s yielded to the 1960s, and the potential value of uranium as an energy source overtook its armaments application, the world-wide boom in uranium extraction, particularly in the US, Canada and Australia, and also elsewhere in Africa, created an over-supply. As a result, by 1965 production in South Africa had fallen to 2 500 tons from the 1959 peak of 6 000 tons. There was a recovery in the mid-1970s, with the world oil price crisis, after which South Africa was producing 14-18 per cent of the world total, but in the 1980s, as the nuclear power industry faltered, the industry declined quietly and steadily. By the early 1990s, only five plants were still operating in South Africa. The fact remains that West Rand Cons, which had ceased production of uranium oxide in 1981, had produced a total of 13 000 tons of uranium.

The Chamber of Mines continued to organise South Africa's uranium output as a collective venture, and set up a uranium sales organisation, the Nuclear Fuels Corporation (NUFCOR), when the commercial market emerged as distinct from strategic demand. In this second generation, the new customers were the commercial nuclear power stations around the world, and South Africa increased its treatment capacity by three times in the late 1970s, with a new emphasis on the working of the tailings at old gold mines and, in particular, a new entrant from Gencor, the Beisa Primary Producing Unit in the Orange Free State, operated by St Helena. Beisa was to become a problem, or rather, a disaster, for Gencor.

Jack Scott's Stilfontein gold mine in the Klerksdorp field on the Vaal Reef, and his smaller Ellaton, were important uranium producers for General Mining in the 1970s; the neighbouring Buffelsfontein, which was brought into production in 1957, was a significant uranium producer from the beginning, and was one of the half-dozen uranium-producing gold mines into the mid-1990s.

The combination of this enormous domestic resource and the steady heightening of international hostility to the apartheid state made it a very hot potato for the mining executives who became involved. Dolf Schumann, for instance, the Technical Director of General Mining after 1965, who served on NUFCOR for years, recalls the high secrecy of those days and remembers that he did not want to get involved in – or be privy to – such secrets as the extent of South African/Israeli collaboration on nuclear weapons technology. And it was less than surprising that, when it was officially announced in 1970 that South Africa had developed its own new process for enrichment of uranium, the world reaction tended to focus on the weapons potential of this alleged technological breakthrough, rather than its potential application to nuclear-power reactors.

It is not easy for a geologist to efficiently protect himself while traversing particularly in long grass country. An emergency usually develops very quickly and as the rifle will normally be carried by a porter, accidents can happen. In Tanganyika we found it desirable to recruit ex-game department gunmen to act as the protectors for each party. The gunmen should never be allowed to shoot except in the case of an emergency and should not be used as hunters to shoot meat for the camp. He should, however, be given five practice shots when first issued with a rifle.

Camps themselves need no protection against elephants. During the day they are unlikely to approach human habitation, and if they do, a slight noise should be sufficient to scare them away. At night they may approach very near to a camp, but although this may be very frightening I have never heard of or experienced trouble in a camp after dark. This is not always the case with buffalo and rhino, and of course lion can be most troublesome at night. When on safari in lion country, it should be remembered that if there are no reports of man-eaters in the area, the lion that one hears prowling around the tents can be considered fairly safe.

Elephant are not normally aggressive and the two chief reasons for a charge are, firstly, that the animal may be wounded or ill, and secondly he may be suddenly encountered at such close quarters that his method of protection is to charge rather than run away. In the case of field parties, if elephant have to be scared off the line of traverse this can usually be done by making a slight noise. But this should not be done at a distance of less than 200 yards. The reason for this being that everything possible should be done to avoid having to shoot. Firing a shot is not a good way of scaring elephant away, and in the case of a wounded animal will frequently produce a charge. If one gets into a tight spot with elephant while driving a car or Landrover, the animal should be scared away by revving the engine and never by hooting.

Giving elephant the wind is a fair way of moving them, but this again should not be done at a distance of less than 200 yards. It must be remembered that a traversing party is not a hunting party and should not be expected to behave like one. If elephant are encountered in thick country at close range, the party should keep close together and move away carefully and not run; it is better at close distance to face it out, rather than turn and run.

If reasonable precautions are taken, survey in elephant country cannot be considered dangerous, the animals are not nearly as aggressive as they look, and if left strictly alone are not likely to cause trouble. The following points should be noted:...

* *If it is necessary to shoot, shoot to kill.*
* *A charging elephant should be shot low in the face, as a general rule well below the eyes, but this depends on how high he is holding his head. The tendency is always to shoot too high.*
* *If after a frontal head shot the elephant does not drop, but turns sharply away as often happens, do not give him one for the road.*
* *A description of body shots should not be necessary for protection purposes as these are only taken as square on from the side. It may in exceptional circumstances be necessary to take a frontal body shot into the chest. This is a good shot but seldom possible.*
* *Always avoid shooting if possible.*
* *If you are in the possession of a rifle, never run out of a tight corner, but if your nerve does break and you run, keep going.*

Memorandum to the Consulting Engineer, 25 September 1958:
Protection of Field Parties.

CHAPTER NINE

THE AFRIKANERS

To go back to General Mining's acquisition of Strathmore, this was also the point at which a new player – indeed, a whole new team – was about to bid for promotion to a first division which for 75 years had exclusively featured the English-speaking members of the Chamber of Mines and of its canteen, the Rand Club in Johannesburg. It is easy to forget what a gulf existed in these post-war years between the 'English' businessmen and the Afrikaner politicians whose National Party government bestrode the country with an unchallengeable authority and a confidence that would never be matched. Dr Verwoerd succeeded Strijdom as Prime Minister in 1958; South Africa became a Republic and left the Commonwealth on 31 May 1961. Stowe McLean, deputising for the sick Sir George Albu at the June 1961 AGM of General Mining, protested that departure from the Commonwealth was a disaster and that the Group accepted with only dismay the break with the Crown, but the mining leaders, with their close links with London, could hardly have been surprised by the way South Africa's isolation was deepening: the wiser among them knew that they must bite the bullet and, for the sake of their shareholders, try to keep some contact with the white majority and with a government which had unprecedented influence over the allocation of contracts, leases and prices. They would have agreed that this situation was unhealthy. They might even have agreed that, if an Afrikaner mining sector did not exist, it would be necessary to invent one.

In fact, there was a lusty contender in waiting (to stay with the metaphor) on the touch line. It was young, and it had begun to win the respect of mining professionals, even though it had learned its skills not in gold but in the dirty and less glamorous side of the game – coal. It was called Federale Mynbou.

The story of Federale Mynbou, whose meteoric success was to be one of the most dramatic of the second half of the South African century, goes

124

back to the 1930s, when Afrikaner leaders realised that the search for political power in their own country must be accompanied by a similar effort to develop their economic base. Santam (and Sanlam) had been founded earlier, in 1918, out of a similar understanding, but historians all agree that the milestone events were, first, the founding of the Federasie van Afrikaanse Kultuurverenigings (FAK) in 1929, whose aim was to promote the Afrikaners' language and culture, and (arranged by the FAK) the first Ekonomiese Volkskongres in Bloemfontein in October 1939, whose aim was to prepare for the economic upliftment of the Afrikaner people, who at this time included 300 000 poor whites, victims of the Depression. This congress created the Reddingsdaadbond, whose function among other things would be to mobilise capital for Afrikaner business. Another direct result of the 1939 congress was Federale Volksbeleggings (FVB), which was to pool Afrikaner capital for the establishment (or takeover) of commercial and industrial concerns.

It has to be said – the point is too central to the story to be ignored, as it used to be by historians – that at the heart of all these organisations stood the Broederbond, the famous Afrikaner secret society whose aim, so successfully achieved over 60 years, was the uplifting of the Afrikaner nation. Again and again, the most senior leaders of the FVB and Federale Mynbou turn out to be Broeders – which was also true, of course, of Volkskas, Sanlam, Saambou, Rembrandt, not to speak of the state corporations like Eskom and Iscor whose co-operation and sympathy were (as the English could hardly be unaware) so helpful to the prospering of Federale Mynbou. The precise role of the Broederbond in promoting the interests of its businessmen members over the next generation is impossible to quantify: perhaps it should simply be noted that this was a network of friends, some of them by now in very high places, and the point of a network, as in many countries and societies, is to make things easier – more feasible – for your brother.

The founder of Federale Mynbou was, indeed, a Broeder – Wennie du Plessis, a diplomat by profession who quit the service when he clashed with General Smuts over his Broederbond membership. He later stood against Smuts in the 1948 election at Standerton and won a sensational victory over the elder statesman. (In due course Wennie du Plessis would be South Africa's ambassador in Washington.) He and his brother Jacques bought a small coal mine called Acme, near Witbank, in 1940, and formed Klipfontein Colliery Pty. They had cash-flow problems and approached FVB, which guaranteed a Volkskas loan and then in 1944 underwrote a share issue. They operated the mine by primitive methods, and it was small-scale stuff, but the brothers found a rather better mine in 1945 at Horingkrans: again, FVB saw it as appropriate to act as underwriter, and on this occasion another Afrikaner group, Bonuskor, which was an investment vehicle formed by and related to Sanlam, sub-underwrote 40 000 of the 100 000 shares. Neither FVB nor Bonuskor appears to have been particularly keen on these initial mining ventures.

At this point a much more important character entered the scene. William Bedford Coetzer had started his career in Barclays Bank in Aliwal North, but by the late 1940s he was the FVB man in Johannesburg, with particular responsibility for mining. He knew perfectly well that the Klipfontein deposits were too low grade to have potential, whereas deposits found at Koornfontein in 1948 were more promising. Coetzer also knew that it would be essential to be accepted by the Transvaal Coal Owners Association (TCOA) and thus get access to its quotas and marketing, if anything were to be built on so thin a foundation. At this point, probably fortunately, Wennie du Plessis went off to Parliament and Coetzer set out to persuade FVB to agree to his constant ambition – the creation of an Afrikaner mining house. The argument would take him until 1953, with the formation of Federale Mynbou Maatskappy Beperk.

To William Coetzer this always seemed an utterly logical development: the Afrikaners were in government, the large majority of the white miners were Afrikaners, and the Broederbond (of which he was of course a member) was committed to storming the heights of the national economy. To Coetzer, it was necessary to think big, and it was also inevitable (and desirable) that the fledgeling Afrikaner businessmen should co-operate with the English sector. As he put it sarcastically in one memorandum, it was wishful thinking to dream of an Afrikaner mining house built on demand for South African coal by Afrikaans-speakers only. But other influential Afrikaners (including Coetzer's colleague, Dr Andries Visser, Wennie du Plessis, and the parliamentarian Jan Steyn) were passionately opposed to co-operation with Anglo American, whether directly or through the TCOA. These three 'purists' even tried to take Koornfontein out of the Group, but they failed and resigned. In 1952 Koornfontein won a quota from the TCOA, after Koornfontein Mines Limited had been floated in 1951 with the support of FVB and Volkskas, and FVB, to its own surprise – since it had no founding mission to get involved in mining at all – found that it had a significant coal mining company.

Coetzer was now about to push through his vision of a proper Afrikaner mining house by putting together the mining interests of FVB, and Bonuskor, on a scale and with a financial backing which would make his plans possible. Public reaction in 1953 was by no means hostile: said the *Cape Argus*, 'it is right and to the good of South Africa that the Afrikaner should play his part in the expansion of our economy. In the competitive society of capitalism, all sections of our people should be entitled to opportunity...' Forty years later one can recognise certain similarities in the tone of voice with which the white business establishment admits the desirability – one day! – of a 'black mining house', just as the financial and technical detail of William Coetzer's manoeuvres in 1948-53 may have lessons for his counterparts today.

William Coetzer was one of the earlier Afrikaner chartered accountants. He came of a fairly humble background and married into a more substantial Afrikaner family. He developed a great ambition to be a first-division mining magnate. His enemies would later say that he was a social climber who aspired to rub shoulders with the heirs of the Randlords. In the latter part of his career, he lost the respect of many of his managers, who did not understand where his particular contribution lay any more and who increasingly suspected him of being principally concerned for his own interests. He enjoyed, for example, his ownership of an island in the Limpopo River and would entertain there lavishly on General Mining's account. But in these early years his vision of an Afrikaner role in the country's mining industry was important. He understood that his fledgeling company would need to be accepted by the established mining houses and for this it would be necessary to demonstrate technical, professional and management competence, and also to build up a necessary range of contacts – but of course, he had available to him certain 'contacts' in Pretoria and Cape Town which were not so warmly disposed to his English-speaking counterparts in downtown Johannesburg.

Federale Mynbou started its life in June 1953 with £1 million in authorised capital: FVB and Bonuskor would, after a period of adjustment, have an equal contribution of £400 000 each, and consideration would be given to asking Sanlam for the remaining £200 000. Coetzer was Managing Director, and Chairman from 1956. The staff was small. The most important hiring, in 1957, was to be a mining engineer, Tom Muller, as Technical and, shortly, General Manager. The Board contained various senior representatives of Afrikanerdom including (after Sanlam became a principal shareholder in 1955) Andreas Wassenaar. (The majority of the directors continued to come from Cape Town.) The Broeders were much in evidence, except that in those days only the insiders would have understood it. In 1958 it was finally agreed that Sanlam would become the third equal partner with FVB and Bonuskor, the authorised capital having previously been increased to £2 million; and in 1958 there was the first public issue and a listing on the Johannesburg Stock Exchange.

Throughout these years, which were accompanied by expansion and new projects, there was frequent pressure on available funds. In an irony which recalls the days of the 1890s, when Adolf Goerz was a close contact of the Deutsche Bank, in 1959 Coetzer had an extended and serious negotiation with Dr HJ Abs (of Deutsche Bank) about the possible establishment of an investment company which would attract German funds. The plan was frustrated – along with so many other projects linking South Africa with the outside world – by the worsening political situation.

With Tom Muller on board and a sympathetic government in power, Federale Mynbou was to prosper and expand. Even before Muller's arrival from Anglovaal in 1957, Federale Mynbou had spotted the importance of Jack Scott's Strathmore discoveries in the Klerksdorp field and had invested in Buffelsfontein; it also developed links with Union Corporation over Erfdeel in the Free State. More important, in 1955 it spotted the potential of the Fairview Consolidated Mine in the Eastern Transvaal near Barberton, and took a controlling position which brought with it the Group's first technical and administrative control of a gold mine. There followed from this a participation with Union Corporation in Winkelhaak, with Anglovaal in the new Zandpan near Klerksdorp, and, in 1960, 10 per cent in the syndicate developing Zaaiplaats in the Free State. In other words, Federale Mynbou had been accepted.

But the breakthrough came not through these marginal gold participations but in two deals in the coal industry where Fedmyn's reputation was already made. The company's technical skills were not denied in the industry – it was running the first fully mechanised coal mines in the country – but it had sustained problems in the 1950s in persuading the Transvaal Coal Owners Association to give it adequate quotas. The solution came with the identification of important deposits at Broodsnyersplaas (near Witbank), a deal with Anglo American, more problems with the TCOA – and then a major arrangement with Eskom, negotiated by Tom Muller between April 1957 and August 1958, to supply a massive new power station at what would be called Komati. The charm of this agreement, apart from its size, was that the contract would be for 30 years, that it fell outside the TCOA, and that it was in partnership with Anglo American. The result was to multiply Fedmyn's coal production by three. But the essential message was that Fedmyn had the contacts to get the Eskom contracts. Similar contracts were to follow: in 1960, for example, Fedmyn moved into Clydesdale Collieries, which was to supply Eskom's Highveld power stations; in 1962 Sasol appointed Fedmyn managers of its Sigma mine; and also in 1962 Fedmyn won the tender to supply Eskom's planned Camden power station, with 1 600 MW capacity requiring 5,5 million tonnes a year; this led to the establishment by Fedmyn of Usutu coal mine.

The second milestone was a meeting in 1960 in London between William Coetzer and the British financier Mr Harley Drayton, who – among many other interests – ran Natal Navigation Collieries. Coetzer had earlier identified Drayton as a potential ally in his ambition to get into gold mines (he had apparently been told by Sir Ernest Oppenheimer, whether brusquely or jestingly is not clear, to go out and find one) and he had even broached with Drayton the idea of a bid for Goldfields, only to be blocked by the caution of his fellow directors. But by now Drayton, with South Africa's departure from the Commonwealth, and in the light of his advancing age, was reducing his South African interests, and in 1962 Muller and Coetzer grabbed the chance to consolidate his three companies with their own so as to create the publicly listed Trans-Natal Coal Corporation, though Drayton remained in the Chair until he died some years later. Natal Navigation was the biggest independent coal mining group in the country, controlling seven mines, with plans to take over three more. FVB agreed to Coetzer's urging, though specifying that 'the Afrikaans character' of the Fedmyn mines be maintained.

Agreement was reached in December 1962 for Trans-Natal to be formed as a holding company with a R1,5 million share capital; Drayton would sit in the Chair but Fedmyn would have management in addition to its 32 per cent interest. Fedmyn thereby discovered that it controlled the largest coal mining company in South Africa, and no one could deny that it had done a splendid deal – just as no one could deny that this acquisition by the Afrikaners was directly related to the desire of a major international financier to get out of the increasingly isolated country. That said, it should be acknowledged that Drayton had been impressed by Fedmyn's coal expertise, as well as by its access to future Eskom contracts. George Clark, who was to become a senior Gencor executive, worked for Natal Navigation at the time of the takeover and to his own surprise became Fedmyn's honorary Englishman. He clearly remembers that Federale Mynbou was aiming for the big league.

William Coetzer was not only interested in coal: on the contrary, he wanted a fully fledged mining-house in which gold would be an essential, but he and Tom Muller, while dreaming their dreams, carried on with Federale Mynbou's expansion elsewhere. They acquired interests in asbestos, for instance, in 1961 taking a position in Msauli Asbestos Mining and Exploration Company (Msauli), and then, in 1961/62, in Griqualand Exploration and Finance Company (Gefco). The Group subsequently disposed of these acquisitions.

Fedmyn was also invited to go into chrome, co-operating in various minor deals and then, in the mid-1950s, with Union Corporation in a move into Chrome Mines – an area where Coetzer's influence in extracting truck quotas from South African Railways was relevant. And Fedmyn was also attracted into and then involved in various proposals for tin and kaolin and, all too soon, for diamonds. The Group also invested in fluorspar, salt and electrolytic manganese. Fedmyn manifestly had the energy, the financing, the skills, the professional reputation, the opportunities, and contacts at the highest level. William Coetzer and Tom Muller were looking for their next and decisive opening. Between 1954 and 1964 Fedmyn's total assets grew from R1,12 million to R19,2 million. It was almost symbolic that in 1961 Fedmyn bought Goldfields' 47 Main Street building in the very heart of the downtown Johannesburg district of the Randlords.

The take-over of General Mining by Federale Mynbou, which dominated the headlines through 1963 and 1964, has subsequently been presented as the wise and magnanimous decision of Anglo American, that is to say of Harry Oppenheimer, to 'allow' – to 'facilitate' – the emergence and arrival of the Afrikaners, after 75 years, into the first division of South Africa's mining houses. These early 1960s were years when the Afrikaners were in unshakeable possession of national political authority, when the continuing domination of the mining economy by the English community (and by the 'Hoggenheimer' empire of Anglo American in particular) was resented by the electoral majority of whites, and when the mining houses would be wise not to antagonise Pretoria and the National Party any further.

Harry Oppenheimer's decision to invite Tommy Muller to dinner in London and suggest a pooling of his General Mining holding with Federale Mynbou's Trans-Natal – with the evident intention of developing the relationship in due course – may therefore be seen as a 'political' and far-sighted move by a statesman of business. It was to be recalled in these terms 30 years later when, for similarly 'political' reasons, there would be talk of the desirability of making it possible for black entrepreneurs in the new South Africa to have 'their own mining house', on the unspoken argument that the cleverest way to defend an unpopular club is to invite your enemies to join. But the story of 1963-4 is much more complicated than that, and the Anglo American motives were not quite so disinterested and philanthropic. At the heart of the strategy of 44 Main Street, the Oppenheimer headquarters in Johannesburg, was the constant and over-riding concern of the Anglo-De Beers empire: the matter of diamonds.

Throughout the 1950s Federale Mynbou, as its reputation developed and as William Coetzer fed his ambition to enter the first division of mining houses, became close to several of these mining houses, including JCI and Goldfields, at least at the level of technical collaboration. No doubt Coetzer and Tommy Muller had their secret ambitions for the future. Coetzer had said to Muller, 'I want this to be a real mining house. What do we need?' Muller replied, 'You have to have a gold mine.' But, except for minor operations in the Eastern Transvaal, gold mines were not available – so Federale Mynbou had to look at the existing mining houses, and they researched all of them, particularly JCI, and eventually decided General Mining was the only possibility.

Federale Mynbou, though still small, was known to be close to government and was approached with all sorts of mineral propositions – including diamonds, the sector in which, of course, De Beers cherished its monopoly control both of production inside South Africa and, through the Central Selling Organisation, of marketing world-wide. Fedmyn's interest was first attracted in Namaqualand in 1960, but the more dramatic opening seems to have occurred off the coast of South West Africa where Sam Collins's Marine Diamond Corporation was developing a Texan-inspired project to dredge diamonds from the sea bed. Jack Scott had always been a diamond buff, and he was probably responsible for General Mining holding 20 per cent in the Collins operation. To one side of this, Fedmyn decided to push on into diamonds, both in Namaqualand and off-shore. De Beers was clearly not going to be amused by these Afrikaner moves into the diamond sector: it evidently took a decision to close the South West African door. Furthermore, Anglo American, having seen how it was in its interest to co-operate with Fedmyn to get an Eskom coal contract, was at the same time increasingly concerned with the frailty of the management of General Mining, in which it held 23 per cent.

The death of Sir George Albu in 1963 must have relieved Harry Oppenheimer of a personal hesitation to assert the authority which had been available for years to the Oppenheimers, thanks to their shareholding in General Mining, if they chose to exercise it. Stowe McLean was immediately appointed to the Chair of General Mining at the end of February 1963 at Harry Oppenheimer's instigation; but manifestly – he was in his mid-seventies – it was a stop-gap appointment: Jack Scott, the other Deputy Chairman, had been passed over by Anglo and would resign in July (he made a point of explaining in public that he was 60 and wanted to do his own thing). Sir Albert Robinson joined the General Mining Board with the plan that he would succeed as Chairman.

At this stage, according to memoranda unearthed by the Federale Mynbou historian, Dr Grietjie Verhoef, there were no clear ideas about the future relationship between Federale Mynbou, General Mining and Anglo American. But on 27 July 1963 William Coetzer was telling his Fedmyn Board in a memorandum that the chief motivation for Harry Oppenheimer's plan for the closer Fedmyn/General Mining arrangement was an acceptable agreement on diamond interests: Coetzer said that Fedmyn had been asked to help De Beers negotiate with Sam Collins's Marine Diamond Corporation (in which Fedmyn had 20 per cent), in which Fedmyn/FVB/Sanlam were evidently seeking control, to the obvious alarm of De Beers. A glimpse of the behind-the-scenes activity is revealed in a subsequent memorandum prepared by Sir Albert Robinson in 1982: 'After a considerable struggle', wrote Sir Albert, he 'had come to an agreement with Collins which put paid to the Afrikaner efforts...'

But Fedmyn, in the early 1960s, had been developing diamond ambitions apart from Sam Collins's operation and, with several other Afrikaner companies, had formed the Terra Marina Diamond Corporation with the aim of obtaining diamond concessions in Namaqualand and on the sea-bed. Sanlam was to be the principal shareholder, and Fedmyn, with 17,5 per cent, would manage the project. De Beers, evidently concerned to maintain its long-standing control of international diamond marketing, asked for a holding in Terra Marina (according to Coetzer's July 27 memo to his Board) but was refused. However, Fedmyn agreed provisionally that Terra Marina's diamonds be marketed through the Central Selling Organisation. This was not surprising – the South African government would certainly have wished it – but De Beers added the request that, should Fedmyn find other diamond propositions, Anglo/De Beers *must* have the option to acquire a 51 per cent interest in them.

This was later detailed in a letter of 13 August 1963 from Harry Oppenheimer to the Fedmyn Chairman. De Beers, wrote Oppenheimer, played a 'vital role' in the industry and it was important it should maintain 'its dominant position in the Central Selling Organisation and in the production of diamonds generally'. Oppenheimer acknowledged Fedmyn's interest in Terra Marina and proposed that the two groups would co-operate in any prospecting or producing activities, but, should Federale Mynbou – or General Mining – become involved in any new diamond venture, it must be offered to a *new* company owned 51 per cent by De Beers, 49 per cent by Fedmyn.

This was clearly an attempt to limit any further inroads by the Afrikaners into the diamond sector, and Fedmyn, if agreeable, would expect a reward. As Dr Verhoef concludes: 'Should Anglo American succeed in arranging the Fedmyn's subjugation to De Beers on a permanent basis, it would be prepared to make it possible for Fedmyn to realise their long-awaited dream of controlling a major mining house, a mining house based on gold...', and, she adds, appositely, 'If the solution of the potential diamond nightmare could be put to rest simultaneously with the new and efficient management of General Mining, then Anglo American's shareholding in

General Mining would also pay better dividends...'

The *other* reasons for allowing General Mining to be taken by the Afrikaners made strong sense – most of all the 'political' bonus of Anglo being seen to accept the Afrikaners' demand for a voice in 'their' South African gold industry, and the more particular 'political' point that an Afrikaner mining-house would have greater hope of government-inspired benefits. But this precise understanding or agreement about the ongoing control of diamonds is clearly central to what ensued. Here again, the point was to be relevant 30 years later: when Anglo American in 1994 instructed JCI to unbundle in order to facilitate and make possible a fuller black participation in its activities, the diamond sector was specifically excluded, 'reserved' for Anglo/De Beers' continuing control.

With this understood by everyone, the negotiations between Fedmyn and Anglo could proceed – and with the all-important benefit of Sanlam's support (in contrast with some hesitation from Bonuskor). The essence of the deal was presented to the Fedmyn Board on 27 July by Coetzer: a new company would be formed (eventually to be called Main Street Investments), held 50/50 by Anglo American/Fedmyn, which would buy from Anglo American its 23 per cent in General Mining and would negotiate with Jack Scott to buy his personal General Mining holding of 7 per cent. The new company would then increase its General Mining holding, via the market, to 40 per cent so as to have unquestioned control. By this time Jack Scott had resigned and had flown himself to South West Africa to look into some new diamond concessions. Sir Albert Robinson, Tom Muller and William Coetzer thereupon moved onto the General Mining Board, and two Anglo representatives stood down. In the words of the *Financial Times* Mining Editor, on 30 September – 'the purport of all these moves appears clear enough... Anglo American, for fairly obvious reasons, including political ones, is happy to take Afrikaners into closer contact with the mining industry. General Mining has been chosen as the vehicle for what looked to be equally strong reasons. They include the possible quietening down of the struggles on two separate fronts, coal ... and diamonds...'

This deal, announced in August 1963, was received positively on the whole. The Afrikaans press noted that this was a good example of collaboration between the two white communities; the English press was complimentary about Fedmyn and about Coetzer and Muller ('they proved themselves to be knowledgeable, able, sincere. They showed themselves to be businessmen who thought and acted in a clean businesslike manner. Conservative yet imaginative and enterprising...' – *Sunday Times*, 10 August 1963 – is there a touch of condescension in this ?) The agreement on diamonds had not been announced, but a couple of papers guessed that some sort of pact was involved. The Fedmyn Board was not unanimously happy, even when the directors were assured that there would be further discussions and negotiations with Anglo. The main opponent was Dr MS Louw (of Bonuskor), who refused to let Bonuskor be included in Tom Muller's agreement on diamonds.

The more difficult – and more important – problem, which was not publicly known at the time but can be seen in the archives, was that Anglo (as expressed in a letter to Fedmyn's Chairman from Harry Oppenheimer dated 27 August 1964 summing up the result of the year-long negotiations) required that if either Fedmyn or Anglo had the opportunity to acquire a 'position in any of the other established South African mining groups in terms of which it would participate in the management of such mining groups or would be given board representation on any boards of such groups, we would discuss the matter with a view to the business being undertaken jointly...' A specific exception was noted for Anglo's relationship with JCI and Rand Mines. Tom Muller replied the same day accepting this record.

This part of the deal – not surprisingly – became an immediate sticking point. After Coetzer had talked with Sanlam and other Afrikaner business leaders, he replied that such a restriction was unreasonable and unacceptable; only when the possibility arose of *control* over another mining group, as opposed to an investment or Board representation, would Fedmyn accept such a restriction. After much coming and going, the agreement was summed up in a letter from Coetzer to Anglo dated 11 December 1964: 'If either your group or ours acquires a dominant position in any of the above mentioned mining-houses, with the exception of Rand Mines and JCI, as far as your group is concerned, then it shall offer to the other group at current market prices, or cost, whichever is highest, a participation of not less than 40 percent of the interest acquired.'

This matter, which surely amounted to an attempt by Anglo to put shackles on Fedmyn's/General Mining's freedom of action, was to become extremely relevant 11 years later when General Mining did indeed cast eyes on another mining house.

The decision to move General Mining and Fedmyn together had obviously been understood by the negotiators from the beginning, but for reasons of political delicacy and staff morale, the announcement, and the implementation, were postponed until August 1964, when 'consummation' (as too many newspapers put it) was made public, together with news of Stowe McLean's retirement in 1965 and the succession of William Coetzer as Chairman of General Mining. (Tom Muller had already become the Managing Director of General Mining.)

At this point, the Afrikaners had to take a view, and there was a significant degree of opposition. *Die Vaderland*, and its editor, AM van Schoor, for instance, saw it as a deathblow for the ideal that the Afrikaner take his place in the mining industry, because Fedmyn, it thought, was doomed to be dismantled, drowned. Afrikaner business ambitions, wrote Van Schoor, 'had been buried in a coffin in 44 Main Street'. Although other comment was more favourable, Harry Oppenheimer was obviously aware that such a split response from Afrikanerdom was undesirable, and – to abbreviate an extremely complex negotiation – in January 1965 he sold another one per cent of General Mining to Fedmyn so that General Mining would become, unmistakably, a subsidiary of the Afrikaner Federale Mynbou. It was Harry Oppenheimer's personal initiative, and people like Tom Muller appreciated what he intended.

The arrival of the Afrikaners into the Chamber of Mines had the important consequence of defusing the ruling Afrikaners' view of the mining industry; Tom Muller's election to the presidency of the Chamber in 1968 must for this reason be seen as a symbolic breakthrough. In 1964, with equal symbolic impact, he had been elected to the presidency of the Afrikaner Handelsinstituut (which represents Afrikaner business nation-wide) in opposition to those members who rejected the new situation; Muller was re-elected the next year, and the point was driven home. He had made his position clear when he said, 'The take-over would probably not have come about but for the integrity and assistance of Mr Oppenheimer. He has been extremely constructive about the whole thing and has shown a genuine desire to assist in creating an opening for the Afrikaans business world to come into the world of mining and finance...' The Cabinet was divided; Verwoerd talked of Hoggenheimer trickery, but the new and decisive voice came from Dr Nico Diederichs, the Economic Affairs Minister, who in effect declared that all was for the best in the best of all possible worlds.

It only remained to carry through various technicalities – a new company had to be formed, for example, and General Mining became a Fedmyn subsidiary with the fuller merger of General Mining and Federale Mynbou's interests, General Mining as the operating company, Fedmyn as General Mining's holding company, and Anglo American represented on the General Mining Board but *not*, ever, represented on the Fedmyn Board! By then, two of Fedmyn's founding Board, Dr MS Louw and CH Brink, had resigned, unable to believe that this was not a sell-out to Hoggenheimer. It is hard to believe they were right.

The result of these dramas was that, by the mid-1960s, Coetzer and Tom Muller were running a mining group which could indeed claim to belong to the first division. They were also having to do this at a time when South Africa's reputation in the world was plummeting, even if attention to events south of the Limpopo was diverted by the Rhodesian UDI, which preoccupied world opinion for some years during which South Africa's discreet support for Ian Smith's regime was an open secret. But at home the National Party was in total control. Coetzer and Muller were at the heart of Afrikanerdom – both were, of course, Broeders – and they could concentrate on their chosen task of sorting out the many problems of General Mining (whose boardroom occasionally served as venue for local Broederbond meetings).

And the fact remains that neither General Mining nor Federale Mynbou, nor their successors, ever subsequently became more deeply involved in diamonds. As for Terra Marina, it eventually finished up in the 1980s as a modest subsidiary of Trans Hex and therefore part of the (Afrikaner) Anton Rupert's Rembrandt group.

In the confidential memorandum Mr Coetzer presented to the Fedmyn Board in Cape Town, July 27 1963, Coetzer's opening words were that the chief motivation for Mr Oppenheimer's co-operation with Fedmyn about the latter obtaining a more substantial shareholding in Genmin was Oppenheimer's condition that an acceptable agreement be achieved on diamond interests. (Confidential memorandum, W B Coetzer – Federale Mynbou Board of Directors, 27/7/63.) Coetzer informed the meeting that AAC wanted an interest in Terra Marina, but it was decided that it could not be granted. This Oppenheimer accepted. Fedmyn was then asked to help De Beers with negotiations with Marine Diamonds, which Fedmyn did, and that resulted in the abovementioned arrangement De Beers could conclude with Marine Diamonds. The next important arrangement with Fedmyn was that Fedmyn had to agree that Terra Marina's diamonds be marketed through the Central Selling Organisation (CSO). Fedmyn only conditionally accepted this proposition, because it demanded that acceptable arrangements first be reached on quotas and prices.

'These arrangements Coetzer did not regard as big concessions made by Fedmyn, since he expected the government to demand a similar arrangement to prevent confusion in diamond sales in future. In an additional letter of August 1 1963, Coetzer mentioned that the AAC intention was to establish a holding company to hold all the Marine Diamonds shares plus those of other diamond mining companies that were operating on the west coast and could be included in these arrangements. Mention was now also made of a request by AAC that, should Fedmyn find diamond propositions outside concession areas, AAC must be given a 51 percent interest in those concerns. (Letter W B Coetzer – Fedmyn Board, 1/8/63)

'Later, when final agreement was reached on the matter of Genmin,

agreement was also concluded on diamonds. The basis of agreement was set out in a letter by HF Oppenheimer to the Chairman of Federale Mynbou, August 13 1963. The letter started off by Oppenheimer reminding Coetzer of "the vital role played by De Beers in it (the diamond industry), and the importance of De Beers maintaining its dominant position in the Central Selling Organisation and in the production of diamonds generally". The letter then acknowledged Fedmyn's interest in Terra Marina, the latter having the concession to prospecting in the areas underlying the territorial waters along portions of the western coastline of the Republic of South Africa and South West Africa. Then mention was made of agreement between AAC and Fedmyn that friendly relations between any company interested in diamond mining in which Fedmyn might participate, and the De Beers Company, would be supported and actively promoted. The agreement also made provision for the fact that Fedmyn would at all stages be prepared to support collaboration between such company and De Beers where it could be shown to be in the financial interest of such a company...

'Probably the most restricting part of the agreement for Fedmyn was that, should Fedmyn or any company over which it exercised effective control, including General Mining, make any new diamond discoveries or be invited to handle any new diamond venture, such discovery or venture would be offered in the first place to a new company to be formed for the purpose, and the capital of the new company would be owned 51 percent by De Beers and 49 percent by Fedmyn. Lastly, it was added that Fedmyn would be expected to use its best endeavours to effect the same arrangements with any company with whom it may be associated. (Letter H F Oppenheimer to Chairman, Fedmyn, 13/8/63)'...

Extract from 'The History of Federale Mynbou Beperk',
by Dr Grietjie Verhoef

CHAPTER TEN

SEPARATE ROOMS

All of this had been happening under the increasingly crippling restraint of the $35 gold price. With new goldfields emerging in the Orange Free State, the Far East Rand and Klerksdorp, it would have been logical to expect the mining houses to press ahead to new possibilities, but there was the un-shiftable brake of the fixed price, made worse by domestic inflation and the first murmurs of unrest from the all-important black labour force. Instead, South Africa's mining houses – not least Union Corporation and General Mining – looked at diversification into industry, property, construction, overseas expansion, anything and everything that was not their root busi-ness, their in-house expertise.

The mining houses were reminded of their real trade when the gold price escaped in 1968. The Tet offensive in Vietnam may have been the last straw which broke the US/European gold pool of central banks dedicated to holding the price at $35 an ounce. The gold markets were closed; the price was released to float. For every mining house executive, every South African mine manager, the situation was transformed. Since then, the gold price has veered between $400 and $800 and back again to under $400 an ounce. More important to the South Africans is the Rand/Kilogram price, as the Rand has lurched against the dollar.

The fact is that times were hard in the General Mining gold mines of the 1960s, as they were in Union Corporation, which is an important part of the background to the transforming events of the 1970s. The gold price made dramatic strides, both forward and back, in the 1970s. The implications of these daily gyrations, in such contrast to the decades of a fixed and immovable official price, impacted, of course, not so much on the immediate revenues from the day's gold, or on the announced ore output, so much as on the locked-in value of a mine's payable ore reserves. When the price languished,

Gold price fluctuations

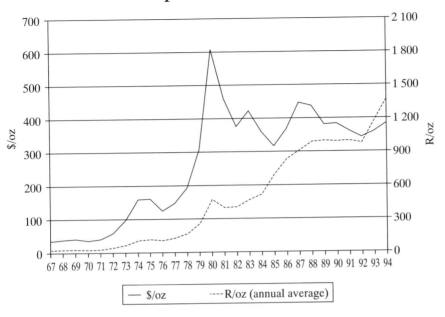

— $/oz   ----R/oz (annual average)

they were left underground and were without value; when the price soared, every mining company – and every local community – re-did the sums to calculate how far their profits, and their very lives, had been extended. This was particularly important for the older mines, some of which still contained large quantities of reef which had been uneconomic to mine at the old price; paradoxically, some of Union Corporation's newer properties were also particularly affected because of their lower grades. However, put at its simplest, the freeing of the gold price encouraged a surge in development and production – which, not surprisingly, gave a new twist to the inflationary tendency of the industry as South Africa entered a new generation of political tension in which the quiescence of the black labour force could not be assumed.

For three years, 1969-71, the free gold market developed gradually: in 1971 the price showed a 15 per cent rise to $40 per ounce, which was not going to be enough to secure a transformation. But in 1972 the price went to an annual average $58, in 1974 it rose to $159; there was a reaction in 1975-6, but the price would then double and re-double and then, in January 1980, it peaked at an extraordinary $846 an ounce (R695), falling back to an average $607 for the year. The consequential impact on profits, on dividends and dusted-off expansion projects was obvious. One immediate result was that Union Corporation felt able to float Unisel Mines, next door to St Helena, whose plant would be used to treat the Unisel ore. This was not a big project, planned to cost R50 million with a target of 75 000 tons a month in a partnership with Selection Trust, and it turned out to be a success even after inflation stretched its target capital expenditure to R84 million.

At the time, Union Corporation, under PM Anderson's son Colin until 1974, had been focusing more on its widespread, even rambling, industrial diversification and distractions. Ted Pavitt had taken over the Executive Chair in mid-1974 and had a preference for diversifying into other minerals rather than secondary industry – but he could not have known that Union Corporation was doomed and that, across the road in General Mining, his mine-magnate colleagues were already planning a new world. Certainly everyone in Johannesburg and London understood that mining had become extraordinarily expensive and that size was going to be all.

In the meantime, General Mining, in its new Afrikaner guise, reporting to Federale Mynbou and thence to Sanlam, also had its problems in the 1960s. In effect, the Group had two very old mines (West Rand Cons and South Roodepoort); one middle-aged mine (Stilfontein, where uranium revenues had faded and where there were faulting problems in its new shaft area – it applied for state assistance in 1970); and Buffels, which was in its prime, though it was going deeper and deeper underground, which was expensive, and it also had to finance expansion of its uranium plant, which handled the highest volume in the country.

General Mining/Federale Mynbou also felt the obligation to diversify. There may have been a logic in that, especially as the South African economy was ripe for import substitution with the government offering protection, but General Mining, it can be seen with the benefit of hindsight, got involved in far too many minor enterprises. Tom Muller and his colleagues in the 1960s went on a buying rampage. It is true that diversification was the fashion of the day, but many of the General Mining acquisitions were short on strategic justification – they bought lawnmowers, golf balls, silk stockings, chutney, marmalade, gas cookers, Marmite, and so on and so forth: in Keith Wallis's polite words, 'a mixed bag of small engineering businesses'. It may be true that 36 per cent of the Group's investments were in the industrial division by 1970, but the 55 or so investments averaged only about R1 million. A more promising move had been to buy Alpha Free State Holdings in 1970, which brought with it Dunswart Iron and Steel, and a minority in the Montrose chrome operations, a pointer to where the future might lie. The leading enthusiast for this General Mining industrial orgy was Herman van Eerden, Chief Executive for Finance and then for Industry.

In a few years' time, Muller's successor, Wim de Villiers, would have to get a grip. Indeed, Sanlam was beginning to worry about its General Mining. Coetzer's influence probably began to wane at this time, though he remained Chairman until 1975 and thereafter continued in the Chair at Fedmyn for years. Muller had not forgotten the criticism he had received from the Afrikaner Establishment for doing a deal with Anglo American and he was also probably dispirited by interference or criticism from within Sanlam. In 1971 he was offered the Chair at Iscor, the state steel concern, and was happy to go. Sanlam promptly put in its master strategist, Wim de Villiers, who would sell 39 of General Mining's lesser businesses in seven months.

Back in Union Corporation, the 1960s stagnation in gold had been accompanied by a difficult leadership situation. PM Anderson had died in 1954 and Tommy Stratten had taken over, the obvious successor as Managing Director in Johannesburg, with the complication that, immediately after his appointment, he fractured his skull in a freak accident on a Union Castle liner in a severe storm. Lord Bracken promised to fly out to Johannesburg to hold the fort, whereupon Stratten made a miraculous recovery – although some of his closest colleagues suspected that he was never the same man again.

Stratten's achievement was to launch Anderson's new gold field at Evander and to transfer Board control of the Group from London to Johannesburg, a tedious, lengthy and technically complex process which, with help from Pretoria, was justified by the need to remove Union Corporation from the British tax system. Stratten had to manoeuvre this exercise past the remnants of Sir Henry Strakosch's generation – Lord Bracken, the London-based Chairman, Clive Temperley (son of a former Chairman) and Eric Fraenkel (Strakosch's nephew), as London directors, Albert Conrad, the London Manager, Lords Harlech and Leathers, Cyrus Pott (of distant Mexico fame), Lewis Douglas (ex-US Ambassador to London, a mining man and a pal of Bracken), and, most effective of all, Sir Charles Hambro. In the event, a batch of these distinguished men was removed by death. Bracken died in August 1958, to be succeeded, temporarily, as London-based Chairman by Sir Charles Hambro – and in September 1962 Union Corporation was at last granted permission by the British authorities to transfer to South Africa. Stratten became Chairman, Harlech and Pott resigned from the Board, and Colin Anderson became Deputy Managing Director. This was another of those fundamental generation changes.

Stratten thereupon could concentrate on happier matters, such as the continued expansion of the Evander goldfield. But he was pessimistic about the prospect of the rise in the gold price, unsympathetic to his managers' demands for new prospecting, and chose to focus on the possibilities of moving into the industrial sector. He already had, as his major experiment dating from before the war, Union Corporation's Sappi, South Africa's first paper industry.

This is not the place to tell the story of Sappi (which has been described by Anthony Hocking in *The Paper Chain*), except to underline its significance in the growth of Union Corporation's, and Gencor's, industrial activities, because some of these followed logically from the early struggles of a paper industry in a country which was not ready to sustain one. Half a century later, when Sappi was unbundled by Gencor in 1994, it quickly demonstrated its maturity and its management drive, in October snapping up SD Warren, America's biggest producer of coated wood-free paper, for $1,6 billion (which was the biggest ever foreign investment by a South African company) and so launching Sappi into the world's top division in pulp and paper, as a dramatic follow-up to the earlier R825 million acquisition of Hannover Papier in Germany.

But in the immediate post-war years, Sappi posed a problem. John Henderson, the young manager who had been diverted by Tommy Stratten to run a munitions plant in the war – South Africa was an important armaments supplier for the Allies and the mining industry operated about 45 munitions workshops – was sent down to the Enstra mill and ordered to make it work. The market was small, the initial process was wrong, and prices were controlled. Henderson would in due course be responsible for all of Union Corporation's industrial interests, but Sappi was a long, hard, expensive slog whose eventual success on an international scale should be recorded as a compliment to Union Corporation and to Henderson, to Basil Landau, and, above all, to his successor, Eugene van As. Sappi was to be a target, in the years ahead, in a number of mysterious stratagems on the part of Anglo American, who had their own plans and ambitions for South Africa's pulp and paper industry.

Part of Sappi's importance to the Corporation was that it inspired a sequence of important industrial diversifications – for example, Kohler Brothers (packaging), Darling and Hodgson (construction and haulage), African Coasters (shipping). The essence of the deal whereby Union Corporation eventually extracted itself from the clutches of the UK tax authorities was that the London assets should be placed in a UK holding company which Robert MacWilliam, one-time manager of the St Helena mine, was to head. There was a flurry of industrial investments in Britain, but this phase was short-lived and a more lasting and profitable investment (though not without some frights and the expenditure of a good deal of management time along the way) was directed into UK property, a substantial operation which involved St Martins le Grand Property Company and, in due course, Greenhaven Securities, which was later to merge with Capital and Counties.

And then, at home in South Africa – where it might have seemed wiser to concentrate – Union Corporation took the surprising decision to take French partners and build the Hendrik Verwoerd Dam on the Orange River. Many years later, Ted Pavitt and Hugh Monro would reminisce about that experience and debate why the Corporation thought it could take on a major civil engineering project. The dam was in trouble from the start, partly because the government's engineers made major changes in the specifications and the Cabinet declined to adjust the contract to take these into account. The French engineers, boasting they had never lost money on a dam, assumed that palms could be greased so that the figures could be made to work out. Ted Pavitt disillusioned them, told them he was not prepared to try to bribe South African officials, and took them to the Rand Club for lunch – where his French guests were furious to be served *Boeuf Wellington*! In the end, the R34 million contract cost R62 million and achieved a R4 million loss for the partners, an experience which, after it was over, the Corporation privately vowed never to repeat – although Monro used to argue that it had been a good experience for his engineers and had kept them busy in between the mine developments in which Union Corporation took such pride.

This was an odd period when the Group was casting about, looking for a role beyond its traditional function in mining and investment. The Corporation was still involved in mining ventures overseas – the San Francisco operation in Mexico, for instance, was still running, and profitably enough until the downturn in metal prices in the mid-1950s. In the end the Group negotiated a Mexicanisation to get out of a no-win local tax situation, and the shareholding was finally sold in the late 1970s. (In 1994, with the purchase of Billiton, Union Corporation would return to South America!)

No one could say that Union Corporation was not *looking*. It had lead-zinc plans in South West Africa, significant chrome plans at home (see below), and the Tsumeb Mine in South West Africa. Its younger engineers discovered that they were sent off to a variety of attractive locations – the ski resort of Kitzbuhel, Spain, Anglesey, an investigation of the mining sites of ancient minerals in Europe, and, most romantic of all, a sustained and doomed attempt to resurrect the tin mines of Cornwall. More seriously, perhaps, a permanent exploration office was established in Australia in 1967.

Far and away the most important achievement of Union Corporation in these years was, in fact, the successful establishment of Union Corporation's stake in platinum (see below). In 1968, with Impala Platinum established, the nightmare of the Verwoerd Dam overcome if not forgotten, and R20 million raised through a rights issue, Stratten decided to hand over as Chief Executive, though he remained Chairman, to Colin Anderson. Some of his colleagues were never to understand why he did it: had he once given a private assurance to Colin's father, the legendary PM? A scion of the Anderson dynasty, a senior figure in Johannesburg's mining-house establishment, four times President of the Chamber of Mines, 32 years in the Corporation, Colin Anderson was in his late fifties and was to preside over a difficult few years. In the damning words of the company historian, Keith Wallis, 'Anderson had no pressing agenda of his own; he saw no need for any major change of direction.' He was frequently ill, he avoided decisions. He had no evident talent or qualification for the job. He was seen by his managers as having a 'hands-off' style, in clear contrast with his powerful predecessors: he seemed happy to rely on his team of Assistant Managing Directors and Senior Managers – Hugh Monro (platinum, the dam and exploration), Jeff Goode (gold mining and Australia), and John Henderson (industry), plus Ted Pavitt (mining), Tony Croad (finance), Ian Greig, Ian Wilson and Lynne van den Bosch. This does not mean that all his lieutenants were enthusiastic admirers of his leadership – many of them learned to ignore him and get on with their jobs – and the result was four years of drift.

At the end of this dispiriting period, Stratten decided to hand the Chair to Colin Anderson and become President. Stratten was reluctant, perhaps because he understood the shortcomings of his successor, but he was drinking heavily and was persuaded that he would be able to maintain some sort of control. Anderson was inclined to carry on as Managing Director as well but was dissuaded by his fellow directors from doing so. Instead the comparatively junior Ted Pavitt – who was very unlike Anderson in personality, style and background, and was significantly younger than people like Monro and Henderson – emerged as Union Corporation's Managing Director in April 1972 and Executive Chairman in 1974. He can scarcely have imagined the dramas that lay ahead.

Ted Pavitt was a mining man by talent and profession. A self-made man from a modest background in the Northern Cape, he had worked his way up the ladder, as shift boss, mine captain, underground manager and consulting engineer, and in the 1960s and 1970s was acknowledged to be one of Union Corporation's most dynamic executives. He had demonstrated his leadership qualities in the war, where he won an MC. He never talked about it, but he won the award for an episode of extraordinary heroism at the crossing of the River Po: pinned down by German snipers, and losing men, Pavitt crossed the river at night, armed only with a revolver, rounded up the snipers single-handed, and brought them back as prisoners. (He modestly insists that this version is fanciful...) He was respected, avuncular, tough, and suspected of being a poor delegator. No one could say whether he would turn out to be a good businessman. He inherited a group whose future, thanks to the revival of the gold price and the coming-good of Impala Platinum, seemed secure. That impression was, in fact, an illusion.

Another thread to the mining story in the Northern Cape and also in the Eastern Transvaal was that General Mining, almost by accident, had become a producer of blue asbestos (crocidolite, on the edge of the Kalahari) and white asbestos (chrysotile, near Barberton). Asbestos was the earliest commercially successful product in the Postmasburg and Kuruman districts, a cottage industry in the early days of this century. The asbestos farmers sent men out into the koppies with hammer and pick to collect the asbestos which the women would 'cob' by hand; every week the farmers sent a donkey cart around the workings to collect the bags of asbestos, and paid them in kind.

Southern Africa is almost the world's only source of blue asbestos. The leading company, Griqualand Exploration and Finance Company (Gefco), British-owned and headquartered in London, dated from 1927 (before that it produced saltpetre); in 1961-2 its collection of small mines was incorporated into Federale Mynbou. In 1961 Federale Mynbou had also taken a minority position in Msauli Asbestos Mining and Exploration Company, which produced white asbestos in the hills of the Eastern Transvaal. Msauli was to be a problem company for years, rarely paying a dividend, struggling against the Canadian and Soviet dominance of the world market for white asbestos. In the 1980s Gencor got rid of its shares in Gefco and Msauli in a management buy-out.

The best thing Gencor (or rather, Union Corporation) did in the otherwise confused 1960s was to get into platinum. Its development of Impala, in the north-west of the country and neighbouring on the established Rustenburg Platinum Mines of JCI, was carried through with extraordinary speed, a tribute to the energy of Hugh Monro and his lieutenants, Byng Jackson and Ian Greig.

Platinum and the so-called PGM (Platinum Group Metals – palladium, rhodium, ruthenium, iridium, omnium) had been identified well before the Second World War in the Bushveld Igneous Complex by Dr Hans Merensky, after whom the Reef that was to be the world's largest source of the metal was subsequently named. Russia and Canada had previously been the principal suppliers of platinum – though it was, in both cases, a by-product of nickel mining. In South Africa, platinum, rather than palladium, was to be the principal metal.

JCI had tied up various platinum interests in a major subsidiary called Rustenburg Platinum Mines and exported the metals for refining in Britain by Johnson Matthey. Union Corporation managed to break into this cosy scene thanks to a group of Johannesburg stockbrokers who believed that it would be possible to exploit the minerals on land owned by the Bafokeng tribe; they patiently acquired mining rights over a significant area of tribal land and, in 1965, after approaching all the mining houses without success, persuaded Hugh Monro to take an option and fund a drilling programme. The results were favourable and, when initial negotiations with Rustenburg and with Charles Engelhard, the American metals magnate, got nowhere, Monro and Stratten decided to go ahead independently, with the technical help of International Nickel (INCO) and financial advice from Hambros Bank, which introduced Union Corporation to a metal trading group run by Samuel Ayrton in London which specialised in platinum. INCO and Hambros both took 10 per cent in a new company which was called Impala, and the South African government's Industrial Development Corporation took another 10 per cent. Conveniently, the East Geduld Gold Mine at Springs was being closed down, and the site seemed appropriate for a PGM refinery (not the least of its benefits was that it was close to Johannesburg's international airport – the shipping of platinum is as tricky a security problem as gold). In September 1967 Union Corporation took the decision to establish a platinum mine with an initial capacity of 100 000 ounces of platinum per annum. Production started in July 1969: a lot of Union Corporation's mining men found themselves moving to the north-western Transvaal. The following 25 years were to take production to over one million ounces per annum, meaning that Impala would be the second largest producer in the West. But it was going to be a turbulent ride.

The first years were fortunate. In May 1971 the US Environmental Protection Agency, following up on the 1965 Clean Air Act, held public hearings in Washington to investigate whether the motor industry was making progress in meeting emissions standards which were to take effect in the mid-1970s. Impala's Monro, Jackson and Greig were already on good terms with General Motors and Exxon. The point was that platinum was known to be one of the finest catalytic agents for accelerating chemical reactions: research was demonstrating that platinum would be the best component of the catalytic converters which were to be necessary to control exhaust emissions, first in America and then in Japan and Europe. A colossal new market beckoned, on top of the already buoyant Japanese market for platinum jewellery, which was being fuelled by the vigorous Japanese economy. By mid-1972 Impala was negotiating long-term supply contracts with General Motors and with Chrysler. In the closing weeks of the year, thanks in part to the newly achieved marketing skills of Byng Jackson, details were announced of an agreement for Impala to supply General Motors with 300 000 ounces of platinum and 120 000 ounces of palladium per year for the period 1974-83. The triumphant Hugh Monro retired a few weeks later; for Impala, the expansion would be full steam ahead. And within 15 years, platinum would become South Africa's second most valuable mining export.

W*im de Villiers was to be one of the most important figures in the business history of white South Africa. He was a bundle of contradictions. He attracted admiration and affection from some, while to others he was a cold fish, an inadequate leader who surrounded himself with yes-men. He preached delegation, but some of his executives would later confess that he was not very good at delegating. The men who worked under him still debate and argue about his true quality. No one ever doubted his high intelligence or his remarkable, near-workaholic stamina. He had no interest in higher culture. There was a vanity in him, a dogmatism which could sometimes become arrogance. A big, burly man, though his health was sometimes in question, he was an Afrikaner from the Free State, not the Cape, which is said to make a difference. He was a member of the Broederbond, though his relationship with his fellow Broeders, William Coetzer and Andreas Wassenaar, originally close, was to be transformed by events. He had a friendship with Dr Anton Rupert and was to be close to State President PW Botha, who eventually co-opted him to the Cabinet.*

An engineer, his early career was with Anglo American, principally in the Northern Rhodesian Copperbelt in the 1960s, but on his return to South Africa he and Anglo seem to have realised that he did not fit in to their elegant English-speaking culture and he went off to the Sanlam group where he became their industrial advisor and strategist. It was a sensible move because Wim de Villiers was above all a self-confessed business strategist and philosopher, and he wrote books to prove it.

There has never been a South African executive who more deserves the honorific of 'philosopher'. He argued that black labour must and could be better utilised. This certainly does not mean that Wim was a bleeding-heart liberal. He published various books in the early 1970s which developed his insight that the crisis of South Africa was a crisis of skills-shortage (this was a decade when South Africa's social structure was visibly breaking down). The top priority, argued De Villiers, must be to develop the 'leader group' (which seemed to mean whites) while introducing massive training programmes for the unskilled and semi-skilled majority. There was, he declared, a fundamental antithesis between the 'Western way of life, based on recognition of the human being and of his right to develop his potentialities to the full', and that of the blacks, which 'does not allow for individualism or renewal, nor for the application of Man's questing intelligence'.

As a few brave journalists pointed out at the time, this was a period of job reservation, migrant labour, pass laws, denial of trade union rights, restrictions on apprenticeship and training, refusal of the democratic vote. In interviews in the mid-1970s, De Villiers gave his answer: black advancement opportunities should be created 'without disturbing sensitive aspects of our socio-political order'; 'the trade union movement is used by far-left Socialists as a political tool and not to improve the worker'. All this was, no doubt, conventional verlig thinking at the time: the essential point, which made him a radical in those days, was that he said he favoured the movement of blacks into formerly white-reserved jobs because it was the only way to maintain the existing order of South Africa's apartheid society – 'it represents the alternative to drastic and radical change, and is in reality a reformist process which leaves existing values intact...'

Wim de Villiers had developed his philosophies first with Anglo and then as industrial adviser to the Sanlam group, which sent him to take over as Chief Executive of General Mining when Tom Muller, who had become a senior and respected member of the Johannesburg mining-house establishment, was persuaded by the Afrikaner establishment to move over to Iscor as Chairman. Wim de Villiers's arrival at General Mining signalled that strategy was to be king, which meant a winnowing out, a rationalisation, of the existing clutter of the Group's industrial diversification. By 1973 General Mining therefore could show how it focused on a portfolio quiver of pipe manufacturing, steel manufacturing, engineering, beneficiation (manganese), mining equipment and oil, to which chrome should be added. Equally important, Wim de Villiers decided to build up a portfolio of gold mine investments, an inspired strategy which coincided with the dramatic rise in the gold price, and therefore a matching rise in profits, dividends, market values. The proceeds of his divestment of the consumer industries were put into a gold portfolio. This was to be Wim de Villiers's war-chest, which he used to take Union Corporation.

CHAPTER ELEVEN

TAKE-OVER

It is hardly possible to imagine that South Africa will ever again see a take-over battle as dramatic, as complex, as impassioned, as extended, as the campaign for control of Union Corporation which opened in mid-1974, and was not finally concluded until nearly two years later. A clutch of South Africa's great mining houses was involved at one stage or other – General Mining, Union Corporation, GFSA (Gold Fields of South Africa), Barlow Rand, while Anglo American hovered on the fringes – and the intensity of the struggle exceeded anything that had gone before. The final result was that General Mining, the Afrikaner outsider, seized Union Corporation, and the South African business world was transformed.

The story started in the middle of July 1974 with screaming headlines in the South African press – 'Financial Giants in R600 million Merger', the giants reportedly being Union Corporation and Barlows. Not for the first time, the headlines failed to get it entirely right. The more modest truth was that the two groups had felt it necessary to disclose a proposal, fairly well advanced, for a merger. This however was to be just the opening shot in a very long and confusing war.

The underlying situation in the middle of 1974 was that both General Mining and Union Corporation had been re-thinking their forward strategies. General Mining, where Wim de Villiers was in full command and enjoyed the support and admiration of his controlling house, Sanlam, could hardly be happy with the knowledge that it was still comparatively small and that its gold mines were few and ageing. But Wim de Villiers had been steadily building up a war-chest: by August 1974 General Mining had a portfolio of gold and other mining shares worth R250 million, by year-end R337 million – and, after paying due attention to the frail chances of mounting a successful exploration programme, he was concluding that the more effective tactic would be to buy in to one of the existing mining houses. Anglo

American and Gold Fields were out of the question. Anglo-Transvaal – the smallest – was family-controlled. JCI was effectively part of Anglo. Rand Mines was part of Barlows. Which left Union Corporation – although it was more than twice as big as General Mining. So De Villiers sounded out Charles Hambro, son of and successor to Sir Charles, who had died in 1964. Hambros, the London merchant bank, had a 45-year connection with Union Corporation and had acquired the Bay Hall Trust shares which dated from post-war reallocation of enemy shares in 1918. Charles Hambro, as a member of the Union Corporation Board, naturally tipped off Ted Pavitt.

The position of the very 'English-speaking' Union Corporation at that time was also one of concern about the future. Pavitt had just taken over as Executive Chairman from Colin Anderson and, although a gold mining man by background, had decided it was necessary to diversify into other minerals (and other countries) and also into industry – but that this process must be done seriously, and on a significant scale. Pavitt realised that Union Corporation was also vulnerable to any group or institution which might build up a stake as small even as 15 per cent – and Union Corporation was an attractive enough proposal to make that a realistic possibility. So Pavitt was not best amused when he heard of General Mining's ambitions. His solution was to accept the logic of some sort of marriage with *another* corporation, *but* to prefer his own choice of spouse – in this case, the (English-speaking) Barlow Rand.

'Punch' Barlow's group was even bigger than Union Corporation, a successful, fast expanding, essentially industrial conglomerate, which 10 years earlier had acquired Rand Mines, descendant of the famous old Corner House mining group, but Barlows' attempts to grow a mining business had not flourished. It therefore seemed to make sense to put together the two groups and, crudely speaking, to rearrange and reallocate their various mining and industrial dowries so that Union Corporation would become the mining division (including Rand Mines) and Barlows would in effect be the joint industrial division. Various meetings took place in secret company flats in the northern suburbs; Harry Oppenheimer (as shareholder in both groups) was consulted and appeared to make no objection from Anglo American, and it was agreed that the deal would be 100 'Unicorp Barlow' shares for every 100 Barlow Rands, and 140 of the new shares for every 100 Union Corps.

The news was broken – with the screaming headlines that suggested a *fait accompli* – on 15 July 1974. Then the objections started, and they came mainly from London, where people like Charles Hambro murmured that surely this looked more like a Barlows' takeover than a merger, and the 140:100 ratio therefore looked poor. There were also European investors who were unhappy because they held their Union Corporation shares for their mining content (where things were looking up, with a stronger gold price and Impala's emerging platinum prospects) and did not necessarily want to dilute them with Barlow's industrial assortment. The complicated result of the merchant bankers' re-negotiation was that the terms were improved by 10 per cent or so, in effect giving Union Corporation shareholders 51 per cent of the new merged company. 'A New South African Colossus!' declared the Johannesburg press. The idea was that Punch Barlow would be Chairman of Unicorp Barlow, ('He's a fantastic, wonderful man,' Mrs Barlow warbled to the reporters) with Pavitt and Mike Rosholt, the Barlow Rand Managing Director, as Joint Chief Executives.

Nothing was to be so simple. On 14 August, Gold Fields of South Africa (GFSA) gave notice that it was launching a take-over bid for Union Corporation.

GFSA was the South African arm of Consolidated Gold Fields, one of the richest of the mining houses, heir of Cecil Rhodes. Gold Fields throughout the century had had a reputation for affluence, style, even arrogance, and it was immediately pointed out that there might be a culture gap between GFSA and the slimmer, less grand, lower-grade-ores Union Corporation – though this need not necessarily matter, of course, if the terms were right. And the GFSA terms were certainly better than Barlows' – about 50 per cent more valuable in price terms, with a mix of an ordinary and preference shares swap, and the analysts and journalists quickly concluded that that was the end of Barlows' ambitions (which were indeed withdrawn in early September). The attraction of the deal to GFSA was clear, while their share price was riding high on the gold price, but from Pavitt's position, it obviously did not satisfy his desire to diversify, since it simply put together two corporations in the same line of mining business. The new group would be very large indeed, in that it would have 14 operating and two developing gold mines, representing 31 per cent of South Africa's output. Still, there were complaints, again largely from London and in particular from Hambros, that the proposal was not quite good enough. And by mid-August, the markets were busy with rumours of *General Mining* activity, but there was silence, for week after week, from Wim de Villiers. 'Why Are We Waiting?' shouted the local headlines.

General Mining was evidently in a dilemma. Since it first dreamed up its ambitions for Union Corporation, two other suitors had appeared; De Villiers had all along understood that General Mining was too small to plan full ownership of the much bigger Union Corporation, all he wanted was control. But he had his war-chest, and he was free to buy in the market. His Chief Executive for Finance, Jan van den Berg, raised an US$85 million loan and arranged to buy Union Corporation shares in New York (avoiding blocked Rands) and Morgan Grenfell and W Greenwell, as General Mining's advisors in London, worked out a strategy of a partial bid made up of a mixture of cash and General Mining/Sentrust shares, with the cash element to be financed by the $85 million loan (Sentrust was an investment company formed of various General Mining subsidiaries).

This bid was at last announced on 30 September – and promptly blocked by the London Takeover Panel under 'Rule 27', which did not permit partial bids unless they were recommended by the Board of the target company. Meanwhile, Ted Pavitt had made it clear to Wim de Villiers that he was no more interested in General Mining's proposal than he was in GFSA's. However, Pavitt's future problem had been spotted: in the early deal with Barlows, he had signalled that he was prepared to go to the altar (to continue the inevitable metaphor), and he presumably had a duty to his shareholders to accept the largest *lobola* (bride price)!

Before then, on 26 September 1974, GFSA's Adriaan Louw spelt out his formal offer – a package of ordinary and preference shares worth 587 cents. Union Corporation said no ('Tough Ted Says No to Tycoon "Sugar"', headlined the *Sunday Times* – 'Sugar' was apparently Mr Louw's nickname and the more popular papers were delighted to find that both he and Pavitt had been war heroes), but many analysts were impressed: 'Gold enthusiasts should grab GFSA's paper immediately,' wrote the *Rand Daily Mail*. On 24 October, to no one's surprise, GFSA improved its offer in various minor details, but won only a lukewarm reception in the all-important London market (the *Financial Times* said: 'Union Corporation shareholders need not fall over themselves to accept the bid...'). On 30 October, again to no one's surprise, the Union Corporation Board rejected the new terms. The next day GFSA responded (all of these exchanges were being conducted in the full glare of publicity) with the effective point that, if the Union Corporation directors were so confident of their glorious future as an independent mining house, why on earth had they recommended the Barlow Rand merger in the first place?

In the meantime General Mining and its advisers, understandably irritated that the London authorities should be the judges in a South African financial transaction (and it should be added that the London Panel was also embarrassed about its role), had been working out a new tactic. At a weekend break in the Kent countryside, Peter Davidson of the brokers Greenwells asked Van den Berg whether General Mining would be prepared to use its $85 million loan facility to buy shares in the market: the intention would be to pick up about 20 per cent or more of Union Corporation, which would block the GFSA offer and also give General Mining the influence it wanted.

In London, the battle between Gold Fields of South Africa, which is controlled by British investors, and General Mining to take control of

Van den Berg phoned Johannesburg and Wim de Villiers flew to London. Greenwells launched a massive camouflaged buying campaign through the jobbers Smith Brothers. In a campaign which was for years to be the stuff of reminiscence in the City of London, General Mining succeeded in rapidly building up a holding of nearly 29 per cent in Union Corporation. (Under London's rules, when a buyer amasses 30 per cent, he has to bid for all the shares – which of course the humble General Mining could not contemplate.) Wim de Villiers then had to sit back and watch what GFSA would do next.

The weakness in the GFSA position was that it was arguing that its *higher grade* properties in times of a rising gold price meant that its shares stood to benefit more than those of a *lower grade* group like Union Corporation. It was slowly appreciated by the analysts that this was a fallacy, because, when the gold price went up (as it was doing at the time) it was the mines which had only just been covering their costs which stood to benefit disproportionately from a large increase in profits per ton. It became clear that the GFSA revised offer in October had simply not been dramatic enough to do the trick – and it was under pressure: by late November the South African press was reporting that General Mining had reached 20 per cent in its open market operations and suggesting, prematurely, that this had slammed the lid on the GFSA bid. On 29 November the papers said that the buyers had reached 26 per cent and were on the way to a maximum 29,9 per cent: on 1 December, 'Genmin Wins the Battle of Unicorp!' (again the headline writers were not quite right).

At last, GFSA was forced to acknowledge that it must raise its offer more dramatically and on 3 December it added R1,20 to its standing bid per share, putting a price of 692 cents on Union Corporation. This was a figure that the Union Corporation directors were obliged to consider very seriously indeed, because it was hard to see how shareholders could look to a better price if the offer lapsed. Ted Pavitt was unconvinced but was overruled by a majority of his directors and agreed to put out a statement of recommendation. 'Unicorp Is Won Over', said the headlines on 4 December – this time more accurately. But the battle had certainly not been won yet. General Mining was sitting on 29 per cent, meaning that GFSA – now with the endorsement of the Union Corporation Board – must look for 51 per cent to put the question of control beyond doubt; that amounted to 70 per cent of the shares not held by General Mining, a difficult target in any long-established share register. The allegiance of some of the larger holders therefore became of crucial importance: Old Mutual, for example (arch-rival of Sanlam, which controlled General Mining), or Charter Consolidated, with a vital 10 per cent and itself controlled by Anglo American. There was furious speculation over the Christmas break: presumably Hambros would follow the Board's endorsement, but Harry Oppenheimer had helped create General Mining in the first place; would he be tempted to intervene again?

At this point, it has to be emphasised that the plot was even more murky than it appeared, although what follows was not publicly known at the time. The role of Anglo American, it seems, was not at all straightforward. According to the later recollections of the senior General Mining financial executives who were centrally involved at the time, Harry Oppenheimer had come to Coetzer and De Villiers *at the time of the first GFSA bid* and had suggested that General Mining might like to enter the battle for Union Corporation in the knowledge that the 10 per cent Charter holding was theirs. These executives insist that this proposal was unconditional. So when Jan van den Berg was buying in the market, he assumed that, unknown to his rivals, he had another 10 per cent up his sleeve (that is, promised by Anglo).

At the turn of the year, when everyone was on holiday and when the General Mining executives really thought they had won, they had another visit from Anglo American. Julian Ogilvie Thompson, one of Harry Oppenheimer's right-hand men, called on Wim de Villiers at his holiday retreat in Hermanus on the afternoon of 5 January 1975, to tell him that Charter was going to accept the GFSA offer (in which the cash element expired in only four days' time). This was a body blow for the General Mining team, which had assumed – both from the original visit from Oppenheimer and from Anglo's willingness to follow the General Mining rights issue the previous October (precisely designed to support the initial entry into the markets) – that Charter's 10 per cent was theirs. All might not be lost, it was intimated, if they agreed to pass on Union Corporation's paper (Sappi) and platinum (Impala) interests. 'You want us to cut up the corpse while it is still alive,' replied Wim de Villiers. His answer was a furious no.

The final battle in the war was to be conducted in a fog of mystery and rumour. On 20 December General Mining had of course publicly rubbished the GFSA revised offer: in a letter to Union Corporation shareholders, the Chairman, Dr Coetzer, declared 'No – 15.7 million times no!' Predictably, Ted Pavitt and 'Sugar' Louw, now finding themselves on the same side, issued a pre-Christmas statement that 'The interests and motives of General Mining may well be different from those of other shareholders' – leaving it to their readers to interpret that for themselves. The deadline for acceptance or refusal was now approaching fast and the newspapers were full of large, paid advertisements from both sides. The language was much rougher than anything commonly heard in the mining-house boardrooms. General Mining actually published a 'Form of Withdrawal' in the press to help wavering Union Corporation shareholders to change their minds. By

10 January it was being reported that GFSA had accumulated acceptances of 30 per cent (which implied that Charter's 10 per cent had indeed been voted for GFSA): by the next day the GFSA total was said to have risen to 40 per cent.

And then – 11 January 1975 – 'Mystery Buyer of Unicorps Comes Back'.

There was furious speculation as to the possible identity of a mystery man. Was it Charter digging deeper into the new Group? Was it 'a large American institution'? Was it a 'gold-bug millionaire'? Was it a friend of General Mining? The vital point in everyone's mind, of course, was that the London Takeover Panel would not tolerate buying by a partner or associate of General Mining. Said the *Rand Daily Mail* on 13 January, 'A powerful, new mystery buyer ... has thrown the whole bid situation back into the melting pot. In a few days of the most aggressive buying seen in London for many a long day the buyer, dubbed The Mystery Man, snapped up an estimated 10 percent of the [Union Corporation] equity...' The Mystery Man was required by Takeover Panel rules to reveal himself the following day. A part of the mystery was therefore solved on 14 January, when Volkskas announced that it had been buying in the market on behalf of a client. So who was The Mystery *Client*? Could it be Sanlam? Lonrho? Slater Walker? The local property millionaire Bernard Glazer? To compound the mystery, on 17 January Volkskas claimed that its purchases were not connected in any way with General Mining's efforts to block GFSA from control of Union Corporation. In a statement which with the perspective of history must be said to be rather odd, Volkskas said it had bought considerably less than 10 per cent of Union Corporation and that the purchases were not on behalf of General Mining, Federale Mynbou, FVB, Sentrust, Sanlam, Bonuskor, or for its own account. This did not succeed in quelling speculation. The question should rather be, was the Mystery Client acting in liaison with – with the knowledge of – General Mining, which would therefore surely be in breach of the City Code of the London Takeover Panel? (Again, there was a question overheard in Johannesburg – why should London decide the rules of a South African game?)

In a little while, the main mystery would be solved and Wim de Villiers's strategy revealed. Trapped under the 29,9 per cent ceiling and bereft of Anglo, General Mining had needed friends – or potential friends – to combat GFSA in the market. Sanlam had been sounded out to help: its Chairman, Dr Wassenaar, who was a close friend of Coetzer, was exceedingly keen on the deal; but Sanlam discovered it could not find the funds it had initially offered. Fortunately for General Mining, it so happened that De Villiers had a personal friend and admirer, Anton Rupert, who controlled and ran the secretive and internationally powerful, cash-rich Rembrandt group from his base in Stellenbosch. Rupert had for some time been interested in expanding in the mining sector, so he decided to enter the fray anonymously, from Switzerland, using Volkskas as his agent, and made DM100 million available. In this particular instance, Volkskas was able to assure the Takeover Panel that the client was independent of the General Mining group – which was true, and it got away with it.

Yet, the full story, as it came to light many years later, was even more tortuous. The essential point is that *there was not one mystery buyer, but several*, both in Johannesburg and overseas. When it was realised in General Mining on 5 January that the Anglo/Charter 10 per cent was 'unsafe' and that General Mining's own shareholding was trapped under the 30 per cent ceiling, an emergency operation was launched – time was desperately short because the cash election option expired on 10 January. That same evening, Wim de Villiers rushed across from Hermanus to meet Dr Wassenaar, the Sanlam Chairman, at Cape Town's DF Malan airport – where Wassenaar was on the point of leaving for Brazil to join a holiday cruise to the South Pole! Wassenaar agreed that urgent steps would have to be taken to neutralise the Charter 10 per cent, which would require an accelerated buying programme at home and overseas, and gave him *carte blanche*. De Villiers contacted Oppenheimer, who (according to General Mining sources) said he could do nothing, because, he claimed, Charter was an independent company. (It occurred to insiders that Anglo might be reckoning that their switched support to GFSA might itself be a deal in return for the Union Corporation's coveted platinum and paper.)

Before he left, Wassenaar contacted Anton Rupert, who was in Europe, to solicit financial support – and the answer was positive: cash would be available overseas, to the level of DM90-100 000. This opened Rupert's door to Jan van den Berg, who then sat down at the Town House, a discreet hotel in the heart of Cape Town, to operate his whirlwind buying campaign, an ingenious and heavily disguised operation by 'Friends' – not just Rembrandt. One of the most important extra players in Johannesburg, the rumoured 'Third Man', was Eric Tenderini, who had a double role: his family London and Dominion Trust acted as one of the pivotal buying agents in Johannesburg (as Greenwell had in London and Drexel Burnham was doing in New York), while Unisec, a Johannesburg investment group of which he was Chief Executive, was an energetic client for Union Corporation's shares.

The dramatic result was that Jan van den Berg and his team managed to 'neutralise' the Charter 10 per cent in three days. In contrast with the Friends' holding of 31 per cent on 2 January, by 10 January (according to General Mining sources) that figure had soared to 41,57 per cent: General

Mining still held its restricted 29 per cent, but by 10 January Volkskas held six per cent, Rupert acting from Switzerland had accumulated five per cent, and Tenderini at that point had 1,5 per cent which would rise to 5,3 per cent a fortnight later. Additional holdings brought that total closer to 47 per cent. By then, 25 January, with the deadline over, the Friends could show 49,87 per cent, mostly acquired overseas (Rupert's holding had risen to 8,65 per cent). Tenderini would later explain that, when his own Unisec resources ran out, he went to Volkskas, where 'bank facilities were made available' to him.

In these circumstances, GFSA obviously could not find 51 per cent and on 25 January 1975 it conceded defeat and announced that its offer would lapse. At this point, Jan van den Berg sent a coded but easily deciphered telegram to Dr Wassenaar on the *Lindblad Explorer* in the Antarctic:

'WEATHER FINE TEMP STEADY 49 POINT STOP KEEPING CLOSE WATCH FOR CHANGE OF COURSE OF WHICH NO SIGN YET STOP MORALE ABOARD SHIP APPEARS TO BE DECLINING PRESENT TEMP UNDERSTOOD TO BE SLIGHTLY OVER 40 AFTER WE HANDLED TWO DEGREE DECLINE STOP THUNDERSTORM IN NORTHERN PANEL NOW NO LONGER THREATENING STOP LOCALS FORMALLY SATISFIED REGARDS JAN.'

Wim de Villiers and his friends now had their control and would proceed to mop up some of the other packets of shares such as Hambros'. He took his time, no doubt conscious that there must be lingering doubts in some quarters about the style of his victory. He was happy to make a gesture to the defeated generals and invited Ted Pavitt and Tony Croad (Union Corporation's Finance Director) to join the General Mining Board; in return he and Jan van den Berg went onto the Union Corporation Board. Charles Hambro stood down – and murmurs were heard about whether Hambros had not been playing for both sides at once. For the moment, General Mining's victorious holding in Union Corporation was presented as a benevolent investment, though everyone understood what had happened. General Mining would also have to pay off its $85 million loan, and immediately started to repair the balance sheet.

The end of the war was facilitated by a change in the London Takeover Panel rules, exempting companies like Union Corporation, which were listed overseas. In consequence Federale Mynbou, in May 1976, after a R74 million rights issue, bought an extra 21 per cent of Union Corporation shares (including the Hambros' parcel and other holdings). Unisec unravelled its position over the next year or two, and Eric Tenderini sold his holding back to General Mining. Rupert decided to stay, subscribing for new shares in Fedmyn as part of the 1976 issue, continuing to build up his position as a 'partner', as did Sanlam, which continued to stipulate that it did not wish to lose 'control'. The result, after a Fedmyn/Genmin exchange,

159

was that General Mining (with Sentrust) finished up owning 50,1 per cent of Union Corporation. Wim de Villiers succeeded Dr Coetzer as Executive Chairman; it had been nearly two years since he had decided that General Mining and Union Corporation belonged together, and he could now concentrate on making the marriage work.

To jump ahead very briefly to complete the tale, in December 1979, to the background of assurances by the two chairmen of General Mining and Union Corporation, Wim de Villiers and Ted Pavitt respectively, that their two corporations had been operating together in total harmony, General Mining was ready to make the logical step and take full control of Union Corporation. A scheme of arrangement was announced whereby the outstanding 48 per cent of Union Corporation was acquired in exchange for a 60 per cent increase in General Mining share capital: Union Corporation thereby became a wholly owned subsidiary with the help of a R190 million General Mining rights issue, and the groups were brought together as General Mining Union Corporation Ltd – which became known as Gencor in 1980. This meant that Fedmyn's interest in Gencor was diluted to 44 per cent, but six months later this was prudently corrected after a rights issue which made it possible to buy an extra holding for R82 million and so recover Fedmyn's 50,5 per cent direct control (with Sanlam and Rembrandt in turn holding 71 per cent of Fedmyn between them). Wim de Villiers, the victor, was the Executive Chairman of Gencor; Ted Pavitt agreed to soldier on as Deputy Chairman – and, sooner than he can have imagined, was to be pushed back into the Chair.

It has been suggested that the silent guest at the feast was Anglo American. Or, to change the metaphor, here, surely, was Sherlock Holmes's dog that didn't bark in the night. After all, Anglo had started off as the largest single shareholder in Union Corporation and also had a long-standing and influential role inside General Mining. Anglo evidently had its eye on Union Corporation's platinum and paper. More interesting still, in 1963-4, when Harry Oppenheimer had brokered the takeover by Federale Mynbou of General Mining, his deal involved a specific undertaking, enshrined in his own words in a letter to Dr Coetzer, dated 27 August 1964, that 'if either Fedmyn or Anglo was able to take a position in any of the other established South African mining groups ... we would discuss the matter with a view to the business being done jointly...', an understanding confirmed in a subsequent, even more specific letter by Dr Coetzer. Surely this clause should have come into operation as soon as General Mining began its tactic to seek control of Union Corporation?

Many years later, the present author was able to put this last point to Mr Oppenheimer. Yes indeed, he replied, he considered that General Mining had reneged on that understanding: indeed, he and his Anglo American colleagues had taken legal advice to see what could be done. But, said HFO, it was thought wiser to let the matter go.

Perhaps this was intended to be seen as another example of a diplomatic decision not to be seen to block Afrikaner ambitions. Except that the Afrikaner executives of General Mining always had their own idea of who had reneged on whom.

The labour situation on the gold mines at this time was largely unreformed. Dolf Schumann remembers how, in the early 1970s, his colleague Pat Dempster, who was in charge of black personnel at General Mining head office, referred to him the situation of a black Fort Hare graduate from the Eastern Transvaal who had approached him for a job...

'Pat came to me because he had no work for the man but felt he simply couldn't just let him go. He had worked out a plan to which I agreed cheerfully and which we then set in motion.

'The man – this graduate – then turns up at a Wenela recruiting post in the Northern Transvaal, wearing only a blanket, in traditional style. He says he wants a job on a mine and has a brother who works at Stilfontein. He is given a medical examination, accepted, introduced to a man who is also going to work at Stilfontein, given a railway ticket, a loaf of bread, a tin of jam, and put on the right train. He then goes through the normal training routine – everything from how to wear boots to how to climb a ladder – and is finally assigned to a gang underground.

'He works there for a week, then disappears. Re-appears at head office, is given an office, and writes down his experiences for me. This turns out to be a true horror story, compounded partly of pure lack of imagination on the part of the authorities, partly the sort of silliness that leads to "initiation" of newcomers to university hostels. I don't want to give examples ... it's too long ago, but a typical one was being chased out at five in the morning for a shift which began at seven, without having anything to eat before going underground.

'With the approval of the head of the Gold Division (I think it was Johan Fritz at the time), and with the approval of the mine manager, I had the report copied and circulated to all our mines and to the Gold Producers' Committee of the Chamber of Mines, where it was discussed. What I remember very clearly was a letter which I received from the manager of one of the mines of the Union Corporation Group. He said he was disgusted and ashamed that the same things might be happening on his own mine, and would I please send my chap to him next time around...

'This move of Pat Dempster's made us all aware of the danger when the chain of command crosses cultural barriers. It was simply not good enough to ask the next man down the line whether all was well in the ranks below him.'

CHAPTER TWELVE

BROEDERTWIS

While the Union Corporation executives licked their English-speaking wounds, and the bilingual Ted Pavitt set himself, stoically, to attempt an adequate relationship with the victorious Afrikaans-speaking General Mining, Wim de Villiers seems to have decided, perhaps wisely, not to force too rapid an amalgamation between the two groups and the two management teams. Pavitt evidently saw part of his role as being to sustain the *esprit de corps* of his Union Corporation people, notwithstanding the painful fact that he and they had 'lost' in the take-over battle. Wim de Villiers may have felt that the rather 'slim' way in which the battle had been won, with all the gossip about the Mystery Buyer and the suspicions of collusion, made a period of tranquillity desirable during which memories would fade and scars heal. Senior executives like Jan van den Berg recalled later that they believed it necessary to give Union Corporation a chance to recover its morale; other managers would remember that they feared at the time that the amalgamation was being postponed for too long. The fact was that for many of the less senior members of both groups, life went on as before. In the end, in 1979, Pavitt, encouraged by his Finance Director, Hugh Smith, told Wim de Villiers that it was time to put the two groups more tightly together: they needed a stronger – a joint – capital base for the big projects ahead: Beatrix and Ngodwana were going to need funding. In 1981 there was a R189 million rights issue to help facilitate the true merger. However, the detail of this issue had been discussed earlier with Sanlam and Rembrandt before it was put to the General Mining Board in 1979, and Sanlam's reluctance to support the issue on the proposed terms led to a serious disagreement between Wim de Villiers and Dr Fred du Plessis.

The first priority for the new Group was to look to the historic core of both operations – their gold mines. The gold price in 1975 averaged $175; by the end of the decade it would be over $600. In 1976 the combined Group was producing 17 per cent of South Africa's gold and 25 per cent of its uranium. The two partners had gold in common: only Union Corporation had platinum, only General Mining had coal.

One of the first new projects, it so happened, was to be a gold mine whose *principal* product would be uranium – Beisa, south of St Helena and the Sand River, at a R200 million capital expenditure estimate, which was given the go-ahead in 1978, though the geologists had done their work there years before. Beisa would turn out to be a problem. On the basis of the newly buoyant gold price, Beisa was followed by a wholly-gold mine next door at Beatrix in 1979, which came on stream in 1981 and reached full capacity in 1985. In financial terms, General Mining was flourishing, paying dividends at 10 times the 1970 level, retaining R100 million of profits, and paying off the $85 million it had borrowed in 1975 to buy the first stake in Union Corporation.

At the end of the decade the 'new' General Mining's gold profile included, in the Free State, Unisel, Beisa, Beatrix and St Helena (which, dating from 1951, was now on to its lower grades); in the Klerksdorp field, Buffels was, as always, strong and Stilfontein was not so certain but had an interesting subsidiary in Chemwes which was extracting uranium from slimes dams. At the other end of the Reef, on the Far East Rand, Winkelhaak was large and profitable and, like Kinross, had been expanded in response to the higher gold price; Bracken and Leslie were both by now reckoned to have a limited life. On the East Rand, Grootvlei was surviving but Marievale was nearing the end (in the event, it lasted until 1992). And, nearer head office, the old war-horse, West Rand Cons, born at the start of the century, was mining ultra-low grade, had given up on uranium, would lose its state assistance in 1982, yet still struggled on.

In the early 1980s, a colossal and unprecedented row erupted within the secretive ranks of Afrikaner business. Gencor – its control, its leadership, its philosophy – was the battleground as the two titans of Afrikaner business, Sanlam and Rembrandt, slugged it out. Exposed on the front-line was Dr Wim de Villiers, and he was to be the eventual victim. Even more startling, the war was conducted out in the public eye, and for much of 1982 the newspapers (the front pages as well as the financial sections) were full of the vituperation and abuse of each side for the other. The headline writers were correct to call this a 'Broedertwis' – for most of the combatants were, or at least had once been, members of the Broederbond.

The tale is worth the telling because it marks the stage at which Afrikaner business may be said to have grown up, in the sense that it had developed a confidence, and a scale of operations, in which it was no longer appropriate or possible to resolve fundamental disagreements in secret meetings of the Brothers; paradoxically, this public and venomous falling-out could be seen as proof of a new diversity, a new breadth of outlook. The Broedertwis must also be located in the changes that had been overtaking Afrikanerdom in this generation: in politics a fundamental chasm had opened some years earlier between *verligte* and *verkrampte*; in the churches the theological underpinning of apartheid had been challenged; in race relations, the Broederbond, cultural affairs, labour and industry, everything was in flux and seemed open to dispute. The 1982 battle for Gencor was further and dramatic evidence that Afrikanerdom was no longer the monolith of earlier years.

It all began early in 1977 when General Mining acquired one-third of a small new computer company in Randburg, northern Johannesburg – Unicom, which had taken over the liquidated Spectro Data and was focusing on the fast-emerging mini-computer sector with its Reality computers and Beehive terminals. It was pretty small beer and would not have merited attention except that its Managing Director was Dirk Wassenaar, son of Dr Andreas Wassenaar, Chairman of Sanlam and the single most influential Director on the General Mining Board. Andreas Wassenaar was one of Afrikanerdom's most influential figures, though this should not suggest that he was a parochial figure: he travelled extensively, published books, and was married to the daughter of a Lord Mayor of London. Born in Middelburg in 1908, he served as a South African Air Force pilot and then trained in Scotland to become an actuary, joining Sanlam in the mid-1930s, where his career was astronomical. It goes without saying that his contacts inside South Africa were unmatched. At the beginning of the affair it was thought that he had put up personal guarantees for his son; in effect, according to correspondence now available, he was the leading family shareholder in the firm, though this was not then clear.

Unicom did not prosper (it is not clear whether Wim de Villiers initially understood the connection between Dr Wassenaar and Unicom's finances). By September 1979 Dr Wassenaar, evidently deeply concerned about the plight of Unicom, broke with his principal partner, an independent businessman called Mr Alfred Street, on terms of extreme bad feeling. Originally Mr Street, who appears to have put up the idea of moving into information technology, had 45 per cent of Unicom, the Wassenaar family 25 per cent, and Gencor took 30 per cent. A letter written by Dr Wassenaar to Mr Street on 12 September 1979 gives the flavour: '...it was your idea to get Genmin in... I swallowed the bait and persuaded Dr de Villiers to take up a minority shareholding... I am ashamed that I have dragged Genmin into a business association with you ... on Monday September 10 I experienced one of the most humiliating moments of my life when I apologised to the

FVB board for this. I had to do this in order to make it possible for me to live with my conscience... I hate to be deceived by a man I called a friend, as much as anybody hates to be bitten by his own dog. I hope we shall never see one another again...'

Several of the most senior General Mining executives at this time were not absolutely hostile to the idea of helping out Dr Wassenaar; they appreciated his strong support throughout the 1974 takeover, they realised he was threatened with personal bankruptcy, and they acknowledged that, for a big corporation, these amounts were peanuts. But they became increasingly worried not only because Gencor was pumping in shareholder loans with the other shareholders defaulting but also about the *principle* of not having these things sorted out through the proper procedures at Board level. Wim de Villiers and Wassenaar at this early stage were still on good terms – Wim was the elected Vice Chairman of Sanlam – though that would change when Wassenaar (according to witnesses) said (words to the effect that) 'I saved you, made you, made you the boss of Gencor. What have you done for me?' A less personal complication was that the detailed discussions for the full and final merger between Union Corporation and General Mining began, at last, in September 1979, so they coincided with the growing in-house worries about the Unicom affair. A rights issue was coming up, for which there would have to be agreement with (Dr Wassenaar's) Sanlam. Dr Coetzer was trying to negotiate with De Villiers and Wassenaar a package of personal financial benefits prior to his own retirement. Anton Rupert was beginning to wonder whether he had a 'partnership' with Sanlam in Gencor as he had apparently assumed. It was all beginning to look very messy.

Unicom struggled on but Wim de Villiers was increasingly worried about what he must by now have realised could be a conflict of interest for his Sanlam Chairman. On 12 May 1980, for instance, his General Manager for Industries, George Clark, had sent him a memo pointing out that Siemens was anxious to negotiate for mainframe and other computers, with the possibility of an important future relationship for Genmin in power station equipment, and that Unicom was 'a conflicting interest': it was, Clark added, a 'small-scale computer agency which does not fit into any of the Group policy guidelines ... this decision must obviously be taken at a level above my own.'

Dr de Villiers, who always prided himself on being a man of principle and integrity, and was being stiffened by his deputy, Ted Pavitt, bit the bullet. On 4 June 1981 a Federale Mynbou Board meeting decided to write off R2 million in shareholder loans, evidently to the benefit of the other shareholders. A little over a year later, at a crisis meeting of Gencor executives (on 10 August 1982), De Villiers gave his version of the personal clash: 'I repeatedly offered to have this issue investigated by an impartial person. When I, in the interests of Gencor, decided not to proceed with this investment, Dr Wassenaar threatened that he would break me. After this I decided not to remain a Vice Chairman of Sanlam. Dr Coetzer concluded the negotiations regarding Unicom with Dr Wassenaar on behalf of management. Dr Coetzer's proposal of an additional R400,000 in management settlement was not acceptable to Gencor's management but was instructed by the Directors. Gencor suffered a loss of R1,925,000 after Dr Wassenaar took over Gencor's interests for R1 as was reported to the Gencor directorate on June 4, 1981...'

At this point Dr Fred du Plessis emerges as the central figure – at first glance a surprising figure in a business brouhaha like this, since he had spent most of his career in the academic world and then in banking. Appointed Sanlam's Managing Director in 1978, Fred du Plessis was an economist, a workaholic, a divorcee, ostensibly apolitical, a professor who had plunged into business. His previous task had been to sort out Bankorp and Trust Bank. He was appointed on 22 July 1982 to succeed Dr Wassenaar as Sanlam Chairman on 1 October – which could only mean that he was immediately in the driving seat. In this capacity, he received a letter from De Villiers telling him that Dr Wassenaar had demanded R750 000 from Gencor as compensation for alleged sabotage by Gencor officials (this probably referred to a computer contract for the University of South Africa): Wim de Villiers continued – 'A committee of Directors then decided to increase management's offer [to buy out his share at par] by R400,000 because in their opinion this would not be in Gencor's interest if its management became involved in a lawsuit with a Director of Gencor who was at the same time the Chairman of Sanlam.'

This is the version of the aggrieved De Villiers, and Dr Wassenaar was reported later that month as insisting that the Unicom disagreement had been resolved and forgotten by mid-1981 and had nothing to do with the fundamental points now at issue. But there can be little doubt that Dr Wassenaar did indeed set out to 'break' De Villiers, who not so long before had been tipped as his successor. There was an argument about share incentive schemes and boosted pension rights, with the confusing implication that Dr Coetzer, who had missed out on the scheme, was being blocked (by De Villiers) from benefiting retrospectively. A rumour was spread that De Villiers's health had cracked, with Dr Wassenaar proposing that he be succeeded in the Gencor Chair by Ted Pavitt: De Villiers protested, produced a medical certificate, and was then required to take another medical with a Sanlam doctor. There was a great deal of lobbying and rumour-mongering, both in the press and in establishment circles. Other senior figures were at risk of being caught in the crossfire: Ted Pavitt, for example, was careful to minute (on 26 January 1982) that at a meeting with Wassenaar and Dr Etienne Rousseau the previous 19 November he had emphasised he would only take over some of De Villiers's executive responsibility with the consent and agreement of De Villiers himself. Dr Rousseau, who took over from De Villiers as Deputy Chairman of Sanlam, only lasted for six months before giving up. Most Gencor executives rallied to their Chairman.

On 17 June 1982, on the very day that Du Plessis was assuring a press conference that De Villiers was doing a fine job and would not be retiring for another two years, Dr Wassenaar and Dr Coetzer were meeting De Villiers to press him to resign and enjoy an improved pension – to which De Villiers immediately replied that this was a matter not of money but of principle and of the interests of Gencor's shareholders and employees, and that to get rid of him they would have to dismiss him. In a subsequent memo to the Federale Mynbou Board, dated 6 July, De Villiers recorded that, sitting in a motor car outside DF Malan airport on 15 June, he had pleaded with Du Plessis 'to convince Dr Wassenaar that he should abandon his vendetta against me. Dr du Plessis said that he would not succeed in this...' Dr de Villiers's memo concluded: 'the integrity of Afrikaner business is at stake'.

It was a long time before South African journalists realised that the Gencor stake in Unicom and the write-off of R2 million never appeared in the Annual Report or the public balance sheet.

In later years everyone who was involved would agree that both Wassenaar and De Villiers had reached a point of personal antagonism where they were out of control. Many of the participants would be able to understand Sanlam's fundamental position – that Wim de Villiers as head of Gencor, their principal investment, was to some degree beyond their supervision – even though they might disagree with Sanlam's views.

But this is where a personality clash arising out of the faltering affairs of a minor computer bureau was – as historians like to say – the occasion rather than the cause of the famous Broedertwis of 1982. The deeper issues related, first, to the role of Sanlam as 51 per cent majority shareholder (and therefore to the protection of the interests of minority shareholders: that is to say, to the responsibilities and obligations of executive directors of a company like Gencor); second, to the different philosophy of other South African holding companies – in this case the Rembrandt group of Dr Anton Rupert, here holding 30 per cent of Gencor and liking to think that it was a partner of Sanlam; third, to the possible ambitions of that second party to outmanoeuvre Sanlam and thus win its own mining house. This was the real battle in 1982 – between Sanlam and Rupert, not between Wassenaar and De Villiers – and, again, it was waged in an unprecedentedly public way, by no one so surprisingly as Anton Rupert, normally discreet, aloof, mysterious, and not at all prone to lashing out publicly in print. The fact that Rupert (who is thought to have left the Broederbond by this time) and De Villiers were close friends would merely confirm Sanlam's worst expectations.

The first shots were fired, out of the blue, on 6 May 1982 at the Federale Mynbou Annual Meeting with a resolution proposing that the number of Directors be increased from 12 to 15. The reason for this resolution was not immediately clear to the public, and Rembrandt and Volkskas (which held a further 5 per cent) immediately opposed, arguing that the matter required a 'special resolution', meaning that it would need a 75 per cent majority as opposed to the 50 per cent required for an 'ordinary resolution'. Dr Coetzer, in the Chair, replied that the resolution would proceed as an 'ordinary resolution', and three Sanlam nominees were thereupon elected. The minority made it clear the issue would have to go to the Courts.

But why, everyone immediately asked, was Sanlam so keen to secure three more directors? Sanlam's answer was that it had to ensure that control of Gencor would never pass to the minorities, and on 17 June Dr du Plessis spelled this out at a special press conference. There was, he explained, a difference of 'control philosophy' between Sanlam and Rembrandt: 'if there is a clash of controlling philosophy the majority shareholder must dictate the situation and that is what the clash is all about'. More precisely, he went on – when asked whether Rembrandt was trying to get deeper into mining: 'All I can tell you is that we cannot accept an interpretation of what happened in 1975 as being a situation where a partnership with a consensus control gets established.'

The transcription of the press conference reveals a very puzzled team of financial journalists. What on earth was Sanlam so scared by? What had Rembrandt been doing? The answer, offered Du Plessis, was that in 1980 – five years after the takeover of Union Corporation – Rembrandt had for the first time referred to a 'partnership' having come into being in 1975 between Sanlam, Rembrandt and Volkskas: 'Sanlam reject this point of view by virtue of the fact that a shareholders' agreement which was drawn up in 1975, made no mention of such a "partnership", and consequently did not spell out the terms of such a "partnership" either... Part of a sentence in the shareholders' agreement itself' – said Dr du Plessis – 'which had read "Rembrandt shall respect the controlling position of the Sanlam group in Mynbou" was deleted, to remove any doubt as to Rembrandt's statutory right as a 25 per cent shareholder, and can in no way be taken as a positive partnership agreement. The opposite is true.' It is true that the 11 November 1975 agreement clearly shows the deletion, initialled by all parties. (The code words used for the sake of confidentiality in the draft documents have a certain charm – Federale Mynbou is 'Labrador', Sanlam is 'Giraffe', Rembrandt is 'Lynx' and Volkskas is 'Aristotelus'.) But journalists and analysts were still baffled as to why the biggest powers in Afrikaner business had gone public about a technical disagreement which would previously, surely, have been settled inside the boardroom.

The Rembrandt response came at once. It attacked Sanlam's declared intention of passing amendments which would give it the power to dismiss Directors of the Boards of controlled subsidiaries: 'Rembrandt ... regards it as important that the boards of controlled companies should be able to maintain a strong loyalty to their own company. Any diminution of their status or powers impairs their ability to look after the interests of their own company as a separate undertaking, especially where those interests may be different from those of the controlling company...'

This of course was evidently a view shared by Dr de Villiers, so the confrontation over management philosophy was inevitably linked to the personality feud: De Villiers's job was now on the line. That situation would have been difficult enough even without the manifest and unusual anger wafting from Stellenbosch, where Rembrandt – remembering, not without justification, that it was its entry into the 1975 Union Corporation take-over battle which had tilted the balance for General Mining and therefore for Sanlam – felt that it was being treated cavalierly. In a most untypical public outburst on 1 August 1982, Dr Rupert declared that 'the threat of Sanlam stretches across the country'; he compared a Director vulnerable to the power of instant dismissal which Sanlam was planning with having a hangman's noose around his neck, and denounced Sanlam for imposing 'dictatorial management'. Dr du Plessis promptly retorted that 'these are not the procedures followed by us at Sanlam ... it is possible for Dr Rupert to experience this nearer home...' All of this was reported with relish by the English-language press.

While the slanging match went on, the Court hearing was scheduled for 17 August. In all this there was a critical distinction between Gencor and Federale Mynbou. Rembrandt held only a token interest *directly* in Gencor, as did its ally Volkskas. Therefore the battle had to be won or lost *in Federale Mynbou* (which had 50,1 per cent control of Gencor) – and in Fedmyn, the joint 35 per cent holding of Rembrandt/Volkskas meant that Sanlam would not be able to win a 75 per cent majority required for a 'special' resolution. Hence the importance for Sanlam that the Court case ruled for an 'ordinary' resolution.

In the meantime the English-language press had floated a provocative theory to answer what remained, to the outsider, the mystery question – why was Sanlam so anxious, to the point of inviting nation-wide hubbub, to appoint its extra directors? 'Sanlam sources' were quoted as saying, sensationally, that Sanlam had discovered that three of its own Sanlam-appointed directors on the Federale Mynbou Board were prepared to switch allegiance and support Rembrandt to seize control of Gencor: 'In effect, Rembrandt had control of Fedmyn'! Hence the urgent need to enlarge the Federale Mynbou Board.

This 'revelation' – although later to be denied by everyone – caused a stir, so much so that Tom de Beer, the Finance Director of Gencor, in an internal memo identified the allegedly 'disloyal directors' as Wim de Villiers, Ted Pavitt and PE Rousseau and showed that their votes, together with those of the Rembrandt and Volkskas Board members, could put Sanlam in a minority of 5:6. De Beer suggested that Sanlam's fear could only be justified in view of 'Sanlam's absolute distrust of Gencor's top management'. He went on to propose a transfer of administration of Fedmyn affairs to Sanlam, and a rationalisation of the existing three-tier structure of Sanlam/Fedmyn/Gencor. (It should be noted that Tom de Beer never believed in this scenario. Nor did Marinus Daling, who was emerging as the man of the future in Sanlam. But there is good reason to think that *Fred du Plessis* believed in the danger that Rembrandt/Rupert was manoeuvring behind the scenes with the intention of seizing control of Gencor. Other senior executives were prepared to believe that Rupert would be delighted to grab Gencor, but most of them later agreed that the possibility of success was highly unrealistic.)

Meanwhile, Wim de Villiers's own position was hardening. On 4 August he wrote formally to Dr Wassenaar himself (who was scheduled to hand over the Sanlam Chair to Dr du Plessis on 1 October). He had apparently been 'instructed' at a recent Sanlam Board meeting that he *must* use his Chairman's discretionary vote at the proposed Gencor's shareholders meeting in favour of the Sanlam position. Dr de Villiers wrote: 'After consideration, I reached the conclusion that I, as Chairman, could not vote in a manner which I did not believe served Gencor's interest... I believe that [the Chairman] should exercise his own unrestricted discretion as Gencor Director and should not have to vote according to an instruction. This discretion, I believe, must be applied in Gencor's interests as a whole and not in the interests of one group of shareholders, even if it is the majority group...'

With their Chairman thus preparing himself for martyrdom, the Gencor executives were in turmoil. On 10 August, Dr de Villiers summoned them to a meeting and promised that Du Plessis and Coetzer would be there. Of the 86 people who attended, no one doubted that majority support was with their Chairman and hostile to Sanlam – and in particular to Du Plessis and Coetzer. Basil Landau, for instance, was reported as saying that the harassment directed over the past two years at Dr de Villiers was 'the most despicable thing I have heard in my life'. (Ominously, Landau was told by Coetzer after the meeting that he had made a grave mistake in speaking up.)

On 10 August De Villiers handed over the Chair to Pavitt and poured out the full detail of what he had been through. He rejected the press report that there were three 'disloyal' directors 'with absolute contempt', and pointed out that Dr Rupert had also described the allegation as ridiculous. Did Du Plessis believe it, he demanded? Dr du Plessis replied, 'No'. And was it not true, he asked Coetzer to his face, that he had been told to resign on the very day Du Plessis was publicly declaring their faith in him? Coetzer looked away and said nothing.

De Villiers must have known that he could not survive. On 25 August he announced his premature retirement. He allowed himself a detailed public statement in which he described Dr Wassenaar's 'sustained personal hostility', repeated his rejection of 'the concept that the Chief Executive Officer should be required at all times to act on the instructions of a majority shareholder, even when in his judgement this would not be in the interests of all shareholders', and reiterated that the allegations that Rembrandt with certain Sanlam-appointed Directors plotted to acquire control of Gencor were totally unfounded.

Ted Pavitt was immediately appointed to the Gencor Chair. That might have seemed the end of the affair, but the two sides continued to abuse each other. Anton Rupert used his Chairman's address at the Rembrandt Annual General Meeting on 26 August to observe that the South African business world had lost 'one of the noblest and greatest among us'. Dr Rupert conceded that 'the outcome was inevitable' ever since in February 1981 Wassenaar had told him he would use 'DuPie' to eliminate De Villiers, and went on to explain: 'We wanted to be investors with a say, not mere stooges... We always regarded ourselves as junior partners [in Gencor] and were regularly consulted until approximately March 15 1982, when at the instigation of Dr du Plessis, Sanlam embarked on a totally new dictatorial management philosophy. Thereafter, everything became different, and the vendetta against Dr de Villiers intensified...' Meanwhile, said Dr Rupert, 'the abominable lie continues to circulate that Rembrandt in collaboration with certain Sanlam-appointed Directors, plotted to seize control of Gencor... Such a thing has never been even considered, let alone discussed.'

The last chapter – surely – came on 3 November when the Rand Supreme Court refused, with costs, the Rembrandt application to declare invalid the Sanlam appointment of three extra Directors to the Federale Mynbou Board which had started the rumpus back in May. The Court ruled that an 'ordinary' resolution would suffice. Dr Rupert commented – and the significance of his words was much debated by veterans of the war: 'In view of the fact that Dr Wim de Villiers has left the Federale Mynbou group, and our action was aimed at retaining his valuable management expertise, my board will probably decide not to proceed with the action.' There was a last protest from Dr Rupert at the 14 December meeting of Gencor – a 'personal appeal' to Dr du Plessis 'not to impose this guillotine clause' which amended the Gencor Articles of Association so as to give Sanlam the power to request any Gencor Director's resignation. Dr du Plessis commented that the suggestion was presumably not intended seriously.

The postscript to the Broedertwis drama is that Dr de Villiers re-emerged in due course to do the state some service. In his days at General Mining in the 1970s, he had somehow found the time to produce famous investigative reports on Eskom, the Post Office, national minerals policy and South African Transport Services, and chaired both Atlas Aircraft and the Armaments Board. In his enforced retirement, he concentrated on a major analysis of South Africa's industrial strategy, and in September 1989 he became Minister of Administration and Privatisation, to which he later added the portfolio of Economic Co-ordination. He died in March 1991 at the age of 69, eulogised by State President FW de Klerk as 'one of South Africa's greatest sons'. According to his friends, he had a reconciliation with William Coetzer on the latter's death-bed in 1989, but he never forgave nor forgot Dr Wassenaar, who survived him by a few months.

Dr Fred du Plessis had been killed in a car crash outside Somerset West in the early hours of the morning of 18 September 1989.

O n 14 August 1982, Wim de Villiers wrote a long letter to Du Plessis: 'Dear friend – ... It is now very clear to me, especially after Tuesday's meeting [with the Gencor managers] that it will no longer be possible or desirable for me to serve on any directorate with Drs Wassenaar and Coetzer in the future. The lack of trust between us is so great that I cannot think of any way to bridge this gap... It is painful to acknowledge, after all the years of loyal co-operation in the interests of Afrikaner business, that I have lost all respect for Dr Wassenaar and Dr Coetzer...'

He then recapitulated the various points at issue over the years. He was willing to continue as Gencor's Executive Chairman until his 1984 retirement date on condition that Wassenaar and Coetzer resign and that the Gencor Board be reconstituted. He offered this as a solution; he can hardly have been hopeful. Du Plessis replied on 16 August, much more briefly, and declining to debate the issues all over again: 'As you know, Sanlam is extremely

concerned that attempts are being made to remove control of Gencor from
us... It now also appears that there are signs that you did not remain
impartial, but actually advanced Rembrandt's position. I do not wish to
elaborate on this point and hoped that it would never be necessary to do
this... It was not Sanlam's purpose to remove you from Gencor's directorate...
It is becoming increasingly clear to me that the current position in Gencor
cannot continue. The continuing friction, the leakage of information to the
press, and the continuous speculation in the press, which you are not trying to
stop, has a very serious detrimental effect... As you are aware, your
co-directors at Sanlam have encountered problems with your unwillingness to
subject yourself to majority decisions... I urge you to subject yourself to
majority decisions of the Sanlam directorate or ... to resign...
With friendly greetings,
[signed] "DuP".'

7, Rembrandt sal uitgenooi word om op sterkte van sy aandeelhouding van 25% twee verteenwoordigers in die direksie
Sanlam sal die beweging in twee sulke.
van Mynbou te benoem en sal die reg tot twee verteen-
verteenwoordigers in die toekoms steun solank Rembrandt se
woordigers behou solank sy aandeelhouding nie onder

20% van die uitgereikte kapitaal van Mynbou daal nie.

25% 37%

8. Rembrandt sal die Sanlam-groep se beheersposisie in
Mynbou respekteer en Rembrandt gee hiermee aan
Sanlam of sy genomineerde 'n eerste reg van weiering
om enige aandele wat te enige tyd in Mynbou gehou
word deur Rembrandt of sy genomineerde of enige lid
van die Rembrandt-groep, te koop, indien hulle dit
wil verkoop.

*he amendments in the original of the 11 November 1975 'Partnership Agreement'
between Sanlam, Rembrandt and Volkskas.*

CHAPTER THIRTEEN

TWO SUCCESS STORIES

Impala Platinum operates, with its neighbours, Rustenburg Platinum Mines and Lonrho (Western Platinum, Eastern Platinum), in a wide and golden valley a two-hour drive from Johannesburg, over the Magaliesberg and side-stepping Brits and the Hartbeespoort Dam. Beyond, there are the Pilanesberg range of mountains, the tourist delights of Sun City, and, eventually, the Kalahari Desert and Botswana. The weather is gloriously sub-tropical. The valley is studded with mine shafts: some 15 of them belong to Impala. There are two reefs, known as Merensky and UG2: the trick is to mine the worthwhile ore. This valley contains a mighty reservoir of platinum-bearing rock – though it must be remembered that, very roughly speaking, it takes ten tons of ore, on average, to produce an ounce of platinum, so this sort of mining has to be on a larger scale than gold.

The complication, which for years bedevilled the Impala management, is that the mine is situated on land owned by the Bafokeng tribe, territory which until the events of 1993-5 was located in the Bantustan homeland of Bophuthatswana. This was to make for a host of problems, which were further complicated by a schism in the Bafokeng chieftaincy and a stand-off between the 300 000-strong tribe and the Chief Minister of Bophuthatswana, the strong-willed Chief Lucas Mangope. Put crudely, this contributed to a problem about the fate of the Bafokeng royalties.

Indeed, there was dissatisfaction on the part of the Bafokeng regarding royalties from the beginning, because the original cession of mining rights had promised that royalties would never be less than 10 per cent of dividends paid by the company. Under South African tax law, Impala deducted its very high start-up capital expenditure in full from profits, and so, for the first few years, losses were consistently recorded and no royalties paid. (A further complication was that Ian Greig, an engaging Johannesburg intellectual, when originally sketching out on a table napkin to tribal representatives the nature of the proposed deal, had omitted fully to explain how the profits/royalties equation worked; the Bafokeng kept the napkin in evidence.) In 1973 Impala, with Greig now Chairman, recognised that this was unfortunate and set up an interim measure to pay the tribe 10 per cent of dividends as advance payments, the system to continue until amounts due under the original formula of 13 per cent of taxable income exceeded 10 per cent of dividends.

The Bafokeng received R700 000 and R900 000 respectively in 1973 and 1974. The payments were R9 million in 1979 and R15,5 million in 1980. Up to 1986 – during periods of fluctuating platinum prices – payments varied between R11,6 million and R20 million. They soared to R96,2 million in 1989. But what was happening to these substantial sums?

Legal proceedings were instituted by the Bafokeng against Impala in the Bophuthatswana High Court based on the company's refusal in 1987, at Mangope's insistence, to accede to a demand for disclosure of certain information related to mining operations. On 30 May 1989, Justice Smith dismissed the tribe's application. Despite an inevitable clouding of Impala's relationship with the Bafokeng as a result of the legal proceedings, the company continued its routine dealings with the tribe. Management could hardly be unaware that, had the Bafokeng succeeded in court, Impala's right to continue its mining operations would have been terminated.

The chieftaincy of the Bafokeng had a history of dissension and internal power struggles. In 1959 Chief Edward Molotlegi had been ceremonially installed; in 1963 he married a daughter of Tshekedi Khama, Regent of the Bamangwata in the neighbouring state which was to become independent Botswana. Chief Edward became identified in opposition to Bophuthatswana's Chief Mangope, and, in 1988, fled into political exile in Botswana, claiming that he feared for his life. His brother George – who had once worked for Impala – was appointed Acting Chief in his place.

With Acting Chief George in power, concerted efforts were launched by Impala to restore its relationship with the Bafokeng. These efforts soon bore fruit. In August 1990, the new Impala Chairman, Brian Gilbertson, reported to shareholders that the Councillors and Headmen of the Bafokeng tribe had unanimously resolved to ask the President of Bophuthatswana (as Trustee of the Tribe) to enter into contracts with Impala, upon terms that had been negotiated over an extended period. These new contracts, executed during March and April 1990, included the extension of Impala's right to mine the existing lease area until the reserves were exhausted; acquisition by Impala of the exclusive right to prospect the adjoining area known as The Deeps, and an option to apply for a mining lease there; an increased royalty of 16 per cent in respect of taxable income attributable to mining The

Deeps; and the right of the Bafokeng to subscribe for up to 7 per cent of Impala equity.

Initially, although Impala would have preferred not to import labour to the mines, the local Bafokeng did not want to work underground. (There is a persistent tale that the Tswana refuse to work at a depth greater than the burial places of their ancestors.) So, although the Homeland government wished to promote local jobs, the company was forced to employ other manpower, partly from Malawi and partly from Lesotho. This led to a series of serious faction fights and tribal confrontations in the mid-1970s, and it was to be years before the Tswana were persuaded to sign on – and even then they were happier in the processing and smelting plants on the surface.

The more positive aspect of the location of the mines inside Bophutha-tswana was that apartheid's restrictive labour regulations did not apply. In 1977, for instance, the independence of Bophuthatswana meant that the South African laws restricting such things as blasting certificates for black miners fell aside, and from then on the company was able to move ahead of the mines inside the Republic, despite the opposition of the white Mineworkers Union. The other side of that coin was that the black National Union of Minework-ers, which made dramatic strides throughout the country in the 1980s, was excluded from the Bophuthatswana homeland. This was a recipe for years of trouble.

Outside the Homeland, there had been a serious dispute at the Springs Refinery in 1984 when the company dismissed 1 300 workers – 80 per cent of the total. These events should be seen in the context of the Group's evolving attitude to black unionism in the mid-1980s. Even more serious, the NUM attempted recruitment at the mines in 1986 – which was a turbulent year for the whole country – and brought on the firing of 23 000 workers, the largest such action ever seen in South Africa. Curiously, Impala was not affected by the 1987 NUM industry-wide strike, but that may have been be-cause the NUM's role inside Bophuthatswana had been dealt a serious blow – and the local Tswana were at last in a majority in the labour force. But 1991 brought a long series of confrontations. From March to Novem-ber there were serious riots, go-slows and underground sit-ins, bombs and necklacings, faction fights, the near-murder of a white General Manager, and stay-aways, arson, and more rioting. Everyone realised that Impala's man-agement was caught up in a politically inspired NUM bid to undermine the Bophuthatswana government of President Mangope; the ANC was taking on Mangope's Bantustan government and using the NUM as its local arm, presenting Impala with evidence that it had 60 per cent signed-up membership at the company. Thirty-five men were killed in the course of the nine months.

The Impala management thereupon set up a major policy review and many changes were instituted in advance of the appointment, in 1992, of a three-man independent Commission to investigate the violence. The Commissioners did not hesitate to identify the central issue: they concluded that 'housing migrant mineworkers in high-density, heavily-regimented compounds is a shocking practice ... hostel life is both a repressed and deprived form of existence ... once any challenge is introduced into such an environment, the mechanisms of social control threaten to break down...' The Commission said that these fundamental abuses were aggravated by a primitive system of labour relations, no recognition of the majority union (the NUM), recognition of a minority rival union (the Bophuthatswana National Union of Mine Workers), very low levels of trust, no effective internal dispute-resolving mechanisms, no external mechanisms, and an ineffective mine security system. Bophuthatswana's labour legislation was designed not to regulate conflict but to suppress it. However, the Commission also criticised the NUM.

The function of the Commission, in effect, was to confirm the shift in management policy. A Workers' Representative Body had already been elected, at the company's instigation, to negotiate the mid-1992 wage settlement, while management and NUM manoeuvred towards a relationship which could survive Bophuthatswana's refusal to recognise the union. Impala's new management under Michael McMahon (who had worked for the competitor, Rustenburg Platinum, until 1988, when he had come to Gencor as Chief Engineer and then Technical Director) had decided that it must dissociate itself from Mangope, and went so far as to pay directly to the NUM the union dues it would have received if it had been allowed to operate in the Homeland – which led to some stormy sessions for the top Impala executives with a furious Mangope. With the hindsight of history, it was clear that the Bantustan experiment was approaching its end. And McMahon remembers the surreal atmosphere in the Bophuthatswana capital of Mmabatho in those days – 'Alice in Wonderland stuff, you were through the looking glass as soon as your plane touched down'. Slowly the NUM – which had been so infuriated and insulted by Gencor in 1986 – and Impala learned to trust each other. It was an example of the traditional mining house coming to terms with a fast-evolving political transformation, and it paid off.

Remarkably, 1993 saw no strikes, no disturbances, in a year when South Africa was swept by nation-wide and politically associated labour unrest. This extraordinary tranquillity extended into 1994, when President Mangope was overthrown. That had its implications for Impala and for the Bafokeng: in August 1994 Acting Chief George's appointment was set aside. This, combined with the reincorporation of Bophuthatswana into South Africa earlier that year, paved the way for Chief Edward's return from exile.

A complex, confidential mediation process between Impala and the Bafokeng had already begun. The Chief, however, appeared to favour another court case. It was he who had previously challenged the existing agreement and had looked into alternative leasing arrangements for The Deeps with Bafokeng Minerals, an associated company of Keeley Granite. The chief's attitude had in the meantime been exacerbated by the acquisition in 1991 by Impala of those rights, such as they were, from Bafokeng Minerals as an adjunct to the acquisition of Keeley Granite itself by Gencor.

Throughout these awkward years, Impala had to concentrate on developing output in response to soaring world demand, not just from the automobile industry but from Japan in particular, where there was an extraordinary boom in the jewellery sector with per capita consumption rising five-fold between 1968 and 1975. Such a dependence on fashion was, of course, dangerous, and would inevitably slump, but by the mid-1970s Japanese car manufacturers had to conform with US international clean air requirements, and, after complex negotiations, in the late 1970s a major relationship had been achieved between Impala and Nissan.

There had been plenty of problems at the mine and also in the transit system (there were a couple of major heists of the metal, at London's Heathrow airport and in Nairobi, for example). But a more serious disaster occurred in 1974 when, following heavy rains at the mine, a slimes dam overflowed and set up an unstoppable mudslide. The tragedy was that the slurry swept aside various surface installations and engulfed the Number 4 shaft: 14 men were killed, and it was a miracle there were not more casualties. It was a reminder that platinum mining – generally thought to be less dangerous than gold mines – sometimes takes its revenge.

The early 1980s were good years. Catalytic converters were increasingly *de rigueur* in the industrial world, and jewellery and investment demand reached new heights. Impala's production, from its 100 000 ounce target of the 1960s, grew to one million ounces by the mid-1980s, but these successes were overshadowed by a period when the company seemed to lose its momentum and also its metallurgical pre-eminence and languished under a blanket of secrecy even more dense than that which normally operates in the platinum industry. After the arrival of Derek Keys and Brian Gilbertson, Impala refocused, firstly on the Karee Mine, across the Bophuthatswana/South African border: almost immediately Impala did a deal with Lonrho, on 1 October 1989, merging Karee with Western Platinum and in return securing a 27 per cent interest in the merged mine and in Lonhro's Eastern Platinum. There were obvious technical synergies in the merger. (The London and Johannesburg Stock Exchanges were frequently swept with rumours of a more fundamental relationship between Lonrho and Gencor, and the two groups did in fact begin to talk.)

Secondly, Impala, which was becoming concerned about the scale of its future reserves, took a majority holding in Messina Limited in 1989, which had platinum rights in the Homeland of Lebowa. (Sanlam had a large interest in Messina and was influential in the deal.) That may have been a miscalculation. With the subsequent faltering of the platinum price, the Messina project would be mothballed a couple of years later, as would the Crocodile River Mine near Brits (Impala had taken 38 per cent of Barplats in 1991). More important, as it turned out, was the successful acquisition in 1990 of The Deeps, the Bafokeng area next door to and east of the existing Impala mining area. Here was the future: The Deeps could be mined from the existing workings, and by the mid-1990s the development was well under way.

Impala reckoned it could weather the grave slump of the platinum market in 1991-2. The problem, in essence, was that although world demand had increased enormously, production had gone up much more – the in-

Platinum

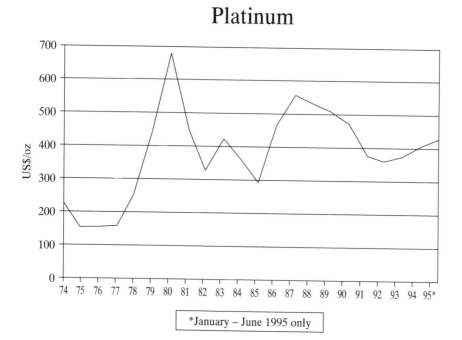

*January – June 1995 only

181

ternational platinum companies had all set up major expansion programmes in 1989-90 but the new capacity came on stream ahead of the expected post-recession demand and, to make things worse, there was gloomy talk of a cutback in PGM demand for catalytic converters. The price fell steeply in 1993, Impala reduced stock, tightened cost controls, mothballed mines – and not so soon afterwards, as the price moved up to $430 an ounce in mid-1995, declared that it would aim to hold production to 1,2 million ounces by 1998. That was a long way from the 100 000 ounce projections, seemingly so bold, of Hugh Monro, Byng Jackson and Ian Greig just one generation before. And in mid-1995 there came an announcement to surprise the markets: that Gencor and Lonrho – as we shall see – had done a deal.

Of course, gold has always been South Africa's glamour mineral. Coal has been the poor relation, unromantic, undramatic, and surely rather boring. But the history of the century reveals how coal has steadily crept up on gold in terms of economic importance – in exports, in share of GDP, in employment, in capital invested, tortoise to hare. Gencor, more than any other group, exemplifies that drama.

Gencor inherited its strong position in coal from General Mining in 1976, just as General Mining had found that coal was the most valuable dowry that Federale Mynbou brought to the 1964 marriage. But in the years since 1985, Gencor focused on coal more intensely, and more successfully, than any of its competitors, because it grasped that coal had a double importance: first, the country's reserves were such that, if the 'political discount' was overcome, there was a prospect of major exports, and second, the coal could be turned into cheap electric power which could be used to set up major beneficiation industries which Gencor intended to dominate. Small wonder that some of Gencor's most effective executives over 30 years had been associated with the development of this so-called poor relation.

Federale Mynbou, as we have seen, built its early reputation and its first-division potential as a mining house on its coal operations. Since they had no apparent hope of a gold mine, William Coetzer and Tom Muller concentrated on winning Eskom contracts: in 1963 their two principal mines were supplying Komati power station (from Blinkpan Colliery) and Ingagane (from Kilbarchan). They were developing mechanical mining and coal processing expertise and it has been suggested that the terrible tragedy at Clydesdale's Coalbrook Colliery – the year Fedmyn moved into Clydesdale – in the Free State in January 1960, which killed 435 men, reinforced Trans-Natal's reputation for mechanical proficiency because it showed the company responding more rapidly than more conservative groups to the consequent shortfall in the nation's coal output. Most important of all, Muller and Coetzer had persuaded Harley Drayton they were his heirs. The result was Trans-Natal Coal Corporation, which by the time of the 1964 acquisition of General Mining by Federale Mynbou was one of South Africa's biggest coal mining companies. Coal now represented 20 per cent of General Mining's income; gold had slipped to 29 per cent! That did not mean that the future looked easy, but by the mid-1970s, following the energy crisis, fast-moving coal technological changes and the development of a serious export capacity with particular hopes of Japan (the Richards Bay Coal Terminal was opened in 1974), the prospects seemed to brighten.

By the later 1970s Trans-Natal had more Eskom contracts on its hands: in 1967 Usutu had been commissioned to supply six million tons per annum to Eskom's Camden power station and in 1970 Optimum was set up to supply Hendrina by 1974. The giant Matla mine, a joint project with GFSA, started operating in 1976. The point about these early Eskom projects was that the price was forced very low and the coal to be delivered was very low-grade: in the words of George Clark, a senior Fedmyn/General Mining coal executive for many years: 'Let's face it, you were dead if you didn't get an Eskom contract. At that time coal wasn't just moribund, you had to exhume the corpse...' Eskom was in a perfect position to demand ultra-cheap coal from huge, dedicated mines, situated literally next door to the generators. There was no alternative customer, but these were 30-40 year contracts with an assured, if low, profit built into them. It was the coal managers of this generation who were beginning to face up to a problem, which was that while everyone agreed that South Africa had immense reserves of coal – perhaps one-tenth of the world's – it was largely low-grade and unexportable.

Optimum was to be particularly interesting. It was intended to be underground but was to become open-cast, with McAlpine coming in as partner to provide open-cast expertise, and itself to be acquired much later by Gencor. There was also a plan for a synthetic fuels project, a favourite of Dr Wim de Villiers, which, perhaps fortunately, never came off. By 1983, Trans-Natal was producing 30 million tons per annum, 60 per cent of which was committed to Eskom, which had been engaged in a colossal expansion of capacity over the previous decade. These Eskom projections were soon to be seen as absurdly and expensively over-ambitious, but the simple fact is that the planners were working to inflated economic growth projections, something like seven per cent; in an industry which had to plan 10 years ahead, it was not so surprising that the economists failed to allow for national growth rates which were to be hammered by international hostility. At the time the scale of these Eskom contracts beggared anything the country had seen before. Optimum, for instance, was scheduled to produce

12 million tons per annum by 1985, half of it for Eskom, at a capital cost of R280 million. There was serious talk among managers that the Group must be prepared to produce 100 million tons per annum of coal by the end of the century.

But these same managers could hardly ignore the wider, political dimension as unrest swept the country and the international sanctions campaign tightened. Trans-Natal's Chairman, Steve Ellis, was quoted in May 1986: 'We are now seeing a return to the situation that existed some five years ago when South African coal was going onto the international market at a so-called political discount – at that time some $5 a ton. A lot of us did a lot of hard work to eradicate that situation but we're coming under the same kind of pressures again. Consumers are concerned not only about the situation here on work stoppages and industrial relations matters, but also about union action in their own countries on imports of South African coal and possible action by their governments.' Ellis candidly admitted that Gencor was lucky in that it had no specific customers in Denmark or France, where cutbacks on South African imports were in force. The size of the danger ahead becomes very clear when it is remembered that at this time other low-cost producers were emerging – for example Colombia – while the directors of Richards Bay coal export terminal, representing the industry, were debating whether to expand to 70 million tons capacity for the years ahead.

At the same time another very different row was going on, to do with Trans-Natal's opening of an anthracite mine in Zululand, just a few kilometres from the Umfolozi Game Reserve. In this case – unlike future arguments with the environmentalists in Zululand – Gencor and the Natal Parks Board managed to work out a happy enough compromise. By the mid-1980s, Trans-Natal was selling 36 million tons of coal from 11 collieries and earning a net income of R110 million.

Coal was bound to be as vulnerable to the world economic cycle as Gencor's other commodity products, but the gloomy and unsurprising situation in the recession of the early 1990s was exacerbated when Eskom's over-capacity came home to roost. Only 22 000 MW of the installed capacity of 36 000 MW were required and power stations were being mothballed and closed down, including Camden, Ingagane, and Komati. More relevant (because the long-term contracts protected the collieries against serious losses), Eskom's future expansion plans looked likely to be set on hold. The immediate effect on Trans-Natal was that Kilbarchan Colliery was closed, Usutu's underground expansion mothballed, Delmas downsized, Ermelo written down. Managers came to terms with the fact that there would be no more Eskom contracts for years. But the silver lining was that Trans-Natal's long-term emphasis on export markets was paying off, just as had happened a few years before: the Group was the country's biggest coal exporter in 1992 (11,6 million tons) and the highest proportional exporter (43 per cent of total sales went overseas). The emphasis was still on expansion – and that was to come dramatically, and controversially, in 1994.

The new generation of Gencor executives who were brought in by Derek Keys in the late 1980s to succeed Steve Ellis and Graham Thompson were spearheaded by Brian Gilbertson and perhaps had a clearer view than their predecessors, who had spent their careers in a lower-scale, more domestic industry. Trans-Natal was understood to be in trouble: apart from various specific problems which would have to be sorted out, the company was too small (which had various implications including the fact that it had only a minor voice in the Richards Bay terminal), and the domestic market, principally Eskom, was stalled. In a Group which Keys was educating to focus on growth, something had to be done. Gilbertson came in as Chairman and the turning-round of the coal division was soon to be described as the take-off platform for his subsequent career in Gencor. He brought in Mike Salamon, who would become Trans-Natal Managing Director in 1989. Their team worked out that there were only two ways to achieve growth in those difficult days of the late 1980s: to buy internal growth (which could only mean to take over Randcoal), and to go offshore. Either or both.

The rationale for the former was to agree that, now that the company had sorted out productivity problems and suchlike, there was indeed a useful long-term business in the domestic market: that is, in power stations. But – since Eskom was not building new ones – that meant buying into companies which already had long-term Eskom contracts: for example Randcoal, which had major collieries like Khutala supplying Kendal power station. (From that point it might be possible to persuade Eskom there were ways of developing power demand through major industrial projects, so long as the electricity price could be kept low.) The rationale for the latter, off-shore possibility was to admit that South Africa's reserves of high-grade, exportable coal were finite, and to conclude that as soon as South Africa sorted out its politics and was permitted to venture overseas again, then Trans-Natal/Gencor would be prospecting and buying around the world, in South America, Australia, Indonesia, wherever. Both of these options were taken up over the next few years.

Rand Mines, once one of the greatest of all mining houses, as part of the Corner House group of the most famous of the Randlords, had been in decline for years. Barlows had never really felt at ease in the mining industry and, after the unbundling of Barlow Rand in 1993, Rand Mines' sole asset was 73 per cent of Randcoal. Without exception, the Trans-Natal/Gencor executives of the past generation had identified Randcoal as 'the parentless child' whose merger with Trans-Natal would make extreme, synergistic sense. A lot of research was done over four years analysing how the two companies could combine in both domestic and export markets. So when Old Mutual, holding 30 per cent of Rand Mines, was persuaded that it made sense to stay in coal so long as it could improve the industry's efficiency, and, in effect, invited tenders for Randcoal, Gencor's Brian Gilbertson and the newly recruited Finance Director, Mick Davis, saw their chance and pounced. Before the rest of Johannesburg had woken up, in the closing days of August 1994, Gencor had grabbed control of Randcoal through a reverse takeover (folding Trans-Natal into Randcoal – Randcoal was to take over Trans-Natal in a share swap of 109 Randcoal for 100 Trans-Natal; Trans-Natal would therefore hold a controlling 49,1 per cent of Randcoal, rising to 54,1 per cent of the merged firm; Trans-Natal would have management control). The result, quite simply, was that Gencor had overnight become the world's third largest coal producer, and the world's biggest exporter of steam coal.

Certain other groups were not best happy with the manner and style of the deal. Liberty Life muttered about inadequate discussions with Rand Mines shareholders, and JCI did not deny that it was disappointed; but Gencor insisted the deal was done. 'The omelette's been made,' Brian Gilbertson was quoted as saying – and there could hardly be any doubt that Rand Mines' biggest shareholder, Old Mutual, had gone along with, and indeed initiated, the Gencor offer.

The implication of the takeover, creating a R5,5 billion coal producer which was soon to be named Ingwe, the Zulu name for leopard, could not be denied, coming as it did just a few weeks after Gencor had bought Billiton. If Billiton had turned Gencor into a world leader in aluminium, Randcoal brought Gencor into the top ranks of the world's coal business.

This could only mean that the emphasis of Gencor's coal operations would turn international: Ingwe had 12 mines in South Africa; combined exports would be 24 million tonnes mainly of steam coal, and the new company would have an allocation of 41,3 per cent of the Richards Bay Coal Terminal capacity (where Anglo American's Amcoal had previously had the loudest voice). Still, 45 per cent of output of the combined Group would go to Eskom. Various mining operations would in due course be rationalised, consolidated or combined. Gencor explained that it expected world demand for steam coal to grow by 50 per cent over the next 10 years – this was a bold projection, some thought, but it took account of the economic take-off of the Pacific/Asian economies, the continuing decline of the European coal industry,

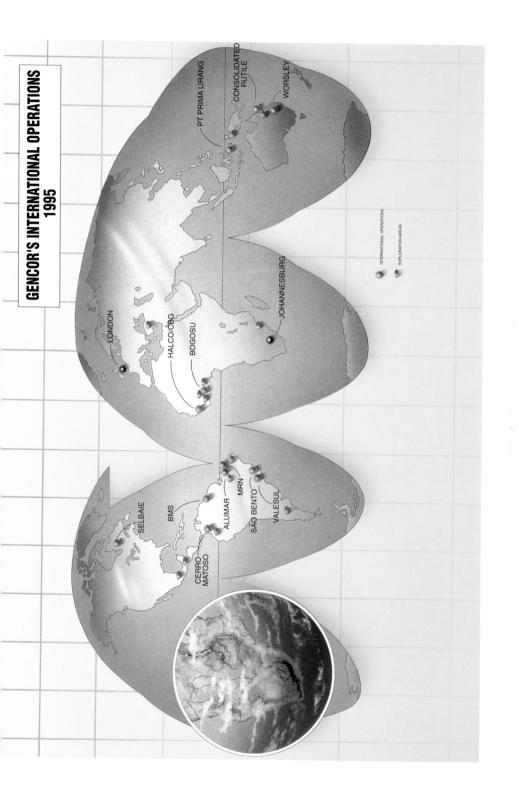

GENCOR'S INTERNATIONAL OPERATIONS 1995

LONDON

SELBAIE

BMS

CERRO MATOSO

HALCO/CBG

BOGOSU

ALUMAR

MRN

SÃO BENTO

VALESUL

JOHANNESBURG

PT PRIMA LIRANG

CONSOLIDATED RUTILE

WORSLEY

INTERNATIONAL OPERATIONS

EXPLORATION AREAS

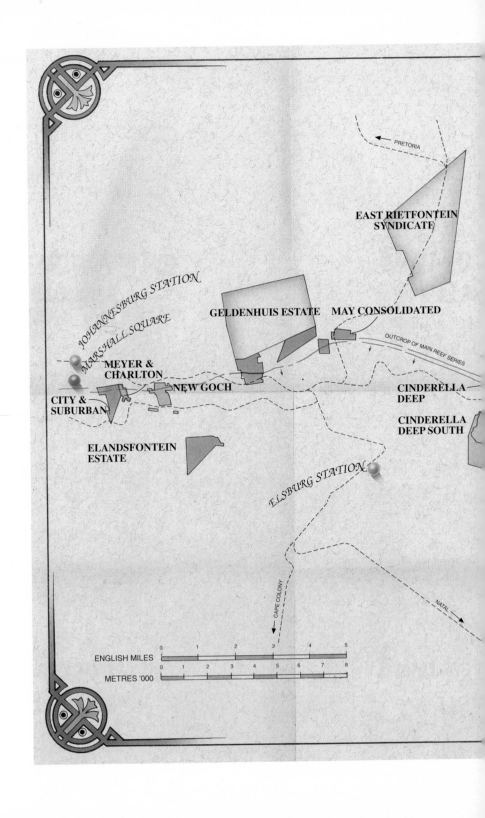

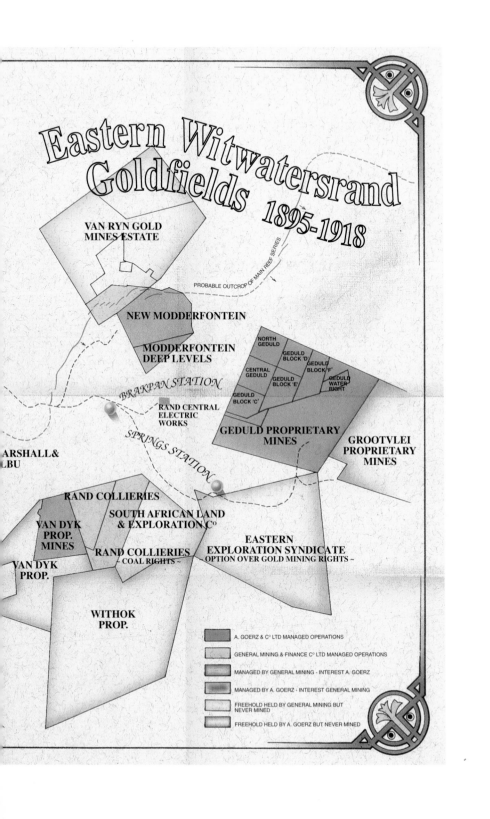

Eastern Witwatersrand Goldfields 1895-1918

VAN RYN GOLD MINES ESTATE

PROBABLE OUTCROP OF MAIN REEF SERIES

NEW MODDERFONTEIN

MODDERFONTEIN DEEP LEVELS

NORTH GEDULD

GEDULD BLOCK 'D'

CENTRAL GEDULD

GEDULD BLOCK 'F'

GEDULD BLOCK 'E'

GEDULD WATER RIGHT

GEDULD BLOCK 'C'

BRAKPAN STATION

RAND CENTRAL ELECTRIC WORKS

SPRINGS STATION

GEDULD PROPRIETARY MINES

GROOTVLEI PROPRIETARY MINES

ARSHALL & LBU

RAND COLLIERIES

VAN DYK PROP. MINES

SOUTH AFRICAN LAND & EXPLORATION C°

VAN DYK PROP.

RAND COLLIERIES ~ COAL RIGHTS ~

EASTERN EXPLORATION SYNDICATE ~ OPTION OVER GOLD MINING RIGHTS ~

WITHOK PROP.

A. GOERZ & C° LTD MANAGED OPERATIONS

GENERAL MINING & FINANCE C° LTD MANAGED OPERATIONS

MANAGED BY GENERAL MINING - INTEREST A. GOERZ

MANAGED BY A. GOERZ - INTEREST GENERAL MINING

FREEHOLD HELD BY GENERAL MINING BUT NEVER MINED

FREEHOLD HELD BY A. GOERZ BUT NEVER MINED

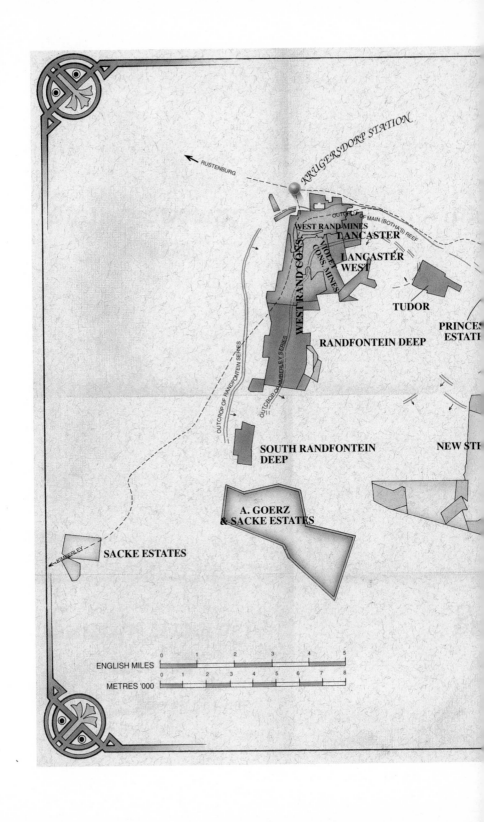

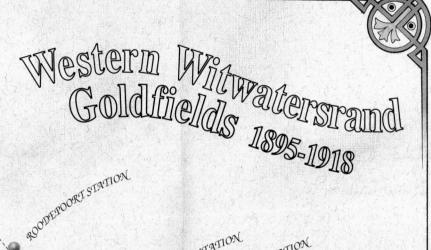

Western Witwatersrand Goldfields 1895-1918

ROODEPOORT STATION

NEW FLORIDA STATION

MARAISBURG STATION

JOHANNESBURG STATION

ROODEPOORT UNITED MAIN REEF

ROODEPOORT CENTRAL DEEP

ROODEPOORT

AURORA WEST UNITED

RAND CENTRAL ORE REDUCTION WORKS

MARSHALL SQUARE

OUTCROP OF KIMBERLEY SERIES

OUTCROP OF MAIN REEF

RAILWAY LINE

DURBAN ROODEPOORT DEEP

NATAL

CAPE PROVINCE

A. GOERZ & Cº LTD MANAGED OPERATIONS

GENERAL MINING & FINANCE Cº LTD MANAGED OPERATIONS

MANAGED BY GENERAL MINING - INTEREST A. GOERZ

MANAGED BY A. GOERZ - INTEREST GENERAL MINING

FREEHOLD HELD BY GENERAL MINING BUT NEVER MINED

FREEHOLD HELD BY A. GOERZ BUT NEVER MINED

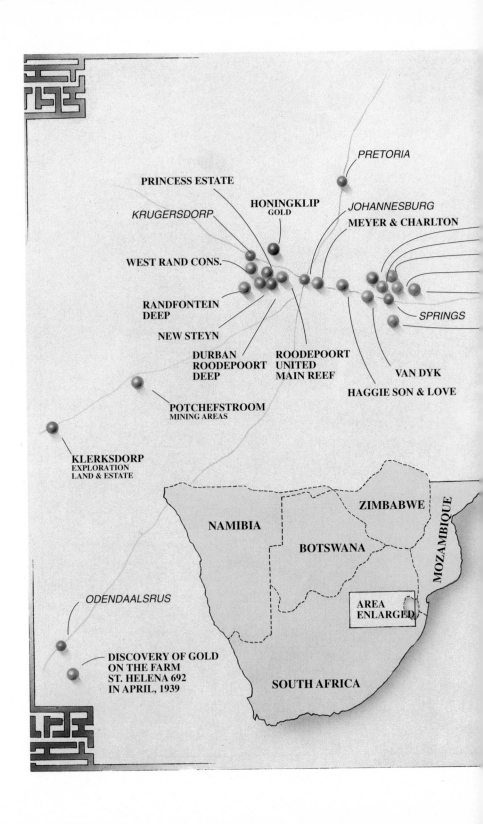

PRINCESS ESTATE

KRUGERSDORP

HONINGKLIP
GOLD

PRETORIA

JOHANNESBURG

MEYER & CHARLTON

WEST RAND CONS.

RANDFONTEIN
DEEP

SPRINGS

NEW STEYN

DURBAN
ROODEPOORT
DEEP

ROODEPOORT
UNITED
MAIN REEF

VAN DYK

HAGGIE SON & LOVE

POTCHEFSTROOM
MINING AREAS

KLERKSDORP
EXPLORATION
LAND & ESTATE

ZIMBABWE

NAMIBIA

BOTSWANA

MOZAMBIQUE

ODENDAALSRUS

AREA
ENLARGED

DISCOVERY OF GOLD
ON THE FARM
ST. HELENA 692
IN APRIL, 1939

SOUTH AFRICA

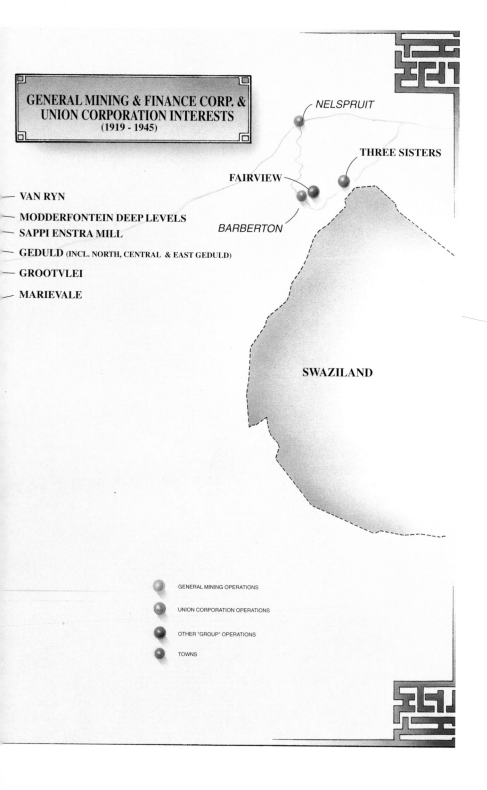

GENERAL MINING & FINANCE CORP. & UNION CORPORATION INTERESTS
(1919 - 1945)

NELSPRUIT

THREE SISTERS

FAIRVIEW

BARBERTON

— VAN RYN

— MODDERFONTEIN DEEP LEVELS
— SAPPI ENSTRA MILL

— GEDULD (INCL. NORTH, CENTRAL & EAST GEDULD)

— GROOTVLEI

— MARIEVALE

SWAZILAND

GENERAL MINING OPERATIONS

UNION CORPORATION OPERATIONS

OTHER "GROUP" OPERATIONS

TOWNS

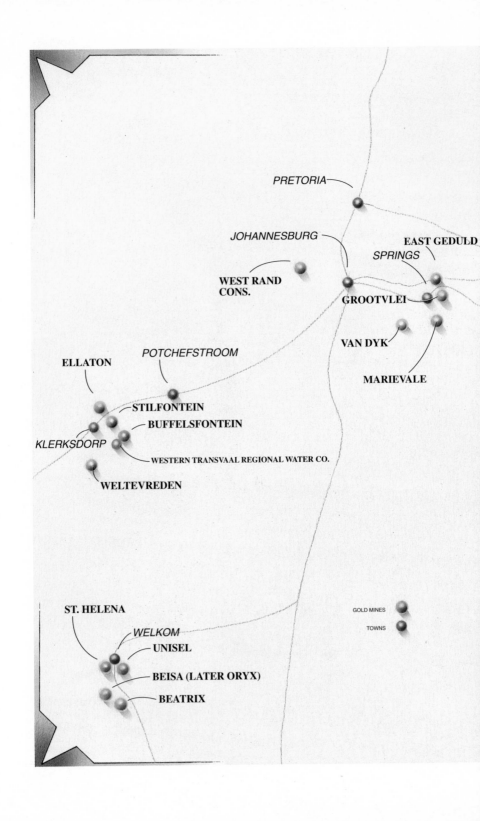

PRETORIA

JOHANNESBURG

EAST GEDULD

SPRINGS

WEST RAND CONS.

GROOTVLEI

POTCHEFSTROOM

VAN DYK

ELLATON

MARIEVALE

STILFONTEIN

BUFFELSFONTEIN

KLERKSDORP

WESTERN TRANSVAAL REGIONAL WATER CO.

WELTEVREDEN

GOLD MINES

TOWNS

ST. HELENA

WELKOM

UNISEL

BEISA (LATER ORYX)

BEATRIX

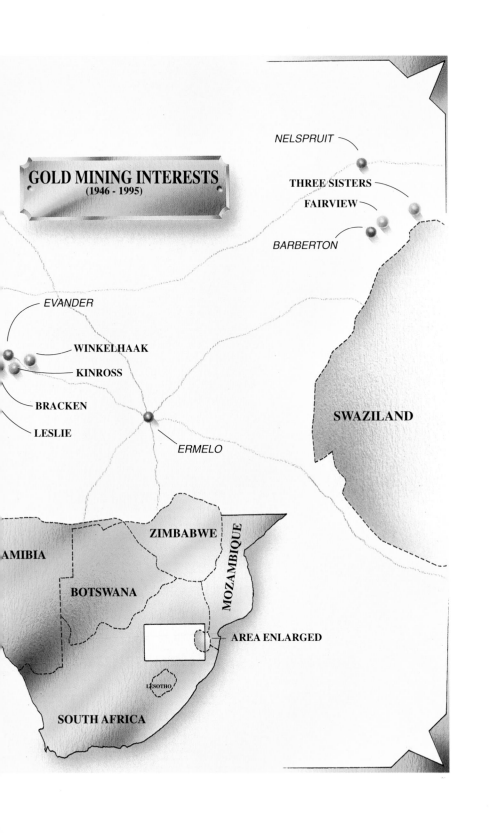

GOLD MINING INTERESTS
(1946 - 1995)

NELSPRUIT

THREE SISTERS

FAIRVIEW

BARBERTON

EVANDER

WINKELHAAK

KINROSS

BRACKEN

LESLIE

ERMELO

SWAZILAND

ZIMBABWE

MOZAMBIQUE

AMIBIA

BOTSWANA

AREA ENLARGED

LESOTHO

SOUTH AFRICA

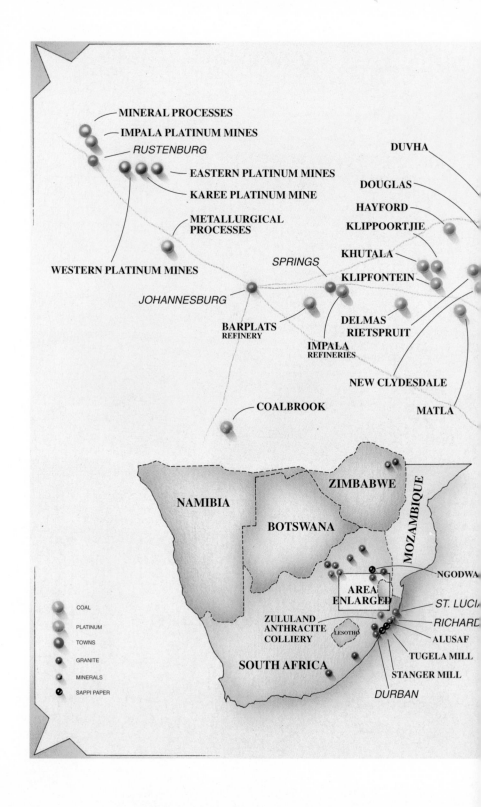

MINERAL PROCESSES

IMPALA PLATINUM MINES

RUSTENBURG

DUVHA

EASTERN PLATINUM MINES

KAREE PLATINUM MINE

DOUGLAS

HAYFORD

KLIPPOORTJIE

METALLURGICAL
PROCESSES

KHUTALA

SPRINGS

KLIPFONTEIN

WESTERN PLATINUM MINES

JOHANNESBURG

BARPLATS
REFINERY

DELMAS
RIETSPRUIT

IMPALA
REFINERIES

NEW CLYDESDALE

MATLA

COALBROOK

ZIMBABWE

NAMIBIA

MOZAMBIQUE

BOTSWANA

NGODWA

AREA
ENLARGED

ST. LUCIA

RICHARD

COAL

PLATINUM

TOWNS

GRANITE

MINERALS

SAPPI PAPER

ZULULAND
ANTHRACITE
COLLIERY

LESOTHO

ALUSAF

TUGELA MILL

SOUTH AFRICA

STANGER MILL

DURBAN

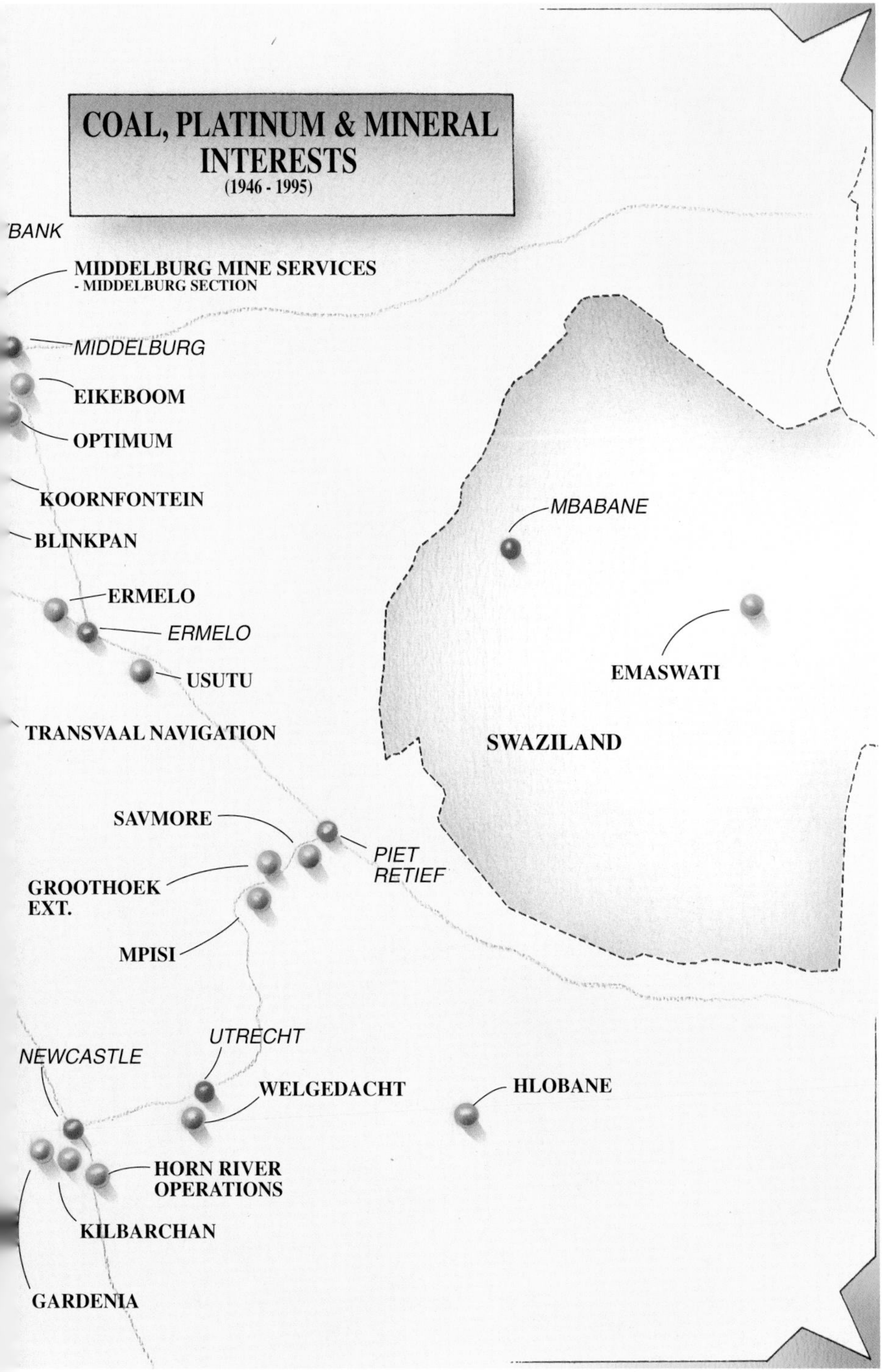

COAL, PLATINUM & MINERAL INTERESTS
(1946 - 1995)

BANK

MIDDELBURG MINE SERVICES
- MIDDELBURG SECTION

MIDDELBURG

EIKEBOOM

OPTIMUM

KOORNFONTEIN

BLINKPAN

ERMELO

ERMELO

USUTU

TRANSVAAL NAVIGATION

SAVMORE

GROOTHOEK EXT.

MPISI

PIET RETIEF

MBABANE

EMASWATI

SWAZILAND

UTRECHT

NEWCASTLE

WELGEDACHT

HLOBANE

HORN RIVER OPERATIONS

KILBARCHAN

GARDENIA

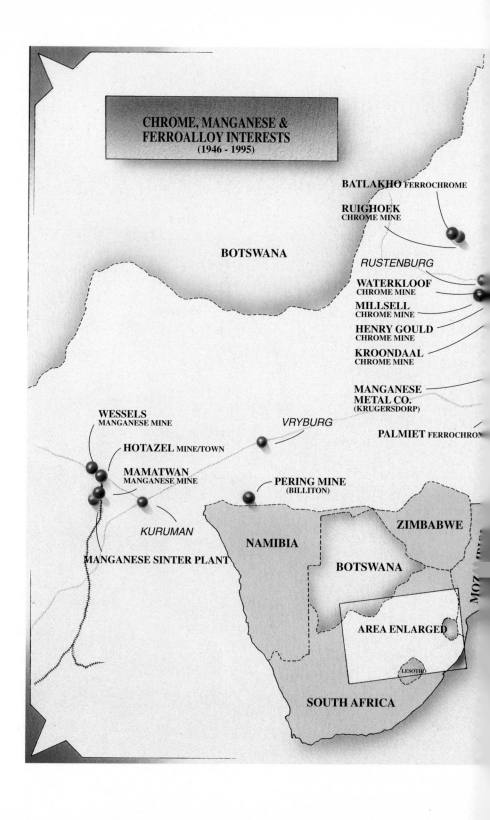

CHROME, MANGANESE &
FERROALLOY INTERESTS
(1946 - 1995)

BATLAKHO FERROCHROME

RUIGHOEK
CHROME MINE

BOTSWANA

RUSTENBURG

WATERKLOOF
CHROME MINE

MILLSELL
CHROME MINE

HENRY GOULD
CHROME MINE

KROONDAAL
CHROME MINE

MANGANESE
METAL CO.
(KRUGERSDORP)

WESSELS
MANGANESE MINE

VRYBURG

PALMIET FERROCHROM

HOTAZEL MINE/TOWN

MAMATWAN
MANGANESE MINE

PERING MINE
(BILLITON)

ZIMBABWE

KURUMAN

NAMIBIA

BOTSWANA

MANGANESE SINTER PLANT

AREA ENLARGED

LESOTHO

SOUTH AFRICA

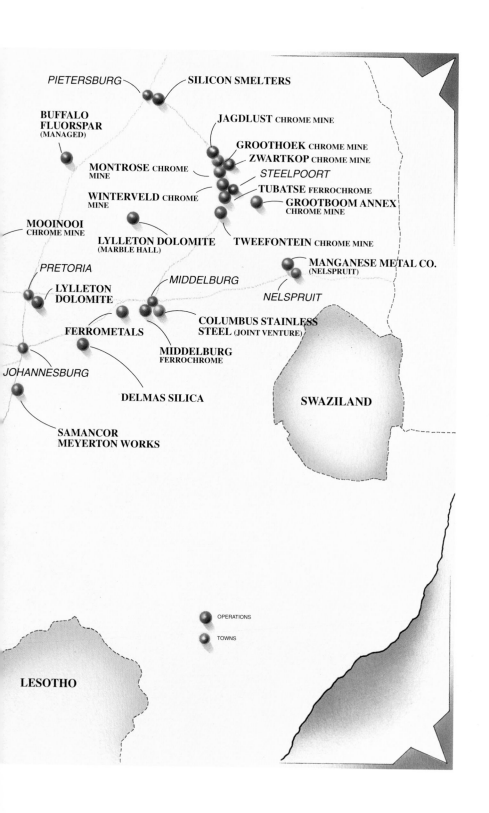

PIETERSBURG — SILICON SMELTERS

BUFFALO
FLUORSPAR
(MANAGED)

JAGDLUST CHROME MINE

GROOTHOEK CHROME MINE
ZWARTKOP CHROME MINE
MONTROSE CHROME
MINE
STEELPOORT

WINTERVELD CHROME
MINE
TUBATSE FERROCHROME
GROOTBOOM ANNEX
CHROME MINE

MOOINOOI
CHROME MINE

LYLLETON DOLOMITE
(MARBLE HALL)
TWEEFONTEIN CHROME MINE

PRETORIA
MANGANESE METAL CO.
(NELSPRUIT)
MIDDELBURG
LYLLETON
DOLOMITE
NELSPRUIT

FERROMETALS
COLUMBUS STAINLESS
STEEL (JOINT VENTURE)

MIDDELBURG
FERROCHROME
JOHANNESBURG

DELMAS SILICA

SWAZILAND

SAMANCOR
MEYERTON WORKS

OPERATIONS

TOWNS

LESOTHO

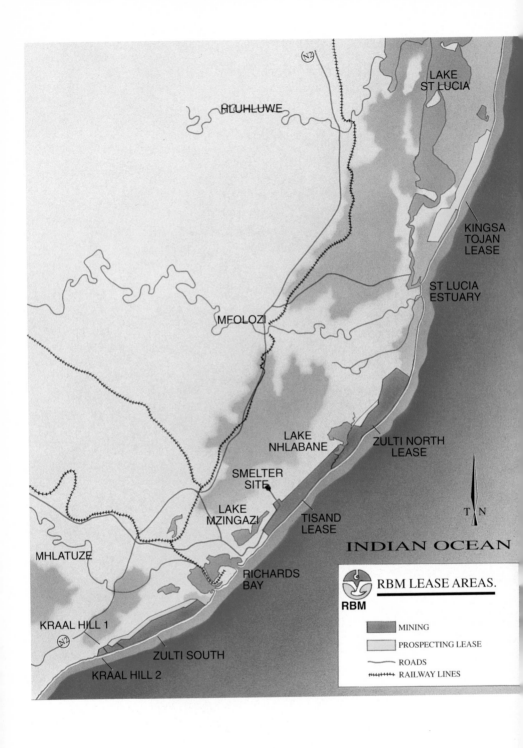

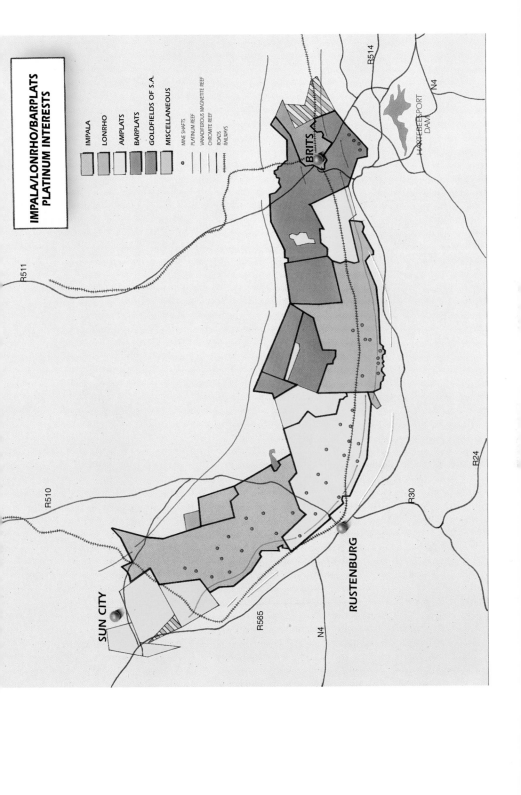

**IMPALA/LONRHO/BARPLATS
PLATINUM INTERESTS**

IMPALA
LONRHO
AMPLATS
BARPLATS
GOLDFIELDS OF S.A.
MISCELLANEOUS

MINE SHAFTS
PLATINUM REEF
VANADIFEROUS MAGNETITE REEF
CHROMITE REEF
ROADS
RAILWAYS

SUN CITY

RUSTENBURG

BRITS

HARTEBEESPOORT
DAM

R511

R510

R565

N4

R30

R24

R514

N4

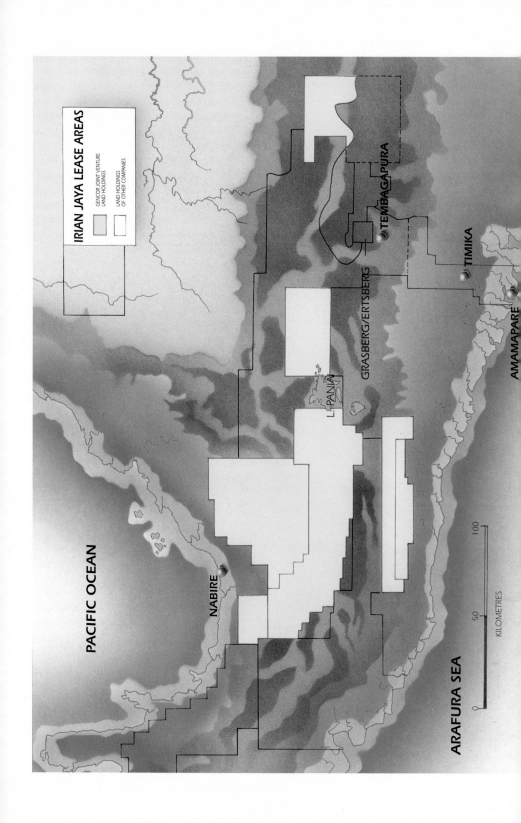

IRIAN JAYA LEASE AREAS

GENCOR JOINT VENTURE LAND HOLDINGS

LAND HOLDINGS, OF OTHER COMPANIES

PACIFIC OCEAN

NABIRE

L. PANIAI

GRASBERG/ERTSBERG

TEMBAGAPURA

TIMIKA

AMAMAPARE

ARAFURA SEA

50   100
KILOMETRES

and the conviction that thermal power generation would at least hold its own against the newly visible disadvantages of nuclear power.

It was a long way from Gencor's first recorded interest in coal – which is a letter dated 10 April 1899 from George Albu in Johannesburg to his brother Leopold in London. He explained that he had a scheme for the Transvaal Coal Trust, which he apparently thought the public might be persuaded would also have gold mining potential: '...a Syndicate has been formed, consisting of Dunkels, Lippert and ourselves ... to purchase from the Co. 50,000 shares for £84,000 cash ... the Company as a Coal Producer has been doing fairly well of late. The profits for April are expected to reach £3,000 ... the Netherlands Railway Company is likely to become a large customer, in consequence of their own Coal Mine (the Springs Colliery) having had to be closed down on account of a fire raging in their mine which they are unable to extinguish... We anticipate that the Coal Trust will again be the largest producer of Coal...'

So, in a way, George Albu was right.

There is a rather boring road that runs from Johannesburg and Pretoria across the flat plateau of the Transvaal Highveld, eastwards towards the steep descent over the Berg. After an hour or two of mealie fields, you come to one of the world's most dramatic coalfields – though the drama is well contained because from the highway you notice only a sequence of distant, steam-plumed cooling towers which rise like cathedrals out of a French provincial landscape. Kendal, Matla, Duvha, Hendrina, Camden, Komati, Ingagane – these are the power stations of the Witbank coalfields. Here is where Eskom generates the electricity which fuels South Africa, and where a few giant corporations like Gencor operate the coal mines – Khutala, Optimum, Duvha, Matla, Usutu, Blinkpan – which, on 30 or 40 year contracts, exist to provide the fuel for the power stations which stand directly next to or above them. Their neighbours are another batch of mines which concentrate on the domestic local market or on the fast-growing export trade, 12 hours down the railway line to Richards Bay or Durban. (There is a touch of poetic licence in this paragraph: Camden, Komati, Ingagane, Kilbarchan, Usutu and Blinkpan have been mothballed or closed.)

Optimum, 35 kilometres across the highway from Middelburg, is one of the best examples. It was conceived in the late 1960s and commissioned in 1970 to supply the adjoining Hendrina power station with its 2 000 MW of output. Eskom originally stipulated an underground mine: the winner of the contract, Trans-Natal, complied but went on to argue that the coal seams were sufficiently shallow for it to be possible to implement open-cast extraction. The three seams of coal lie no deeper than 60 metres below the surface.

Trans-Natal brought in South Africa's first dragline in 1971, in collaboration with McAlpine. A few years later Eskom had been convinced, and the underground shaft was abandoned in 1982.

The secret of Optimum is that it is extraordinarily large in scale and uses equipment so enormous as to be near-indescribable to an amateur. This is the playground of the world's biggest collection of Marion walking draglines – there are seven of them, and they seem to be on the scale of a ferry ship, yet are operated by one man. They move in a scarcely stopping, 24-hour, clumping crawl across the veld, tearing out the overburden, and exposing the successive coal seams, in 50-metre parallel strips which can go on for 5 000 metres. Viewed from the vantage point of the air-conditioned control cabin, the bucket looks like a Meccano toy from your childhood, yet it could easily hold a couple of bakkies, and it whips around faster than any bakkie could manage. Far below, down on the exposed seam, the men drill their holes and prepare for the regular blasting. Then it is the turn of the giant trucks and the conveyor belts to carry the coal to the plant, where it is separated between the demands of the Hendrina power station, just across the road, or the railway trucks which lead to Japan or wherever.

Optimum is a favourite of the industry because it became the country's first multi-product mine when in 1983 Eskom agreed that the success of the open-cast method was such that it should be allowed to develop its own export market for the higher-grade, washed coal. From Trans-Natal's point of view, the charm of the scheme was to be able to cream off the better grades which were not needed by the power station and send them to the coast for export. It was a success. Ten years later, the 5-6 million tons that were consumed every year, according to plan, by Eskom, were being matched by approximately the same volume of low-ash steamcoal for overseas markets, plus just under a million tons from the related and adjacent Eikeboom operation for inland.

Behind the draglines comes the infilling. The topsoil is replaced, the land is replanted. There are farms, a lake, a brave new expanse of low bush, some fruit trees, even some game – and in the distance, the steam clouds of the Hendrina towers against the clear-blue Transvaal sky.

CHAPTER FOURTEEN

SAMANCOR

The Samancor operation in and around Hotazel is very big: after all, it is the world's largest producer of manganese ore, containing 80 per cent of the world's reserves in a 40-kilometre stretch of scrub-bush. The Mamatwan open-cast mine, for example, is almost larger than the imagination can encompass: the circumference of its main pit is nearly five kilometres, the ore body is estimated at up to 17 *billion* tons (able to supply more production years than need ever be calculated), and the excavation proceeds at about 25 metres per year, with the overburden meticulously replaced as the giant bulldozers move on. It's a simple concept: they just dig out the black manganese ore, crush it on site and deposit it on the two-kilometre conveyer belt, and they will carry on doing this for the next century and more. It might be seen as a licence to print money, but the operation is not without problems.

The existence of both iron ore and manganese in the remote and barren area adjacent to the Kalahari Desert in the Northern Cape had been known for many years; the deep black of the outcrop ores stood out against the yellow of the Kalahari sands, but there seemed no realistic way of exploiting them; anyhow, there was more interest in asbestos mining and farming in the region, and, most of all, in the local belief, only occasionally proved, that there were diamond pipes to be found. The first geologist to show serious interest in manganese was a colourful ex-army officer, Captain Thomas Shone, who was well into middle age when he came to live in Postmasburg in 1922. Three years later, with a couple of partners from Johannesburg, he founded Union Manganese Mines and Minerals Limited – and here is an odd, co-incidental link with Gencor, because one of the partners was John Dale Lace, the dashing magnate who had first built Northwards, the grand house on the Johannesburg Ridge which was by now occupied by the Albu family. But there was still no sign of the essential railway line, nor, equally important, of a South African steel industry to supply the demand for either the iron ore or the manganese.

However, that was about to change with the creation of the state-owned South African Iron and Steel Industrial Corporation (Iscor) in 1927 under the leadership of a young man who would become South Africa's foremost industrialist, Dr HJ van der Bijl. The geologists began to take a keener interest in the region (only 20 years later would Iscor buy the local farm called Sishen and set up an enormous iron ore export operation) and a group of businessmen from the Rand, separate from 'Skipper' Shone, bought mining rights over a number of farms near Postmasburg and set up SA Manganese Limited. Neither company had made much progress – and a sensible proposal of a merger fell through – until the British Swiss International Corporation showed interest in importing the ore to Europe and proposed to negotiate with SA Railways for a new branch line to Postmasburg. A deal was done with Union Manganese to start a new company called the Manganese Corporation 1929 Limited. The railway, vital to the region's prospects, was opened in November 1930.

By this time, the world was in deep recession, which inevitably brought a complete collapse of the manganese market. Mining operations closed down in both companies. Out of this confusion Captain Shone emerged in 1932, surprisingly, as Chairman of his rival, SA Manganese, though he later returned home to Postmasburg as Managing Director of the operations there. One of Captain Shone's protégés was the young Fred Bamford, who had come into the mining industry via the Stock Exchange. He was to represent, and lead, the second generation at SA Manganese as European demand slowly resumed (particularly from Germany, and thanks in particular to the arms race), while the export trade was aided by South Africa's departure from the gold standard. The company paid its first dividend in 1936. The South African government was now keen to promote base metals and agreed on another extension of the railway line, as far as an important prospect at Lohathla and Gloucester. This led to an amalgamation of the old Manganese Corporation with the smaller Gloucester Manganese, thus forming the Associated Manganese Mines of South Africa Limited, to be universally known as Assmang. The manganese industry was at last emerging.

The new government interest brought to the scene the second of the crucial figures of this second generation. A young geologist called Leslie Boardman was sent out by the Geological Survey to make a detailed study of the district. Boardman was told to focus on the less-awkwardly located manganese deposits because he was thought to have a heart condition. He took two years, travelling rough, and, among much else, identified the iron ore deposits at Sishen, though no one paid much notice at the time.

Dr Boardman would return, and with dramatic effect.

At this point Dr van der Bijl of Iscor also entered the scene when he set up African Metals Corporation Limited (Amcor) in 1937 to make semi-processed products in iron and steel. Amcor therefore needed the manganese which played a crucial role in the production of steel, partly because it is an essential de-sulphurising agent, partly because it is an important agent in making alloys. SA Manganese was by this time suffering gravely from the loss of its German market, and the approach from Amcor was providential. The relationship between the two companies, which started with the exchange of shares and directors, together with Van der Bijl's assurance that all the manganese requirements of Amcor and Iscor would be bought from SA Manganese, would eventually lead to their merger, in 1975, as 'Samancor'. In the meantime, with the coming of the Second World War, Amcor's expansion was dramatic, based first at Vereeniging and then Meyerton: it became necessary to clarify the extent of South Africa's manganese deposits.

Leslie Boardman therefore found himself back in the Northern Cape in 1940, investigating the distinctive hill called Black Rock, which is north of Sishen and 120 kilometres from the railhead at Lohathla. SA Manganese had been unable to find even the £6 000 asked by the prospector who held the options on the local farms, so Assmang had stepped in, just before Boardman's arrival, and, deciding there might be enormous manganese reserves in the vicinity, immediately started to mine Black Rock. For these first couple of war years, both the producing companies flourished, until a serious slump in 1942-4 when German U-boats interrupted shipping and even at home there were problems with rail capacity.

By the late 1940s, iron ore production was being developed to meet growing demand at Amcor's pig-iron blast furnace at Newcastle. Amcor and SA Manganese set up another partnership to form Manganor Iron Mining Limited with Fred Bamford as Chairman (he had lost a foot while fighting in the Western Desert, victim of a German shell which may have contained his own manganese) – and both companies realised they would be needing more manganese, since Lohathla was low-grade and had had its problems. The result was the third return of Dr Leslie Boardman, who was persuaded to leave the Geological Survey and join Amcor. He went back to the Black Rock area, this time with one of the magnetometers which had recently proved themselves in tracking the western extension of the Rand Gold Reefs (though he was not able to operate – at least officially – on the three farms adjoining Black Rock because they were Assmang's reserves).

By 1954 SA Manganese had decided to open a new mine on a farm called Smartt to work a high-grade ore for Amcor's ferro-alloy operations. Smartt was 110 kilometres north of Lohathla on the route which passed Sishen on the way; the manganese ore had to be carried to the Sishen railhead by heavy truck; the road was appalling. To make things worse, the ore body at Smartt turned out to be inconsistent. And then Dr Boardman struck again. A farmer had come to him to report that a local water diviner, 'Siener' van Rensburg, a gravedigger from Lichtenburg, had been hired to look for water on his new farm called Hotazel. The diviner had found no water but, he insisted, plenty of black rock. Although Boardman did not believe that Hotazel was on the line of ore, he took his magnetometer and got a reaction so extreme that he thought the instrument might be broken. But the boreholes would soon confirm that Boardman had stumbled on an extraordinarily large deposit of rich manganese ore.

This was the real start of the modern-day manganese industry of the Northern Cape. South African Railways was persuaded, after complex negotiations with Bamford, to extend the line in 1960 by 80 kilometres to Hotazel on the basis of SA Manganese funding. (This railhead would later service Assmang's Black Rock operation, as well as the subsequent SA Manganese expansion in the area.) The Hotazel open-cast mine opened in 1959; it was eventually closed down in 1991, but Hotazel remained the centre of the mining industry in the area. (The story goes that at the opening ceremony the Minister of Mines, Jan de Klerk, father of a later State President, refused to refer to the locality by name because he thought it a blasphemy.) In 1963 another open-cast mine was developed at Mamatwan, 20 kilometres to the south, where the ore ratios were even higher and the reserves limitless. In 1966 Fred Bamford took over as Chairman of SA Manganese.

As it happened, the Hotazel operation had its share of problems. It had a top layer of 48 per cent manganese/14 per cent iron which was seven metres thick, then a 27-metre layer of banded ironstone, then a second layer of manganese which was intended for Amcor (the top layer was for export). The problem was the ironstone, which defied the drills. The ore grades were also more erratic than had been expected. Mamatwan was geologically much simpler: beneath the yellow sand cover there was a 50-metre layer of pale limestone – no problems with benching – and then (an extraordinary sight from an aircraft, or for that matter in good colour photographs) a 20 metre deep slab of perfect black manganese, waiting to be dug out of the great hole in the desert. The hole moves slowly forward, remaining the same size, because the exhausted benches are backfilled and rehabilitated as the machines move slowly on.

Mamatwan was soon to be producing one million tons a year. In the meantime, Assmang was working Black Rock. SA Manganese thereupon decided – in view of the limited life of the two incline shafts and one vertical shaft of Hotazel itself – to develop the world's largest *underground* manganese mine, at Wessels, in 1973, just beyond Black Rock and north-west of Hotazel where the ore lay 300 metres deep and where rights had been secured 20 years before. Again, there were unexpected problems – in this case, and ironically in view of the conditions on the surface, there was too much water. It never dried up, as the experts had promised it would; in due course it would be pumped into Hotazel to help solve the town's chronic water shortage. (If you live in Hotazel you have two separate water supplies, one of which is treated sewage, for use only in the garden and for just one hour a day.)

By the 1970s, SA Manganese had become the world's biggest producer of manganese. Amcor was said to be the largest single consumer. A full merger of SA Manganese and Amcor – in 1975 – had an obvious logic to it and the new title, SA Manganese Amcor Limited, was universally shortened to Samancor.

To take the story forward, the entry of Gencor into the subsequent control of Samancor was controversial. In 1977 Iscor, which had a 40 per cent stake (because of its original role in Amcor) offered its Samancor shares to the private sector. Anglo American, Gencor and Barlow Rand were all interested. Thereupon the Minister of Economic Affairs, Chris Heunis, presumably because Anglo American looked to be the winner and the government did not favour that prospect in those days of ideology and isolation, intervened and blocked the sale. Anglo and Gencor carried on buying in the market, and Anglo, evidently irritated, set up its own mine, Middelplaats Manganese.

Next, Anglo sold Middelplaats (at a loss) to Samancor in return for shares which brought Anglo's holding in Samancor to 24,6 per cent, later (through the market) to 31 per cent. (Middelplaats was closed in the next recession, as were the long-surviving Lohathla and Manganore mines.) The Gencor response in 1983 (or perhaps it should better be described as the government's response) was to do a direct deal with Iscor from which it emerged with 50 per cent and therefore control (a figure to be adjusted over the next 10 years to 46 per cent). This *fait accompli* was achieved in secret and was much criticised in the Johannesburg business community. In the words of the *Financial Mail*, 'There was widespread indignation at the time on the nature of the secret agreement between Iscor and Gencor to maintain control over Samancor. Anglo was clearly not aware of it, while many questioned Iscor's action in selling off assets belonging to the taxpayer without an open tender for bids which could have raised more money.' But the plot was rather more complex than it appeared: in the summarising words of the same *Financial Mail* article: 'The Gencor-Iscor deal had its roots in a fight over a reduction in level of the sales of coking coal Iscor had contracted to take from Gencor's Hlobane Colliery. Gencor threatened legal action and the outcome was that Iscor took the Hlobane Colliery and the Gencor-controlled Dunswart Steel Works, while Gencor took 50.25 percent of Iscor's wholly-owned subsidiary African Metals [Amcor] which, in turn, held 39.6 percent of Samancor...' – all of which, reflecting as it did the extraordinarily complicated and incestuous relationships of the South African business world, will come up again in a later chapter.

Anglo American did not, in fact, pull out of Samancor in disgust, as many people expected, and there continued to be a significant and high-powered Anglo presence on the Samancor Board - which continues to this day, representing Anglo's holding of about 28 per cent. The more substantial result of 1983 was that Gencor transferred its chrome mines to Samancor.

It is just one – yet another – of the many examples of South Africa's mineral riches that almost three-quarters of the world's economic chrome ore reserves are found in the Bushveld Igneous Complex, which extends like a great saucer under the dry grassland of the Transvaal. Gencor's eventual exploitation of them, first through General Mining then through Samancor, was a good early example of the strategy that was to be introduced to various sectors – to add value to the primary resources by processing and beneficiating, with the advantage of low-cost labour and with cheap electric power which itself was a consequence of the country's enormous and easily mined coal deposits.

The original Gencor connection with chrome involved all three of the founding elements of the Group. General Mining had become involved in 1954 when it bought the company which owned the Montrose Chrome Mine at Lydenburg in the Eastern Transvaal; Federale Mynbou had a small shareholding in Chrome Mines of South Africa; and Union Corporation managed Chrome Mines, which had good deposits in the Northern Transvaal and also had mines in the Steelpoort district in the Eastern Transvaal. In 1974, General Mining acquired Chrome Mines from Union Corporation. The subsequent history of the chrome industry – the second principal activity of Samancor – appears to be bewildering in its detail of acquisition and amalgamation, but in essence it was a rationalisation of dozens of operations of varying efficiency, conceived in particular by Jan van den Berg, the General Mining Finance Director. Their strategy was to close down minor and scattered operations, most of which had been under-capitalised and under-mechanised, and to focus on the fundamental point, which was that South Africa had colossal reserves of chrome but they were mainly low-grade. Once the new argon-oxygen decarburisation process had been developed in the late 1960s, South Africa's chrome was viable. Eventually Samancor's

Chrome Mining was reorganised, for obvious geographical reasons, in 10 underground mines, into Eastern Chrome Mines (with capacity of 1,3 million tons a year) and Western Chrome Mines (1,7 million tons). There would be four alloy plants.

Tubatse Ferrochrome, near Steelpoort, was a R46 million joint venture with the American firm Union Carbide, which had the technology and had been looking for partners. In 1976 Tubatse was built on a 51/49 Gencor/Union Carbide arrangement. It was an ultra-modern and highly efficient plant, designed to produce 1 ton of high-carbon charge chrome from 2,5 tons of chrome ore and 3 500 kwH of electricity: it had a maximum capacity of 140 000 tons per annum of charge chrome. This turned out to be over-ambitious, especially when the next world recession arrived, and by the early 1980s Tubatse was operating at, or under, half capacity. In 1985 Union Carbide pulled out and Samancor took over: these were years when many multinationals were disengaging from South Africa even if in some cases their reasons were strategic as well as political. But in 1989 and 1990, with economic recovery, two new furnaces were built, making it the second largest ferrochrome plant in the world, and another furnace was planned for 1996. (In the meantime, Ferrometals, between Johannesburg and Middelburg, originally an Amcor Ferrosilicone operation, installed new furnaces in the 1970s, and by the mid-1990s had become the world's largest ferrochrome plant, with a 370 000 ton capacity. Additionally, after the 1991 Samancor take-over of Middelburg Steel and Alloys, it acquired Palmiet Ferrochrome west of Johannesburg and Middelburg Ferrochrome.)

Ferrochrome is an alloy of chromium and iron which is an essential element in the manufacture of stainless steel: it is the chrome which gives stainless steel its anti-corrosive quality and also its appearance. Samancor was to become the world's largest producer. But the problem for chrome exports, as for manganese, is that they – which is to say the great bulk of Samancor's activities – are desperately vulnerable to the world's economic cycle. Nothing can be done about that. A recession impacts most deeply on the carbon-steel industry, which happens to be the principal end-user of both manganese and chrome. So the mid-1980s were bad for the two sectors, the late 1980s were wonderful, and the early 1990s were bad again. Mike Salamon, who had been given this hot potato of a job, remembers 'an absolute collapse of the chrome market'. But in this last case the natural pain was seriously exacerbated by the coincidental break-up of the Soviet Union and the dumping of chrome and steel scrap as the CIS States (and also China, to make things worse) abandoned sensible pricing in the scramble for foreign exchange. For instance, Kazakhstan, always a major competitor, was dumping chrome and ferrochrome on a scale which forced Samancor to cut back to, and below, 50 per cent capacity, with mountainous stockpiles. The South African defence in 1993 included an alliance with Nippon Denko, under which the Japanese bought half of a ferrochrome furnace, guaranteeing product from Tubatse's No 5 furnace in the Eastern Transvaal while Nippon Denko closed its high-cost charge chrome furnaces at home; the management of the Chrome Mines was rationalised; half the furnaces were closed; there was retrenchment of labour. One day, no doubt, things would look up again as the world economic cycle passed on. As they did: by 1995 Salamon could say: 'We are running everything flat out.'

The manganese division's plight in the same situation in the early 1990s was not quite so traumatic, partly because in this case the CIS competitor (the Ukraine) is a very low-grade though high-volume producer. Here the South African defensive strategy was to focus on the downstream, to turn unused ferrochrome furnaces to manganese alloy production, to do a deal with the French in which Samancor took a stake and set up a joint venture (on the chrome side, an important long-term supply arrangement was reached with Ugine of France, involving a four per cent acquisition). There was also a timely fillip to the balance sheets with the purchase by the IDC of a one-third interest in another of South Africa's biggest industrial development projects, Columbus, with the result that Samancor, the IDC and Anglo American's Highveld Steel became equal partners in the stainless steel Joint Venture.

Stainless steel is made of iron, chrome and nickel. It therefore became a classic example of South Africa's industrial challenge of the later decades of the century – to progress from extraction/export of the country's minerals to beneficiation/export. Gencor was at the heart of the Columbus project from the beginning. The livelier minds in Samancor had been dreaming of a move into stainless steel for some years: the argument today seems self-evident. In view of the fact that South Africa was a major coal producer, what should it be doing to stop sending its minerals – in this case its chrome – overseas, where the real money was being made in their beneficiation? The Alusaf smelter project was a response to a similar conundrum. For Samancor men like Fred Boshoff, the logical solution was stainless steel. He was charged with setting up a pre-feasibility study and at the end of 1988 took it to the Samancor Board.

The directors of Samancor, including representatives of Anglo American, were undeniably aware of the potential importance of the ferrochrome industry world-wide. It emerged that Anglo had also been thinking about stainless steel – and, in view of the enormous investment that any project would entail, the sensible decision was to investigate a joint venture between Samancor and Anglo's Highveld Steel and Vanadium. The managers began thinking of a greenfield site, and were talking about a R3 billion project with a 500 000 tonnes per annum output, which would make it the world's fifth largest producer. After much lobbying, they knew they could get the accelerated tax write-offs from government which might make it feasible. But South Africa already had a small 120 000-ton producer – Middelburg Steel & Alloys, which belonged to Barlows. It had always been in the back of the minds of people like Boshoff that it would make good sense to get hold of the technical and marketing skills that already existed in this small local market. And Barlows was known to be disillusioned with the problems of its mining arm. These included a ferrochrome operation which had spent R300 million on a unique process which never worked properly.

In mid-1989 Samancor first went to Barlows – who said no. The Columbus partners therefore continued with the planning of a completely new plant. Then, in mid-1991, on the brink of a final decision, they went back to Barlows at the highest level, and a R1 billion deal was done. Columbus Joint Venture took the stainless steel business of Middelburg Steel & Alloys and thereby had a basic facility at Middelburg; Samancor acquired its ferrochrome operation. As a minor consideration, the partners reckoned the plant they had acquired would help bring down estimated costs. (A subsequent twist in what was bound to be a complicated financial arrangement was that, to finance their part of the deal, Anglo American sold in the market most of its own shareholding – 5,8 per cent – of Gencor, having politely asked Gencor if it would mind. Derek Keys, the new Gencor Chairman, replied, in the press, that he was rather tickled that R600 million of his shares could be placed so easily. The older generation of observers enjoyed remembering that the Anglo stake was a legacy of 30 years ago when Anglo made possible the elevation and arrival of General Mining to the first division...)

There followed a tricky amalgamation between Columbus's greenfield plans and the existing Middelburg Steel & Alloys facility (inevitably, there were job casualties). The final go-ahead was given in December 1992 and a skilful engineering feat was launched in which, notwithstanding the rigorous technical requirements of stainless steel manufacture, the giant new Columbus was built adjoining and around the existing Middelburg operation without disruption of production over just two years. It was one of South Africa's biggest ever construction projects, carried through in the depths of recession, and coming through – just in time for Gencor's centenary – at the same time as the other big project, the Alusaf second smelter, in mid-1995. The first stainless steel from Columbus was tapped in May 1995. Full capacity of 500 000 tonnes was projected for 1998.

There was an interesting coincidence between the political and industrial developments over this period. The Joint Venture had been conceived at a time when South Africa was still obstructed by international sanctions. The original plan therefore required an international partner: the idea was that South Africa would handle the 'hot end' while the cold-rolling would be done off-shore, where sanctions might be evaded. As the months of negotiations passed, majority rule (and therefore the end of sanctions) became an ever-stronger possibility. Then, very near final agreement, the intended partner (in Taiwan) fell away at the end of 1991. The South Africans had mixed feelings. They had the project to themselves, but the magnitude and exposure of the deal were terrifying: the political situation was by no means clarified, the investment was huge, this was a highly cyclical commodity business, and (unlike aluminium) there was no terminal market for stainless steel. The two partners decided that it was necessary to bring on board the government's Industrial Development Corporation and, at the December 1992 announcement, the IDC became a third and equal partner in a R3,5 billion project, though it was understood that it would in due course probably want to reduce its stake to 15 per cent. Each partner put up R970 million and the balance would come from suppliers' credits. And as one of the more cynical South African executives commented, the Taiwanese partner who never came to the altar finished up with a great deal of technical expertise. It had been, said Fred Boshoff in mid-1995 in his bluff way, a gamble. But it was going to work because South Africa had been re-admitted to the world.

Hotazel – a wonderfully appropriate name for the place! – is the archetypal mining-company town. It has sat for 36 years on the edge of the Kalahari Desert, not far from the Botswana frontier and more than 1 000 kilometres from its main export terminal on the far side of South Africa in Port Elizabeth. There are about 250 houses (the manager, suitably enough, occupies the only one with two storeys), laid out very neatly in this strange, not unbeautiful landscape of red soil, yellow grass, cattle, windstorms, local koppies and distant hills. It is very hot indeed in summer, and very cold in winter.

Only Samancor people live in Hotazel: there is a Dutch Reformed Church, one shop, a cafe, a liquor store, a bank that opens only briefly, one doctor, a small hospital, a sports and recreation club, a couple of schools, and not even a South African Police presence. Older children are usually sent off to school in Potchefstroom or Kimberley. Afrikaans is the main language amongst the whites. People say they adjust to this strange life and come to like it – the Kalahari sunsets, the braais, the peace and quiet of the stoep at evening. Samancor's people tend to stay.

A quick 60 kilometres down the road there is the town of Kuruman, an important district centre for the Hotazel families. This is the self-styled 'Oasis of the Kalahari', a surprise to the stranger because it is a staggeringly green little town to flourish in this semi-desert region. That is explained by its extraordinary source of water: the Eye, a rocky outcrop which sits in the heart of the town, pleasantly presented in a municipal garden, and gushes a never-faltering torrent of clear water, 16 million litres a day, to irrigate the trees and lush gardens of this oasis. Just outside, there is the Moffat Mission, also green and irrigated, where the Revd John Moffat established his church for the London Missionary Society in the 1820s on the so-called Missionary Road that led to Central Africa, and where, in 1840, David Livingstone proposed to the Moffat daughter, Mary, under an almond tree whose dead stump still stands, just, in the garden outside the church.

CHAPTER FIFTEEN

THE NEW MEN

When Ted Pavitt succeeded Wim de Villiers as Chairman of Gencor in August 1982, he was 64 and could not have been too surprised when he was told by Sanlam's Dr Fred du Plessis that he was to be a caretaker. There followed not, as one might have expected, a brief interim period of a few months, but three and a half years which Pavitt long afterwards would describe as the most miserable of his life. They were also to be pretty miserable for some of his senior colleagues (technically, Pavitt became 'Non-Executive Chairman' after less than two years, but it made very little visible difference). Those years were to be seen by many – managers as well as observers – as a time of drift and lack of direction for the Group, as Pavitt chaired a Committee of Five of the Executive Directors who shared out responsibility for the various operations: Tom de Beer (finance), Johan Fritz (mining), Hugh Smith (investment), George Clark (industry), Basil Landau (paper and other industries).

In subsequent years, when Gencor's management style had been transformed, the failings of this period in the early 1980s became exaggerated to the point of unfair myth, with much talk of headless chickens and suchlike: it was easily forgotten, for example, that the company's results recovered by 1985 and the Corporation's asset base doubled during the period of 'Committee' rule. But it could hardly be denied that the early 1980s were grim, with the economy in recession and the Rand plunging. There were serious foreign exchange losses in some of the subsidiaries such as Kohler, Tedelex and Kanhym, requiring recapitalisation and rights issues. (Memories would later differ about why Basil Landau in the end negotiated a deal at so high a price.) The acquisition of Tedelex for R11 a share in 1983 – to drop to R2 two years later – was to be particularly criticised. These were tempestuous years for Impala, which also had to reveal a R60 million stock loss. The Gencor share price lagged – and all of this must be set in the wider context of fast-growing political tension throughout South Africa, of hardening international isolation, and of an increasingly violent labour situation in which Gencor developed its reputation as 'Public Enemy Number One' of the black trade unions.

Pavitt had taken the job principally out of a sense of loyalty to the Group and to his colleagues; he had observed with alarm the damage done by the fight to the death between Wim de Villiers and Andreas Wassenaar, between Sanlam and Rembrandt. But he cannot have anticipated the degree to which Sanlam, newly determined to demonstrate its control after the row with Rembrandt, would keep him on a tight rein, or the length of time Dr du Plessis would take before he sorted out a new succession. Afterwards, Pavitt would admit that he had told Du Plessis he would prefer to get rid of four of his five Executive Directors – and was firmly told he would do nothing of the sort. Why did Du Plessis let the situation drift for so long? Perhaps because he had been so alarmed by the inter-Afrikaner trauma of the Broedertwis and would risk no more scandal or publicity? Perhaps because after Wim he did not want to risk another powerful Executive Chairman at Gencor? Perhaps because he was so overwhelmed with Sanlam's other business responsibilities that he could not give more of his time to Gencor? In the end, in 1985, influenced by his right-hand man Marinus Daling (later to become Chief Executive of Sankorp and, in due course, in late 1993, Chairman of Sanlam), he called in the American consultancy firm Arthur D Little to draw up an analysis of Gencor's management structure.

The Arthur D Little report has been seen, in full, by very few people, and – as is frequently said of management consultants – is described by those who saw it as confirming what the client wanted to hear (except that it made the absurd suggestion that the only person capable of filling the central and essential role of Executive Chairman of Gencor was Dr du Plessis himself!) But the report signalled the need for a new age, and gave Sanlam the impetus – the excuse? – to ring the changes. Marinus Daling recommended to Du Plessis a local chartered accountant, an independent business consultant whom he had encountered on the Samancor Board – Derek Keys – and things would never be the same again.

The best single illustration of the atmosphere (and the dangers) of this period of rule by Committee is found in the most delicate aspect of the Group's activities at the time – on the labour front, where Gencor's plight can be encapsulated in the row between the Head of Mining, Johan Fritz, and his senior expert on industrial relations, Naas Steenkamp. This clash can even cast light on the great debate in white South Africa in that decade. Here were two characters, two Afrikaners, destined to do battle. Fritz was an able mining manager by background, a Christian Scientist, an authoritarian of legendary repute (he would issue dinner invitations which specified that his guests should arrive at three-and-a-half-minute intervals so that he could greet each one in turn and offer them orange juice or water, and woe betide anyone – like Steenkamp – who failed to arrive exactly on cue). He had no visible sympathy for the demands of the fast-emerging union movement. He believed – and would say so publicly, even at times of extreme industrial unrest – that mine labourers must be ruled as if they were in the army. And, to add a sadder element, he was convinced that he was the obvious successor to Ted Pavitt, though all of his colleagues knew that he was deceiving himself.

Naas Steenkamp was the opposite in almost every respect. He was amiable, gregarious, well-connected, and not at all a miner. His first career had been in diplomacy and, like many in that profession, he would always be suspected – no doubt unfairly – of manipulation and intrigue; his enemies thought – and said – that he was 'deep'. When he joined General Mining in 1966, he became very close to Wim de Villiers, who seems to have valued his diplomatic skills as well as his principal role in the Group's public relations. He was to become an influential member of the Wiehahn Commission, which would rethink South Africa's archaic labour relations in the late 1970s. So it was natural for Steenkamp to be nominated by Gencor to move towards the Presidency of the Chamber of Mines, which he would occupy twice. But first he had to survive Johan Fritz.

At a time of political and labour turmoil in South Africa, there was bound to be tension between an executive who saw his principal role as maintaining production and a negotiator who was looking for politically acceptable solutions. That this tension turned into a bitter clash was made inevitable by the very different characters of the two men concerned. Fritz, with a German background, in fact was not politically *verkrampte* and certainly not as hidebound as his critics would later claim; he nevertheless had a 'Prussian' instinct for control and autocratic management. (He imposed just as strict a discipline on himself, as when, for example, he insisted on attending a heavy schedule of meetings in the week when he and his wife were desolated by the loss of their eldest son in a botched mercenary coup attempt in the Seychelles.) In contrast, Steenkamp had arrived at a very different appreciation of the speed at which change had to take place, as well as the need to be aware of and take into account the public perception of Gencor which Fritz (and, to a much lesser extent, Pavitt) regarded as secondary to the need to keep the industry and the Group running.

The clash between Fritz and Steenkamp, and between two very different views of where South Africa's future lay, came at the end of Pavitt's chairmanship – fortunately for Steenkamp. He had observed with growing horror the reluctance of the head of the Group's most important division to move with the times. In September 1985, for instance, after Gencor had dismissed 1 100 striking workers on its gold mines, mainly at Marievale, Fritz had blithely declared in an interview with the *Financial Mail*: 'it is important to remain consistent with black employees and not vacillate. Blacks have a different cultural approach. They want to know exactly where they stand, otherwise they lose confidence in you... Mining operations are conducted more in a military manner than other industrial activities. This is due to the relatively unsafe natural environment...' These sentiments would have been understood by George Albu, no doubt, but 90 years later the political turmoil in South Africa had reached such a fever point that Gencor's reputation for hard-line labour policies was by far the worst in the Chamber. It had certainly not been forgotten that it was Gencor which in January 1984 had allowed a row about the dismissal of seven workers at Impala Refineries to escalate overnight into a confrontation which led to the Courts, and it came as no surprise at all when in January 1986 Impala fired no less than 23 000 workers at its platinum operation in Bophuthatswana. It was not altogether unexpected that Gencor, and Gold Fields, were declared 'enemy companies' by the NUM – and it hardly helped matters when Gencor admitted that, like Anglo American and Anglovaal, in at least one of its mine compounds it had installed a nerve gas system capable of responding to worker unrest.

In the early months of 1986, Ted Pavitt requested Steenkamp to give him his view on Gencor's image with reference to its industrial relations practices. Steenkamp replied that labour decisions were over-centralised – that is, taken at head office, not by local management – 'and made on the basis of dogmatic conviction without sufficient exploration of alternatives and without sufficient weighing of the consequences... Our approach appears to be based almost exclusively on two items of belief: blacks are different and have to be treated differently; the most fundamental consideration is the maintenance of discipline and order. This approach has been assiduously followed in style, word and deed, and has had a profoundly negative effect on the regard in which Gencor is held... We cut a somewhat foolish figure. We are seen as making a virtue of being hawkish, paternalistic and anti-[black] union and being rigidly doctrinaire in the process...'

Not surprisingly, Fritz was furious. 'The memo is a most serious inditement [*sic*] of my leadership and management performance, and a matter which I am obliged to consider very carefully', he wrote to Steenkamp on February 1986. 'As a matter of urgency, please substantiate the various allegations with specific written facts...' Steenkamp could only oblige. In a memo dated 10 March 1986 which sums up the South African debate about labour in that period and reveals the gulf between the two schools of thought, he wrote: 'Our practice appears to be based on: the fundamental assumption that labour, like machinery or electrical power, is a commodity; denial that there are circumstances under which workers may justifiably withhold their labour; and insistence that the common law right to dismiss an employee, who is in breach of his contract of employment, prevails over any right to strike... ; assumptions that race determines peoples action's and reactions... Gencor top management did not consider alternatives to labour confrontation or make proper assessment of the cost of decisions such as the Impala firings ... the Principles of not negotiating with striking workers have been elevated over the interests of these employees and of the Group: the attitude towards unions was essentially antagonistic and unconstructive... We have focused attention on Gencor as a target for political activities', he argued: Gencor had been publicly branded 'an enemy of the people'.

Steenkamp realised by now that Fritz was determined to get rid of him. His only hope was to play for time – because Pavitt had in the meantime commissioned an investigation of Gencor's industrial relations from two outside consultants, Professor Dawie de Villiers and Mr RV Sutton. Fritz would be stalled until they delivered their reports, which eventually arrived in late April. But – providentially for Steenkamp and his team – on 14 April Dr Fred du Plessis came up from the Cape to summon Gencor's senior managers and tell them that Ted Pavitt was stepping down and that Derek Keys would take over in May with a brief to restructure. Johan Fritz was astonished that he had been passed over, and within days announced he would be taking early retirement – but added he would carry on until August to help Keys. Steenkamp was therefore not yet entirely safe because, although Fritz presumably no longer had unilateral power to fire him, he would certainly continue to try, and indeed he put up a note to his fellow directors enumerating Steenkamp's vices and (as he explained to Steenkamp to his face) urging that he be dismissed.

Against this background of bitter in-fighting (and in the context of nationwide political and labour turmoil), Professor de Villiers and Mr Sutton reported on Gencor's image. The Professor, who was no radical, declared that Gencor's industrial relations decisions – which were determined at corporate, executive-director-level and not, as the company sometimes claimed, with maximum decentralisation – 'have ignored the socio-political realities of our times... It is quite clear that relations are deteriorating... If not rectified a catastrophic polarisation is likely to take place which can only have disastrous consequences for Gencor as a whole...' Gencor was out of line with the rest of the industry, said the Professor, in its resistance to raising minimum wages, in opposing black upliftment, and in the very bad conditions on its mine compounds. He urged 'the earliest possible action as the socio-political climate in South Africa, the strategic importance of the mining industry, and the public image of Gencor following Marievale and Impala, make the Group more than a prime target for both activists and unionists...'

Mr Sutton weighed in in similar terms. Gencor had been labelled 'a bad employer with no regard for Blacks' well-being and it has been targeted for further action; the Group had been placed on a collision course with Black political developments which in turn implies some disturbing consequences...' Mr Sutton added: 'Implacable resistance to increases in minimum wages, which is now part of the Gencor image, will inevitably be interpreted as anti-black pro-apartheid.' He referred to 'the cynicism which is evident in respect of the leadership', and recommended Gencor take urgent steps to improve its image, particularly in respect of minimum wages; there should be a far-reaching re-investment in black housing, and a major bid to develop a more co-operative relationship with the black labour movement.

These two confidential documents were on Derek Keys's desk when he arrived. Steenkamp had been saved in the nick of time, and the rest of the decade would be devoted to the effort to transform Gencor's labour image and its relations with the new black leadership, personified in the NUM's Cyril Ramaphosa. In June Keys announced his new team and said to Steenkamp, 'I want you to be an angel of light!' (to which Steenkamp apparently replied that he feared he had no wings). Johan Fritz went into retirement.

Derek Keys in 1986 was a 55-year-old South African chartered accountant, English-speaking but with excellent Afrikaans and Afrikaner connections, a committed Christian, apolitical, whose early career had taken him from the Industrial Development Corporation to independent consultancy, which brought him directorships with National Discount House, Malbak, ASEA, Samancor and Sappi, and various advisory jobs on government bodies. He had only one early connection with General Mining – Sir George Albu was Chairman of a Barclays Scholarship Committee which interviewed the schoolboy Keys and gave him a bursary! To the Gencor staff, he was a largely unknown quality; he had no evident connection with the mining industry, except for the Samancor directorship, and he was not surprised to discover on his arrival that he was assumed to be a mere 'bean counter'. He was to go through Gencor like a dose of salts and – a very different achievement – he was to win extraordinary popularity throughout the Group before, less than six years later and to his own astonishment, he was accosted on the first tee by FW de Klerk at a Presidential Golfing Day and invited to step into the Cabinet.

The Committee system was immediately disbanded. Fritz went first. Basil Landau had already been negotiating his own departure before Keys arrived, and stayed on, he would explain, only to see the completion of Sappi's massive Ngodwana project. George Clark decided it was time to step down and retire to the Cape. Tom de Beer was a valued fixture, and Naas Steenkamp, as we have seen, was to have his own role at Head Office – he was sometimes described as Keys's Minister of Foreign Affairs.

From the beginning Keys was determined to decentralise and to delegate. He knew that Gencor needed a change of team, and devised an elegant, not-too-painful solution whereby the older, less energetic generation could stay on, if they wished, as Senators, with an essentially advisory role – Hugh Smith was one of them – while the younger team of Chief Executives could be promoted to the daily direction of the various divisions. Sometimes Keys changed the metaphor and called them coaches and athletes. He set up a management system which could be illustrated with two circles, one within the other, the inner group reporting to himself, and he had a system of executive councils, which he would attend but not, as a rule, chair. He became famous among his executives as well as visiting journalists for his ability to keep his desk empty, to gaze out of his top-floor window, and to *think*. (In researching this book I managed to elicit only one fractionally critical comment out of all the Gencor people I interviewed, from barons to secretaries: Keys was, said one retired senator, 'a strategist, not a manager...') He was quoted as seeking 'an environment that is supportive of enthusiasts', in which the Group would contain 'a number of centres of momentum'.

His team, in those next years, was to include Steve Ellis, as Head of Mining (a mining man who had come through the ranks, particularly via the Coal Division); Tom de Beer at Finance; Eugene van As at Sappi; Grant Thomas, brought on board to run the industrial interests, who was an early protégé of Keys from Malbak; and Bernard Smith, who had behind him a precocious, high-flying career at JCI and a spell with BP International Minerals in London, and had returned to Johannesburg in 1985. Smith was appointed by Johan Fritz to run Operational Services, 'in order to allow him to fire in from the flank, which is his preferred way of contributing', as Keys would later put it, after Smith had played a noteworthy role first in creating the Engen Division and then in setting up the Billiton deal which was to be Gencor's transformation after Keys had gone on to greater things.

Keys had brought with him a particular knowledge of Malbak, which he had put together in the 1960s and 1970s, and which would control Gencor's industrial portfolio, much slimmed-down from the wild diversifications of both General Mining and Union Corporation in the previous generation: leading South African companies grouped around Malbak in 1987 included Carlton Paper, Kohler, Haggie, Union Carriage, Chemico, Protea Chemicals, Sentrale Chemiese, Kanhym, Malcomess, Blue Circle, Hall Longmore, Tedelex, Ellerine, Malbak Motor Holdings, etc – the list could run on. All the Gencor industrial holdings went into Malbak except Sappi and Trek (which was later used as a vehicle to acquire Mobil and merge both into Engen). In effect, Malbak was Gencor's own industrial conglomerate with its own separate and expert management; these were the areas in which Gencor's mining men had rarely felt confident, and this was to be the last of various attempts by the mining house throughout the century to tackle the manufacturing-industry sector. It was to be the barony of Keys's protégé, Grant Thomas.

But Keys's most important hiring was to come a little later. He realised that he would one day need a new head of the mining side, to succeed Steve Ellis who, on his own admission, was a hands-on type who would not relish the Senator option. Keys asked Bernard Smith if he knew of anyone; Smith remembered that in his JCI days at Rustenburg Platinum he had a scientist-turned-manager called Brian Gilbertson. The introduction was effected and in 1988 Gilbertson arrived at Gencor. From this appointment would follow a whole new generation of Gencor executives – and the day would eventually come when Gilbertson, by now Gencor's Executive Chairman, would bring Keys back, his political career happily behind him, as Chairman of Billiton.

The Derek Keys legacy to Gencor, it is often said, was the 'unbundling' of the Group which occupied the headlines throughout the early 1990s. The true story is not quite so simple, because Keys would later say that he was always a little ambivalent about whether or not it was a good idea to unbundle the Group into its component parts. He first broached this idea at one of his brainstorming sessions of top executives at Gencor's Magaliesberg retreat: he distinctly remembers that he reckoned he was flying a balloon. He thought that 70 per cent of his motivation was to get rid of the conglomerate discount which was believed at that time substantially to devalue the share price of a pyramid organisation, and 30 per cent was his preference for making Gencor a smaller target for big predators; he was also aware that there were negative aspects to Gencor becoming too big an element in Sanlam's portfolio.

Public (and in-house) reaction to the idea was divided. Brian Gilbertson recalls that the debate dragged on and on, with Keys returning to the theme from time to time. The political background was, of course, relevant to the argument – there was now a prospect on the horizon of a new government which might well want to break up the great white conglomerates – but this factor tended to fade as less was heard from the ANC of more radical policies such as nationalisation. The business world was not easily convinced of the merits of unbundling. Anglo American, for instance, pooh-poohed the concept, and there were people who saw no point in disbanding the empire and deliberately going down the league of quoted companies. Although Keys had always taken care to stay on close terms with Sanlam in Bellville, keeping them informed of investment and other strategy decisions, he says he took his unbundling initiative without direct reference to Marinus Daling, who was Chief Executive of Sankorp and would move into the top seat at Sanlam – but Daling was to prove very much in favour, so much so that Keys afterwards felt it would not have gone through without his support. Keys would later add, modestly, that he had not foreseen what he later reckoned would be the biggest benefits brought by unbundling – the unleashing of the entrepreneurial energies of the liberated younger executives like Gilbertson and Eugene van As, who would eventually lead the slimmed-down Gencor into the wider world.

Ironically enough, it was not to be Keys (translated into government in early 1992) but Brian Gilbertson, his successor, who would implement the unbundling – which is to say the break- up – of Gencor. There was no shortage of speculation that Gilbertson was not best pleased to find that his first task was to dismember his new organisation: he would later admit that, like Keys, he had been in two minds – but he was persuaded that, on balance, it was the sensible strategy, and he was going to be adequately eloquent in preaching the virtues of the strategy. He proposed, he said in August 1992, to halve the size of the Group: the benefits would be, first, to give the Group a clearer resource focus (eg for separate activities such as Sappi); second, to release for Gencor shareholders the 10 or 20 per cent discount inherent in a pyramid structure; and, third, to achieve a smaller Group which would appear to be politically more welcome in the new South Africa. He admitted that the loss of size might weaken Gencor's chances of major international projects (a fear which was to be dramatically disproved two years later).

Over the months ahead, unbundling became the central topic of business debate on Johannesburg. It was widely agreed that the process might release entrepreneurial energy – one of Keys's earlier convictions – but would it really turn out to unlock the discount on net asset value for shareholders which the analysts (and Gilbertson) thought might be as high as 20 per cent?

Marinus Daling (who, as Sankorp Chief Executive, was the biggest player in the game) was quoted as saying that the vital issue was to create corporate structures that went on adding value and that this process required a high degree of specialisation and focusing (he was speaking in May 1993 in the context of what he was at pains to stress was a reconciliation between Sanlam and Rembrandt). Gencor's unbundling was, everyone agreed, a revolutionary move for South Africa, although it was granted that there was an international trend to move away from conglomerates.

In May 1993 it was announced that Gencor would distribute its holdings in Engen (under Rob Angel), Genbel (under Tom de Beer), Sappi (under Eugene van As), and Malhold (under Grant Thomas) (this was later amended, with Gencor retaining 20 per cent of Malbak), thus leaving Gencor as an essentially mining group containing Gengold, Impala Platinum, Richards Bay Minerals (50 per cent), Samancor, Trans-Natal, and the Alusaf and Columbus projects. Gilbertson would later explain that he held onto 20 per cent of Malbak as a precaution, so that he would have adequate financial liquidity available for the future financial deals he was planning: 'Malbak is just cash as far as I'm concerned.' He was also conscious that Malbak contained various strong brand-names which might be tempting to foreign investors.

All of this required a major financial reorganisation. Genbeheer, which had existed to hold 54,8 per cent of Gencor, distributed its shares in Group companies to the shareholders and liquidated itself in November 1993. The two principal shareholders in Genbeheer, Sankorp (54 per cent) and Rembrandt (25 per cent), would in future hold just under 40 per cent of Gencor and 35-40 per cent in all the former Gencor subsidiaries. Old Mutual, Liberty Life, and Southern Life would thereafter hold 9-12 per cent each. Marinus Daling was quoted as saying that Sankorp and Sanlam's future role in the unbundled Gencor companies would be the same as before.

The question was posed: would the Gencor unbundling in fact succeed in unlocking value for the shareholders? The answer would soon turn out to be positive. In the centenary year, two years later, a simple calculation would show that the holder of 1 000 Gencor shares worth R11 250 just before unbundling would (if he had not dealt at all) be holding a cocktail of Gencor, Engen, Genbel, Malbak and Sappi which, on 1 June 1995, would have been worth a total of R18 400.

Derek Keys's contribution to Gencor was not, of course, limited to a thoroughgoing reorganisation of the corporate structures or the initiation of a debate on the unbundling which, it turned out, would have to be carried through by his successors. His senior colleagues all describe how he per-

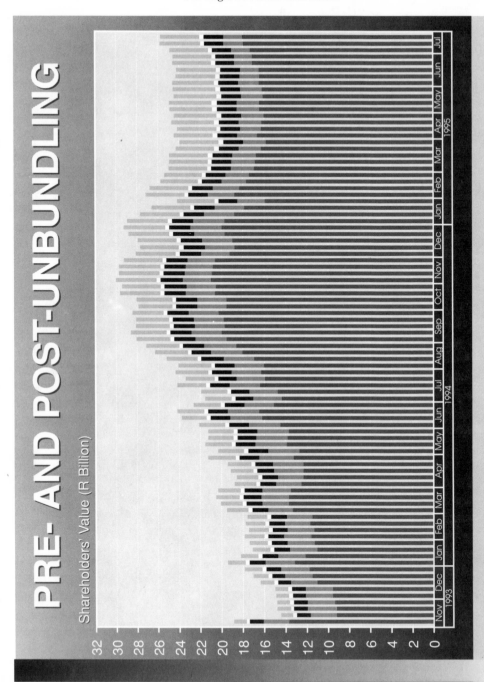

PRE- AND POST-UNBUNDLING

Shareholders' Value (R Billion)

Sappi
Malbak
Genbel
Engen
Gencor

suaded them to identify the critical issues which the Corporation had to face (labour relations were an obvious example: the Kinross disaster of September 1986, when 177 men were killed, followed by a second Gencor disaster at Ermelo in April 1987 with 34 deaths, and then a third at the St Helena gold mine in August 1987 when 62 lives were lost, all had a grim impact on public opinion and, in turn, on Group thinking).

One way in which Keys redirected the organisation was to focus attention on a 'mission statement'. This is an area where management consultants thrive, and it is easy to be disrespectful. But in Gencor's case, Keys, Gilbertson and the others spent many hours thrashing out a mission statement which implied, and necessitated, a fundamental change in the direction of the Group. According to subsequent annual reports, Gencor's mission – and one wonders what George and Leopold Albu would have thought! – reads, inter alia: '*Aim*: real growth as one of the world's foremost natural resource groups... Acting as entrepreneur in starting or acquiring major resources ventures... *Goals*: ...a higher than average return for our shareholders... *Style*: we encourage the creation and development of independent, entrepreneurial and participative management...'

The point about this – and this was in the closing years of apartheid, when South Africa was still blockaded in its laager, with majority rule and international respectability still only a distant hope – is that it put the focus on *growth* as the single great essential. The implication of making such a statement was that you *wanted* to grow, you *intended* to grow, that you were therefore by definition prepared to take greater *chances* than you might have considered in the past, that you would not be content to sit back and wait for something to turn up, that you would do your damnedest to find new things to do. It is entirely possible to argue that this is what Gencor has been doing in the 1990s. (And critics would no doubt add that this is a mission which implies a high-risk strategy – not for nothing has Brian Gilbertson been accused, blamed, praised, for being a gambler...)

With the arrival of majority-rule government, Gencor's prompt and public commitment to support the Reconstruction and Development Programme (RDP) was obvious and logical. The Group emphasised its commitment to ensuring decent housing, clean water and electricity for all its employees, and promised particular attention to education. The Gencor Development Trust, which was to manage the Group's activities in the RDP area, devoted more than half of its budget to education, ranging from support for pre-school education to full-time adult education: the announced objective was to have 80 per cent of the Gencor workforce literate by the year 2000.

But it is important to reiterate that in the late 1980s South Africa was not yet set free. The brighter South African managers were aware that mining possibilities at home were no longer limitless – the gold price had jammed, while costs continued to rise; even coal had its limits, in terms of exportable higher-grade reserves. Part of the answer would be beneficiation, using the country's surplus electric power reserves to process the raw materials for export, and Gencor was planning to be heavily involved in this, but the new entrepreneurial spirit of the Keys-Gilbertson group demanded that, somehow, Gencor must look offshore. As Keys's new team travelled the world, they became ever more conscious that there were things going on, technologies being developed, projects being launched, of which the isolated South African mining industry knew next to nothing. And as Brian Gilbertson began to say, 'The Lord put the mining deposits in certain places. He put some great ones here in South Africa, but he didn't put all of them here...'

The problem was that South Africa was still the pariah of the world. Senior managers like Bernard Smith (with his exploration responsibilities) and geologist John Raubenheimer were becoming increasingly frustrated, but it was difficult in those days for South Africans to travel to many countries and even the projects that were investigated had to be conducted under cover of Australia or (as in a gold prospect in the United States) London. So most of the exploration budget was still being spent inside South Africa, where everyone knew that the future possibilities were limited, especially after the recognised problem of finding new platinum reserves had been tackled. The tradition of Union Corporation – to keep on finding the *next* mine – was faltering at home, yet when people like Gilbertson travelled to South America or the Pacific Rim they came back knocked off their feet by the discovery that mining projects were going on on a scale which South Africa knew nothing about. Their conclusion was that Gencor – and South Africa – *had* to break out of the laager.

This decision was given overwhelming force by a fast-growing realisation that South Africa's traditional mainstay, the gold industry, had gone into a decline from which it would only be rescued by a serious rise in the gold price – and no one could rely on that. The problems emerged with new force in the later 1980s when the gold price jammed somewhere short of $400 an ounce. The Rand fell, political tension intensified, international hostility grew apace, labour relations became a nightmare, and costs soared. The men in the hot seat at Gencor, after the departure of the hard-line Johan Fritz, were to be Steve Ellis and Gary Maude.

Gary Maude was a Northern Englishman, relaxed and talkative, often described by his colleagues as 'a terrier', who over a 30-year career in South Africa had become 'Mr Gold'. His background was in Union Corporation

– he was one of the Johannesburg mining engineers who took pride in Union Corporation, its technical strengths and its reputation for opening a new mine every two years (as they used to say), and he also had experience at Impala Platinum. Maude was involved in a whole series of these new projects in the Free State ('where we were sinking two shafts in the mealie fields and creating a new community'), in the Far East Rand and in Buffelsfontein, where he was the first Union Corporation manager to take over a General Mining mine. As a Union Corporation man, he observed the fading-out of the sense of *esprit de corps* in the early 1980s, when the merger with General Mining at last began to bite. He was an admirer, and junior, of Ted Pavitt, and was a good example of the Group managers who were deeply disillusioned in the 1980s – he even tried to resign in 1986 because of his exasperation with the management of Impala, where he had been attached as Technical Manager – and who were then re-motivated by the arrival of Derek Keys as Chairman. He would later say that it was the nature of the Group's response to the St Helena disaster of August 1987 which persuaded him that there was a new and transforming determination at the top to let the managers get on with their jobs and accept responsibility on the ground. In essence, Maude's eventual and difficult role, first as Managing Director and then Chairman of Gengold, was to supervise and slow the decline of the gold division.

By the late 1980s he was seeing the problems of the gold industry very clearly and drawing bold conclusions. In 1985-8 costs were rising at, probably, 30 per cent per annum – an impossible situation when the gold price was becalmed. Maude's painful conclusion, with Gilbertson as his Chairman, was that costs must be cut and the industry's traditional rule of fixed costs must be challenged. Steve Ellis and he supervised a fundamental change of emphasis: what would matter in future was not the 'tons of rock milled' in the monthly statistics, but 'kilos of gold' extracted. There was a small revolution in that. For example, too much rock was being hoisted which contained insufficient gold to justify its subsequent treatment. That must stop – Unisel, for instance, had been hoisting 110 000 tons per month, which was cut to 70 000. This might be explained as cutting out unprofitable work on the mine, but, as Maude always admitted, it also meant cutting labour, sometimes savagely (he laid off 3 500 men at Unisel in six months).

These were the problems of the existing mines, but his first real taste of a dud mine had come not in gold but in uranium. He would later recall how Beisa was planned after the uranium price shot up from $4,50 a pound in 1965 to $42,50 in 1980. They had found good uranium values south of St Helena in the Free State, so he designed a mine based on uranium. Beisa was all along seen in the industry as a risk untypical of Union Corporation.

Ted Pavitt admitted this when he was quoted as saying of Beisa that mining was 'the gamble of the possible... It all revolved around the rather favourable financing conditions made possible by the consumers, and our own view of the uranium market...' Fair enough. The uranium price then plunged to $10, the main Japanese customer 'walked away', as Pavitt would put it, and Maude would afterwards reminisce about 'a grand opening party in 1981, and a grand closing party in 1982'. But that was not the end of the story. Beisa was allowed to flood, so that water came within 60 metres of the surface over the next three to four years. In 1986 it would be de-watered – to discover the mine was in good condition – and would be extended 500 metres deeper as the Oryx Gold Mine, which would lead to new problems for Maude and for Gencor in the 1990s...

The decision to push through with Oryx – it might be noted that there was a Group tradition of naming its mines after the antelope known in South Africa as the gemsbok, reminiscent of the unicorn, the symbol of Union Corporation – was based on the fact that it would save two years and a lot of money if they could access the reef by going lower from the Beisa shaft, although it was not exactly in the best place for the Oryx ores. But the real problem was that the timing of Oryx turned out wrong: the planning calculations had been made in 1987-8 on a forecast gold price of R85 000 per kilogram. The gold price was on the point of taking a bad beating, and in 1995 it stood at only R45 000. Yet another problem at Oryx was that the first reef turned out to be desperately low-grade and unable to cover marginal costs. Gencor decided to press on and hope for production by 1997. The financial analysts, with good reason, were talking of 'Gencor's problem child'.

Behind this difficult period there was a fundamental strategy: that you *must* close a mine, without sentiment, if it has been losing money for three full months (a dying mine needs enough remaining funds to cope with the closure, otherwise it would have to be declared bankrupt). There were mines in the Group, and in the country, which were old and facing an inevitable closure one day: Marievale, for instance, the old faithful, which lasted until 1992, Bracken, which went in 1993, and the famous West Rand Cons which was sold off in 1992.

So Gary Maude won a new reputation in the second half of his career as the man who closed down whole chunks of the industry and was responsible for the loss of 45 000 jobs in his Group. He kept on proclaiming his faith in a higher gold price even while he would explain the problem – that in 1979 the world had produced 900 tons of gold, and 15 years later it was producing 2 300 tons. No wonder the price continued to hold back, however much demand was said to be rising in the Far East. Gold, Gary Maude was saying in 1995, was a very cheap commodity now, at a bargain basement price...

Well, he would, wouldn't he? So said some of the cynical outsiders and no doubt it was a cheap crack and unfair to Gary Maude's integrity. But he could not deny that South Africa's gold industry, having dominated the world for more than a century, was in a long-term dilemma because the mines of the Rand had become distinctly high-cost in comparison with the more accessible reserves elsewhere in the world, now that it was no longer possible for the Randlords and their heirs to mine their deep-level reefs with ultra-cheap black labour.

By 1995 the figures were an inescapable proof that the industry was in a long decline. In 20 years, the country's share of Western gold production had fallen from three-quarters to just over one-quarter; South Africa's gold mines had become among the most expensive to work; more than one-third of the industry's 1986 work force of half a million men had been retrenched. Not so surprisingly, labour relations in the mines in this New South Africa were not good, output per man was low, and 'continuous mining' was denied (not just because there were so many public holidays but because of an absurd overhang of President Kruger's Calvinist and century-old prohibition of Sunday shifts). There was still no sign of a break-out of the gold price over the $400 barrier, promised for so many years by the ever-optimistic executives of downtown Johannesburg. All of this, of course, also had major fiscal implications for the state, but at least there was the beginning of a debate about the wisdom of the fundamental and historic South African arrangement whereby the mining houses bled off substantial (sometimes very substantial) 'head office' management fees from the individual mines. Just as Gencor in the late 1980s had been quick to understand that the fundamentals of gold extraction had changed, so in mid-1995 it announced a dramatic change in policy with a restructuring of its gold division to grant its mine managers much greater freedom from the traditional head office's hierarchical authority.

No one expected South Africa to discover a new, accessible and economic gold reserve at home. So the logical – necessary – answer for South Africa's mining houses, whose engineers' expertise in gold was unmatchable, must be to go offshore. Until the early 1990s, that was not an option. In 1994, with the end of apartheid, South Africa's gold miners could venture out – and Gencor's men had the opportunity offered by that year's take-over of Shell's Billiton mining arm. And so, in July 1995, Brian Gilbertson announced that the Gencor/Billiton gold assets would be restructured into two parts – overseas and domestic. Tom Dale would be responsible for the 10 mines operating in the Wits Basin, most of which could only be described as 'mature', that is, nearing their end, with the implication that there would have to be various mergers. Gary Maude, while remaining in overall control of Gengold, would join the Billiton Board and concentrate on developing the Group's international gold operations and ambitions in countries like Brazil, Ghana, Indonesia and Turkey. Somewhere, under the rainbow – that must be where Gencor's gold future would be found.

A *short distance beyond Barberton, tucked into the soft green hills of the Eastern Transvaal Lowveld, is the Fairview Gold Mine. Note the truth of the name: it must be the most beautifully situated gold mine in all of South Africa. Fairview and its community used to be perched high up on the summit, safe from the malaria of the valley, but after the Second World War they were brought down-slope, and now the mine buildings cling to the steep mountainside and the shafts appear to burrow directly into the cliff face.*

This is a very old mine and also, in technological terms, a very modern one, because it is today the site of Gencor's pioneering Biox process, the place where bugs are used to extract the gold by 'eating' the ores. Fairview dates from the Barberton gold rush of the 1880s: these hills are pock-marked with hundreds of old-time workings and shafts dating from Jock of the Bushveld times, with romantic and evocative names like Three Sisters, Sheba, Olifantskloof; where the view goes on forever and you glimpse the ruins of dynamite stores and manager's bungalows in the bush. Most of these mines have today been amalgamated, or abandoned, or at best mothballed to await a new gold price.

Fairview was first brought to Gencor as a small part of Federale Mynbou's dowry to General Mining in 1964: today it covers 41 mines on the Fairview property, which, after much consolidation, are now worked from a single shaft. Fairview is also unique in Gencor's gold stable because it is wholly owned, is not separately quoted on the world's stock exchanges, and is not a member of the Chamber of Mines. (Under the July 1995 reorganisation of Gengold it was to be transferred to the Billiton 'international division'.) For much of the century there has been pessimistic speculation about its life, yet in 1995 it is producing one-and-a-quarter tons a year from 14-gramme grade, mining 13 000 tons of admittedly high-cost ore a month, and its local geologists keep on finding new possibilities in the vertical reef, so that no one is talking of closure. Fairview is of course a pipsqueak operation by the standards of South Africa's massive gold mines on the Rand, but the Gencor managers will tell you that this is mining as difficult and interesting as anywhere else in the country. It deserves to be repeated that the mountain and its valley below are stunningly beautiful.

The problem has always been the refractory nature of the gold ore which, unlike the deep-level ores of the Rand, is locked into sulphide minerals like arsenopyrite, which cannot be dissolved in cyanide and so had to be roasted and put out emissions of pyrite sulphur dioxide which blackened the green hillsides under the stack and, so the locals believed, were harmful to health. The Barberton pollution became so inescapably bad, as can still be observed years later, that the Gencor metallurgists had to do something. This was the cue for Gencor's discovery of the bugs, the bacteria, the bio-hydrometallurgy employing the Thiobacillus ferrooxidans, *a peculiar life-form which obtains energy from the oxidation of insoluble and inorganic sulphide minerals. Therefore, there is no resultant pollution and the gold thus unlocked can be processed by the conventional cyanide system.*

The metallurgists like to say that the use of bacteria in dissolving copper ores was known to the Romans in Spain. The tradition was picked up again by General Mining in its operations at West Rand Consolidated after the Second World War, when uranium was found to be extractable from underground water. This phenomenon was noticed in the late 1970s by an unsung General Mining scientist, Eric Goldblatt, then manager of General Mining's central laboratory, who in the words of Dr Alan Haines, Gencor's chief executive for Mineral Technology, starting fiddling around with bugs and convinced his colleagues and bosses that there was something in it. With Barberton an increasing problem, says Haines, 'We decided it was time to engineer the process.' Microbiologists and chemical engineers were brought in and the period the bugs required to open up the ore in the leaching process was reduced, early in the 1980s, from 15 to 4-5 days. A pilot plant was started up at the laboratories in 1984, the process was shown to work, a full-scale plant – a world first – followed at Fairview in 1986, the conventional roasters were de-commissioned in 1991, and today Fairview's ore is entirely treated in the un-spectacular Biox tanks on the hillside. You cannot see *the bugs as they break up the sulphides – they are one-tenth of one millimetre long, constantly dividing, non-toxic, and the tanks appear to contain a rather unpleasant, dirty-grey slurry.*

The irony, after this Gencor breakthrough (because no one else in the world had taken new technology so far), is that this is of little use to the rest of South Africa's gold mines because, quite simply, most of their ores do not need it. The answer is to export Biox to parts of the world where the gold-containing ores are difficult and refractory. Gencor's own Brazil operation at São Bento was a case in point from 1990, but the bigger commercial attraction lies in the licensing of the process elsewhere and to other companies, where the offer of a licence for the secret process may be used to achieve not just cash benefits but also offshore alliances which might in turn lead to exploration opportunities. The large Ashanti Goldfields plant in Ghana and several operations in West Australia are the best-known areas where Biox has been licensed. The new relationship with Billiton would presumably offer new opportunities.

Most exciting of all, Gencor's metallurgists think they have extended the Biox process to the point where the bugs will be able to cope with nickel. That would be another major world breakthrough.

CHAPTER SIXTEEN

DOWN IN RICHARDS BAY

Richards Bay used to be a remote fishing village on the Indian Ocean coast of Zululand, 180 kilometres north of Durban, on the way to Mozambique. Population (white) about 60; one of the poorest, least developed areas in South Africa. In the late 1960s, as part of the government's decentralisation policy – which was one of the pillars of second-stage apartheid, aiming to take industries (and therefore jobs) away from the Transvaal industrial heartland and out to the Bantustans, or at least to their 'border areas' – it was realised that Richards Bay could become one of the African continent's finest deep-water harbours, a perfect growth point from which to export South Africa's coal and minerals. It would also create jobs. The focal point of Richards Bay would be an aluminium smelter.

The first aluminium was cast at Alusaf's bush-site at the Bayside smelter in 1971 with an initial output of 52 000 tons which was increased to 170 000 tons in 1983. The noteworthy point about Alusaf, then and in the years ahead, was that South Africa, which is so rich in almost every mineral, *has no domestic source of bauxite*. (Put very crudely, four tons of bauxite produce two tons of alumina, a white powder which is smelted in electric pots to produce approximately one ton of aluminium.) Alusaf's operation therefore required the importation of alumina from Australia or wherever, to be passed through reduction cells aligned in giant potlines in which colossal volumes of electricity would convert the semi-raw material into the shining, reflective, non-corrosive, environment-friendly, recycleable, lightweight, non-toxic, high-conducting metal which was fulfilling so many functions in the modern world, from aircraft to beer cans to cooking foil to building components.

Even in this initial Bayside project, more than half of the output was exported; in the subsequent expansion at next-door Hillside, the entire production was to be exported. In other words, the charm of the Richards Bay

218

aluminium development was that it offered a way of exporting South Africa's excessive and surplus supply of electricity; to put it differently, it was a device for exporting South Africa's *coal*, which fuelled the Eskom power stations which had been constructed in the alarmist, isolationist years of the 1970s so as to produce a costly over-supply of electric power capacity. It was a bonus that the building of the Bayside smelter was to be a catalyst for the rapid economic development of the Richards Bay region.

The IDC had been the government vehicle for this development project, with a substantial 38,6 per cent minority shareholding held with the technical collaborator Alusuisse and local finance houses like Sanlam and Southern Life. With the arrival of privatisation in the late 1980s, spearheaded by the former General Mining managing director Dr Wim de Villiers, in the Cabinet from 1989, Alusaf was an obvious target. Gencor at this point identified aluminium as the major growth area in both international and domestic markets, and in August 1989 bought a controlling interest of 30,7 per cent in Alusaf from the IDC for an effective R270 million (it would rise to just over 40 per cent). Gencor was concurrently engaged in raising, successfully, R1,47 billion in a rights issue (as was Federale Mynbou, for R826 million). Ironically, this turned out to be the peak of the aluminium price: the eve of the world economic recession of the early 1990s when aluminium prices plunged and the very future of Bayside was clearly in question. Alusaf's operating income would fall from R170 million in the 1990 financial year to R7,4 million in 1993. Equally alarming, Bayside was 20 years old and would need a major rejuvenation if it were to survive. Moreover, something had to be done about the level of fluorine emissions.

The Gencor/Alusaf response can only be described as bold: it decided not merely to upgrade Bayside but to build another, separate – and double-sized – smelter in Richards Bay; it would cost R6,4 billion, it would be the biggest aluminium smelter in the world with a capacity/output of 466 000 tonnes per annum, the equivalent of four per cent of the world market; and it would be South Africa's biggest ever private sector project.Again, the guiding principle was to import all the alumina into Richards Bay harbour, to smelt it with Eskom electricity, and, this time, to export *all* the aluminium as ingots, through the same harbour. There would be 1 000 extra jobs at Hillside, and a spin-off in employment throughout the region and indeed throughout the country. Dr Fred Roux had been recruited from JCI in mid-1990 and was the youthful Gencor Executive Director in the Alusaf Chair; Rob Barbour was Alusaf's Managing Director.

And again, the project would stand or fall on the price of Eskom's electricity. Aluminium smelting is a 24-hour, 365-days-a-year process: if the power supply fails, the pots solidify and the result is total disaster. (Hence the need for double supply lines, and hence the interest of power companies in smelter contracts, because here is a customer for life!) Eskom had, in the past, been reluctant to offer preferential rates to one company, on the argument that it could hardly then resist special pleading from other customers. The consequence was that Alusaf at Bayside had been paying a tariff 35 per cent higher than the average in the world aluminium industry. But now the Alusaf negotiators could point out to Eskom that it had a surplus capacity of 8 000 MW out of its installed capacity of 38 000 MW, that six of its 15 coal-fired stations were in mothballs – and that the new smelter was looking for a contracted supply of a colossal 800 MW (equivalent, the newspapers always explained to their readers, to the combined consumption of Cape Town and Port Elizabeth), a demand which was uniform across 24 hours.

Early in 1991 Rob Barbour spelt out to Eskom that if there was no breakthrough then he was prepared to close down all or part of the existing smelter, which would be a blow to the state corporation: it was essential that the power generator acknowledged that Alusaf was a unique customer. Eskom bowed to the argument and offered a 38 per cent reduction, cutting the 2,7 US cents per kwH which Alusaf had been paying to the world average of 2 US cents. But the additional element, after intense negotiations, was an ingenious deal whereby this electricity price was linked to the world aluminium price on the London Metal Exchange. Hillside would pay on a variable tariff, with its power costs falling if the LME price fell and rising when the LME price went up. The 2 cent price would be predicated on an LME price of $1 800 a ton; if that LME price halved, for example, or doubled, the electricity price would drop to 1 cent or would go up to 4 cents. There was a long-term contract and Eskom in a very real sense thereby became a partner in the project, standing to share in the risks or profits with Alusaf. The ageing Bayside smelter, whose future viability had been in doubt in 1990, would also benefit because it would enjoy the new price once Hillside was in production.

Fred Roux's philosophy behind this Eskom deal was that Alusaf would not have to forecast – to guess – the future aluminium price. He simply would have the assurance of knowing that he had one of the lowest-cost smelters in the world and, while he would be ceding to Eskom a share in the good years, he knew that he would survive in the worst years. And of course, Eskom were delighted to be offered a mechanism for exporting the surplus electricity which was the legacy of the erroneous growth projects and investment decisions of the previous generation. (Incidentally, why did Alusaf go for the option of a double new smelter? Because they had done their calculations at a forecast aluminium price of $1 650, and found that their sums did not work out – whereas the economies of scale with a double-smelter made sense.)

The second element in the Hillside formula was to tie up the alumina supply, which would account for 25 per cent of Alusaf's costs. Alusuisse, the traditional partner of Alusaf, would continue to supply Bayside but appeared anxious to reposition its world-wide operation and distance itself to a degree from aluminium. Contracts were instead signed by Alusaf with Alcoa and Billiton (the minerals branch of Royal Dutch/Shell) for 900 000 tons per annum of alumina: prices were again linked to the LME price and, in an additional bid to limit the risk factor of so colossal a scheme, long-term deals (not unusual in the industry world-wide) were set up in which both Alcoa and Billiton, on 20 and 15 year supply contracts, agreed to buy back about half of the refined aluminium, setting the metal price against the alumina supply price. (As we shall see, the relationship with Billiton would change significantly in 1994, opening all sorts of possibilities, not just for up-stream supply and international marketing, but for down-stream developments world-wide.)

Thirdly, Gencor had to raise the money, which at one stage became a major problem. The main Gencor Board, after initial hesitation, announced its approval for the smelter project in November 1992. Total estimated costs were R6,5 billion, including a large contingency element: interest charges were reckoned to raise that figure to R7,2 billion. Equity funding was set at R2,7 billion, with Gencor committing R1,125 billion so as to continue to hold 40 per cent of Alusaf, and IDC another R875 million. Fred Roux and Rob Barbour had to go out and find R800 million of equity. Alusuisse had been reducing its stake as it distanced itself from primary production. Eventually eight South African institutions, mainly Sanlam and Old Mutual, put up R500 million, though only after a long negotiation and after a hesitation in the later months of 1992 which delayed the final go-ahead. Genbel, IDC and Eskom itself (with R300 million) had to come in to complete the deal. The balance of the funding would come in the form of loans from a consortium of South African banks guaranteeing other foreign loans, tax credits and export credits, particularly from France, whose Pechiney was supplying the state-of-the-art smelting technology with its highly automated AP30 system, overseen by a strong French team in Richards Bay. The new respectability of South Africa on the international scene was crucial, because Pechiney would not otherwise have been willing to collaborate. Alusaf was also helped significantly by government tax amendments (Section 37 E of the Income Tax Act) to allow concessions on capital spending which could be claimed immediately so that the tax credit in effect became part of the project's initial cash flow.

221

As its 1994 deal with Billiton would later confirm, Gencor had decided to go very big indeed into aluminium. After all, aluminium had become the fourth biggest commodity market in the world, exceeded only by coal, oil and gas. Hillside alone would supply four per cent of the world market, and no one was pretending that the local South African demand was going to be of any significance in that future total. But world demand was estimated to be rising by 400 000 tons a year, which suggested room for a South African expansion after the spurt in ex-Soviet supplies in the early 1990s had slowed down. The secret of success would be found in the ability to operate as a low-cost producer: hence the vital importance of the electricity and alumina contracts and their sliding-scale link to the world price. Alusaf was prepared for a break-even price as low as $850 a ton: by June 1995, when production started, the aluminium price was over $1 600 and Gencor executives were jubilant. Curiously enough, Alusaf was going to perform as happily when that price was low; when the price went up – as it did, to Gencor's unconcealed glee, in 1994-5 – its profitability would be checked by what were in effect profit-sharing arrangements with its suppliers.

But on the ground, in Zululand, these things were theoretical. Alusaf had had an argument with the Richards Bay locals about the siting of the megasmelter at Hillside. An independent Environmental Impact Assessment was therefore set up in 1991, as a result of which Alusaf agreed to move its

Aluminium

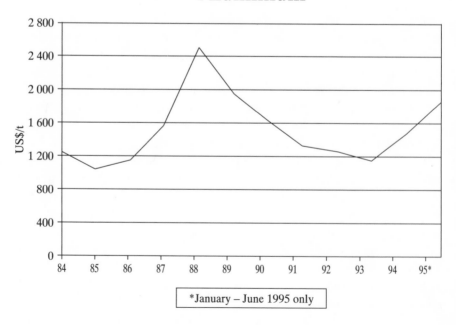

*January – June 1995 only

proposed site for the new smelter: thereafter, the building of the vast industrial complex went ahead with such energy that it came in five months early and an extraordinary R1,25 *billion* under budget. The explanation was that it pays to build in a recession – the economic climate was very bleak, the suppliers and contractors were anxious for work, and Roux and Barbour discovered that the estimates were coming in from the contractors up to 25 per cent lower than they had expected. The first aluminium ingot was cast at Hillside in July 1995.

Today, the fishing village of Richards Bay must have 30 000 residents. The new community, evidently the outcome of careful town planning, is dominated by Alusaf but is not a company town in the sense that everybody works for the same company, because there are a variety of other major players – the Richards Bay Coal Terminal, for example, Indian Ocean Fertilisers, Richards Bay Minerals only a short drive to the north, and plenty of small businesses which have been attracted to this formerly sleepy, even soporific northern outpost of Natal.

There are good beaches, lush semi-tropical vegetation, plenty of game parks within easy reach, a busy little airport, a new shopping centre. Many of these people are recent arrivals from the Transvaal or farther afield. Some of them complain about the traffic (which, after Johannesburg, is absurd) and about the weather (it can be very hot and humid and the wind is sometimes a curse). There is also much talk about the pollution: visitors are invariably assured by the locals that Richards Bay has the highest prescription rate in South Africa for antibiotics, though this is ridiculed by the scientists. The problem is alleged to be the fluorine gases emitted from Bayside's open pots, which the doctors say have no effect on humans but undeniably harm vegetation. Alusaf has committed itself to holding the emissions from the *two* smelters below the *previous* level of Bayside, hence technical measures to dry-scrub the gases so as to recycle them into the alumina. The fluorine emission from the Hillside technology is planned to be one-tenth of Bayside's.

So here is a new segment of South Africa. Big factories are rarely things of beauty, but the Hillside smelter, all in crisp 'blue grotto' paint, and camouflaged with thousands of emission-resistant trees, is no great eyesore. The pylons come looping down from the Transvaal, the ore-carriers arrive on schedule in the harbour, the Zulu workers are trained to increasing levels of sophisticated skills: everything will depend on the world's requirements of this favourite metal of the twentieth century.

In the 1990s Gencor discovered that it had walked into the biggest environmental row that South Africa had ever seen. The enterprise involved was Richards Bay Minerals (RBM), working the mineral sands of the North Zululand coast, in which Union Corporation had taken a 25 per cent stake in the 1970s, to be increased by Gencor to 50 per cent early in 1993. The other 50 per cent shareholder was Rio Tinto Zinc. RBM comprises two companies: Tisand – which does the mining – and Richards Bay Iron and Titanium, which does the smelting. (It would later be a source of confusion, so it should be said at once that RTZ also has mineral sands prospects in Madagascar and Gencor (not RBM) has promising prospects in the far north of Mozambique at Moebase. In Natal the two groups worked together.) The decision which provoked the green protest was RBM's plan to mine the dune sands on the eastern shores of Lake St Lucia.

Mining is, by definition, an environmentally destructive industry. For generations, that was accepted. The grotesque landscape of Johannesburg and the towns of the Reef, for example, where scores of dusty yellow mine dumps are only recently being levelled and grassed over, confirms what was always understood as a fact of life, the inevitable consequence of an economy based on riches extracted from under the ground. Strip-mining of coal created a different ecological eyesore, as have diamonds, manganese, chrome, and the rest. Slowly, in the past generation, the world's mining houses have come to acknowledge that public opinion requires that they minimise their depredations: at best, they must agree to *make good*, as far as is technologically possible, the damage caused by their extractive processes. In some situations and creations, this will be even more desirable than in others. In a manganese mine on the edge of the Kalahari, for example, the creation of an enormous hole in the ground like Samancor's Mamatwan was not really going to cause a public outcry; perhaps the Big Hole in Kimberley is acceptable today for sentimental reasons. But in an idyllic landscape on the shores of the Indian Ocean, by contrast, the miners were going to have problems.

It would be hard to think of a more delicate area for dredge-mining than the coastal dunes of North Zululand. The area around Lake St Lucia was set aside for protection as early as 1895; the Natal Parks Board, since its formation in 1947, has succeeded in consolidating various adjoining areas and has set its sights on the creation of the Greater St Lucia Wetland Park of 280 000 square hectares. This area is one of the world's major breeding grounds for birds; the lake is an equally important habitat for fish; the eastern shores house the largest numbers of hippo and reebok in Southern Africa, together with 450 vertebrate species, 44 red data challenged species, and so on and so forth. But the black sands of the Zululand coast have always been known to contain minerals, and it may or may not be apocryphal that Shaka and his Zulu warriors made their spears from the minerals they found in the dunes which run parallel to the sea for many kilometres and rise to a mini-range of 200 metres.

In the 1970s – after the 1967 decision to build a modern port at Richards Bay – the commercial exploitation of these sand dunes became feasible. The Canadian firm Quebec Iron and Titanium (QIT), whose main experience was on the St Lawrence River in Quebec, was looking for a higher quality of ilmenite, which is smelted principally to extract titania dioxide slag, which in turn is a feedstock for pigments. The higher-quality ore was found in Zululand, on the Tisand lease area immediately north of Richards Bay. In 1974 QIT (to become part of RTZ) and the Industrial Development Corporation (which had been the Canadians' partner in the project) were joined at IDC's suggestion by Union Corporation, which was respected for its mining expertise and had experience of beach sands through an Australian connection. Union Corporation took 25 per cent, and the consequent company, named Richards Bay Minerals, started production of ilmenite, rutile and zircon in 1978. There was rapid expansion through the 1980s; by the end of the decade there were four furnaces and production of titania dioxide slag had risen to 1 million tonnes per annum. After early smelting problems had been sorted out, it was a very profitable business.

All of this was achieved with deliberate discretion. They were years of international sanctions against South Africa and, because these were strategic minerals for the West, they were exported – over 90 per cent of output has always been for export – with the precaution of a corporate profile so low as to be close to invisible. As an additional security, the RBM management took particular pains to implement the so-called Sullivan Principles (the American code of guidance for employment conditions in the apartheid period) to an extreme degree. (That did not seem to avert various difficult and violent strikes, as in late 1994.) So it was all the more confusing for everyone in Johannesburg when this obscure but surprisingly sizeable mining company, operating out in remotest Zululand, was called to account for its apparently logical development plans.

RBM held the Tisand lease, extending 17 kilometres north of Richards Bay (an area containing the smelter), and the Zulti South lease, a similar distance to the south of the town. Beyond Tisand there was Zulti North. All of these were scheduled to be mined for 17 years, and then rehabilitated with the professed intention that no one would know the miners had ever been there. South Africa's conservationists never made a serious protest about those initial leases. But when RBM looked farther north – to the narrow strip between the eastern shores of Lake St Lucia and the Indian Ocean, the so-called Kingsa Tojan lease – then all hell broke loose. Gencor appeared not to worry;

as late as April 1993 it raised its holding to 50 per cent when it bought out IDC and the minorities. (Late in 1994 the Gencor stake in RBM was *technically* transferred to Billiton as part of the complex merger/takeover of the Shell mineral operations.)

The environmental row was first unleashed in 1989 when RBM applied to convert its existing prospect leases north of the St Lucia Estuary to mining leases. (This development from prospecting to mining has usually been an uncontested and logical process in South Africa.) The campaign to Save St Lucia began as a nation-wide – and essentially white, middle-class – 'Green' protest which then travelled overseas. The argument has been raging ever since, so much so that this has become one of the classic confrontations between international business and the world-wide Green movement.

It has also become a dialogue of the deaf. Both sides have lucidly expressed and carefully argued positions. Neither side, it soon became clear, was going to budge. So the issue was referred back to government, where, of course, a fundamental change of authority was in process – from minority to majority rule, and, equally relevant, a shift in the relationship between national and provincial authorities.

The company started from the position that (a) this was a desperately poor region of South Africa where job creation was vital, (b) the mining process would be completed in a short-term 17 years and the landscape would then be restored, and (c) that it had the technology to return the dunes to their original state. It added a welter of statistics, promoted through an expensive public relations budget, to show how the region and its people were benefiting not just from jobs in RBM but from the schools, hospitals and social services which were donated by the company.

The Greens replied (a) that RBM's expansion into the eastern shores of St Lucia would create only 159 jobs, (b) that the eco-tourism projects proposed by the Natal Parks Board would bring more benefits over a longer period (and more jobs), (c) that there was plenty of titanium in South Africa and no need to mine it in this of all places, (d) that it was impossible to drive a massive dredger 30 metres deep through the coastal dunes without damaging the delicate ecological balance of the area, and (e) that a mining operation would not only lose South Africa its international status as a Ramsar Wetland of International Importance (named after the 1990 convention in the Iranian town of that name) but would destroy any hope of success in the on-going application to have St Lucia designated a United Nations World Heritage Site, with consequent loss of tourist revenues. Several senior Gencor directors, the newspapers reported mischievously, had signed petitions against the St Lucia project.

226

The argument developed. RBM insisted that it could rehabilitate the dunes to a point where a recent mining episode would be forgotten. It showed photographs, and produced scientists, to demonstrate that the dunes would recover; it had experience of nearly 17 years to show how, first, you replace 95 per cent of the sand/soil (that is, minus the five per cent of minerals that have been removed), then you mould this into the approximate shape of the original dunes, then you cover with the original top-soil, then you sow a temporary ground cover, then you plant *Acacia karoo*, which develops rapidly so that you have a cover under which the original habitat can re-establish itself – not just vegetation but birds, mammals, insects, the lot.

These dunes are young, explained the RBM men – perhaps only 10 000 years. Dunes are *always* changing: this would be just another minor diversion in their development. As for the slumping of dune-cliffs into the sea, which the environmentalists had highlighted – well, that was always happening and had nothing to do with the mining operations 80 metres inland, as could be seen from the fact that slumping occurred many miles from any dredger.

The Greens would have none of it. How could you remove five per cent of the sand/minerals, they argued, and maintain that nothing had changed? How could you destroy a giant dune and then rebuild it with bulldozers and be confident that you had not altered the subtle, centuries-old geology which had filtered rainfall so slowly through the sands that, in a dry season, it was still replenishing the creeks and sustaining the hippos and the crocodiles and the myriad life of the estuary? And what about the noise of the dozers and dredgers, and the glare of the floodlights, in a 24-hour operation in what was supposed to be a wilderness of tranquillity?

Nonsense! replied the company. It was absurd to suggest that St Lucia was a pristine and unspoiled area. Since the 1950s, 5 000 hectares had been given over to commercial forestry. Apart from the non-indigenous appearance of the state pine forests, there was the massive din of all the forestry operations – and it was agreed that it would take 20-plus years to run down the existing forests, with all the chain saws and draggers that that would entail. As for the argument that a mining project would kill the prospect of a World Heritage Listing, look at Australia, where the siting of a uranium mine within the Kakadu National Park had been no problem.

'That's a lie!' replied the Greens (for by now the debate had become heated). The Ranger mine was *not* inside the Kakadu Park. And, they repeated, why do you have to target this particular site, when there is titanium all over? Look at the Namaqua Sands project near Saldanha Bay, for example, on the opposite side of the subcontinent, where Anglo American was developing its own minerals sands project on a 150-kilometre stretch of strandveld without any particular public protest. The fact is, they said, and kept on saying: 'St Lucia is unique and is *off-limits*!'

This was not – to repeat – an argument which RBM was going to win with the affluent white intelligentsia of the northern Johannesburg suburbs, and certain company executives may have privately accepted that fact. But the debate was going to be seen rather differently by the new, black leaders of the country, whether at a national or a provincial level. One complicating factor was the existence on the sidelines of the tribes which had been evicted from the area in the 1950s and 1960s, and who, with the arrival of majority rule, wanted to return to their ancestral lands. The embarrassing fact was that the prospect of the return of peasant scratch-and-burn farmers to the St Lucia shores appalled *both* the Greens *and* the RBM scientists, who had spent 15 years proving they could recreate an unspoiled environment. However, in the new political climate that now seemed a very possible prospect. The white holiday-makers wanted to return to their fishing, hiking and sailing on and around St Lucia; the provincial administration was likely to be more concerned to maximise job creation and tax revenue – which were more dramatically available in the short-term from RBM than from the Natal Parks Board; meanwhile, the local population simply wanted to go home. As for the businessmen, they were painfully aware that their share in RBM was responsible for perhaps 20 per cent of Gencor's profits: we were talking about some of the Crown Jewels.

The government decision late in 1989 was to set up an Environmental Impact Assessment, principally directed by the CSIR. The Greens were always sceptical about this, alleging that it was funded by the company, and their suspicions were proved right, they thought, when the EIA report was published early in 1993 and explained that 'the area is a vital part of the conservation network in Africa, for a number of important reasons. These include the size of the undisturbed area, the unique nature of the estuary, the area's coastal location, its declaration as a Wetland of international importance, and its potential to support big game and to attract tourists...' – and nevertheless concluded that 'it is possible to gain maximum value by developing eco-tourism concurrently with mining'. The EIA then seemed to draw back: 'The problem would be a simple one if all costs and benefits could be reduced to monetary terms. In the case of mining on the Eastern shores of St Lucia, however, costs of impacts such as visual quality, the sense of place, and a sense of wilderness, are almost impossible to evaluate. This leads to the notion of willingness-to-pay...' And the EIA summed it up in these stark and commercial terms: 'Would South Africa be willing to pay, in other words forgo by not mining, R153,5 million in order to avoid the predicted impacts on the environment?'

But this was not the end of the process. The next stage was a Review Panel of five distinguished men, headed by a respected Judge, Richard Leon, which took its own evidence in November 1993. George Hughes, boss of the Natal Parks Board, seized his chance to argue for the conservation/tourism development of the area without mining, and pointed out that no decision should be taken until the land claims to the district had been resolved: he said permission to allow the project on a Ramsar site would 'impact upon the integrity of the nation'. Dr Jack Goedhals, for RBM, maintained that the Kingsa Tojan lease area was a major ore reserve by world standards and there was no alternative for an industry growing at 2-6 per cent per annum: there were no other deposits in the country, he said, which were on a similar scale and economically viable. If eco-tourism could go hand in hand with the present, noisy, forestry operations, he did not see why tourism and mining at St Lucia could not co-exist.

Judge Leon's conclusion focused on the 'sense of place' argument. His panel decided that no mining should be allowed at St Lucia – 'mining the Eastern Shores would cause unacceptable damage to a place which is special because of its rich history, ecology and biological diversity, and the significance it has in the eyes of its many visitors... The area has a unique and special sense of place... Because of its special value, St Lucia is too precious to risk...' Acknowledging the silent threat of a return of the original population, Judge Leon urged that 'the original inhabitants should receive adequate land in adjacent areas and money in compensation as a matter of urgency'.

This might have seemed a crunching defeat for the company, but by this stage the political background was in flux and the Leon recommendations were rapidly to be overtaken by events. The decision about St Lucia would – it appeared at the time – be handled at provincial level. Or would it? Surely it was too important to be delegated by the national government? Meanwhile the Natal Parks Board application for World Heritage status for St Lucia was pending. The company agreed it did not propose to start mining until the year 2001: 'What's the hurry?' asked the protesters. Well, said the company, we are responding to a world demand for titanium oxide which is rising at 2-6 per cent a year from a present base of 3 million tons: we have to know where we are going to find our raw materials.

To which replied the Greens (for the umpteenth time) – the South African beaches are full of titanium, you don't have to invade St Lucia, you might even move your machines to Mozambique where you'd be welcomed.

The debate would run and run. But as the majority rule government entered its second year in power, it seemed more and more inevitable that the decision would have to be taken by the Cabinet at national level – unless the company, at this late stage, suffered a change of heart.

D*rive north out of Durban on the toll road up the coast; after an hour or so the sugar cane yields to timber, then you emerge on the fast road from Empangeni towards the smoke-stacks and polluted air of Richards Bay. Across the coastal plain, by-passing the town centre, and after another 15 kilometres up the coast, this time through densely populated KwaZulu bush, you are into Company Territory – the RBM Lease Area, its schools, its clinics, its traffic regulations, and its hordes of workers and children – and another smelter belching black dust and flying a silver flame, with heavy security everywhere to remind you that they have had labour problems here.*

They mine the sand dunes not in a wide and undiscriminating swathe, but along a narrow spaghetti strip above and away from the sea, between avenues of untouched indigenous forest. You climb to the top of the dunes and then you see a rather grotesque sight, a pond several hundred metres long, with a sort of mobile factory floating on it, linked to shore by a scramble of heavy tubes carrying water, slurry, concentrate, whatever, and yoked to a dredger which, like a swimming-pool suction-cleaner, burrows around haphazardly near the sand cliff, soaking up the sand from many metres down, blasting water at the cliff so that it crumbles and slips into the water, the whole caboodle moving forward by six metres a day while the mineral sands are slurped back into the processor plant. Ahead, there are machines to strip out the trees and the topsoil, to stack the soil for its eventual reinstatement. Behind them, the ochre sand – minus its five per cent of minerals – is stored, ready to be returned and pummelled into approximate dune shapes, then stabilised, watered, covered with the old topsoil, given a quick and temporary first-year vegetation, protected by terraces of windbreak netting, replanted by regiments of Zulu ladies, until, urged on by the Natal coastal rainfall, the natural vegetation returns. The secret lies with the acacias, the pioneer karoo, which sprout rapidly, build up humus levels, produce the nitrogen, welcome back the wildlife and the plant species. The acacias grow thick for the first five to seven years, then they thin out and other indigenous plants and trees emerge. After 15 years the revived forest looks undeniably impressive. Is anything missing? How many species have been lost? Do the indigenous trees falter because they are growing out of a churned-up, shallow, minerally depleted soil? RBM says no. Their scientists agree. The Greens mutter darkly.

The ugly part is the scar while they are mining – a gross, ochre quarry of naked sand, gouged by tyre tracks, topped with giant machines spewing water and slurry. Even here, there is not much noise (the ponds are quiet, the motors are electric), though it could hardly be described as a tourist paradise. It is not exactly Wilderness.

This is the ultimate test of the mining industry. Can it pass through these giant sand dunes in one of Africa's most precious sanctuaries, extract its minerals, reconstitute the landscape and its ecology, and leave that wilderness unspoiled? And will it – should it – will it really want to – be allowed to try?

CHAPTER SEVENTEEN

BREAK-OUT

Brian Gilbertson was given just 10 days to prepare himself to step into Derek Keys's shoes as Executive Chairman of Gencor. In January 1992, after Keys's golfing encounter with State President FW de Klerk – which led to tears from Mrs Keys, prayer by Mr Keys, and second thoughts by Mrs Keys – FW returned from Taiwan and offered Keys the Ministry of Trade and Industry (to which the Finance Ministry would be added four months later). Gilbertson had been one of Keys's chief lieutenants, successively Executive Director in 1988, Deputy Chairman of Genmin in 1989, Chairman of Genmin in 1990, and he was not unaware that one day he would be a contender for the top job, but he had never dreamed that elevation would come so soon and so abruptly.

Gilbertson was an outsider. He was not a mining man by background, nor even an accountant, but a scientist. Born in the Eastern Cape, he became a physicist who took his first degree at Rhodes on a CSIR bursary which tied him to that organisation until he was 'bought out' by JCI, which was interested in trying to apply to mineral exploration his expertise in a particular field of optics and mathematics. Bernard Smith – whose career was to be interlaced with Gilbertson's – was running the JCI mining division and gave him a job in 1970 (he was to be briefly diverted by a role with America's NASA space project). His physicist's skills failed to find any mines, as he admits, so he was moved to Head Office and developed a successful career which took him to the JCI Board in 1986, when he was made Managing Director of Rustenburg Platinum Mines, and then – through Bernard Smith, who had by this time left JCI, moved to London, and returned to Gencor in South Africa – he was hired by Derek Keys. It was made clear that Keys was looking for someone of the next generation to run Gencor's mining arm; it was also clear that, if he was a success, he would be in the running, eventually, for the top job.

Gilbertson's response was not inevitable, although it had been rumoured that he did not always see eye-to-eye with his Chairman at Rustenburg; he had made it to the top, was engrossed in that job, did not know Keys or Gencor – but the chance of running Gencor's mining division in a year or two (there had to be a delay because there was a 'restraint of trade' on him – the gentlemanly stipulation that he would have to steer clear of platinum for 18 months) was an irresistible temptation. Gilbertson settled down quickly in Gencor and rapidly emerged as one of Keys's most promising lieutenants. He was given a sequence of tough jobs – sorting out the Trans-Natal coal operation, which was in trouble at the time, and sharing the gold mines with Colin Officer. It was a running-in period before he was permitted to return to platinum and take on the chairmanship of Impala. After that there was the Genmin Chair when Steve Ellis stepped down.

An unpompous, cultured, private man, he developed an unexpected skill at public relations, and soon his photograph, with its shock of thick, increasingly salt-and-pepper hair, was a regular feature in the financial press. But he was inevitably thought of – invariably referred to – as Derek Keys's protégé. With Keys's translation to high office, Gilbertson would have to show that he was his own man.

Gilbertson had arrived at Gencor only after Keys had imposed a new structure and dynamic. The industrial arm had been identified and strengthened, but the mining side was not yet entirely sorted out; Steve Ellis, Gilbertson and Colin Officer shared various responsibilities, and Impala Platinum, from which Gilbertson was initially barred, was in a particularly odd state, a distant island of Union Corporation nostalgia hidden behind the traditional secrecy of the platinum industry and drifting towards technical obsolescence. Keys had made his generational changes to Gencor's top team, but as the 1990s brought the opening of South Africa to the world, Gilbertson was able to complete and extend the break with the past. There was to be an unashamed emphasis on new men: the old guys departed, and sometimes they went without over-extended ceremony. Gilbertson inevitably earned a reputation as a hatchet man. He was unrepentant, content to say that he needed a new (and by definition younger) team, and happy to boast of the quality of his new executive chiefs. The process was enlivened by the apparent frequency with which he hired former colleagues from JCI – Dr Fred Roux to run Alusaf, Michael McMahon, and Mike Salamon (from Shell SA to Trans-Natal) to join Bernard Smith, who had been with JCI many years before. Gilbertson always denied that he was targeting JCI and insisted that everyone approached him (McMahon had not been looking for a job – he was about to move to Canada and innocently asked for a reference!)

Gilbertson's aim was to break the system where executives expected to fill their desks until retirement and their deputies expected to succeed them. Keys's legacy to Gilbertson, of course, had been 'unbundling'. Whatever Gilbertson's original doubts, he had now been convinced, and he got on with it. The compensating fact was that Gilbertson and his new team were already engrossed in the great plan for Gencor's international expansion. They had identified Billiton, and knew that its parent, Royal Dutch/Shell, was interested in a deal.

On 2 February 1990, State President FW de Klerk took the podium in Cape Town's Parliament and made the historic announcement, utterly unexpected only a short time before, that apartheid was to be ended, Nelson Mandela and his colleagues released, the ANC and the other liberation organisations unbanned. For South Africa's businessmen, and none more so than the new leaders of Gencor, it was the signal that they would soon be able to target the world, relieved of the barriers of economic sanctions and political opprobrium. In this transformed atmosphere, Gencor was to get to work on the major business deal which was to mark South Africa's return to the international community.

The timing of President de Klerk's extraordinary about-turn was particularly welcome to these South African businessmen. John Raubenheimer's geologists, for example, had launched a major exploration programme in 1987 as one of the ways to achieve Gencor's new mission of aggressive growth. Raubenheimer, Genmin's chief executive for Mineral Resources, had been given five years to come up with something special and, after three years' work which had perforce been focused mainly inside the country, he was convinced that it would be necessary to go international: he therefore prepared to concentrate on four areas – the South American Cordilleras, West Africa, the Pacific Rim, and North America – and over the next few years he presided over a very dramatic growth of Gencor's prospecting department. Bernard Smith, his immediate senior, was also convinced that the Group would have to look offshore for growth (his own apprehension about unbundling was that it might have made Gencor too small to do a big deal overseas).

Smith, who had returned to South Africa in the gloomy days of 1985 and had devoted most of his time since then to growing the energy interests of the Group by buying Mobil for a remarkably low price, developing Engen, and managing the Mossgas project (from which Gencor would in due course, and wisely, disengage) appears to have been more convinced than some of his fellow Directors that it was possible to operate internationally even while sanctions remained in force. It was Smith who had been keenest on the mysterious possibility of a merger between Lonrho and Gencor

Northwards, on Johannesburg's Parktown Ridge, was the home of the Albu family from 1912.
Designed by Sir Herbert Baker, it was renovated by Gencor in 1995 and restored to its former
Edwardian splendour.

Top left: The Fairview gold mine, near Barberton in the Eastern Transvaal, was one of the legacies of Federale Mynbou to General Mining and then to Gencor. Today it is the home of the 'Biox' process in which the refractory gold-bearing ore is treated by 'bugs'.

Bottom left: These micro-photographs show how *Thiobacillus ferrooxidans* attacks the sulphides in the treatment tanks. The bugs, less than a tenth of a millimetre long, open up the ore in a non-toxic, non-polluting process.

Above: The moment of the opening of the sluices of the H F Verwoerd Dam. This was an unusual project for Union Corporation to take on in the 1960s. The group was not to repeat the experience.

Top: Impala Platinum, near Rustenburg, in 1979. President Lucas Mangope of Bophuthatswana (left) with Ian Grieg, Impala Chairman, one of the Gencor executives who had originally negotiated the project.

Bottom: Ted Pavitt, Executive Chairman of Union Corporation in the 1970s, seen where, as a professional mining engineer, he was most at home – on site.

Opposite page: A Sappi forest in the Eastern Transvaal in the 1960s. Sappi would eventually be 'unbundled' from Gencor in the 1990s, to become a major pulp and paper industry in its own right.

Above:
The beginnings of the Beatrix gold mine in the Free State – Ted Pavitt (right) and Gary Maude (left) survey the new shaft.

Right:
Gary Maude (right), originally of Union Corporation, was to become South Africa's 'Mr Gold' in the 1980s, when he had to push through major retrenchments in the industry.

Hotazel, on the edge of the Kalahari Desert, is the Samancor base and the archetypal company town.

Blasting at the 'Big Hole' of Samancor's Mamatwan manganese mine, where the dark grey strata of manganese contrast with the yellow of the Kalahari sands.

Optimum open-cast colliery, where the landscape is rehabilitated after the walking drag-line has stripped out the coal seams. The Hendrina power station, supplied by Optimum, is in the background.

Right: The world's biggest aluminium smelter, Alusaf's 'Hillside', completed in 1995 at Richards Bay. The older smelter, 'Bayside', is in the background.

Top: Gencor is actively involved in the development of the communities around its mines. In 1994 alone, the group established 31 small farmers and allocated 900 hectares of redundant mining land for agricultural development. Here farmers display some of their produce.

Bottom: A rehabilitated forest on the coastal sand dunes of the Richards Bay Minerals lease area, 15 years after the titanium in the sands was mined by dredger and the area replanted.

Opposite page: The first 'tap' of stainless steel at the Columbus Joint Venture in Middelburg, May 1995. The partners are Gencor, Anglo American and the Industrial Development Corporation.

Irian Jaya: one of Gencor's exploration teams at work in the Komopa/Dawagu area, where there are hopes of a major copper-gold prospect. Surrounded by the local population, 'Indiana Jones' style, are Gencor partnership geologists (left to right) John Smart, Dale Hancock and Andy Jackson.

Left: Visiting the Irian Jaya venture in mid-1995: Gencor Executive Chairman Brian Gilbertson (right) and Head of Mineral Resources John Raubenheimer (left) in the company of one of the local population.

Gencor's spectacular new Head Office in Johannesburg's mining sector was completed during the centenary year and opened by President Nelson Mandela in September 1995. The site has always been the corporate home of Gencor and its founders and the new building incorporates some of the architecture of the early headquarters of General Mining and Union Corporation.

Executive directors in the atrium of Gencor's new head office. (Left to right, back row) Colin Officer, Executive Director, International; Mick Davis, Executive Director, Finance; Derek Keys, Chairman of Billiton; Michael McMahon, Chairman of Impala Platinum. (Left to right, front row) Brian Gilbertson, Chairman of Gencor; Gary Maude, Chairman of Gengold; Dr Fred Roux, Chairman of Alusaf; Mike Salamon, Chairman of Samancor.

which was mooted, and discussed, at various times. Derek Keys, who was brought together with Tiny Rowland by Smith – and at one point was offered the chairmanship of Lonrho by the controversial ex-Rhodesian tycoon! – would afterwards say that he never took the idea seriously so long as Tiny was anywhere around, but Smith was intrigued by the synergies that might arise from a reverse take-over, and believed a deal was available. (He was once ordered out of Rowland's London house in pouring rain because he had undiplomatically referred to the possibility that Lonrho might pass its dividend!) On Lonrho, Bernard Smith would eventually be proved right, at least in part, and it was he who would be directly involved in driving through the subsequent deal with Billiton – and who, ironically, would leave the Group in consequence.

It can be said that the Billiton deal arose indirectly out of the ambitious Alusaf plan to build a massive new smelter at Richards Bay. Early in 1992, while the feasibility study was going on, the Alusaf Chairman, Dr Fred Roux, and his colleagues focused on the need to ensure alumina supplies for their project. One of the potential international suppliers was Billiton, although they had not been in close contact in the past because Billiton was wholly owned by Royal Dutch/Shell, which preferred not to be seen doing business with apartheid South Africa. As everyone in the mining industry knew, the oil majors at that time were keen to get out of minerals and Shell was no exception. It occurred to Fred Roux that here was a large, wide-ranging, international mining company, unlisted and owned by an oil group which did not seem very interested: he began to wonder whether an alliance might make sense – but that was as far as it went at the time, and Fred Roux had a host of other concerns to do with his new smelter.

Later that year, however, a London consultant came to Gencor to say that it believed it could persuade Shell to sell Billiton. One relevant factor was that, although majority rule was still more than a year away, South Africa was now manifestly set on the path to radical change: Shell need no longer have political qualms about doing a deal with a South African mining house. Nevertheless, the initial contacts were conducted with great discretion. Detailed negotiations began early in 1993: they were appallingly complicated and difficult, and were to drag on, with frequent crises, until November 1994. As Fred Roux would later sum it up: 'It was always very, very difficult – because we couldn't take money out of the country.' To put it slightly differently, Gencor set out to buy a major international mining company, admittedly containing very high-quality assets which no one doubted would make a good match with Gencor's portfolio, without having the money.

The Gencor team was led by Brian Gilbertson, of course, with Bernard Smith, whose reputation for stubborn tenacity made him a natural as the man whose job would be to make the deal work. Billiton was a collection of mining operations spread throughout 15 countries round the world, particularly strong in bauxite, alumina and nickel, starved of exploration funds by a parent company which appeared to have lost interest in its mining arm. But Billiton was split up into an assortment of local operations: there was no identifiable 'Billiton', for which to bid, and much of the complexity of the 18 months of negotiation would stem from this.

The problem was that, because the South African Reserve Bank would not permit it to export the funds to make the purchase – the Reserve Bank officials were 'very tough', Gilbertson recalls – Gencor had to raise the money offshore. It knew that it had about $300 million of non-core assets in Europe, largely in the shape of TransAtlantic Holdings – a relic of Union Corporation's near-forgotten activities in the London property market of the 1950s – and some North Sea oil and gas interests. The original asking price for Billiton was in the region of $1,8 *billion*. How to fund – to bank – the balance?

One possible solution was to find an international partner, and in April 1993, out of the blue, Peter Allen of Lac Minerals – a Canadian gold mining company – came to Gencor and suggested he was interested. Brian Gilbertson was tempted; Bernard Smith was worried. (Some of their colleagues date their eventual falling-out to this period.) In September 1993 Lac abruptly pulled out, and the Gencor proposal was in deep trouble.

At this point Gencor fielded its fourth star player. Mick Davis was a very young (35 at the time) high-flying and ambitious accountant who had just departed from Eskom, the state electricity institution, because, as he would candidly explain, he had been passed over, to his astonishment, for the Chief Executive's job in April 1993. Brian Gilbertson knew that he had a gap in his team, on the financial side, and Mick Davis was persuaded to join, on condition that he would not only be Finance Director but would be given a wider management responsibility, in this case as Chairman of the Trans-Natal coal division. He wanted to start at once, but Eskom asked him to stay until the end of the year. As it happens, in September 1993 he had an emergency telephone call from Gilbertson and flew to London that night. He was pitchforked into the Billiton negotiations.

Suddenly, following the disappearance of Lac, Gencor was struggling, in Mick Davis's words, 'to work out how we could make the thing pay... We suddenly found we were in a position where we couldn't afford to fund the transaction...' But with the benefit of hindsight, it can be seen that the situation had changed in the course of 1993, because Shell had discovered, as negotiations proceeded, that it *wanted* the deal to work out (and indeed, there was plenty of evidence that Billiton's employees, who had been feeling underesteemed by Shell, were also keen). Both Davis and Bernard Smith realised that the loss of their proposed partner gave them the opportunity to persuade Shell to come in on the financing of the sale. Eventually this proved true: Shell proposed a loan, Gencor said it couldn't afford it, and in the end, after eloquent talk from Gencor about its Reserve Bank problem, Shell put up $300 million in bonds.

It was always clear that everything hinged on whether or not Gencor could bank the transaction. Mick Davis, whose responsibility that was, always promised Gilbertson that it could be done. He was proved right in the end, but only after many months of nail-biting uncertainty, with deadlines extended again and again into 1994, right up to the very end of October, when at the moment of signing the Reserve Bank changed its mind about an earlier point of detail and had to be argued round by a frantic Mick Davis. Throughout these months, there was a particular argument about Richards Bay Minerals, which the international banks, not surprisingly, demanded as security. Davis and Gilbertson put their foot down. Giving RBM as security would not be permissible in terms of Reserve Bank requirements. Anyway, Gencor could not put at risk one of the principal jewels in its crown – if the joint project went wrong, it would be bad enough, but if that failure led to the loss of RBM, then the consequences for Gencor would be disastrous. In the end, after long and fierce argument, the banks agreed to accept the security not of RBM's *assets* but of its future *dividends*. RBM was injected into the newly created Billiton International but definitely not sold or pledged.

So the eventual deal was, in crude summary, that the size of the purchase was reduced to $1,14 billion, for which Gencor put up the $300 million of its offshore, non-core assets (a figure which rose to $335 million and gave Davis his first grey hairs); the banks (UBS, Barclays, Credit Suisse, Dresdner) put in $510 million of debt financing, though with no recourse to Gencor; and Shell took on $300 million of exchangeable bonds whose fine print amounted to a three-year interest-free loan. RBM and São Bento (in Brazil) were injected into Billiton International, though RBM's management was not affected.

Mick Davis had his bad moments, particularly when he discovered he would have difficulty coming up with all of the $300 million-plus, but he was saved when he discovered a facility with JP Morgan which was linked to TransAtlantic but which the Reserve Bank agreed could be shifted to Gencor. As Davis would afterwards say, it was a fantastic deal – 'No one can appreciate how precariously balanced this whole transaction was – we were coming to the party without the capacity to do the deal.'

In November 1994, it was at last confirmed that the deal would take effect on 1 December. Gencor, for $1,1 billion, was buying the larger part of Billiton's operations in the 15 countries: bauxite and alumina in Australia, Brazil, Suriname and New Guinea; the Cerro Matoso nickel mine in Colombia; gold mines in Ghana and Indonesia and Brazil; copper and zinc in Canada; various exploration ventures world-wide. Important, too, was the Billiton marketing and trading operation based in Europe. In the course of the negotiations, as it became necessary to cut the cloth of the deal according to the funds available, and as various prescriptive rights were exercised, the copper prospect of Collahuasi in the Chilean Andes (where Anglo American's Minorco had rights), the Boddington gold operation in Australia and, eventually, an Irish alumina refinery, Aughinish, fell away.

The result was heavily weighted towards aluminium – which was ironic, because South Africa has no commercial bauxite! – and it became an immediate talking point that Gencor was staking its future on a recovery in the aluminium price, and indeed on the very future of the metal. The negotiation had been conducted through the industry's bleakest period for many years. Now, the price was recovering strongly, and there was to be much talk of 'Gilbertson's gamble' paying off. More soberly, there was copious analysis of the synergies available to the new grouping: Billiton alumina, for example, to feed Alusaf's new smelter at Richards Bay; Columbia's Cerro Matoso nickel for Gencor's new joint venture in stainless steel at Columbus in the Transvaal; and of course, the Billiton marketing expertise to spearhead Gencor's drive into the world. The new Gencor was now firmly focused, world-wide, on gold, platinum, aluminium, coal, ferro-alloys, titanium, nickel. The back-room boys were soon to be setting up project teams on copper, iron ore, nickel and (offshore) gold – with mineral sands, zinc and even diamonds next in line. There had been democratic elections in South Africa in April 1994. By Gencor's centenary year of 1995, the Group had indeed rejoined the world with vengeance. The financial analysts – and the domestic and international press – were positive. 'Prometheus Unbound', declared Warburgs, in an unusual flight of fancy.

There was just one shadow over the Billiton celebrations. Bernard Smith, who had handled so much of the detail of the negotiations, apparently believed he had been assured of the Chief Executive role at Billiton. When, at the Annual General Meeting at the end of October 1994, it was announced that Derek Keys, who had left the Cabinet a few months before, would become Chairman of Billiton International, and that the young David Munro would be sent to Holland as Managing Director (Munro was only

39; after a spell as a JCI mining engineer he had climbed the Gencor ranks through Trans-Natal and Samancor), Smith quit, though he remained Chairman of Engen. No one had forgotten that it was Smith who had been responsible for bringing his younger protégé, Brian Gilbertson, to Gencor only seven years before. The best explanation is that Smith and Gilbertson had been moving in different directions in their ideas about the future structure of the new joint group. Smith seemed to favour turning Billiton into a listed overseas arm (rather like Anglo American's Minorco), while Gilbertson came round to the view that, with South Africa no longer polecat of the world, this sort of distinction was unnecessary and a restructuring along commodity divisions extending world-wide would be more effective. Indeed, as 1995 proceeded, it became more and more clear that this was what would happen. But the news of Bernard Smith's departure was overshadowed by the celebrations inside Gencor when it was understood that their previous Chairman, Derek Keys, was, in a sense, coming home. The photograph of Gilbertson and Keys, grinning like schoolboys, seemed to say it all.

The centenary year of 1995 was a time for planning a complex consolidation between Gencor and its new offshore arm. Appropriately, Gencor in September moved into its new head office at 6 Hollard Street in the heart of Johannesburg's business centre. There had been a series of downtown Johannesburg headquarters of varying grandeur over the years, always on or around Marshall Street; the new building, opened by President Nelson Mandela in September 1995, amalgamated several of the surrounding buildings, and continued the 40-year tradition that Gencor has – and uses – a helicopter pad on its roof in the very heart of the city.

The reverse take-over by Trans-Natal of Randcoal, described in an earlier chapter, demonstrated that, even after the exertions with Billiton, Gilbertson and his team were full of energy. The aluminium price climbed steadily to $1 000 a ton in early 1993 and then beyond $1 900 in mid-1995, seeming to confirm that Gilbertson had pulled off his Alusaf gamble in Richards Bay. The Columbus Joint Venture stainless steel project came on stream as planned in April 1995. The new Alusaf smelter was a remarkable R1,25 billion under budget and cast its first ingot in July, six months ahead of schedule. There was talk in Johannesburg of the fantastic promise of a copper-gold prospect in Irian Jaya – and in this Third World country there was no need to conceal a South African origin any longer, President Mandela was an honoured guest in Indonesia. Gilbertson and his lieutenants were touring their new empire, marvelling at, and challenged by, the scope of the world's new mining industry. The executives of Gencor and Billiton were getting to know each other, working out how they could best co-operate, whether in exploration or in technology or in supply contracts.

History has lessons to teach and there were people still around who could remember how, in the mid-1970s, the big merger between General Mining and Union Corporation had not been implemented briskly enough – which in retrospect had surely been a mistake. This time no one doubted that Gencor and Billiton would be restructured rapidly, and almost certainly along commodity lines. But these things take a certain time. How would the new commodity-based divisions be set up? Would Billiton be given an international listing? What to do about Alusaf? How long would South Africa's exchange controls continue to be a complication? When would the Billiton head office be moved to London, as was surely logical? What would the new command structures be? Would Gencor itself one day move offshore?

And then there was yet another announcement, to crown an extraordinary 12 months. On 20 June 1995 Brian Gilbertson and the German financier Dieter Bock – who had only recently, and with great and public difficulty, managed to oust Tiny Rowland from the leadership of the diversified but African-orientated conglomerate, Lonrho – announced that Lonrho and Gencor planned to merge their South African platinum interests so as to create a new company with an output of 1,6 million ounces a year, which would challenge Rustenburg Platinum as the world's top producer.

The news came as a surprise, which was in itself rather odd since there was every sort of logic in bringing together the nearby properties in the valley that lies between the Magaliesberg and Botswana. Indeed, Impala already held 27 per cent of Lonrho's West Plats and East Plats, and everyone in the platinum business knew that Gencor and Lonrho had been talking, on and off, for years about a rationalisation. There had been what Michael McMahon, Impala's Chairman, describes as a 'dalliance' dating back to the mid- and late 1970s, when Lonrho seemed disposed to sell but Tiny's reluctance to cede any of his territory (as Bernard Smith would later discover) was always a problem. Discussions between the two groups intensified in April/May of 1994, and Gencor executives realised they might be able to do business with Bock, but Tiny only faded from the scene at the end of the year. In May/June 1995 there was a flurry of activity and the deal was done.

For older Gencor men, it had its ironies because, back in the 1960s, Impala had originally had an option over part of what became the Lonrho ground, and again, in the 1970s, Impala passed up the opportunity of buying this Lonrho operation because it did not consider itself short of reserves (which was a mistake) and decided it did not need what it thought to be the lower-grade ores of West and East Plats. Twenty years later, the partnership made sense: the Lonrho mines were burdened with debt, while Impala was cash-rich. There were all sorts of synergies available to fascinate the engineers on both sides. Impala had already realised that it could postpone a new and very expensive vertical shaft to mine its next development area, The Deeps, until the year 2007; in the meantime it would concentrate on much cheaper incline shafts, which also had the benefits of producing ore at once. Even in the secretive world of platinum, the managers knew each other – they were neighbours – and would be able to learn from each other.

The odd part of the deal, at first glance, was that in the new holding company Lonrho, not Impala, was to hold a majority of one share over 50 per cent. The explanation was that this was an accounting requirement of Lonrho's so that the London company could consolidate the earnings of this subsidiary. To Gencor this did not matter – the counterbalancing point was that Impala had the chairmanship of the operating Board, and so the casting vote,

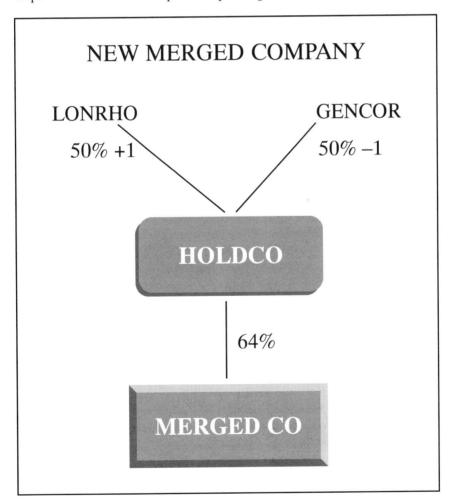

which meant that the Gencor-appointed Chairman would appoint and control the management of the joint project.

Meanwhile, the platinum price was holding at $420,30, steady but dull. Engelhard had just announced an invention for spraying a car's radiator with a catalytic coating which could turn an ordinary motor into a device to vacuum away carbon monoxide and smog to a height of about five metres above the street as it drove along. Managers at Impala believed that this 'PremAir' system could work, even if the news was a few years premature and it would need a big step to make it commercially viable as well as environmentally essential. And with Dieter Bock in command at last in Lonrho, who knew where the two groups might yet co-operate?

G *encor's head office in Johannesburg had worked up a theme to celebrate the centenary. 'GENCOR – 2000' it was called, and looked into a crystal ball to project the Group's world position at the millennium. (Fifty years earlier Sir George Werner Albu would surely have called in his spirit medium!) The answer was:*

Gencor 2000
The world potential

	World ranking
Ferroalloys	1
Coal exporters	1
Platinum	2
Mineral sands	1/2
Coal producers	Top 3
Gold	Top 3
Aluminium	Top 5
Stainless steel	Top 10
Nickel	Top 10

Break-out

Could this really be possible? Were the South Africans aiming, innocent, for the stars? It was a long way, but it was also a direct line, from those two German brothers, penniless and still in their teens, bumping across the Karoo in an ox-wagon to seek their fortune in Kimberley.

POSTSCRIPT

That was the history: so – what of the future?

What could be more dramatic than one of the adventures being played out in the centenary year by Gencor's geologists, this particular example high in the tropical rainforests of the inaccessible and unexplored mountains of Irian Jaya, where there is talk of the world's biggest untapped deposits of copper and gold?

Irian Jaya is the western half of New Guinea, governed as a province of Indonesia since the 1960s. It is almost entirely undeveloped in terms of infrastructure, and is home to a tiny population of one of the most 'primitive' societies on earth – headhunters, cannibals, Papuan-Melanesian (not Asiatic) by race, animist (or Christian where the missionaries have reached them), the women topless, the men still wearing the 'koteka' penis gourd. This is where Gencor has come face-to-face with the Stone Age.

The central highlands of New Guinea attract the geologists because they are the region where the Pacific and Australian tectonic plates collided and created a frenzy of geological activity many millions of years ago. The best prospects are found in the 'roots' of eroded volcanoes. But it is diabolically difficult to access this terrain: the helicopter has been the miners' salvation. Gencor first got interested in the island in the late 1980s, through its Australian subsidiary, and its first reconnaissance was launched in 1988; after a delay while mining laws were rewritten, major exploration began in 1992. Gencor is today the majority shareholder in a complex partnership with French, Australian and local interests (see Appendix). So it may be said that, whatever the Irian Jaya project achieves in the twenty-first century, it has a symbolic importance as a postscript to this History: South African miners are venturing out into the world after long years of apartheid-enforced isolation to take up a role in the development of the Third World. It should be added that here is evidently a territory where the arrival of the mining in-

244

dustry in a land of such unspoiled beauty might well become a subject for future protest from the environmentalist movement, however delicately the mining engineers proceed – as the Gencor geologists will wearily admit, and contest.

The best clues to the potential of the Gencor project in Irian Jaya come from their neighbours, PT Freeport Indonesia (PTFI), a wholly owned subsidiary of the American, New Orleans-based mining company, Freeport-McMoRan Copper and Gold, which was the first to tackle the cloud-covered forests and mountains of New Guinea – and made a staggering commercial success of it. PTFI began drilling in 1967 on a tiny 10 kilometre concession area, Ertsberg – a black mountain of copper ore rising 180 metres above the surrounding terrain, which had first been discovered in 1936 by a Dutch geologist-mountaineer, after which his survey report was filed and forgotten. The company had to instal the entire infrastructure from scratch: it built a harbour, an airport, an hotel, etc, at its headquarters at Timika, and its company town, Tembagapura, and was operational in 1973. It had pretty well mined out Ertsberg by the mid-1980s, leaving a 360-metre water-filled crater; then, only two kilometres away, it found the real bonanza, Grasberg, said to have the world's largest gold reserves. It is also said to be the world's second largest open-pit copper mine, and its ore reserves are reckoned at over *one billion tons.*

To indicate its size, in 1995 Freeport was planning to mine 150 million tons which would deliver 36 million tons of ore containing 1,26 per cent copper and 1,35 grammes per ton of gold. Copper output for 1996 was planned at over 1 billion pounds – and there would be 50 tons of gold *as a by-product.* Moreover, it was all low-cost production; the only complication was that the ore, after milling and flotation on-site, had to be piped as a slurry concentrate literally down the mountain for 120 kilometres in 13-centimetre pipes to the coastal plain, where it was de-watered and loaded onto carriers to be taken off to smelters around the world.

Small wonder the Gencor geologists got interested. They did a discreet reconnaissance programme in 1988, under Australian cover, identified the most promising 10 000 square kilometres, and applied for permits. All these things took time, even after the South African 'political' problems had departed.

Gencor's men were faced with what John Raubenheimer could only describe as 'horrendous logistics'. There are no wheeled vehicles in the interior, not even bicycles. The samples are taken to Jakarta and Australia to be assayed. The group was restricted to 12 expatriates (half of them are French) and had to rely on Indonesian geologists and local labour. There are, in 1995,

245

four base camps – Komopa, Dawagu, Obano and MogoMogo – all in the vicinity of Lake Paniai (some of which accommodate wives and even children), plus four or five temporary 'fly camps'. The geologists – who are *6 400 kilometres* from their head office in Jakarta, the capital city of this same country – are totally dependent on helicopters which drop them into tiny clearings in the forest canopy so that they can enlarge these and construct rough plank platforms which are sometimes too small even to support both of the 'copter's skids, so the rotors continue to spin and the pilot pirouettes on the narrow shelf for the prospectors to jump off onto the safety of dry (or rather, very wet) land. To the layman, this is terrifying stuff: the mountainside is near-sheer, the clouds swirl ever lower, the blades of the 'copter literally chop at the foliage, the streams from which the best samples are taken run swift and jagged. Perhaps the pilots are the true heroes of this first stage of the project.

After the heat and high humidity of the coastal plain, the prospecting areas at 1 500-2 800 metres are less oppressive, but it rains most days (five metres a year) and the cloud cover is a constant danger for the pilots. The timber line is abrupt at about 3 000 metres, and then there is savagely jagged rock interspersed with brief patches of alpine heath, rising to one of the world's three equatorial glaciers. It is magnificent and beautiful: the mountain ranges emerge again and again, for countless kilometres, above the dark mass of the impenetrable forests, rising even above the constant confusion of scudding cloud and the plumes of tropical storms; but for even the toughest and keenest young geologist this can only be described as a hardship post. At least there isn't malaria, once one moves away from the coastal plain.

The locals are no longer hostile, but communication is not easy. There are difficulties, for example in persuading the village headmen to allocate labour for long enough to become an experienced team – and then they cannot always travel freely from one steep valley to another, where the tribal rivalries are still intense. It is rumoured that head-hunting continues to be a valid part of the local culture. But the missionaries and the miners appear, at last, to be having an impact on such things as traditional costume – more and more of the tribespeople have been taking to a ragged form of Western dress over the past few years. The greater problem is that the Indonesian government has a policy of 'trans-migration' which entails importing many thousands of Javanese volunteers to Irian Jaya and settling them in smallholdings. They are better educated and tend to take the newly created jobs; they are also Muslim, which can lead to tensions with the part-Christian Papuans.

By mid-1995, the Gencor partnership was beginning pre-feasibility studies which would take a minimum three years or so. It must be emphasised that no one yet has any idea of the extent of the mineralisation: people like Andy Jackson, one of Raubenheimer's exploration managers, can only say, 'We know we have a resource, and it indicates a fair tonnnage.' In Johannesburg's bars, people speculate about 100 million tons of ore at the very least – but Freeport has at least one billion tons – and no one knows whether the copper or the gold will eventually prove the greater prize.

Then comes engineering design: it is not yet even clear whether Gencor will take its ore to its present base at Nabire on the north coast or south to the Freeport harbour at Amamapare – nor whether it will use slurry pipes or instead use trucks on the new dirt road the government is building across the island. After exploration, there will be five years or so for the construction phase. No one in the company is denying that Irian Jaya is looking good. But Gencor will be well into the next century before it can prove it has yet another winner.

Gencor Organisational Structure
(September 1995)

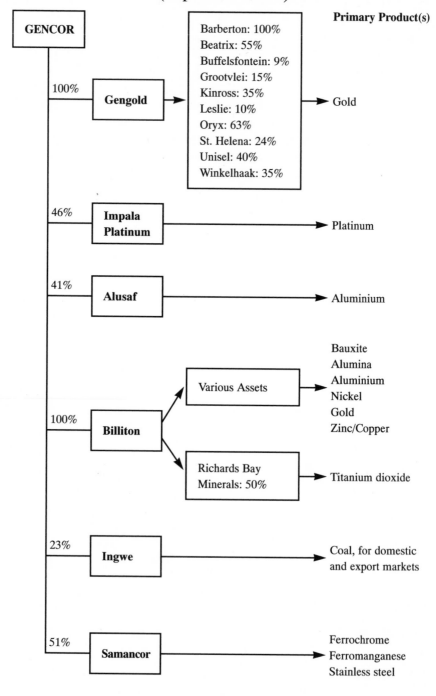

Primary Product(s)

GENCOR

100% — Gengold →
Barberton: 100%
Beatrix: 55%
Buffelsfontein: 9%
Grootvlei: 15%
Kinross: 35%
Leslie: 10%
Oryx: 63%
St. Helena: 24%
Unisel: 40%
Winkelhaak: 35%
→ Gold

46% — Impala Platinum → Platinum

41% — Alusaf → Aluminium

100% — Billiton →
Various Assets →
Bauxite
Alumina
Aluminium
Nickel
Gold
Zinc/Copper

Richards Bay Minerals: 50% → Titanium dioxide

23% — Ingwe → Coal, for domestic and export markets

51% — Samancor →
Ferrochrome
Ferromanganese
Stainless steel

Major investments
(September 1995)

COUNTRY	OPERATION	PRODUCT
Australia	Worsley Mine & Refinery (30%)	Bauxite
		Alumina
	Consolidated Rutile (25%)	Mineral sands
Brazil	MRN (15%)	Bauxite
	Alumar Refinery (36%)	Alumina
	Alumar Smelter (46%)	Aluminium
	Valesul Smelter (41%)	Aluminium
	São Bento (95%)	Gold
Canada	Selbaie (100%)	Zinc
		Copper
Colombia	Cerro Matoso (52%)	Nickel
Ghana	Bogosu (81%)	Gold
Indonesia	Prima Lirang (90%)	Gold
Sierra Leone	Sierra Rutile (12%)	Mineral sands
South Africa	Barberton (100%)	Gold
	Beatrix (55%)	Gold
	Buffelsfontein (9%)	Gold
	Grootvlei (15%)	Gold
	Kinross (35%)	Gold
	Leslie (10%)	Gold
	St. Helena (25%)	Gold
	Stilfontein (10%)	Gold
	Unisel (40%)	Gold
	Winkelhaak (35%)	Gold
	Impala Platinum (46%)	Platinum
	Ingwe (23%)	Export coal
		Domestic coal
	Samancor (51%)	Ferrochrome
		Manganese alloy
	Columbus Stainless Steel (33%)	Stainless steel
	Alusaf (41%)	Aluminium
	Richards Bay Minerals (50%)	Titanium slag
Suriname	Mining Joint Venture (76%)	Bauxite
	Refining Joint Venture (45%)	Alumina

Holding structure
for Irian Jaya Projects

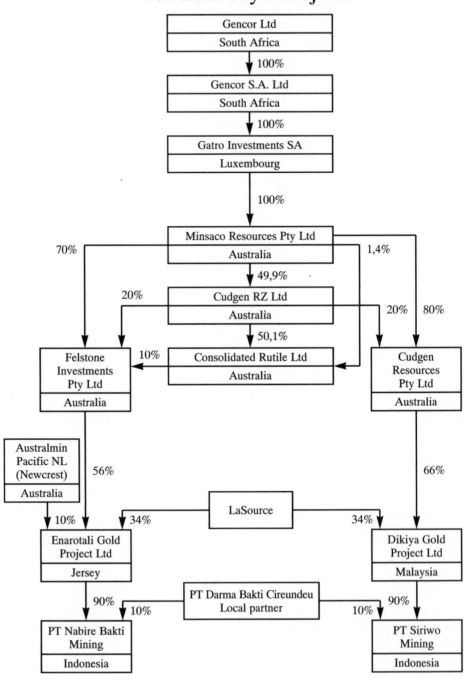

FURTHER READING

Some of the readers of this book may be interested in some of the books which follow. This list is confined to aspects of the Gencor story and does not pretend to be either scholarly or exhaustive, but all the books mentioned here are interesting, in some way or other ... JDFJ

VI Allen (1992), *The History of Black Mineworkers in South Africa*
Andrew Boyle (1974), *Poor Dear Brendan*
Luli Callinicos (1981-), *A People's History of South Africa* (3 volumes)
Diana Cammack (1990), *The Rand at War 1899-1902*
Hedley A Chilvers (1929), *Out Of The Crucible*
AP Cartwright (1962), *The Gold Miners*
— (1965), *The Corner House*
— (1968), *Golden Age*
— (1971), *The First South African*
Louis Cohen (1911), *Reminiscences of Kimberley*
— (1924), *Reminiscences of Johannesburg*
TRH Davenport (1977), *South Africa, A Modern History*
Andrew Duminy & Bill Guest (1987), *Interfering in Politics:*
 A Biography of Sir Percy Fitzpatrick
— (eds), *FitzPatrick: Selected Papers (1888-1906)*
Paul H Emden (1935), *Randlords*
Vernon February (1991), *The Afrikaners of South Africa*
JP FitzPatrick (1899), *The Transvaal From Within*
Laurie Flynn (1992), *Studded with Diamonds and Paved with Gold*
S Herbert Frankel (1922), *An Economist's Testimony*
— (1938), *Capital Investment in Africa*
Martin Gilbert (1976), *Winston Churchill, vol 5, 1922-39*
Sir Harry Graumann (1934), *Rand Riches and South Africa*

Timothy Green (1982), *The New World of Gold*

Theodor Gregory (1962), *Ernest Oppenheimer and the Economic Development of Southern Africa*

John Hays Hammond (1935), *The Autobiography*

WK Hancock (1962), *Smuts: The Sanguine Years*

Norman Herd (1966), *1922: The Revolt on the Rand*

JA Hobson (1900), *The War in South Africa: Its Causes and Effects*

Anthony Hocking (1973), *Oppenheimer and Son*

— (1983), *Kaias and Cocopans*

— (1987), *The Paper Chain: The Story of SAPPI*

Duncan Innes (1984), *Anglo American and the Rise of Modern South Africa*

Alan H Jeeves (1985), *Migrant Labour in South Africa's Mining Economy, 1890-1920*

Edward Jessup (1979), *Ernest Oppenheimer: A Study in Power*

Mendel Kaplan and Marian Robertson (1986), *Jewish Roots in the South African Economy*

— (1991), *Founders and Followers*

CW de Kiewiet (1937), *The Imperial Factor in South Africa*

— (1941), *A History of South Africa: Social and Economic*

Gerhard de Kock (1954), *A History of the South African Reserve Bank*

Robert V Kubicek (1979), *Economic Imperialism In Theory and Practice: the Case of South African Gold Mining Finance, 1886-1914*

John Lang (1986), *Bullion Johannesburg*

— (1995), *Power Base*

Greg Lanning (1979), *Africa Undermined*

Merle Lipton (1985), *Capitalism and Apartheid*

CE Lysaght (1979), *Brendan Bracken*

William MacDonald (1931), *Pioneers of the Golden Rand*

Roy Macnab (1987), *Gold Their Touchstone*

Richard Mendelsohn (1991), *Sammy Marks: the Uncrowned King of the Transvaal*

The Milner Papers (vols 1 & 2)

Jill Nattrass (1981), *The South African Economy*

Thomas Pakenham (1979), *The Boer War*

David Pallister *et al* (1987), *South Africa Inc: The Oppenheimer Empire*

Lionel Phillips (1924), *Some Reminiscences*

— (1977), *All That Glittered: Selected Correspondence 1890-1924*

Mrs Lionel Phillips (1900), *South African Recollections*

W Randerson (1965), *Notes on the History of Union Corporation, 1888-1918* (unpublished)

Eric Rosenthal (1946), *Gold Bricks and Mortar*
— (1970), *Gold! Gold! Gold!*
— (nd), *The Rand Rush: 1886-1911*
Samancor (1977), *Kalahari Wealth: The Story of Manganese*
Saron & Hotz (eds) (1955), *The Jews in South Africa*
JHP Serfontein (1979), *Brotherhood of Power*
Leonard Thompson (1990), *A History of South Africa*
Sheila van der Horst (1942), *Native Labour in South Africa*
Jean van der Poel (1951), *The Jameson Raid*
Charles van Onselen (1982), *Studies in the Social and Economic History
    of the Witwatersrand, 1886 – 1914,* vols 1 & 2
G Verhoef (1992), *The History of Federale Mynbou Beperk*
    (unpublished)
Keith H Wallis (1992), *The Progenitors: Gencor and its Predecessors*
    (unpublished)
Peter Warwick (ed) (1980), *The South African War 1899-1902*
AD Wassenaar (1977), *Assault on Private Enterprise*
John Wentzel (1975), *A View From The Ridge*
Geoffrey Wheatcroft (1985), *The Randlords*
Ivor Wilkins, Hans Strydom (1978), *The Super-Afrikaners*
Monica Wilson & Leonard Thompson (eds) (1969), *The Oxford History
    of South Africa* (vols 1 & 2)
Francis Wilson (1972), *Labour in the South African Gold Mines 1911-69*
David Yudelman (1984), *The Emergence of Modern South Africa*

(The manuscripts by Wallis and Verhoef mentioned above are available at
Gencor head offices in London and Johannesburg.)

GENCOR: A CHRONOLOGY*

Year	General Mining and Finance Corporation Limited	Federale Mynbou Beperk	Union Corporation Limited	The Context
1895	GMFC registered by George and Leopold Albu on 30-12-1895.			Jameson Raid 29-12-1895: Jameson forced to surrender. Railway link: Transvaal to Delagoa Bay officially opened.
1897			A Goerz & Co Ltd registered by Adolf Goerz 27-12-1897. Lord Battersea: Chairman Amandus Brakhan: MD, Johannesburg.	Industrial Commission set up in March 1897 to investigate the state of the mining industry. 19-11-1897: Formation of re-amalgamated Chamber of Mines of the Republic of South Africa.
1899			Geduld Proprietary Mines Ltd incorporated 28-3-1899.	Anglo-Boer War: 11-10-1899 to 31-5-1902.
1900			Death of Adolf Goerz.	Production from mines lost during war.
1901	Meyer & Charlton re-opened.			

* Based on research by Dr G Verhoef and Dr L van Meurs

Year	General Mining and Finance Corporation Limited	Federale Mynbou Beperk	Union Corporation Limited	The Context
1902	Controlling 9 gold mines, including Meyer & Charlton, West Rand Cons.		Mining activities start in West Rand. A Goerz & Co listed on London Stock Exchange. Henry Strakosch MD in London.	Treaty of Vereeniging: 31-5-1902.
1903	Relations with A Goerz & Co deteriorate.			S A Customs Union abolishes all internal customs barriers.
1904			Van Dyk floated.	Arrival of Chinese labourers on mines.
1907	Dresdner Bank of Germany raises new capital for General Mining 1906-7.			White miners strike. Louis Botha becomes Prime Minister of Transvaal.
1908			Into Mexico. Geduld Proprietary Mines Ltd begins producing gold.	National Assembly engaged in drafting new constitution for SA.
1909-13	Opens 3 deep-level mines: serious losses.			
1910				Union of South Africa: 31-5-1910. Final departure of Chinese labourers.
1911				The Mines and Works Act enshrines a colour bar.
1912	Albu family buys Northwards.			
1913				Miners' Strike.
1914-18				First World War.
1915			Modder Deep in production.	*Lusitania* sunk: anti-German riots.

Year	General Mining and Finance Corporation Limited	Federale Mynbou Beperk	Union Corporation Limited	The Context
1917			Buys German-held shares.	
1918			Name changed from A Goerz & Co Ltd to Union Corporation Ltd. Controls 5 gold mines.	End of First World War. Agreement between Chamber of Mines and SA Industrial Federation on black/ white ratio on mines.
1919				28-7-1919: Treaty of Versailles: SWA awarded to SA as a C-mandate under League of Nations supervision. Botha dies – Smuts succeeds as PM.
1921	German shareholders bought out by GMFC.		PM Anderson recruited as manager.	Continuing economic depression.
1922	West Rand Consolidated – CS McLean as General Manager.			General Strike; Rand Rebellion.
1923			Sir Henry Strakosch becomes Chairman (based in London).	
1924				Pact government: Hertzog in power.
1925				UK, SA return to Gold Standard.
1926			East Geduld mine developed.	
1927			PM Anderson joins UC Board.	
1928				Iscor established.
1930-38			Grootvlei developed.	World-wide depression 1930-32.

Year	General Mining and Finance Corporation Limited	Federale Mynbou Beperk	Union Corporation Limited	The Context
1931			East Geduld comes into production.	Statute of Westminster 1931: SA achieves sovereignty. UK leaves Gold Standard.
1932				SA leaves Gold Standard: Dec 1932.
1933				Fusion of National Party and SA Party.
1934			Marievale mine developed.	
1935	Sir George Albu dies: 27-12-1935.			
1936	Sir George Werner Albu becomes Chairman.		Sappi established.	Hertzog's two segregation acts: Representation of Natives Act and Native Trust and Land Act.
1938	Leopold Albu dies. Swap shares in gold mines with Rand Mines: also representatives on Boards. GMFC moves into OFS.		Van Dyk re-opened. Free State goldfields discovered by UC geologists. Grootvlei comes into production. Marievale begins producing gold.	
1939				Partnership of National Party and SA Party disrupted 4-9-1939. Smuts leads South Africa into war.
1939-45		Federale Volksbeleggings Beperk established by W du Plessis.		Second World War: Commodities and foodstuffs scarce, but good overseas markets for gold, wool and diamonds.
1940		Klipfontein Collieries founded: Acme mine.		

Year	General Mining and Finance Corporation Limited	Federale Mynbou Beperk	Union Corporation Limited	The Context
1943		FVB approached for financial assistance. Broodsnyersplaas coal deposits found.	Sir Henry Strakosch dies 30-10-1943.	
1944	'Geoffries' floated (General Exploration Orange Free State Ltd).			
1945			Brendan Bracken Chairman, PM Anderson Deputy Chairman.	
1947			First shaft sunk at St Helena.	
1948		W du Plessis leaves FVB.		United Nations Charter. National Party government 26-5-1948.
1949				Sterling devaluation.
1950	GMFC takes over Ohlthaver Group – gold, platinum engineering, sugar.	FVB decides to form separate mining company, Federale Mynbou.		
1951			First gold produced in Free State by St Helena. Discovery of gold at Evander in Eastern Transvaal.	Separate Representation of Voters Act of 1951: removes Coloureds from voters' roll.
1952	West Rand Cons produces first SA uranium.			
1953		Federale Mynboumaatskappy Beperk incorporated on 16-6-1953.		

Year	General Mining and Finance Corporation Limited	Federale Mynbou Beperk	Union Corporation Limited	The Context
1954	GMFC takes over Strathmore group: Stilfontein, Buffels-fontein, Ellaton. GMFC share issue: AAC increases interest in GMFC. GMFC aquires new interests in diamonds, fluorspar, chrome.		PM Anderson dies November 1954. TP Stratten becomes MD.	DF Malan retires as Prime Minister. JG Strijdom takes over.
1954-62	Buffelsfontein comes into production: 1957.		Development of Far East Rand mines at Evander.	May 1959: Bantu Investment Corporation of SA established and Border industries concept accepted.
1955		Acquisition of Barber-ton Fairview (gold). Sanlam joins as shareholder.		
1958		Name change: Federal Mynboumaatskappy Beperk to Federale Mynbou Bpk 12-6-58.	Bracken dies: 8-8-1958.	Dr Verwoerd succeeds Strijdom as Prime Minister.
1959		JSE listing of Fedmyn.	Chairman: Sir Charles Hambro.	Promotion of Bantu Self-Government Act of 1959: greater authority to blacks in homelands.
1960			Sappi developing. Other industrial investments.	Referendum: 52% of voters in favour of Republic. Sharpeville: 21-3-60, ANC banned.
1961		Coal mining expansion.		Republic of South Africa comes into being and SA leaves Commonwealth.

Year	General Mining and Finance Corporation Limited	Federale Mynbou Beperk	Union Corporation Limited	The Context
1962		Harley Drayton's coal interests merged with Fedmyn as Trans-Natal. GEFCO acquisition.	September 1962: UC granted permission by British authorities to move to Johannesburg.	
1963	Sir George Werner Albu dies: 18-2 63. New Chairman: CS McLean.	Mainstraat Beleggings/Fedmyn takes management of GMFC. Fedmyn remains as holding company.		Rivonia treason trial: Nelson Mandela jailed.
1963-64	GMFC taken over by Mainstraat Beleggings/ Fedmyn. AAC becomes partner of Fedmyn via GMFC. Chairman: WB Coetzer, MD: TF Muller.			
1965		Anglo American sells 1% in Mainstraat Beleggings to Fedmyn to cede control.	Option taken in platinum exploration. Chairman: TP Stratten, MD: CB Anderson.	Rhodesian UDI.

Year	General Mining and Finance Corporation Limited (Holding company: Fedmyn)	Union Corporation	The Context
1966	Sentrust formed from investment companies.		Dr Verwoerd assassinated: 6-9-1966, BJ Vorster succeeds as Prime Minister. Lesotho and Botswana achieve independence from Great Britain.
1967	Trek Beleggings Bpk established.		
1968			Gold price floats. Swaziland independent.
1969			Herstigte Nasionale Party founded: 24-10-1969.

Year	General Mining and Finance Corporation Limited (Holding company: Fedmyn)	Union Corporation	The Context
1970	Coal: Japanese coal contract. Building of Richards Bay Harbour.		
1971	TF Muller succeeded by WJ de Villiers as MD. Chairman: WB Coetzer. GMFC strategy changes. Sells unprofitable industrial interests.		Bantu Homelands Constitution Act of 1971.
1972		New MD: E Pavitt. Chairman: CB Anderson.	
1973		Unisel floated south-east of St Helena.	
1974	GMFC acquires 29,9% shareholding in UC. GMFC has 51% shareholding in Tubatse Ferrochrome (Pty) Ltd.	Executive Chairman: E Pavitt.	
1975	GMFC obtains 50,1% in Union Corporation.	Controlling interest acquired by GMFC but separate entities maintained.	
1976	Executive Chairman: WJ de Villiers. Deputy Chairman: E Pavitt.		Soweto uprising: 16-6-1976. Transkei becomes independent.
1977			Bophuthatswana becomes independent.
1978		Beisa Mines (uranium) development begins.	PW Botha succeeds BJ Vorster.
1979	GMFC acquires remaining minority shares in UC.	Unisel begins production.	

Year	General Mining Union Corporation Limited (Holding company: Fedmyn)	The Context
1980	Effective amalgamation of General Mining and Union Corporation begins. WJ de Villiers first CEO of Gencor. Name changed to General Mining Union Corporation Limited (Gencor): 2-7-1980.	Sanctions build up.

Year	General Mining Union Corporation Limited (Holding company: Fedmyn)	The Context
1982	'Broedertwis'. WJ de Villiers resigns. E Pavitt CEO Gencor, Dr FJ du Plessis Chairman of Sanlam (holding company of Fedmyn).	National Union of Mineworkers (NUM) (black mineworkers) begins negotiations with Chamber of Mines (representing the mining houses). Negotiations between Mineworkers' Union (whites) and Chamber are still continuing.
1983	Group reorganisation: devolution by 'committee'. Gencor takes control of Samancor.	New constitution.
1984	Chairman: E Pavitt, with Committee of Five executive directors.	
1985		International financial constraints as sanctions intensify.
1986	23 000 dismissed at Impala. Kinross mine disaster. Derek Keys becomes Executive Chairman: end of diversified structure. Malbak group joins Gencor.	State of emergency.
1987	Participation in Mossgas.	
1988	Brian Gilbertson recruited 1-3-1988 as Executive Director.	
1989	Name change from General Mining Union Corporation Ltd to Gencor Ltd: 25-9-1989. Reorganisation of subsidiaries. Takes 30,7% in Alusaf. Dr Fred du Plessis (Chairman of Sanlam) dies in accident. Fedmyn changes name to Gencor Beherend Beperk on 25-9-1989.	FW de Klerk succeeds PW Botha.
1990		FW de Klerk announces release of Mandela, legalisation of ANC: 2-2-1990. Namibia achieves independence: 21-3-1990.

Year	Gencor Limited Holding Company: Gencor Beherend Beperk until 1994, now Sanlam/Sankorp	The Context
1991	Tension at Impala.	Constitutional negotiations.

Year	Gencor Limited Holding Company: Gencor Beherend Beperk until 1994, now Sanlam/Sankorp	The Context
1992	Derek Keys appointed to Cabinet and succeeded by Brian Gilbertson as Executive Chairman. Samancor/Highveld Steel and Vanadium announce Columbus Stainless Steel project. 'Unbundling' announced. Alusaf smelter expansion announced.	
1993	Gencor increases RBM stake to 50%: Gencor Beherend Bbk name change to G B Corporation Ltd: 15-11-1993. Unbundling from Gencor of Engen, Genbel, Malbak and Sappi: effective 1-9-1993.	
1993-94	Gencor/Billiton negotiations concluded November 1994.	
1994	Trans-Natal/Randcoal merger to form Ingwe. G B Corporation Ltd succeeded as largest shareholder in Gencor by Sanlam/Sancorp.	Democratic elections: 27-4-1994. Government of National Unity: interim new constitution: all homelands again incorporated in SA.
1995	Derek Keys returns as Chairman of Billiton. Columbus Joint Venture on-stream. Alusaf Hillside smelter on-stream. Merger of Lonrho's and Impala's platinum interests. Gencor centenary.	

INDEX